The Wines of Chile

The Wines of Chile

by Peter Richards

MITCHELL BEAZLEY

The Wines of Chile

Peter Richards

First published in Great Britain in 2006
by Mitchell Beazley, an imprint of
Octopus Publishing Group Limited,
2–4 Heron Quays, London E14 4JP.

ISBN 1 8453 3122 2
ISBN 978 1 8453 3122 1

A CIP catalogue record for this book is available from the British Library.

Set in Berkeley.

Printed and bound in England by Mackays, Chatham.

Contents

Maps

viii *Chile, from Elqui to Malleco*

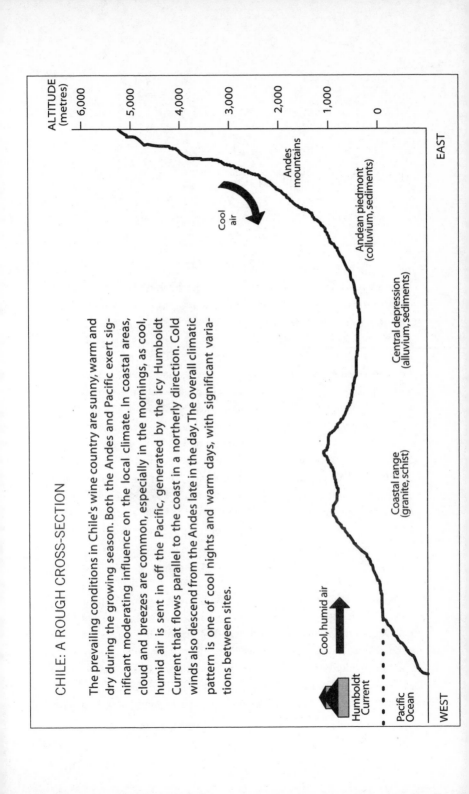

CHILE: A ROUGH CROSS-SECTION

The prevailing conditions in Chile's wine country are sunny, warm and dry during the growing season. Both the Andes and Pacific exert significant moderating influence on the local climate. In coastal areas, cloud and breezes are common, especially in the mornings, as cool, humid air is sent in off the Pacific, generated by the icy Humboldt Current that flows parallel to the coast in a northerly direction. Cold winds also descend from the Andes late in the day. The overall climatic pattern is one of cool nights and warm days, with significant variations between sites.

ALTITUDE (metres)

6,000

5,000

4,000

3,000

2,000

1,000

0

EAST

Andes mountains

Cool air

Andean piedmont (colluvium, sediments)

Central depression (alluvium, sediments)

Coastal range (granite, schist)

Cool, humid air

Humboldt Current

Pacific Ocean

WEST

Acknowledgments

I am greatly indebted to many people who have helped me write this book, but one sticks in the mind more than most – the thief at Liguria. This watering hole in Santiago has long been known for its lively atmosphere and ample wine list, and one evening I availed myself a little too freely of its bounties and failed to notice the sudden absence of the bag that contained my passport, cash, bank details, and driving licence. What was worse, I was just about to set off on a round-Chile trip to visit wineries, which would have been impossible without these items.

But I had a secret weapon. Prior to the bar, I had been interviewing a winery owner, who had given me a bottle of wine to taste. It was this bottle that proved to be my saviour. The thief, it later turned out, had clearly been so thrilled at managing to steal such a fine bottle of wine that he completely ignored all the valuable items in the bag and simply tossed it over a wall into an old lady's garden. The old lady duly returned the bag to me and I learned a priceless lesson. Always carry a bottle of fine Chilean wine in your bag.

This book would simply not have been possible to write without the invaluable support of Wines of Chile. The teams in the UK and Chile have been unceasingly supportive, helpful, responsive, and patient and they have enabled me to spend extensive time on the ground in Chile. For all of this I am enormously thankful. Wines of Chile does a tough and often thankless job incredibly well and they deserve recognition for it. Special thanks and appreciation go to Michael Cox, Pilar Valverde, Ricardo Letelier, Georgina Nunn, Anita Jackson, and Karen Sutton.

Particular thanks must also go to the real protagonists of this book, the wineries. Ever since I began to visit Chilean wineries, as a rank amateur in the wine business, I have always been hugely grateful for the courteous, welcoming, and professional reception I have enjoyed in Chile's numerous wineries. Winemakers, viticulturists, winery owners, and all related staff have been generous with their time, hospitality, and wines to a humbling extent, and have never sought any special treatment in return. For this I would like to extend a sincere vote of thanks.

I would specifically like to thank all those who have gone way above and beyond the call of duty to help me research the book. They are, in alphabetical order: Fernando Almeda, María José Alvarez, Carlos Andrade, Marina Ashton, Ana María Barahona, Sven Bruchfeld, Tim Burford, Eduardo Chadwick, Oz Clarke, Sam Combes, Carlos Cousiño, Ana María Cumsille, Felipe de Solminihac, the team at *Decanter*, Cristobal Duke, Alvaro Espinoza, Mariano Fernández, Matías Garcés Silva, Felipe García, Karen Gilchrist, Daniella Gillmore, María del Pilar González, Guy Hooper, Adolfo Hurtado, Andrew Jefford, Ernesto Juisan, the Kingston family, Isabel Lazaeta, Gustavo Llona, Jen MacDonald, María Luz Marín, Francesco Marone Cinzano, Francisca Marshall, René Merino, Rodrigo Millán, Aurelio Montes, Max Morales, Yerko Moreno, Felipe Müller, Irene Paiva, Marcelo Papa, Alvaro and Javier Paredes, Pedro Parra, Sergio Reyes, Jaime Roselló, Andrés Sánchez, Carlos Serrano, Eduardo Silva, Alfonso Soto, Rafael Tirado, Aída Toro, Miguel Torres, Felipe Tosso, Patrick Valette, Paula Vigueras, Eduardo Wexman, Corrina Wilson, and María Pía Yovanovic. Thanks also to Alejandro Hernández, who provided the inspiration for the cross-section diagram on p. ix.

Fond thanks are also due to Hilary Azzam, who commissioned this book in the first place. Also to Susanna Forbes for her thoughtful stewardship of the book as it came together, Margaret Rand for her support and guidance, Pat Carroll for some brilliantly sharp-eyed proof reading and invaluable advice, and Susan Keevil for both enlightening me and saving me from many pitfalls through her diligent and perspicacious copy editing.

On a personal note, I would like to thank Steve Anderson for giving me a job in Chile in the first place. My family has, as ever, been a constant source of support. Finally, I dedicate this book to Susie.

Preface

First times tend to be memorable, for better or worse, because they mark watersheds in our lives. I still remember the day I first went to visit a winery. I had recently arrived in Chile to work as a journalist; it was an exciting, nerve-racking, often bewildering time in my life. First, I got to know the office and my new home, which became familiar and comforting territory. But Chile has a particular way of getting under your skin, and before long I was itching to explore farther. There was just one small problem. Where to begin?

I think, even then, I knew the answer to that question. Wine was one of the few things I had associated with Chile before I arrived so it seemed a natural place to start. Before I knew it, I was being flung around the front of a thundering *micro* bus trying to ask the driver as politely as possible to let me know when we arrived at the winery. It was a balmy day and the sun's warmth was insistent through the threadbare curtains. I dozed off, and woke to the sight of an aggravated driver glaring back down a near-empty bus. I got off, and the bus promptly disappeared. The road was empty; all I could see were vines stretching into the distance and the gates to a grand-looking winery. I hesitated. This felt odd, it was not my world. I took a deep breath and pushed open the gate.

It was a defining moment in my life because, since then, wine has become my world. Not long after my first winery visit I was commissioned to write a guide to visiting Chilean wineries and so set off on a fascinating and frustrating trip around the backwaters of Chile's wine lands in the company of several notepads and a leaky old BMW. It took six months and a good deal of patience to visit over 100 wineries. By the end, I felt not only ready to murder Chile's rural road-sign department, but also privileged to have got to know the country in a way that few are lucky enough to experience. It was the beginning of the path that has led to this book.

It is an exciting time to be writing about Chile. Since 1990 the country has undergone a profound and exhilarating process of change and development. This has been manifested nowhere more starkly than in its wine industry, which has flourished and, in doing so, transformed itself in little over a decade and a half. That process of change remains ongoing, though it seems the fundamentals of Chile's new wine era have been established: viticultural expansion into marginal areas, ever-increasing diversity of grape varieties, a newfound will to experiment and explore, and a drive to craft wines that speak increasingly of Chile as well as the cheap and cheerful wine that has won it so many friends all over the world. The face of Chilean wine is changing and the purpose of this book is to document this vinous evolution.

This book is first and foremost a reference guide to Chilean wine in the modern era. At its heart is a comprehensive series of profiles on the country's most significant wine producers, and throughout I have endeavoured to provide information that will serve those interested in Chile and its wines, whatever their knowledge about wine in general. There are 129 producers in the book, 82 of which have major profiles – and of those wineries profiled, I have visited all but seven, many of them on more than one occasion. As a result, most of the material I have used in the book is original, gathered in the course of my time in Chile, though I have also drawn on a range of sources, from historic writing to fresh material such as geological maps and the latest industry studies.

This is a reference book with a difference, however. I am very aware that wine writing can be dry and uninspiring – surely a crime given the stimulating subject matter – especially in books that delve into as much detail and have as little pictorial relief as this one. As a result, I have tried to make the book more readable by providing all-important context wherever possible and attempting to bring Chile's people, places, history, and present-day realities to life in a way not often seen in wine reference books. Specifically, Part I aims to do this as well as the individual sections in each regional chapter entitled "A Picture of…"

Similarly, I have not refrained from offering my opinion on key issues or producers. I hope and trust that this approach is taken in the spirit in which it was meant, which is to stimulate debate and ultimately help raise awareness of Chilean wine as well as foster improvements in the wines themselves. I do not offer these opinions as definitive or final judgments; they merely reflect my personal views based upon a good deal of research (interviews, tastings (often blind), visits etc.) and a desire to be as objective as possible. Any criticism is constructive in intent and I have attempted, wherever possible, to counter-balance these comments. I hope that these forthright opinions make the book more readable and, ultimately, engaging.

The structure of the book is based on a region-by-region exploration of the subject, with wine producers discussed as part of a particular wine-growing area. This is a new way of looking at Chilean wine but one that has become increasingly relevant as its winemakers have begun to explore and express the country's significant regional diversity in ever more lucid ways. Chilean wine is an increasingly diverse subject, and the structure of the book is intended to reflect this as well as allow a detailed exploration of why this is the case.

To help with orientation, within this region-by-region structure there is a total of ten maps, all of which incorporate topographical relief, which is crucial to understanding the country's wines. Chile is a notoriously difficult country to map in book format, especially given its shape and length, and it has suffered in the past from under-representation on this front as a result. However, good maps are an invaluable tool when it comes to understanding any wine country; hopefully, those in this book will prove a helpful initial guide. (I believe that this is, to date, the most comprehensive collection of maps in any English-language book on the subject.) By way of a footnote, there are many other maps available that offer a more detailed and enlightening picture of the country – Origo's fold-out version being a particular case in point (www.origo.cl).

Despite my best efforts and those of my excellent editorial team, there will be errors in this book, all of which are my personal responsibility. In addition, things are changing fast in Chilean wine and thus some information will soon be out of date, such as vineyard statistics and details on winemakers, who have an annoying habit of changing jobs just after books are written. However, I have tried to offer an accurate picture of the Chilean wine scene at the time of writing as well as concentrate on the fundamental issues that will remain of ongoing relevance.

Finally, this book can never be an adequate substitute for visiting Chile and experiencing its extraordinary nature and wines at first hand. It was certainly an experience that marked my life in an indelible way, as it has done to many others, Charles Darwin and Che Guevara included. It is an experience I cannot recommend highly enough.

Peter Richards
London, May 2006

Part I

Introduction

"Of bee, shadow, fire, snow, silence, foam,

of steel, line, pollen was built your tough,

your slender structure."

Pablo Neruda, *Tina Modotti ha muerto, Residencia en la Tierra*

Chile is an extraordinary country. It is a thin strip of land, averaging less than 180 kilometres (112 miles) in width yet stretching over 4,300 kilometres (2,600 miles) along South America's southwest extremity. Its slender territory is hemmed in between the towering peaks of the Andes in the east and the vast Pacific Ocean to the west. The northern extremities are windswept, desiccated desert, but in the far south the air teems with rain and sea spray as the country fragments into bitter, iceberg-strewn Antarctic waters at the southernmost tip of the Americas. In between these extremes lies an intriguing, diverse, extraordinary world.

Such is the range of Chile's natural features that it almost seems too much for one nation to contain within its borders; it is certainly a challenge to try to put it into words. A Chilean friend once told me how his country's weird and wonderful nature was the result of divine thrift. It was, I was informed, all down to the fact that when God was nearly finished making the world, He had bits and bobs of everything left over –

desert, mountain, ocean, lake, river, glacier, plain, island – and so He cobbled them all together and tacked them onto a part of the world where no-one would notice. This was Chile.

I have always been fond of this story, not just because of its wonderful imagery but also because of the way in which it reveals a common feature of the Chilean character: self-effacing, imaginative, cheerfully fatalist. The Chilean novelist Isabel Allende put it in the following terms: "we're a people with poetic souls. It isn't our fault; that one we can blame on the landscape. No one who is born and lives in a natural world like ours can resist writing poetry. In Chile, you lift up a rock, and instead of a lizard out crawls a poet or a balladeer." (*My Invented Country, A Memoir.*)

Having been lucky enough to live and work in Chile, to get to know its people as well as travel across its extensive territory, I can safely say two things. Firstly, I still have much more to learn and, secondly, it is hard to remain detached from Chile once you get to know the country and its people. It is at once a fascinating, frustrating, endearing, and contradictory country, where the memory of violence, both natural and human, is seldom far from a serene surface. It is a country that is worth getting to know.

One way that people have got to know Chile better in recent years has been through its wine. Although it is only ever a limited and vicarious introduction, it nevertheless affords some sort of an insight into the country, its climate and geography, soils and people. It is this vivid and varied picture that I hope to capture in the following pages and in doing so lend what momentum I can to the enjoyable task of creating an ever-greater understanding and appreciation of Chilean wine as well as the country and culture.

This introduction is not intended as a comprehensive picture of Chile. Rather, it is an attempt to situate Chilean wine in a brief and general context of nature, history, politics, geography, economics, society, and gastronomy. Wine is just one small part of Chile's big picture but it is nonetheless an element of increasing significance, renown, and interest both at home and abroad. This, then, is the beginning of the story.

A BRIEF HISTORY

Chile's earliest beginnings are thought to lie in the Palaeozoic era, around 300–400 million years ago, when tectonic activity caused by the collision of the Nazca and South American plates raised land from the ocean. Chile's oldest landscapes are to be found in the far north and on the summits of the coastal range of hills: this was the first land to rise from the waters. Some two to three hundred million years later, by which time dinosaurs were widespread, similar tectonic forces pushed up the Andes mountain range and Chile as we now know it slowly came into being.

Since then, the activity of volcanoes, earthquakes, and natural erosion has further moulded Chile's form. Glaciers and rivers have scoured and deepened valleys; winds and rains have slowly worn away the rocky hillsides; volcanoes and magma vents have added their ash and lava to the changing landscape. The country is continually reminded of the underlying forces that have given rise to its lands: earthquakes are common, as are active volcanoes. Much of the country – around eighty per cent – is mountainous.

Chile's climate is governed by two major factors: its mountains and ocean. Variations in altitude and exposure create differences in local climate (in the Andes, for example, higher means cooler and wetter). In central and northern parts, which are of most relevance to wine, the ocean plays a crucial role in determining the weather, primarily because of a cold Pacific water mass known as the Humboldt Current that runs northward along the coast from southern Chile. In combination with the Pacific anticyclone (a stable high-pressure system that prevails in much of Chile's central and northern areas), this cooling influence in the ocean creates a temperature inversion, with cool air trapped beneath a layer of warm air, which prevents the formation of high rain-bearing clouds.

While this makes for clear, dry weather inland for much of the year, it also gives rise to morning fogs and low cloud cover as well as afternoon breezes, especially in areas on the westerly side of the coastal range or inland areas where these hills are less obstructive. These cooling afternoon winds are also a feature of the mountainous east, where cold air moves down the hillsides from altitude. The overall effect in much of central Chile is a temperate climate, with sunny, dry conditions for much of the year followed by a short, rainy winter. (It is often referred to as a Mediterranean climate, though winemaker Ed Flaherty has suggested the term Eastern Pacific Cold Ocean climate as a more accurate alternative, noting the greater similarities between the Chilean and Californian climates.) During the grape-growing season, conditions during the daytime are usually warm and dry, turning cool at night.

Humans are believed to have started settling in the Americas from before the end of the last Ice Age. This may have been as early as 50,000–60,000 years ago, with people arriving either via the Bering land bridge from Asia or by sea from Polynesia. In any case, evidence exists to suggest that humans had reached the southern tip of South America by 12,000 BC. Indigenous cultures such as the Chinchorro, Molle, Ona, Diaguita, Aymara, and Mapuche subsequently developed within what are now Chile's borders. In the fifteenth century, the Inca invaded and assumed control over northern Chile, though they were not able to conquer the Mapuche in the south. It was a similar story when the Spanish arrived in the mid-sixteenth century.

The first conquistador to lead a foray into Chile was Diego de Almagro in 1535. This was a short-lived incursion, however, and in 1540 a new expedition under Pedro de Valdivia was launched. He founded Santiago in 1541. For the next three centuries, the settlers would be at violent loggerheads with the Mapuche, the border between them for much of this time being formed by the river Bío Bío in the south. Nonetheless, the conquerors were determined to settle the land and did so by not only installing themselves but also encouraging émigrés from Spain to set up homes and establish managed estates. What was effectively slave labour was provided by the now disenfranchised indigenous underclass. The Mapuche were not officially defeated until 1881, though, when the overwhelming firepower of the Chilean army was finally brought to bear. The Mapuche had the majority of their land confiscated – estimated to be around five million hectares, or ninety-five per cent of what they had previously counted as their own – and were moved to reservations. This territorial issue remains an ongoing source of conflict in Chilean society.

With the arrival of Europeans, wine vines became part of Chile's scenery for the first time. These were most probably from Spain although some may also have originated in the Canary Islands (there are conflicting accounts of these first moments of American viticulture). Part of their function was to provide sacramental wine for the Church, whose mission it was to convert indigenous people and maintain a strict religious observance amongst the settlers. (The variety known as País in Chile, also called Mission in California, is thought to have been the chief ingredient of such Communion wine.) The presence of vineyards on the landscape reinforced the permanent nature of the colonizers' settlements.

Among the country's most historic winemaking areas are the north (Copiapó, La Serena) and central parts (Santiago) as well as southern lands around Concepción and Maule. In the north, the rumbustious Francisco de Aguirre had set up vineyards by 1550, while Juan Jufré was granted the Macul estate to the southeast of the nascent Santiago in 1564, which he planted to wheat, barley, and vines. Such estates were not only the beginning of wine culture in Chile, they also established a balance of power that has proved enduring – that of a dominant, wealthy minority controlling the country's politics and purse-strings.

By the early nineteenth century, popular revolutions in North America and France together with Napoleon's victory in Spain had sown the seeds of independence in Chilean minds. A Chilean junta was set up in 1810 and formal independence from Spain was finally achieved in 1818. Upheaval in Europe also gave rise to a wave of immigration at this time, one by-product of which was an increased European influence on Chile's vineyards. This trend was compounded by the spread of phylloxera across Europe from the 1860s onwards, devastating European wine production and leading to widespread unemployment. Many winemakers headed to more promising pastures in the New World, including Chile.

It was this European and Chilean cross-fertilization, backed up by newfound riches from a booming mining industry in Chile's northern territories, which led to the foundation of Chile's modern wine industry. A new era of international travel among Chile's landowning classes had brought them into contact with European and, specifically, French wines. The result was a concerted programme of imports of European noble vine stock, including Cabernet Sauvignon, Malbec, Carmenère, Chardonnay, Semillon, and Riesling. The first imports are thought to have taken place in the 1830s, and by the latter half of the century the Chilean wine industry was flourishing. It was at this time that what are the historic Chilean wineries of today were founded, including Cousiño Macul, Concha y Toro, Undurraga, Errázuriz, La Rosa, Santa Rita, Carmen, and San Pedro. Exports took off and production rose – this was the Chilean wine industry's first heyday.

The boom was not to prove enduring, however. By the mid-twentieth century, world wars and economic crises had taken a severe toll on Chile's economy. Alcoholism was rife among Chile's working classes, fuelled by cheap and abundant wine that now was struggling to find a market. As a result, Chilean authorities took a hard line, imposing taxes and capping vineyard growth. It led to a period of sustained depression in the Chilean wine industry, which started in earnest in the thirties and lasted until the eighties. It is worth noting that during this period, in the sixties and early seventies, an initiative known as agrarian reform was introduced, aimed at splitting up Chile's large estates and reapportioning land to the country's less affluent citizens. This was, of course, bitterly opposed by the landowners and led to a severe downturn in the wine industry.

The process of land reform ultimately came to a decisive halt after the coup in 1973, when a military junta including army general Augusto Pinochet seized power from the president, Salvador Allende. Chile remained under military rule until 1990. It was a period of history that has proved immensely divisive for Chilean society and remains a source of considerable internal conflict within the country. The transition to democracy in 1990 was, however, surprisingly smooth and successive Chilean governments have handled these issues with delicacy and responsibility, enabling the country to make significant progress since. One of Chile's main barriers to development, however, remains the steady polarization of its society, though perhaps more in economic than political terms today.

Although the eighties saw the beginnings of a revival in the Chilean wine industry, it was not until the nineties that this process really started to take off. With the return of democracy, foreign markets opened up and investment and expertise from abroad started to flow into Chile. The wine industry bloomed. The national vineyard doubled in size between 1995 and 2002. Total wine production rose from 282 million litres in 1991 to 668 million in 2003. Exports grew from 43 million litres in 1990 to 355 million litres in 2002. Where in 1980 nearly ninety per cent of Chilean wine exports went to other Latin American countries, by 2002 over half were being sent to Europe, with North America and Asia also prominent recipients. Although growth is still ongoing, it is at a steadier rate now than before. Nonetheless, this has been Chilean wine's second coming.

THE CONTEXT TODAY

Chile's economy remains export-driven and focused on several key commodities. Mining is by far the country's most dominant economic activity, with copper alone accounting for around thirty-five to forty per cent of total exports, with other minerals such as molybdenum (used in the manufacture of stainless steel) and lithium also being big earners. Beyond this there are, in descending order of importance, chemical products, fresh fruit, forestry products, wood pulp, and salmon. Wine ranks around seventh in terms of overall net export value (around two to three per cent of the Chilean total) but is a growth sector. Chile's total exports in 2005 were worth nearly forty billion US dollars – in the same year, wine shipments generated US$877 million. (These were both record figures.)

The early twenty-first century has been marked by strong economic growth for Chile. This has been fuelled principally by demand from China for raw materials such as copper and has led to economic prosperity and a reduction in unemployment. However, Chile's economy remains vulnerable to shifts in global demand as well as currency fluctuations. In addition, analysts have warned that complacency is a real concern, as is the structure of the economy. As an example, a government report in 2005 revealed that one per cent of Chilean firms accounted for eighty per cent of income, a polarizing trend that had been accentuated over the previous decade. Government figures also showed that, in 2005, ten per cent of firms accounted for nearly half of Chilean exports by value – and of this ten per cent, over two-thirds were in the mining business. Strategic planning and diversification have been consistently highlighted as areas for improvement in the Chilean economy.

As one winery owner put it to me, Chile is now looking "to take its second step toward development". A stable and prosperous economy, progressive politics, and improved infrastructure have laid the foundations but now more underlying issues need addressing, such as the social divide and poverty. In 2005, the annual Human Development Index report by the United Nations Development Programme ranked Chile as the world's thirty-seventh most developed country (out of 177) but also noted the country's poor record in terms of inequality and income distribution. Although the divide between rich and poor is a global problem, it is marked in Chile, where it is estimated that nearly half of total earnings go to the wealthiest ten per cent of society while, as of 2003, over twenty per cent of the population was living below the poverty line. Within this picture, education remains a high priority for improvement, not only to promote social equality but also to build up the broad skill base necessary to develop a successful and growing economy.

Chile's environment remains under threat from growing industry and development. Pollution is a major issue, not only in Santiago but also in other areas of the country where toxic discharges, improperly managed waste, and other unpalatable industrial contamination provide regular reminders of the need to implement strict environmental regulations on all industries – including wine. Conversely, there also needs to be flexibility and logic built into the system so that regulation does not end up penalizing growth. Fresh water represents a key environmental issue. Chile's centre and north are arid lands that have increasing demand for water for both industrial and agricultural use – their situation needs careful management if it is not to end in disputes, shortages, and lasting environmental damage. To make matters worse, the process of global warming seems to be placing extra pressure on the situation.

A similar balance of regulation and flexibility is required from Chile's wine appellation law, a system drawn up in 1994 that uses the country's administrative regions as the framework for demarcating the various different wine regions, such as Maipo and Maule. (For reference, Chile has thirteen administrative regions, which have both numerical denotations (I–XIII) and names – *e.g.* Valparaíso for Region V.) Though this system deserves criticism for being too broad-focused and with administrative rather than wine-growing divisions at its heart, it has nonetheless provided a serviceable structure within which Chilean wine has been able to evolve in a relatively progressive manner. However, as there is an ever-greater focus on individual wine-growing sites in Chile and a consequent need to provide a regulatory structure to cater for smaller-scale developments, there will be increasing pressure to reform this system.

Chile's is a young wine industry, still in the throes of development. The same could be said of its fine dining scene. Traditional Chilean gastronomy has consisted either of heavy-handed European imitation or hearty dishes such as corn pie, meat pasties and sickly-sweet desserts. There have been notable changes since the nineties, however, when chefs started travelling more, experiencing a range of world cuisines and focusing their attention on Chile's natural attributes. The result has been the emergence of an identifiable modern Chilean cuisine based on an exquisite range of seafood and fish (some of which is unique to Chile and the direct result of the Humboldt Current's fertile waters) in combination with the fresh fruits and vegetables that the country excels in producing. New chef and sommelier associations, competitions, culinary concepts, international events, and a newfound sense of confidence are all aiding development in this regard. It is a process still in incipience but, as with its wine, Chile is starting to discover and assert its identity in its food. It is to be hoped that as both Chilean cuisine and wine develop in tandem they can feed off each other's success.

Tourism is becoming an increasingly important part of Chile's economic activities. The wine industry is beginning to capitalize on this and develop its own wine-tourism initiatives and infrastructure. It is a great opportunity for Chile's wineries to develop customer loyalty and promote their wines as well as for smaller producers with less widespread distribution to access a ready market. For those visitors who do make the trip, it is an excellent way to get to know the wines as well as the country.

As a country, Chile is undergoing a profound and exhilarating period of transition and development. This is also true of its wines and wine industry. One winemaker described it to me in evocative terms as *el destape chileno* – a phrase that conveys both shedding of clothes as well as liberalization and revival. (A *tapa* is a lid so *destapar* is literally to take the lid off something.) It is an exciting time.

2

Viticulture

"Terroir is all about typicity. It's like, if your foot smells, be proud! Because it's your foot."

Enthusiastic Chilean viticulturist

"Chile has got to think big."

Dr. Yerko Moreno, agronomist and viticultural consultant

This is not a long section. Wine-growing and viticulture in Chile are simply too vast and complex a topic to cover in one general overview and this is why I have opted instead to explore the issue in more depth through a region-by-region approach in Part II. This section is more of a general introduction to the topics that will be explored at greater length later in the book.

Chile is not a young nation in viticultural terms. Wine grapes have been cultivated here since the mid-sixteenth century; noble varieties arrived from France in the mid-nineteenth century. But it was not until the nineties that a new viticultural era began, one that has radically altered the country's wine-growing scene and brought about a new awareness of Chile's vinous potential.

The two quotations above embody the viticultural aspirations of this modern Chilean winemaking era, characterized by a newfound sense of ambition, the search for identity and diversity, and a fundamental re-evaluation of the country's wine-growing realities. It is precisely this incipient viticultural revolution that invites a closer look at the country's winemaking regions, with its wine producers considered as part of this context. It makes a new format for a wine book on Chile but one that is intended to reflect this process of ongoing and profound change in Chilean wine.

THE CONTEXT

Chile is often described as a viticultural paradise. This is an enviable label and in one sense accurately reflects the country's many natural advantages for wine-growing, as well as its tremendous potential for diversity and quality. On the other, it is a somewhat dated description given that Chile clearly has many viticultural challenges, especially those new ones thrown up as the country's vineyard continues to expand into new and uncharted territory.

To recap on Chile's basic geography, the country has four major features that appear across its slender form along an east–west axis. These are the Andes in the east, which lead down to intermittent plains or valleys which, in the centre of the country, form a central depression, known in wine terms as the Central Valley. This in turn is broken up by hills that run parallel to the coastline, where the Pacific Ocean forms the country's western limit. The climate during the growing season is dry with cool nights and warm days. Conditions are cooler and more humid in those westerly areas directly affected by the ocean, but humid conditions tend to stop at the coastal hills. Soils are varied in texture and profile but are mainly alluvial clays, loams, sands, and silts on the flat land with gravel and stony content near rivers or in piedmont areas, and decomposed granites and raised marine sediments in the hills.

Historically, Chile's vineyards have occupied those lands where viticulture has proved practical and relatively easy – hence, perhaps, the reputation of a viticultural paradise. The country's central flat lands that lie in the depression between the Andes and coastal range are often warm, fertile, and dry yet with ample river water for irrigation. This situation began to change in the eighties and nineties when Chile's viticultural horizons began to be pushed back by growers eager to expand the country's vinous range beyond cheap-and-cheerful wines produced in easy viticultural territory. It was becoming clear that Chile's natural array of climates, soils, altitudes, and exposures would make a sound basis for vinous diversity.

By the nineties, the political, economic and viticultural situation in Chile was ripe for growth, which duly happened between 1995 and 2000 when the country's vineyard underwent a massive expansion, effectively doubling in size. As well as consolidating in its traditional central heartlands, Chilean viticulture pushed up into the hills and toward the country's limits in all directions in the search for diversity: in the north (Elqui, Limarí), the east (Andean foothills), the south (Malleco, Bío Bío), and west (San Antonio, Casablanca). The trend for expansion has continued since, albeit at a slower rate. New areas either under development or slated for such include Huasco (north of Elqui), Choapa (between Aconcagua and Limarí), coastal areas of Aconcagua, Maipo, Colchagua, and Maule, Andean territories farther east as well as sites to the south of Malleco.

The prime driver behind these changes has not only been the realization that Chile offers great diversity in its natural conditions but also the will and means to exploit them. The rate of change has meant a steep learning curve for the country's wine-growers and -makers – all of whom agree that there is much yet to learn, explore, and achieve.

KEY ISSUES IN CHILEAN VITICULTURE

Viticultural expansion has led to a re-evaluation of Chile's wine territory. Where before the general rule was that north equates to warm and dry, the south to cool and wet, it is now clear that the east–west axis is of more significance in viticultural terms. There are four major zones in this regard. The first covers the plateaus and slopes on the western side of the coastal range, where cloudy, humid mornings and stiff afternoon breezes are the norm. The second is the eastern side of the coastal range, where temperatures tend to be very warm except in the sites that are exposed to some oceanic influence. The third is the central depression and the fourth is the contact zone between this flat land and the Andean foothills in the east, where conditions are warm though moderated by mountain downdraughts and southerly winds. Within all of this, there are crossovers, variables, and exceptions, all of which give rise to a naturally multifaceted and diverse wine-producing country.

A system of informal terminology is now commonly used to qualify the traditional wine appellation system. Thus, the terms Alto, Medio, and Costa are often appended to the regions to differentiate (respectively) between the higher eastern territory, the warm central areas, and the coastal-influenced vineyards in the west. It is generally a helpful system and there are calls for it to be enshrined in Chile's wine appellation law, drawn up along broad-brush political lines in 1994 and now showing its shortcomings. This may prove difficult to impose, however.

The fact is that Chile's range of soils, exposures, altitudes, and local climates means that there is significant diversity even within these more precise designations. In order to be more meaningful, the system would have to be more specific still. Though Chile is understandably reluctant to commit itself to any sort of restrictive appellation framework, it does seem that the logical conclusion to the recent viticultural advances is to develop a system that allows for ever-greater specificity while not penalizing those producers with a broader focus. Time, experience, and consensus will all be needed before this can become a reality.

Water and irrigation are of increasing importance in Chilean viticulture. Irrigation is needed in most of the country's vineyards because the growing season is so dry. The one major exception to this is the broad swathe of dry-farmed agriculture in the south and west known as the *secano*; in addition, some established vineyards on flat land need little irrigation due to the presence of high water tables. Traditional irrigation techniques in Chile are flood or ditch methods using river water. Modern drip irrigation systems were first introduced in the 1990s and enabled the development of hillside vineyards. The advantage of drip is the control it affords over the vineyard, while extensive irrigation methods are thought to help control soil pests such as nematodes. A more recent innovation is underground irrigation, aimed at reducing waste and encouraging deep root growth, which is being trialled by the likes of Almaviva.

Chile's newer vineyards are often in areas that have less ready access to water, especially in the arid north and hilly west of the country where river water is scarce. Wells are often the only source of water in these parts but increasing pressure on aquifers has meant that in some areas, such as Casablanca, moratoria have been placed on the issuing of further water rights. (In Chile, water rights must be acquired in order to irrigate land; these can be purchased from authorities or existing owners.) More effective sourcing, use, and retention of water are called for if this issue is not to slow development in key areas.

Chile has enviable natural advantages for wine-growing, such as good solar exposure, frequent winds, low ambient humidity and rainfall, as well as geographical isolation. All of these factors help reduce the incidence of pests and diseases in the country's vineyards, giving Chile a reputation for relatively trouble-free viticulture. However, there are threats in the vineyard, and these include vine weevils (*Naupactus xanthographus*), red spider mites (*Brevipalpus chilensis*), and mealybugs (*Pseudococcus*), as well as nematodes and ground pearls, (*Margarodes vitis*). Downy mildew is rare but oidium (*Oidium tuckeri*) and botrytis (*Botrytis cinerea*) are common, especially in rainy vintages and in more humid areas such as near the coast. Viruses such as leafroll are also present.

Sound vineyard preparation and management are effective means of controlling most of Chile's natural vine threats, hence the growing trend toward organic viticulture or its lesser form, integrated management. The use of natural predators, cover crops, organic manure, and other non-synthetic methods is now widespread. In order to sell and market their wines as organic, wineries must achieve certification from an institution accredited by the market in which they sell (the EU, for example, has several such bodies, including IMO, Ecocert, and BCS). Many wineries in Chile are, however, reluctant to certify their wines as organic due to the paperwork and costs that this process entails. There is also a widespread fear that labelling wines as organic will mean they are pushed into a niche that producers have little interest in exploiting. As a result, there are a number of producers that farm along organic lines but do not sell or label their wines as organic. This is surely an opportunity missed; Chile has a significant chance to communicate its viticultural bounties to the world in this way and add value to its wines in markets that are decidedly receptive to organic produce, such as the USA and the EU. On the other hand, Biodynamic viticulture has now taken a firm hold in Chile. Biodynamics is like an extension of the logic of organics, in which not only are synthetic products avoided but cosmic cycles are taken into account and homeopathic methods used to promote vine health. The main practitioner of Biodynamics in Chile is Emiliana Orgánico and its winemaker Alvaro Espinoza, owner of Antiyal. Given that the precedent is now there, it is likely that other wineries will adopt these methods in the near future. The certifying body for Biodynamics is Demeter, based in Germany but with international reach.

One viticultural curse that has yet to afflict Chile is phylloxera (*Phylloxera vastatrix*). It is still unclear why this root-sucking aphid has either not reached or, more likely, has not taken to Chile's soils and vines. Nonetheless, as a result the vast majority (almost certainly more than ninety-five per cent at the time of writing) of Chile's vineyard is not planted on rootstock, a situation that is unique in the modern wine era. Vines on their own roots are likely to be healthier and longer lived than those on rootstocks. As for whether the wine from ungrafted vines is any different from that of grafted vines, it is very difficult to say. There are few direct comparisons that can be made but, on the few occasions that I have been able to, it seems only in those cases when the rootstock is poorly chosen, and vigour or ripening is adversely affected, that the difference is significant. Nonetheless, there are those who assert that non-grafted vines do produce purer, more intense character in the wines.

Even so, rootstocks are becoming increasingly common in Chile. Partly this is insurance against any possible future outbreak of phylloxera, although mainly it is for other reasons. These include a desire to achieve greater homogeneity in the vineyard (ripening times, canopy growth) and better adaptation of plant development to soil type (promoting vigour in poor soils and reducing it in fertile sites). They are also being used to aid root development in varieties such as Merlot and protect against soil-related issues such as salinity or pests (nematodes, margarodes etc.). Rootstock trials are ongoing across the country, a necessary though time-consuming process. Many producers, including big guns such as Concha y Toro and Santa Rita, are now routinely incorporating them into new plantings.

The advent of vine clones has been decisive in improving the quality of Chile's vineyard. Before the 1990s, most new vines were developed from Chilean field selections, which were often of uncertain origin and limited quality. Imported material has allowed the development of purer, healthier, and more diverse vineyards in addition to bringing new varieties into the country. The success of varieties such as Sauvignon Blanc and Syrah has been a direct result of successful clonal imports and Pinot Noir is also benefiting. Nonetheless, field selections remain an important element within Chile's overall diversity, not least because of Chile's draconian plant-import laws, which considerably restrict access to foreign clonal material. It should be added that there are Chilean viticulturists who decry the use of clones as a trend toward international homogenization.

A good deal of research is being carried out into the country's different soil types. This is a subject that has traditionally received little attention in Chile so it is good to see winemakers working to provide accurate information of direct relevance to wine production. *Calicatas*, or holes dug into the ground in vineyards to study soil profiles, have become increasingly common sights in recent years. This improved understanding of soil types, textures, and properties has led to better matches between varieties and sites as well as vineyards being developed in more interesting and diverse soils – Torres' Empedrado vineyard in Maule on Carboniferous slate is a case in point. This will be an interesting aspect of Chilean viticulture to follow in the coming years.

By way of brief and general background, in its traditional viticultural territory in the central depression, Chile's winemaking soils are largely the result of gradual erosion by glaciers and rivers. Clays, loams, silts, and sands are to be found, often in deep profiles, with coarser, rocky, and gravel material in areas near rivers or at the base of slopes in what are known as colluvial soils. More diverse soil and bedrock types are to be found in the west of the country and in the coastal range. These areas contain some of the country's oldest rock formations, dating back over 300 million years to the Palaeozoic era, largely intrusive granites though with some raised marine sediments and even metamorphic rocks such as slate and schist. In the raised and hilly sites, bedrock is often close to the surface and relatively unaltered though decomposed as a result of weathering. These tend to be more diverse, complex, and less fertile soils than those found in the central depression.

As regards vine-training and trellis systems, two-thirds of Chile's vineyard is managed on an *espaldera* or simple wire-trained system, in which fruiting shoots are trained upward from canes in what is known as the vertical shoot position. A little over ten per cent is on *parronal* (pergola), wherein the canopy and fruit are arranged in a roof-like structure, while a further eighteen per cent is head-trained or free standing. For the rest a variety of other methods – most commonly Lyre or split canopy training – are employed to counter vine vigour in fertile areas. Pergola training is often used in the warmest areas to protect from sunburn; it can give very high yields but under the right management can give quality at a basic level. Machine harvesting is prevalent for the simple wire-trained systems, although the relatively low cost of manual labour means that hand harvesting remains widespread.

Differences between vintages have become increasingly relevant for Chilean wine. This is not due to any inherent climatic changes; rather it reflects how the country's vineyard has expanded into more marginal territory and thus variations in annual conditions have had a more marked effect on the wines. However, two significant climatic variables to bear in mind in this regard are the El Niño and La Niña phenomena. These are caused by temperature fluctuations in the eastern Pacific, where warm surface waters bring El Niño and its attendant rains, while a general cooling of the ocean top gives rise to La Niña and its dry, arid conditions. An example of a La Niña vintage would be 1999, whereas El Niño hit the 1998. In general, Chile's viticulturists are becoming progressively more adept in dealing with the variations between years, whether it involves rain, drought, frost, or heat.

There are a variety of challenges that lie ahead for Chile's wine-growers. A major task will be to reduce alcohol and over-maturity in the grapes, as the search for complexity leads to ever-longer hang-times and later harvests. Greater attention to irrigation and canopy work will be needed with care to avoid over-exposing fruit, and cooler, more marginal areas that give naturally longer seasons (such as in coastal territory or farther south) will need to be sought out. Another challenge will be to address quality issues in the existing plantations: separating mixed vineyards (such as Merlot and Carmenère, *see* p. 21), replacing inferior clones (Sauvignonasse), grubbing up others like País, and generally replacing those varieties that are ill-suited to local conditions, a legacy of the generalist approach that has been too common in Chile. This will be a long-term task.

It seems likely that there is further growth to come in Chile's vineyard. A government study published in 2005 predicted that this trend could see Chile reach 180,000 hectares by 2014. (As of 2004 the total was 112,056 hectares.) It is to be hoped that this expansion is steady and considered, unlike that between 1995 and 2000, when the country's vineyard doubled in size as a result of the rush to export wine. Measured progress is necessary in order to maintain a balance of supply and demand as well as to ensure viticultural standards are kept high in such matters as sourcing adequate plant material and site selection. In addition, there are a variety of ongoing research projects, both private and publicly funded, that should provide much-needed data for further development or improving existing vineyards.

A final, brief word on Chile's viticultural calendar and relevant dates. The seasons are the inverse of the northern hemisphere so spring in Chile begins around October-November; the hottest summer months are January and February; autumn roughly equates to April and May. Although there are variations between varieties and regions, bud-break usually takes place in September, flowering and fruit set in December, veraison in January. Harvesting begins in late February or early March and continues until May.

GRAPE VARIETIES IN CHILE

Cabernet Sauvignon

This is Chile's most planted grape variety by some distance, accounting for over a third of the national vineyard and nearly half of all red vines. Its plantings have more than trebled since 1995 and its growth continues – so while old Cabernet Sauvignon vines do exist in Chile, the majority are relative youngsters. The flipside of this is that Cabernet is now planted in a far greater variety of sites than before, which has meant an increasingly diverse offering in wines, from fresher fruit styles from the south, west, and north, and more structured, ripe, stately versions from the east.

Deep colour, black fruit, and firm structure are the hallmarks of Cabernet Sauvignon; in Chile, there is often an added earthy or minty edge. Because its structure can sometimes be austere (fresh acidity, firm tannins), Cabernet benefits from ageing and blending – Carmenère and Syrah make good blending partners in Chile. In general, Chilean Cabernet is made in a variety of styles, from simple, fresh berry-fruited wines that are among the best in the world at this level to more complex, ripe, and structured versions.

Cabernet Sauvignon is a vigorous vine that does best in poor, well-drained soils and in areas that experience a long autumnal maturation period (its home is Bordeaux's maritime climate). Because Chile's vineyards have traditionally been in the centre and east of the country, the best sites for Cabernet have been toward the Andes (Puente Alto, Pirque, Totihue) or farther south (Curicó, Maule, Itata). However, new sites in more coastal areas (Limarí, Maipo, Colchagua) are starting to give good results, generally fresher in style than the more continental eastern parts. Where Cabernet struggles in Chile is in the fertile and hot central areas that give high vigour and yields and, without proper care and attention in the vineyard and winery, can result in fruit with harsh, green tannins and overly high alcohol levels.

It is good to see Chile's Cabernet Sauvignon becoming increasingly diverse, with wines made in different styles but ever more assured in their own ways. More work is still needed in the vineyard to ensure it is not overripened or too vigorous. In the winery, it is important to get extraction levels right and avoid astringency. Blending should be used more than it currently is, either between sites or with other varieties, to give this grape more flesh and breadth. Conversely, a small proportion of Cabernet blended with other varieties that lack structure (Merlot, Carmenère) can also generate a useful synergy. Balance in a wine must be the overriding aim of any Cabernet winemaker and when this is achieved in Chile, the results can be excellent.

Merlot

Officially the country's second most planted variety, Merlot has become something of a conundrum for Chile. On the one hand, the success of Chilean Merlot around the world has been phenomenal. On the other, it is now clear that most of this success has been down to Carmenère, which until 1994 remained formally unidentified in Chile's vineyard and as a result was sold as Merlot. It is generally accepted that much of what is currently registered as Merlot is still Carmenère – estimates range from thirty to eighty per cent – though the country's commercial departments are reluctant to abandon the lucrative Chilean Merlot niche and thus many wines remain a blend of the two, if not mainly Carmenère.

As the two varieties have been increasingly separated, it has become apparent that Merlot consistently underperforms in Chile. The exact reasons are as yet unclear but the symptoms include a lack of root development, frequent heat stress and dehydration, sensitivity to soil-related issues, big grape clusters, and a falling-off in flavour and colour in the latter parts of the season. As a result, wines made purely from Merlot are often vegetal or raisined with dry tannins and short palate presence. Work is being done to correct this. Rootstocks are being used and new clones increasingly planted. Greater attention is being paid to soil profiles at the time of planting and cooler, more humid climates such as San Antonio and Bío Bío are being targeted as better suited to this grape. Irrigation is being adapted to prevent dehydration.

It is perhaps not surprising that Merlot is proving such a headache for Chile's wine-growers. It is a challenging variety to grow well, attaining quality in only very specific sites (in Pomerol, where Merlot reaches its apotheosis, a matter of metres can be the difference between great and simply good wine). In addition, there is very little Merlot around the world planted on its own roots, as most is in Chile. As a result, there is much to learn, and I would applaud those growers persevering on this front. Good versions of pure Merlot from Chile are few and far between but they do exist and are worth hunting out, from producers such as Gillmore, Calina, Casa Lapostolle, Veramonte, and Carmen. Its best versions show ripe red and black fruits – often with dark chocolate, herbal, and leathery hints – and a fresh acidity. It also works well in blends.

Carmenère

Carmenère represents both a challenge and a golden opportunity for Chilean wine. It is a difficult variety to vinify well and demands effort and attention both in the vineyard and winery. Nonetheless, Chile is starting to demonstrate that Carmenère can make exceptional wines, often in a range of styles, and there seems little doubt that more and better things are to come from this variety in Chile.

Carmenère was originally one of the mainstays of Bordeaux but it fell out of favour after the phylloxera blight swept the region in the 1870s due to its unreliable yields, late ripening, and susceptibility to disease. It came to Chile in the mid-nineteenth century and was commonly propagated alongside Merlot (many vineyards at this time were a mixture of varieties, with Malbec and Cabernet Franc also common). Although it is claimed that the two varieties were confused, in reality most wine-growers recognized the difference, with Merlot known as "Merlot Merlot" and Carmenère as "Merlot Chileno". It was not until 1994 that Carmenère was officially identified in Chile, however, and since then the process of separating the vineyards has been progressing. It is a necessary job because the two varieties have very different viticultural needs.

Carmenère is a vigorous vine that is also very late ripening (it is often harvested in Chile in May, the equivalent of November in the northern hemisphere). As a result it needs deep soils of moderate fertility and sites that are sunny and warm but temperate, dry, and relatively free from late-season rains. It has a tendency to produce bunches that are uneven and poorly set. Genetically speaking, it is related to Cabernet Franc.

Chile's winemakers have made good progress with Carmenère. The issue is that if it is planted in too cold an area, or harvested too early, it can give virulently green flavours. On the other hand, over-mature and over-extracted styles are equally unsuccessful. The challenge is to find the perfect medium, where the variety retains its attractive, savoury qualities but is also ripe and complex. The timing of harvest is crucial (picking the right moment is a skill that comes with experience), as are low yields, good canopy management, and simply selecting the right sites. In this regard, Carmenère's best-performing sites in Chile are those in the warm but moderate parts of the coastal range, such as Peumo, Apalta, and Isla de Maipo. Some of the best wines show ripe, black fruits with savoury notes of grilled red pepper, roasted herbs, tar, and paprika, with a broad, smooth, and round palate. Because the variety tends to give low acidity (especially when harvested late), it is commonly acidified or blended with a more structured variety like Cabernet Sauvignon.

Given that Chile started focusing on and developing Carmenère as an individual variety only in the mid-nineties, the progress made has been tremendous. There is undoubtedly more to do but it is good to see clonal selection programmes underway as well as other research initiatives. Carmenère is not unique to Chile – it is grown in France and Italy, among other places – but it is the only winemaking nation to have appropriated it successfully as its own variety. As such, it represents a significant point of difference.

Sauvignon Blanc

Overtaken by Chardonnay as Chile's most planted white grape in the 1990s, Sauvignon Blanc is now reasserting its claim to be the country's top white variety. Its resurgence is due to two major developments in the latter part of that decade: the advent of better plant material and the discovery of better vineyard sites.

Although it seems strange to say it, until the nineties there was very little pure Sauvignon Blanc in Chile. Most of Chile's plantings were the inferior Sauvignonasse (also known as Sauvignon Vert), a vine that is thought to be related to Italy's Tocai Friulano, and which in Chile can give some fresh character when young but is light on the palate and takes on a dried, vegetal character not long after bottling. Much of Chile's Sauvignon vineyard (some estimates are as high as eighty-five per cent) is still planted to this mediocre variety, most notably in parts of central Chile such as Curicó. It is a situation that needs addressing – Chilean wineries should not be selling substandard varieties as Sauvignon Blanc nor should they persist in their widespread cultivation.

Sauvignon Blanc performs best in a cool to moderate maritime climate where its flavours and acidity can develop slowly without losing freshness. It is a variety for which site and clonal selection, viticultural work, and harvest times are decisive in the quality of the final wine. If the site is too warm, the fruit too exposed, or the harvest too early or late, the wine can lack character. In the winery, care is needed to retain aromatics by avoiding oxidation, while palate complexity can be added by working with the lees and even careful contact with oak. Chile is making good progress on all of these fronts.

The first modern, certified Sauvignon Blanc clones are thought to have arrived in Chile in the late eighties; the first instalments (including Clone 1) came from UC Davis, California, while French stock (Clone 242) was also subsequently brought. This innovation, combined with planting in more coastal areas such as Casablanca and San Antonio, has made for a sea change in Chilean Sauvignon, with cleaner, crisper flavours emerging, and classic Sauvignon characters of herbs and zesty citrus fruit coming forward. San Antonio in particular has pioneered a more food-friendly, broad, and complex style of Sauvignon, with roasted grapefruit, nettles, and a warm-stone character.

The country's range of Sauvignon Blanc is improving and looks set to develop further as other suitable vineyard areas emerge, such as Limarí and Bío Bío and more recently the maritime territories of

Aconcagua and Colchagua. As a result, Sauvignon Blanc is currently one of Chile's most exciting varieties.

Chardonnay

Chile has been relatively successful in producing middle-of-the-road Chardonnay made in a ripe style often with a touch of oak. This is still a style the country does well, although recent adjustments in the winery as well as new vineyard areas have led to improvements at the top end among Chile's better producers.

The issue of balance in Chardonnay is increasingly important to Chile's wine producers. Changes in winemaking have included carrying out less malolactic fermentation, in order to retain crisp malic acid to balance the ripe character of the wines. There is more of a focus on the type of oak being used, with the percentage of new oak being reduced and fermentations now occurring in barrel for better integration of flavours. Whole-bunch pressing is becoming more common and there is a greater willingness to become less strictly reductive in winemaking, and experiment more with the styles being produced. It is true to say that too many Chilean Chardonnays are still too creamy and sickly, lacking structure and balance, but in general the move is away from this style.

Improvements have also been made in the vineyard. One of the problems with Chardonnay in Chile has been that, unlike Sauvignon, it has struggled to find terroir that has been an instant hit. However, there is undoubted progress being made – winemakers are enthusiastic about the prospects for Limarí, which gives an understated but structured style of Chardonnay, as well as San Antonio (slightly sweeter and spicier fruit), and coastal Casablanca. Southern climes are also beginning to show good results, and cool yet continental conditions in the likes of Bío Bío and Malleco are giving vibrant, food-friendly Chardonnays. Even newer vineyards are being developed in both western coastal areas and higher into the Andean foothills in the east. Time is needed but there is more to come from Chilean Chardonnay.

Syrah

Also known as Shiraz, this variety has emerged from nowhere to stake an increasingly convincing claim to be Chile's signature red variety. Given its success, it is sobering to think that as recently as the early nineties no Syrah whatsoever was planted in Chile. The first nineteen hectares were officially registered in the 1996 vineyard census and rapid growth followed, with Syrah accounting for 2,754 hectares by 2004. As such, it represents only around three per cent of the national vineyard, but this will surely change in time.

Why has Syrah done so well so quickly in Chile? The answer lies partly in Chile's climate and soils – Syrah thrives in the poor but complex granitic soils and continental-style climate with warm days and cold nights. In addition, Syrah's timing was impeccable given that, when it arrived on the scene in the late nineties, Chile's viticulturists were working at a better level than before: they were looking to research and find the best Syrah clones, plant on hillsides, and explore more marginal territory. The result was that even with underage vines, Syrah got off to a flying start.

After only a decade of existence in Chile, Syrah has already developed a range of styles. There are those from the warmer sites, such as Aconcagua, Colchagua, and Cachapoal, which tend to be broad, warming, and spicy. On the other hand, there are those wines made in a more cool-climate fashion, which show lively berry fruit and engaging, complex notes of fresh meat, herbs, pepper, and flora. Top regions in this regard include Limarí, San Antonio, and Casablanca. Other styles are to be found between the two, with Syrah often showing toasty, meaty, and bitter nut character from a range of sites. New areas such as Choapa and Elqui are providing further diversity and more are sure to come. It is telling to see that John Duval, former winemaker of Grange, the iconic Australian Shiraz, is now working on a Chilean Syrah project.

Other Grape Varieties

In the past, Chile has been criticized for its limited spectrum of grapes. While valid, it is an increasingly outdated criticism given the steadily growing diversity in the nation's vineyard. There is also clear potential for future development. It is true that there is still much to do in terms of fostering diversity and improving the planted stock, but the success of varieties such as Viognier, Riesling, Gewurztraminer, Pinot Noir, Malbec, and Petit Verdot point to diversity being one of Chile's future strengths. Given the country's varied terroir, it seems there are few varieties that could not ultimately prove successful here.

One task for Chile is to deal with the irredeemably mediocre vines that are its historic legacy. The large hectarage of País, Torontel, Chasselas, and Sauvignonasse needs reducing, as does that of Moscatel and Semillon, which, while they have the potential for quality and often crop up as old vines, are usually planted in ill-suited sites. There are others on the list, one of which I would pinpoint as the Tintoreras, vines used to give colour to wines and little else.

For whites, Viognier is a grape that has great potential in Chile, having adapted well to the country's continental-style climate and granitic soils since its first appearance on the scene in 1998. It copes well even in Chile's warmer areas. The challenge for winemakers is to retain balance while also ripening the variety fully to gain complexity, which means considered site selection and careful handling in the vineyard and winery. (Otherwise, Viognier can easily fall into overripeness and become alcoholic and flabby.) Currently, the best examples from Chile show a tantalizing blend of fleshy, exotic fruit as well as white pepper and floral notes together with a fresh, balancing acidity. Areas such as Bío Bío, Casablanca, and even Colchagua are already proving to be successful with this variety. There will certainly be more to come in the future.

Other aromatic varieties showing good potential in Chile include Riesling and Gewurztraminer. These are made in a pleasantly subdued style in the far south (Bío Bío) as well as more aromatic styles in coastal territory such as Casablanca. Both are being planted in San Antonio and they may also prove suitable farther south in the coastal range where slate soils are to be found. Experience and skill are needed in the vineyard and winery to make good wines from these varieties, but producers like Cono Sur have made excellent early headway and there seems to be a bright future for both in Chile.

Marsanne and Roussanne have been planted on a small scale since 2000, and Pinot Gris is also now starting to make an appearance in the Chilean vineyard. Chile is also one of the few significant outposts for the rare Sauvignon Gris, which is grown by the likes of Casa Marín, Casa Silva, and Cousiño Macul.

Among the reds, Pinot Noir is still a work in progress for Chile's winemakers. Notable advances have been made of late but the essential problem is that much of Chile's Pinot vines are selections of uncertain origin that can give forceful but often chunky, simple, and inelegant wines. These can make passable inexpensive bottlings, but for better wines the goal of achieving delicacy as well as complexity has largely proved elusive.

In the past, much of Chile's Pinot Noir was used for sparkling wine production and was planted in unsuitably hot, fertile areas. However, selected clones are now appearing on the scene, planted in promising sites in the western coastal range as well as in the far south – with high eastern parts also an interesting option. Either way, Pinot needs a long season and then kid gloves in the winery – adapting to these require-ments has been a learning curve but Chile's better winemakers are now getting there. Growing experience as well as vine age and clonal diver-sity should lead to improvements in the future.

Promising Bordelais varieties in Chile (as well as Cabernet Sauvignon, Merlot, and Carmenère) include Cabernet Franc, Petit Verdot, and Malbec. While Petit Verdot is mainly being used in blends to add colour, acidity, and tannin, Malbec is proving its worth as a stand-alone variety. Its style varies according to local conditions, from perfumed and sleek-fruited in cooler, more humid climes such as Bío Bío to sturdy black-fruit flavours with complex notes of dried flowers and graphite in warmer areas. There are several examples of old-vine Malbec in Chile that are real treats and these are most commonly found in areas from Colchagua south. Carignan is another variety that gives wines full of rustic, bitter-fruit power from old vines in southern Chile and examples of this are increasingly prevalent as winemakers hunt down these often small, remote parcels. Other Mediterranean reds that are more recent newcomers to Chile's shores include Mourvèdre and Grenache, both of which are still in the early stages of their development in the country. This is also the case for varieties such as Sangiovese, Tempranillo, Zinfandel, and Nebbiolo, all of which are now being produced commercially but largely remain works in progress. That said, Sangiovese is showing some initial promise in the hands of a few growers (Errázuriz, Casa Tamaya, Canepa) and the old-vine Zinfandel of TerraMater is also worth hunting out. Petite Sirah is another minority variety in Chile that is worth mentioning, and it is used both as a blending partner for its tannin and colour as well as in the odd varietal wine such as Carmen's Reserva.

3

Winemaking

"It takes a lifetime to learn how to make wine. And then you die."

French winemakers' proverb

Winemaking in Chile is not a topic that has received much attention over the years. Perhaps the country's reputation as a winemakers' paradise encouraged the misconception that its oenologists had little to do between vineyard and glass. But it is clear that winemaking has changed significantly over the last few decades.

CHANGE AND CHALLENGES

The traditional style of Chilean winemaking was common as recently as the seventies and eighties. A chronic lack of investment together with an insular mentality meant that winemaking for many Chilean producers was a crude and haphazard business. (This was a situation by no means unique to Chile; Bordeaux-based consultant Michel Rolland notes that when he started out, "Winemaking was not about making good wine, just about stopping it being bad.")

Vinification was a fast and furious affair. Pressing was quick and brutal; fermentations were short and hot; maceration times were kept to a minimum for fear of bacterial spoilage; filtering was conducted as early and comprehensively as possible. By contrast, maturation and was often a drawn-out affair, with wines routinely kept for years in large wooden vats. (The most common wood used at this time in Chile was not actually oak but raulí, a species of southern beech.) It is safe to say that cellar hygiene was not the uppermost concern in the wine-maker's mind. The resulting wines were often pale, thin, and oxidized.

It was not until the eighties that things began to change. The man credited with the change is the Spanish winemaker Miguel Torres. He established his eponymous winery in Curicó in 1979 and began to import modern winemaking technology such as stainless-steel tanks and pneumatic presses. His example of rigorous cellar hygiene, making white wines reductively, gentle pressing, and temperature-controlled fermentations proved influential. Other producers adopted similar strategies and so the eighties and early nineties became a time of significant investment and renovation.

Torres was one of the first high-profile foreign winemakers to invest in Chile but more were to come, especially after the country's seventeen-year period of military rule came to an end in 1990. French and American investors and winemakers became commonplace in the nineties. As did small oak barrels, extended maceration times, commercial yeasts, and other useful winemaking tools.

This was the era of the winemaker, and the effect on the wines was dramatic. Gone were the thin, pale wines of before: now Chile started turning out concentrated, ripe wines made in a modern, international style, often by a new breed of prestigious winemaker. This was the first major step toward improvement.

Winemaking in Chile today is diverse and increasingly complex. This is good to see (if not to try to document) because it means that winemakers have been moving away from a one-size-fits-all approach, toward a more multifaceted and flexible system. Challenges still remain, however.

Chilean winemakers are often criticized for their reluctance to innovate, and for a lack of self-belief. Another point of censure has been the tendency for Chilean winemakers to make safe, even standardized wines. Added to this, more than one foreign winemaker working in Chile has expressed their surprise at how Chilean winemakers are more often found in the office than getting their hands dirty in the winery or vineyard.

All of these criticisms are justified. However, it is necessary to put them into context. Chile is a relatively young winemaking country; its modern wine era began in earnest only in the 1990s. The learning process is at an early stage and, frankly, it is testament to the quality of its winemakers that Chile has made such good progress.

Enthusiasm and experience are the key qualities needed now – and Chile has a new generation of winemakers for whom working abroad and at home to gain perspective and experience is a prerequisite, as is a desire to work first and foremost in the vineyard. The best among them have the confidence and ability to experiment, foster diversity, and develop their own styles in both whites and reds. As a result, Chile's winemaking is becoming increasingly assured and successful.

It is encouraging, for example, to hear Adolfo Hurtado say, "Our greatest aim now is for 'drinkability'. People are tired of big, oaky, alcoholic wines they can't finish. As a winemaker, my aim is for elegance and finesse above all." Felipe Tosso is also moving away from excesses. "We're constantly experimenting and doing vinification trials to work for better balance in the wines; in the past we've been too macho in our winemaking," he says.

Rafael Urrejola puts it in similar terms: "I'm trying to make wines that invite you to have another glass. In the past, winemakers have almost competed to produce the biggest, most extracted wines, but I aim more for restraint and complexity." Andrés Sánchez defines his style as "simple and traditional – our wines have to have good balance even if it means they can be more difficult at the start and take time to open up. We have good raw materials so there's not much need to intervene." The final word goes to Jean-Pascal Lacaze: "Trying to eliminate all the imperfections in a wine is a mistake, because great wine is about a blend of perfection and imperfection."

These speak of a less formulaic, less interventionist style of winemaking emerging in Chile aimed at making increasingly complex and individual wines. Nevertheless, all of these winemakers concede that there is much still to discover and that Chile has much more to give.

WAKING UP THE WINERY

Around three-quarters of Chilean wine production in any given year is red. The rest is almost all dry white, with a small but growing amount of rosé. Some sparkling wine is produced, mainly for the domestic market. A few sweet wines are made in a mid-weight style. There are further oddities around – port-style wines, a Carmenère made in a *passito* style, University-made brandy – but they remain rare. This, then, is the general context of Chilean winemaking.

Alcohol is a major issue, just as it is for virtually every other wine-making nation. In the search for ever-greater complexity in wines, grapes are being left to hang longer on the vine to achieve full phenological ripeness. The downside of this is that, especially in warm areas or vintages, sugar levels can be worryingly high by the time of harvest. This can lead not only to over-alcoholic wines but also to stuck fermentations because the sugar levels are too high for yeasts to work properly.

This issue is being addressed both in the vineyard and the winery. Getting it right in the vineyard (by planting in cooler sites) is clearly the best long-term solution because reducing alcohol in the winery is not easy. One option, albeit illegal, is to add water. Blending is another. There are also more technological processes available to the winemaker which effectively consist of removing sugar or alcohol from the wine via fractional or osmotic procedures, whereby machines are used to adjust the overall ratio of the wine's individual constituent parts to achieve a required result. Though these are not yet widespread in Chile, they may well become so in the future.

Another way of tackling the issue is with work on yeasts. The widespread use of cultured yeasts in the modern wine industry helps ensure reliable fermentations and give predictable flavours and aromatics in the wines. By their very nature, such yeasts are very effective in converting sugar to alcohol (the usual rate is for seventeen grams of sugar per litre to yield one per cent alcohol by volume). As a result, some Chilean winemakers are now looking to work with less efficient yeast strains that will generate less alcohol and are conducting experiments to see how this might best be done. They are also calling on the yeast industry to develop more products to this end.

It is not just the quest for lower alcohol that is motivating the focus on yeasts. A small but growing number of Chilean wineries are undertaking what are known as "wild fermentations" or fermentations in which no cultured yeasts are inoculated and only ambient yeasts carry out the fermentation. The aim is to achieve greater complexity of aromas and flavours, although wild ferments can prove a headache for winemakers because they can lead to reduction (in which the absence of oxygen in the wine can cause reactions that lead to undesirable aromas and flavours) as well as to stuck and unfinished fermentations. Nonetheless, this growing trend, led by the likes of Errázuriz and Viña Leyda, is important in the search for ever-greater complexity in Chilean wines, and as such should be encouraged.

Contrary to their less than confident past, it does seem as if this is a time of experimentation and learning for winemakers, with an increased willingness to depart from the modern oenologist's rule book and try new things. Small-batch fermentations are common. Reductive (*i.e.* oxygen-free) winemaking regimes for some whites are being relaxed to encourage greater complexity and ageworthiness. Techniques such as co-pigmentation are being trialled by producers like Errázuriz: a small proportion of white grapes are fermented with red in order to extract greater colour and add complexity – for example, Viognier with Syrah. Stainless-steel barrels are being used as anaerobic maturation vessels for varieties such as Sauvignon Blanc, to allow extended lees contact and thus better mouthfeel – Córpora and Kingston are both using them. Casa Lapostolle has even introduced a policy of hand-destemming for its top Clos Apalta wine, a process that involves sixty people hand-picking the grapes from their bunches in order to ensure no stalks or leaves make it into the fermentation vats.

A more widespread though still relatively modern procedure is that of micro-oxygenation. The idea is to mimic effects of barrel ageing on a large scale by bubbling small amounts of oxygen through a tank of wine. As well as softening the texture of the wine, winemakers use this technique to stabilize colour and reduce pyrazinic or green aromas in reds. Micro-oxygenation can also help yeasts multiply before or during fermentation. It is becoming increasingly common to see Chilean winemakers using this procedure, especially for the more commercial wines and varieties such as Carmenère. It is particularly helpful for wines that are naturally high in phenols (*see* Glossary), which Chilean wines can be. However, even its best results do not match up to the quality achieved by barrel ageing.

Acidification is routine in Chile, where, due to the warm climate, both red and white grapes often lack the necessary pH levels to ensure stability and freshness in the bottle. It is commonly carried out before fermentation with tartaric acid and in general is a technique that Chilean winemakers have mastered well. In those cases where it is heavy-handed, the wines can be prickly on the palate and the tannins angular in the reds. Some winemakers also assert that it has a negative effect on wines' ability to age in the bottle. Blending with more acidic fruit is one alternative to acidification. Another technique is to work in the vineyard to ensure a better, lower pH in the fruit come harvest – or simply growing grapes in cooler areas.

For those who choose not to acidify, and who work with low-acid musts, there are risks. Because acid acts as a stabilizing agent, it helps prevent spoilage – the alternative is to ensure rigorous cellar hygiene. A good example of this is Casa Lapostolle, where Michel Rolland has encouraged "meticulous work: topping up barrels, using only top-quality oak, and working with sulphur dioxide". This is an aspect of cellar work where Chile is improving but more work is needed because a significant though small proportion of wines still show defects from poor cellar hygiene.

One topic related to cellar hygiene and currently the subject of much debate in Chile, as elsewhere, is brettanomyces (*Brettanomyces bruxellensis*). This is a species of yeast found in any winemaking environment and can give an animal (some have termed it "farmyard") character to wines. It is especially prevalent in high-alcohol, low-acid reds such as those found in the Rhône and in many New World countries. Many modern winemakers deem it a fault because if "brett" contaminates a wine and is not checked by sulphur addition or fine filtration, it cannot be controlled and may end up multiplying and spoiling the bottle, especially if storage conditions are not ideal. On the other hand, there are those winemakers and drinkers who admire the complexity that, in small concentrations, brett can bring to red wines.

It is a debate that looks set to run. Both opinions exist within Chile's winemaking community, though the general trend is toward greater cellar hygiene and a reduction of brett as much as possible. Winemaker Arnaud Hereu has worked on reducing it at Odfjell. "We had brett problems here at one stage and so worked hard on our hygiene, cleaning our barrels for longer and harder, for example – and from the next vintage we noticed an immediate improvement." Francisco Baettig of Errázuriz describes his work as mainly preventive, using specific microbiological tests to check tanks and barrels regularly and, if any show brett presence, racking and cooling the juice and correcting with sulphur. "All winemakers in Chile should be working like this," he says, "because otherwise they're working blind and can end up over-correcting." Both, however, admit that they find a small percentage of brett character in some wines good for complexity.

Another issue that winemakers have been paying particular attention to of late is extraction in red wines. Chile's natural conditions often give notably high concentrations of polyphenols in the skins of its red grapes. (Polyphenols are a large and complex group of compounds that occur in grape skins and have a significant influence on the appearance and flavour of red wine; they include tannins and the colouring agents known as anthocyanins.) As red wines are kept in contact with the grape skins before, during, and after fermentation, the longer this maceration process is conducted, the greater the extraction and the higher the polyphenolic content in the wine. If there has been too much extraction, the wine will be harsh, chewy, and aggressive on the palate and, whatever the winemaker says, will never regain its balance. The fact that fruit from young vines can lack natural balance (and the majority of Chile's vineyards are still relatively young) can also compound the problem. On the other hand, some extraction is needed to give the wine concentration, character, and the ability to age. Extraction is a tricky issue to get right, especially in Chile.

Too many Chilean wines are still over-extracted. Although an easy mistake to make in Chile, it is still reprehensible, especially at the lower levels where drinkers are looking for straightforward, uncomplicated pleasures. It is simply a case of sloppy winemaking. Happily, however, over-extracted wine is becoming less common as the country's better winemakers look to refine their macerations. San Pedro's Irene Paiva, for example, notes that the compounds extracted from maceration when alcohol is present tend to be harsher – as a result, she is now letting her wines macerate before they ferment, in a much gentler process. This is an increasingly common practice in Chile and one also favoured by Felipe Tosso of Ventisquero, who comments, "We're trying to move away from excesses, easing off on the extractions to give the wines balance." Hot fermentations can also give harsh extraction, which is why winemakers like Almaviva's Tod Mostero are aiming to reduce fermentation temperatures.

Where winemakers still tend to give full rein to their extractive instincts is in those rare cases where the vines are old. As Torres winemaker Fernando Almeda says of the winery's old-vine Cabernet Sauvignon, Manso de Velasco, "If we get grapes of this quality, we feel we must extract as much as we can." Either way, achieving balance in the finished wine must be the overriding concern for winemakers.

Oak is a commonly used winemaking tool across the world in its many formats. It was a relatively late arrival in Chile – before the eighties, barrels in Chile's wineries were almost exclusively made from raulí or beech wood. Nonetheless, Chile's winemakers were swift to adjust and are now adept at using oak, from chips and staves at the lower end to add a touch of roundness and complexity to the basic wines up to small oak barrels for the maturation of top-end whites and reds.

At one stage it was common to find over-oaked Chilean wines, with Chardonnay a particular victim. This is less the case now, as the more forward-looking producers are using barrels as tools for giving subtle complexity via slow oxidation and integration of flavours, rather than simply as imparters of flavour *per se*. In part, this means putting the right wine in the right barrel – if either element is too weak the resulting wine will be imbalanced.

At Concha y Toro, Marcelo Papa has a cold barrel room for Chardonnay.

It's to inhibit malolactic fermentation in order to retain acidity, which we need. Also, we want to avoid using sulphur as much as possible as it can extract oak flavours. We're aiming for a slow oxidation and gentle extraction to set the wines up to develop in the bottle. We used to ferment our Chardonnay in stainless steel then give it some short oak ageing. But we looked at Burgundy and California and realized that with the best wines it wasn't just a question of oaky flavour – it's all about how complete the wine is in the mouth. We match the wood and the toast to the fruit, be it from Limarí or Casablanca, or Maipo. As a result, we've been able to turn our Chardonnays around.

It is also good to see Chilean winemakers becoming more demanding and knowledgeable about their barrels and the coopers that make them. At Altaïr, winemaker Ana María Cumsille is experimenting with seven different types of cooper making similar barrels to find the best. Casablanca-based Casas del Bosque is working with consultant David Morrison to source barrels direct from coopers in order to sidestep brokers and have greater control over their products.

Although blending is a relatively common practice in Chile, it is still an under-used technique in red wines. This has partly been the legacy of a vineyard lacking in diversity (in 2004, over forty-five per cent of red vines were Cabernet Sauvignon). Ironically, its absence is particularly obvious in Cabernet Sauvignon, which can in some cases be linear and austere if not blended, and Merlot, which on its own can lack structure. Even Pinot Noir and Syrah benefit from blending different sites or plots of the same variety, often within the same vineyard, as happens in Burgundy or the Northern Rhône, though a combination of young vines and inexperience with these varieties in Chile has slowed progress in this regard.

Nonetheless, Chile's vineyards have seen increasing diversity since the mid-nineties, both in terms of varieties planted and sites available. Take a wine such as Purple Angel, created by Aurelio Montes in 2003 after he noticed the obvious synergies between his Carmenère fruit from Apalta (broad, structured, ripe) and the recently planted Marchihue region (juicy, fresh, spicy). Concha y Toro's Terrunyo Carmenère is mainly sourced in Peumo but is lent structure and backbone by a percentage of Cabernet Sauvignon from Pirque. Valdivieso's

Caballo Loco is a big blend of varieties and regions. There are many other successful examples.

There are, of course, blends that don't work. In particular, I have found in Chile that Sauvignon Blanc resists any attempt to blend it successfully, though, interestingly, little has been tried in conjunction with Semillon, a variety that has plenty of history in Chile but which rarely makes top quality-wine because it is planted in sites that are too warm. Among the reds, Pinot Noir has much the same characteristic. I believe that experimentation is a good thing with blends, because what doesn't work somewhere else might well work in Chile, but winemakers should not be tempted to bottle the results simply for the sake of novelty.

Making single-varietal, single-site wines successfully is one of the most difficult challenges in the wine world. It needs time, experience, and experimentation. There are wines like this made in Chile that are very good; however, for the majority, blending is a sound option while techniques are being honed, whether it be for top-level or commercial wines, or across varieties or sites (or even vintages, in small measure). Winemakers such as Alvaro Espinoza, Adolfo Hurtado, and Marcelo Papa are masters of this art: if you look closely, you'll most often find their wines are carefully thought-out blends of some sort. It is a good skill for a Chilean winemaker to have.

Winemaking and viticultural consultants are a common feature of the wine world and Chile has its fair share. On the one hand, such consultants have a highly beneficial role in providing perspective, experience, and guidance for wine producers. On the other, they are often criticized for encouraging a prescriptive and formulaic approach to winemaking. The best are those who manage to strike the right balance between the two and the only way to judge this is in the wines they help produce.

Many consultants in Chile are foreign, though there are an increasing number of Chileans in the same role. The likes of Eduardo Silva, Felipe de Solminihac, Alvaro Espinoza, Yerko Moreno, Pedro Izquierdo, and Philippo Pszczolkowski are all Chileans working as consultants (Patrick Valette also qualifies as a joint Franco-Chilean national). It would be good to see more such Chilean consultants emerging both at home and abroad as the country develops in confidence and winemaking scope.

ICON WINES

The term "icon wine" is one that arouses a range of emotions, from passion to anger and confusion. Some view these wines as standard-bearers, highly desirable for their quality and scarcity. Others criticize them for excessively high prices. There are those who, quite rightly, question what the term actually means.

An icon wine is an ill-defined concept but essentially denotes a wine made in limited quantities and sold at a high price. There is a strong element of associated prestige to the product (the Greek *eikon* means image). The term conveys little about the wine itself – it could be red or white, a blend or single variety or even single vineyard. There is also an inference of high quality in the term, though in reality this is not always the case. It is most often used in reference to New World countries and, as a result, for better or worse, any discussion of Chilean wine involves mention of icon wines.

Chile's purveyors of icon wines argue that it is important for Chile to develop a presence in the top echelons. They add that their wines compare favourably against far more expensive wines from Bordeaux, California, or other regions that command high prices. Perhaps the most prominent example of this was the Berlin tasting organized by Errázuriz in 2004. In this memorable blind tasting by European journalists, two Chilean wines (Viñedo Chadwick 2000 and Seña 2001) took the top two spots above such vaunted names as Châteaux Lafite, Margaux, and Latour, and Italy's Sassicaia, Solaia, and Tignanello, all of which sell at higher prices.

There is undoubted justification in these arguments. Chile can and does produce exceptional wines. But, comparisons aside, are these Chilean icons really worth the money, especially given that the wines usually have comparably little track record and are often made from relatively young vines by winemakers who admit they are works in progress? And where is the market – for Bordeaux has its *place*, a system of merchants and brokers experienced in selling wines in great demand at high prices, and Napa has its auction scene for cult wines?

The jury is still out. My feeling is that Chile can and will succeed in these price categories – indeed, already is in a few exceptional cases – but there is an inherent danger in rushing into these things. It would be better to take time to develop these wines and the vineyards that supply them before releasing wines that, if they ultimately disappoint, may not only damage a winery's reputation but Chilean wine in general. Chile's best strategy is a long-term one aimed at persuading customers to covet these wines by force of quality alone and take their pricing lead from there.

HOW WELL DO CHILEAN WINES AGE?

I wanted to touch on this issue as a result of a tasting I was lucky enough to attend not long ago. It was on a chilly March evening in 2005 at the Chilean ambassador's residence in London. The ambassador, Mariano Fernández, a renowned wine-lover, opened eleven bottles of Chilean red wine, the oldest a 1976 and the youngest from 1990. Just three producers were on show: Canepa, Santa Rita, and Cousiño Macul. It was a rare treat because there are few Chilean wineries with such historic stock available for tasting.

It was a fascinating insight into how Chilean wines made at this time had aged – which was surprisingly well. Although they struggled to match up to food (the wines were delicate and evolved, showing dried fruits and spices), it proved that, though winemaking and viticulture at the time were still quite traditional, the wines had the wherewithal to age and develop.

There was an obvious question that arose as a result of this tasting. If this was how Chile's red wines of yesteryear have aged, when winemaking techniques were very different to today (less concentration and ripeness, more oxidative wood ageing before bottling), how are the modern wines going to develop? Indeed, is Chilean wine worth laying down?

It is difficult to give a definitive answer to the first question yet; the second would be a qualified yes. Chile's modern winemaking era has been in full swing for only around a decade and there are few examples to draw on. However, from the many tasting experiences I have had of wines from the mid-nineties onward, several conclusions are apparent.

The first is that the nineties were a time of learning for most Chilean winemakers and so results from this decade are variable. Hot and dry years such as 1997 and 1999 often encouraged winemakers to go over the top in extracting or ripening; such wines are disappointing. By contrast, a rain-affected year like 1998 found many Chilean winemakers ill-equipped to cope, and most wines are dilute. Many wineries at this time in Chile were new and finding their way with their vineyards and winemaking style. Nonetheless, good wines were made in Chile in the nineties, notably from mature vineyards with experienced winemakers, and these have continued to age well.

It seems safe to say that the Chilean wines best suited for ageing are those that are concentrated yet balanced, in which all the principal elements of acidity, tannin, alcohol, and fruit are in harmonious equilibrium. As Chile's winemakers are increasingly making wines in this style, there are good grounds for optimism as regards their ability to age and develop in the bottle. A vintage such as 2005, touted as exceptional for reds, may prove decisive in testing Chile's mettle. It is already clear that many of the better Chilean red wines are developing further complexity in the bottle over the short to mid-term, which is encouraging. More time is needed before the effects of long-term ageing can be assessed.

Part II

Regions and producers

Welcome to the heart of this book – a detailed exploration of Chile's wine regions and producers.

This is the first book about Chilean wine to explore the country by region. I wanted to take this approach for one simple but important reason. Chilean wine has been undergoing a period of exhilarating change and progress in recent years and one of the most significant results of this has been the emergence of wine regions bearing different, individual characteristics. Understanding these regions and terroirs is therefore now an essential part of understanding Chile's wines and wine producers.

What follows is a region-by-region breakdown of Chilean wine country, with producers profiled at the end of each regional section. In all of this, my overriding concern has been to be informative, practical, and readable. Hence the mix of easy-reference details with analysis as well as some all-important local context: social, natural, economic, and so on.

Producers are listed in alphabetical order within each regional section. Each producer is assigned a regional home on the basis of where its main wine focus is. In practical terms, this is almost always where its main winery is based. Producers who are not based in a region but are doing significant work in the area are included in the Noteworthy section that comes before the producer profiles.

This is not an exhaustive listing of Chile's wine producers. I have selected those included for importance, for wine quality, or simply for having something worthwhile to contribute to the big picture. I have conducted extensive tastings and interviews, pursuing a long and thorough programme of research and analysis, in the course of which I have visited around 120 different Chilean wineries. (Of the eighty-two with major profiles I have visited all but seven, many more than once.)

Although I have tried to be as objective as possible in the assimilation and presentation of these results, the judgments about wines and producers expressed in this book are inevitably personal and should be taken as such. It is difficult if not impossible to separate the personal from the objective in a book as detailed as this and I believe it makes for more worthwhile reading if opinions are expressed, whether or not the reader may agree. In addition, where I have allocated criticism it is always constructive in intent and I have endeavoured to present a counter-balance of positive recommendation.

Regarding the brief particulars provided for each wine producer, contact details are either office or postal addresses, rarely the winery itself. (For reference, a Casilla is a PO Box.) Vineyard statistics refer only to land actually owned by the winery, not purchasing contracts, so it is not uncommon to see wineries with no hectares to their name. Grape varieties detailed are the most significant ones within a winery's portfolio. Production refers, as accurately as humanly possible, to output in litres. There are 129 wine producers detailed in this book.

Over time, details included in these pages will inevitably change. The Chilean wine industry has been evolving at breakneck speed over the last decade and shows no sign of slowing down. Wineries change hands; winemakers move jobs (something that in Chile seems to happen with alarming regularity); new projects are undertaken and new wines made. There is no avoiding this and I have instead tried to give an accurate and vivid portrayal of the industry at one point in time as well as concentrating on the fundamentals in order to give the book as much long-term relevance as possible.

A FEW GENERAL WORDS ABOUT CHILE'S WINE PRODUCERS

Chile has over 250 registered wineries. The country's typical, traditional wine producer conforms to a certain basic model. Its main features tend to be ownership of extensive land holdings, a wide range of alternative grape sources, and a portfolio of wines that runs from basic domestic plonk to top-end export products. Many wineries were first established in the mid-nineteenth century by a wealthy land owning Chilean family.

This type of estate still dominates Chile's wine industry. Concha y Toro, Chile's largest winery, is one of them – along with its subsidiary wineries, it accounts for around twenty per cent of total Chilean wine output. Its three traditional competitors have been San Pedro, Santa Rita, and Santa Carolina. Similarly influential Chilean wineries have been the likes of Undurraga, Tarapacá, Errázuriz, and La Rosa.

However, the nature of Chilean wine producers has been changing since the nineties. This has been a boom time for the Chilean wine industry and as a result new wineries have sprung up in abundant fashion. Within this growing industry, the level of corporate ownership has stepped up, foreign investment has increased, and there has been a lot of consolidation.

New large-scale producers are emerging to challenge the traditional hegemony of the big four – Via, VEO, and Ventisquero, for example. At the other end of the spectrum, the nineties saw the emergence of Chile's first small-scale terroir-focused producers (offering an alternative to the top-of-the-range wines produced by the big wineries). The first such were Almaviva, Aquitania, Antiyal, Domus Aurea, El Principal, Gillmore, and William Fèvre. The increase of their kind has been a positive growth trend and more recently they have been joined by Altaïr, Casa Marín, Garcés Silva, La Reserva de Caliboro, Matetic, and Neyen.

Foreign investment, both in the form of joint ventures or direct ownership, has increased diversity. The majority of foreign investment has come from two countries: France (forty per cent) and the USA (twenty per cent). Other significant investors include Spain, Canada, Switzerland, Germany, Italy, the Netherlands, and Norway. Foreign capital is also present via public stock listings, as in the case of Concha y Toro, for instance. Foreign expertise has also proved influential.

Chile's established players have been consolidating by setting up or acquiring subsidiary operations. Examples include Concha y Toro (now owners of Cono Sur, Emiliana, Viña Maipo, and fifty per cent of Almaviva), Santa Rita (Carmen, Terra Andina, forty-three per cent of Los Vascos), San Pedro (Santa Helena and joint ventures Tabalí and Altaïr), and Tarapacá (Misiones de Rengo, Viña Mar, Casa Rivas). This trend is expected to continue.

It is also worth noting that Chilean wineries have made significant moves into Argentina from the nineties onward. All four of the major producers listed previously have wine investments here, respectively: Trivento, Doña Paula, Finca La Celia, and Tamarí. Other wineries such as Montes and Santa Carolina are developing trans-Andean projects. A significant and growing proportion of Argentine wine production is now accounted for by these Chilean investments.

The issue of corporate ownership in the Chilean wine industry is a complex one. This is largely because, while corporations and companies have taken an increasing interest in the wine trade in recent years, many of these institutions are themselves controlled by private, often Chilean, investors. Thus, while San Pedro is majority owned by CCU (Compañía de Cervecerías Unidas), in turn CCU's holding company Quiñenco is controlled by the Luksic family. It is a pattern that occurs in several other major wineries and thus makes it difficult to separate the corporate from the private in practical terms. For the meantime, it is safe to say that private, often home-grown family investors remain the dominant force within the Chilean wine industry.

A final word about a relative rarity in Chile: the co-ops. Most of these were formed in the mid-twentieth century when times were hard for small growers. Only a handful survive now (Los Robles in Curicó and Lomas de Cauquenes in Maule are examples). Quality has traditionally been lacklustre but new legislation since 2002 has helped drive a change toward greater efficiency and competitiveness.

1

The North

Chile's arid, sun-bleached northlands evoke certain time-worn images. The desiccated highland plains of the Atacama Desert. Salt flats teeming with impossibly pink flamingos. The odd steaming geyser. Vast open-pit mines as well as abandoned nitrate stations, forlorn and statuesque, that tell the story of immense mineral wealth beneath the surface. Volcanoes and observatories. Extensive, profitable citrus and avocado plantations. And pisco, the heady brandy whose grapes are grown under rainless skies and distilled in burnished copper stills.

Until very recently, wine wouldn't even have made the most modest appearance in this vivid tableau. But, thanks to the sustained efforts of a committed number of wine pioneers in Limarí and, latterly, Elqui, fine wine is now firmly on the map in the north and looks to have a very bright future. It took around a decade from the first incursions in wine in 1993 for the north finally to hit the big time, but it has done so in ebullient fashion.

THE ATACAMA REGION AND AREAS TO THE NORTH

Although the Atacama Region (III) does not yet officially possess any wine vineyards, it is worth dwelling briefly on its principal characteristics because there may well be developments here in the future. (Indeed, Chile's far northern reaches have been used for wine in the past – what is perhaps Chile's oldest wine press can be found in a town called Matilla, near Iquique in Chile's northernmost Region I, up toward the Peruvian border.)

The Atacama Region is not, as its name may suggest, the region that plays host to the Atacama Desert proper. That is farther north; this region is more of a gateway to the Atacama Desert. Grape growing is focused in the south, in the two sub-regions of Copiapó and Huasco, both of which are centred on transverse valleys created by a river course from east to west. There are 8,740 hectares of vines in the region, over ninety per cent of which supply table grapes and the remainder are used for pisco.

The Chilean Andes are at their mightiest here (Ojos del Salado, 190 kilometres (118 miles) east of Copiapó, is the tallest peak in Chile at 6,863 metres (22,615 feet)) so development is largely restricted to the western half of the country. Being on the fringes of the Atacama Desert, this is an arid and sun-blasted region, though, as in all Chile's grape-growing territory, the cooling influence of the Humboldt Current ensures moderate conditions near the coast. In both valleys, the maritime influence prevails some distance inland, a climatic feature that could prove conducive to wine development. Agriculture and irrigation networks are well established in both areas.

There are two incipient wine developments worth mentioning. The first is the news that Ventisquero is looking to plant experimental vineyards in the coastal reaches of the Huasco Valley on land owned by parent company Agrosuper and originally intended for pork and olive production. The other is perhaps a sign of even more extreme things to come, because the 2005 vintage saw the production of the first wine from the Atacama Desert. As reported in Chilean broadsheet *El Mercurio*, the wine came from some 800 vines grown around twenty-two kilometres (fourteen miles) northeast of Antofagasta, Region II (around 600 kilometres (372 miles) north of Copiapó – farther north than the limit of the Atacama viticultural region). The project, which started in 2001, is being conducted by Corporación Gen, whose stated aim is eventually to commercialize the wine. The newspaper reported that the wine tasted "like sherry".

THE COQUIMBO REGION

Coquimbo is Chile's northernmost wine-producing region and contains three sub-regions: Elqui, Limarí, and Choapa.

This is a transitional zone between the desert conditions of the north and the more Mediterranean climates to the south. Climatic conditions vary between the different areas, though in general this is a region of clear skies, intense sunlight, and very low rainfall. Despite this aridity and plentiful sun, it is helpful not to get too caught up in the concept of desert or semi-desert climates, which might give the impression of searing Saharan heat and sands. The reality is very different for much of the wine-growing areas of Coquimbo, which tend to be of a more moderate maritime climate due to the cooling influence of the Pacific Ocean.

As in the Atacama Region, the Andes are an imposing presence, though here even more so because they divert to the west, bullying their way across the country toward the coast, and merge with the coastal range. This makes for an inaccessible and varied landscape across much of the region – a factor compounded in the south by the fact that Chile's narrowest point occurs at the latitude of Illapel in the Choapa Valley: here, the country is just ninety-five kilometres (fifty-nine miles) wide from the Argentine border to the Pacific Ocean.

Choapa is the least important of the three areas in wine terms, though it is far from devoid of potential. There are 109 hectares of registered wine vineyard and Choapa's sole fine wine exponent to date is De Martino, which sources Cabernet Sauvignon and Syrah from seventy-five hectares (fifty-four Cabernet and twenty-one Syrah), supplied by six of the valley's eight growers. De Martino winemaker Felipe Müller considers Syrah to have the best prospects here, and the one Syrah of his from this area that I have tried certainly points to some excellent potential in this little-explored region.

Choapa is a steep-sided, winding valley and Müller believes that the best quality is to be found in its higher reaches on rocky hillsides around the town of Salamanca. "We are having our best results from a place called Llimpo, twelve kilometres (seven miles) from Salamanca, which is at around 810–840 metres (2,660–2,750 feet)," says Müller.

Here we are in the hills but this is where the Andes are closest to the Pacific so in the afternoons we get an ocean breeze that helps lower tem-

peratures and gives a unique characteristic of ripeness and freshness to the fruit.

He adds a final exhortation, "We need new areas in the valley to be planted [so more people can] taste the results." (A new reservoir project near Illapel, announced in late 2005 by outgoing Chilean president Ricardo Lagos, may be further encouragement for wine development.)

For now, however, it is Elqui and Limarí that have the highest profile in the north. Although they are dealt with at length below, it is worth drawing a general comparison between the two, as they have quite different natures. Where Elqui is a steep-sided narrow valley that burrows its diligent course westward toward the coast away from the imperious mountains, Limarí enjoys what Elqui does not: an expansive plateau of relatively flat land stretching between the mountains and the low coastal hills. Where Elqui is about drama and energy, Limarí is a more sedate environment. (Incidentally, the name "limarí" translates as "that which rolls along".)

The Coquimbo Region contains 21,707 hectares of vines, of which 10,233 are used for table grapes, 9,282 for pisco, and just 2,192 (ten per cent) make wine. Limarí accounts for three-quarters of the region's wine vineyard, with over ninety per cent of it planted to red grapes and some forty per cent grown on pergolas.

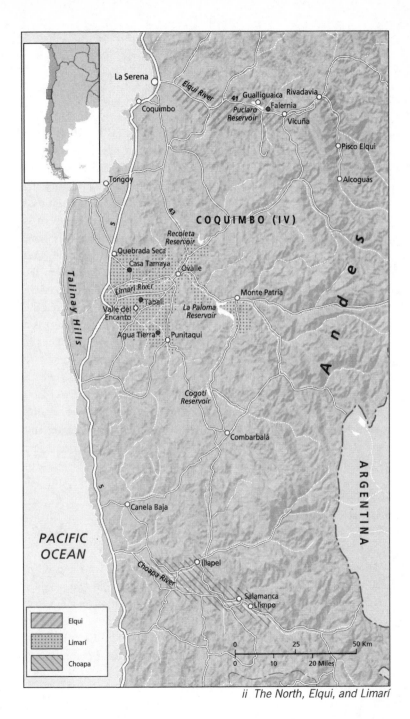

ii The North, Elqui, and Limarí

1a

Elqui

BRIEF FACTS
Vineyard: 451ha (90% reds)
Main grape varieties (ha): Cabernet Sauvignon (185), Merlot (49), Chardonnay (34), Carmenère (32), Syrah (29)
Climate: warm, dry temperate with 70–100mm (2.8–4 inches) annual rainfall and high sunshine levels
Soils: alluvial sands and loams with gravels in places; decomposed granite hillsides

INTRODUCTION

The Elqui Valley has developed something of a contradictory reputation in recent times. On the one hand it is a well-maintained agricultural oasis in the midst of mountainous desert conditions, producing all types of fruit, vegetables, and pisco with the aid of an efficient irrigation network. Its famously clear skies and lack of light pollution endear it not only to farmers but also to astronomers, and several international observatories can be found here. Its credentials are further boosted by being the birthplace of Gabriela Mistral, Chile's first Nobel-Prize-winning poet.

However, Elqui also raises eyebrows. The New-Age-style mysticism and its devotees that have become a staple in the region (due to supposed convergences of cosmic and telluric energy and even UFO contact) provoke dismay or derision among more conservative Chileans. A similar reaction has greeted news of recent ventures in the cultivation of algae and ostriches. And as for wine, the consensus of opinion until recently had it that wine made in the Elqui Valley was either destined for distillation or the least discriminating palates.

Such scepticism was challenged abruptly in 2005 when, at the second annual Wines of Chile Awards in Santiago, in front of the assembled Chilean wine industry elite, a wine from the Elqui Valley beat all other competition to the coveted "Wine of the Show" award (it was Falernia's Alta Tierra Syrah 2002). Eyebrows went through the roof, followed closely by a wine rush north to see just what was going on in this remote and somewhat derided valley on the fringes of the Atacama Desert. This wasn't by any means the first occasion on which Chile's true potential for fine wine was shown to be greater than many had previously imagined – Casablanca had done much the same thing previously. But it was a welcome addition to the momentum that had already been built up by Chile's new areas and was recognition of the country's growing viticultural ambition.

Elqui had a head start when it came to wine-growing because it already had an established vineyard of its own. Indeed, as one *elquino* commented to me, "Most people in this valley live off grapes, whether they be for pisco, table grapes, or wine." The valley has 5,341 hectares of vines, of which just over 3,000 hectares are planted to table grapes, and 1,846 hectares are used for pisco. These have traditionally been the main uses for grapes in the valley, until the late nineties with the arrival of Falernia and the wines that would change the reputation of Elqui.

A PICTURE OF ELQUI
There is a ghost winery in the Elqui Valley. It's hard to miss as you drive up the modern, single-lane road that glides along the valley's southern wall. There, down to your left, sitting forlornly in the shallow waters on the edge of the Puclaro reservoir, lies a jumbled pile of massive round-walled concrete vats, the odd one strewn and toppled in careless fashion, like the discarded solitaire set of a giant. Among the vats is an abandoned metal staircase, mottled in colour between vibrant green and rusty brown, leading up from the water and into nothingness.

Farther on, a mass of dead pergola vines processes haplessly away from the water's edge.

The encroaching water that laps around these statuesque repositories is both an end and a beginning. Where there once was an old winery, there is now a new one. It is located a short distance farther along the road, at the Gualliguaica crossroads, from where you can see the village of Gualliguaica itself. The village lies just over on the far bank: several neat lines of glinting metal roofs and an orderly series of green gardens process modestly along the reservoir edge. But this is not the original Gualliguaica, it is a reincarnation. The old one lies at the bottom of this man-made lake, puzzling at its newfound status wherein the world has suddenly become muffled and murky. A ghost town, to keep the ghost winery company.

THE NATURE OF ELQUI

Elqui is a steep-sided, dramatic river valley whose watercourse runs from the Andes in the east to the Pacific in the west. Water flows off the Andes, which include some of Chile's highest peaks at up to 6,250 metres (20,500 feet), into several rivers. Two of these flow in high-walled, steep valleys that snake down and form a confluence that becomes the Elqui River at Rivadavia – they are the rivers Claro (southern, Pisco Elqui branch) and Turbio (northern, Guanta branch) and their valleys make up Elqui's split head.

The river Elqui then flows down past the valley's main town of Vicuña and into the Puclaro reservoir. Along this route, spanning over twenty kilometres (twelve miles) past Puclaro, the verdant valley floor is rarely more than a brief horizontal interlude between grave and imposing hilly walls. After this, the valley begins to peter out, the plain gradually opening until the hills become a distant memory by the time the river empties into the Pacific at the coastal town of La Serena.

Conditions can vary significantly between the different parts of the valley. For example, the valley's westerly entrance enjoys a relatively maritime climate, characterized by morning mists and moderate conditions with average summer daytime temperatures of 24–27°C (75–81°F) and nights of 10–12°C (50–54°F). Farther inland, the climate develops significant temperature fluctuations between hot days and cool nights. In the middle of the valley, summer daytime temperatures average 27–32°C (12–14°C at night) (81–90°F daytime, 54–57°F night) and this effect becomes more pronounced to the east.

Winds are a constant during the afternoons in the valley proper, drawn in off the coast by the rising hot air in the central valley, moderating temperatures somewhat. (The power and regularity of the wind can be seen in the profusion of windbreaks in the valley, such as harried cypress trees and weather-beaten nets, as well as in the windsurfers on the reservoir.) Cool air also descends from the Andean heights at night.

One common feature of the valley is its aridity and high levels of sunshine. It receives negligible rain during the growing season (70–100mm (2.8–4 inches) as an annual total) as well as enjoying an average of 300 clear days per year in the inner valley. Soils vary from alluvial silts, loams, and gravels found near the river to sandier soils and decomposed granite on the slopes. Some raised marine sediments, including limestone elements, are to be found at the valley mouth.

VITICULTURE AND WINES

The Elqui Valley is not only a varied and complex landscape, it is also still in its infancy in wine terms. This means firstly that it will take time for the region to discover its true potential, and secondly that both generalizations and predictions are difficult. Nonetheless, it is worth trying to tease out some initial conclusions.

Winemakers like Elqui for its lack of rain and reliably clear skies. Irrigation, a necessity in these semi-desert conditions, is effected by drip systems in the majority of the vineyards – the exception being for the traditional pergolas. (Water is mainly sourced from the Puclaro reservoir, which was installed in 2000 to service the lower valley from its 200 million cubic-metre capacity.) All of this gives winemakers a certain control over the growing process and, along with the regular winds in the valley, helps keep the vineyard healthy. (It also means that organic cultivation is a viable option, for which Falernia (*see* p. 58) is now certified by IMO Switzerland.) The valley's variety of soils, climates, and exposures also allows for good diversity of fruit character, a feature that should become more pronounced as more vineyards are developed and the vines adapt to their conditions.

Any discussion of the region's wines must to a certain extent centre on what is, to date, the only winery in the region: Falernia. This Italian-influenced project has produced some noteworthy wines in its first few years of existence, the best of which offer tantalizing glimpses of complexity and individual character.

Syrah certainly seems to thrive here, producing wines of Northern-Rhône-like meaty and spicy complexity, underpinned by the sleek, ripe fruit that is the hallmark of the region. Factors that may contribute to this include granitic soils, hillside plantings, and a varied climate that allows judicious blending in the winery. When asked his thoughts on the matter, Falernia winemaker Giorgio Flessati simply shrugs and says, "It's the character of the area." The winery has certainly managed to reproduce this style of wine in subsequent vintages after its award-winning Syrah first publicized this distinctive Elqui style. Given time and more hard work, Syrah looks to have a bright future here.

Of the other reds, I have yet to taste enough Cabernet, Merlot, or Pinot to form any firm conclusions on their potential. As for Carmenère, it has hitherto proved less than convincing, often making wines with a somewhat green, bitter, and hollow character (which may be why Flessati is experimenting with adding raisined grapes, *see* p. 59). It would be surprising, however, if there wasn't some kind of a future for Carmenère in Elqui, given the region's plentiful sun, long growing season, and, in certain places, the kind of deep soils that this capricious and late-ripening vine needs.

For the whites, there seems to be good cause for optimism. Wines of exaggerated character are already being made from Sauvignon Blanc in the cooler, westerly part of the valley, though more needs to be done to add depth and breadth, as early examples have tended to show well initially but age prematurely. When I tasted at Falernia in late 2004, a selection of Chardonnay barrel samples from its Titon vineyard indicated in their impressive balance and structure that there may be considerable potential for this variety in the valley. Riesling and Viognier may also prove sound bets for future development; indeed, Falernia is conducting trials with both in the valley.

CASE STUDY: VINEYARDS THAT CHART ELQUI'S DIVERSITY

Falernia's three main vineyard estates are sited at strategic points along this narrow valley: one at its mouth, one at its centre, and one high in its mountainous eastern reaches. They provide an insight into the valley's diversity.

The 125-hectare Titon vineyard is planted in the terracotta-tinged soils and rolling hills of the valley's westerly beginnings, with a cooler and more humid climate than inland in the valley proper. This neat, undulating vineyard was little more than dusty hillside with the odd desultory pergola until an ambitious planting plan was implemented in 1998, with the aim of arriving at 200 hectares. The first crop was taken in 2000 and plantings include Cabernet Sauvignon, Merlot, Carmenère, and Sangiovese, though so far it seems that the best results have come from its Syrah, Chardonnay, and Sauvignon Blanc. White grapes are generally planted in the lower land, reds farther up into the hills, where it is hotter.

San Carlos vineyard is located near Elqui's focal town of Vicuña and the Falernia winery. Here, daytime temperatures are warmer than at Titon though moderated by the consistent afternoon winds that funnel up the valley from the coast and cool air descending from the Andes at night. Carmenère is planted on the flat land and steep hillside plantings of Syrah are giving some excellent quality fruit, a programme Falernia should look to develop further. In addition, some forty hectares more of Syrah and Carmenère were recently planted in rocky, sandy soils on what was the river bed.

Then Guanta vineyard. At between 1,700–2,000 metres (5,600–6,600 feet) above sea level (Titon is a mere 350 metres (1,100 feet); San Carlos 500 metres (1,600 feet)), Guanta is breathtaking. Its location is high above the Turbio River, in Elqui's mountainous easterly reaches where the valley is cleaved in two by the soaring masses of inscrutable grey rock. At the end of a long and vertiginous dirt road, the green stain of the vineyard is dazzling against the barren rock face and the sky's intense blue. Clouds float by, close at hand; the air is crisp and loaded with the scents of sweet fruit and spices. Ten hectares of Pedro Jimenez are planted here and some are in the process of being grafted to Syrah and Carmenère. The winery has plans for expansion here, with another 100 hectares plantable, and it will be fascinating to see what will prosper in this fierce climate.

Noteworthy

Though Falernia dominates Elqui's wine production, there is other activity afoot. Far into the valley's remote eastern extremities, an ambitious new wine project is being developed under the auspices of viticulturist Eduardo Silva. Silva has been an advocate of exploring uncharted viticultural territory in Chile and is planting vines at high densities on terraced land between 1,700 metres and 2,100 metres (5,600–6,900 feet) near Alcoguás. Syrah, Carmenère, Sauvignon Blanc, Chardonnay, Cabernet Sauvignon, and Merlot are the grape varieties going in.

Several other wineries, including Cono Sur, are beginning to test the waters in Elqui, buying fruit to evaluate the prospects. Laroche Chile has used Elqui Sauvignon Blanc and Carmenère in its range.

Producer profile

FALERNIA
Ruta 41 km 46, Vicuña. Tel: +56 51 412254. Email: info@falernia.com.
Website: www.falernia.com
Established: 1997. Vineyard: 320ha (Syrah, Pedro Jimenez, Carmenère, Sauvignon Blanc, Cabernet Sauvignon). Production: 4 million litres.
Falernia is a pioneering and somewhat maverick winery. It has been single-handedly responsible for putting Elqui on Chile's fine-winemaking map and has the potential to take things further, provided more progress is made in the vineyard and the restraint shown in winemaking is continued.

Owned by the Olivier family, Falernia is essentially a joint project between cousins Aldo Olivier, a successful pisco and papaya producer of Italian origin though long-time Elqui resident, and Giorgio Flessati, a winemaker based in Italy's Trentino region. Its first bottled wines appeared in 2000 and, whilst a large percentage of the winery's production is still sold as bulk, Falernia is slowly shifting its emphasis toward bottled wine as its stature grows both domestically and on export markets.

The winery is the first to be established in the Elqui Valley and is a suitably eye-catching construction complete with timber exoskeleton that sits in landscaped serenity on the blustery banks of the Puclaro reservoir, a short distance west of Vicuña. Vines cluster around the winery on the narrow valley floor and bustle a short distance up the hillside on the valley's southern wall: this is the San Carlos estate, one of the three major vineyard blocks owned by Falernia in the valley (*see* Case Study p. 57).

As well as producing some highly promising Syrah, Chardonnay, and Sauvignon Blanc, Flessati is not averse to experimentation. In the 2004 vintage, he used raisined grapes to add a *passito*-style touch to his varietal Carmenère, creating a dense, sweet-fruit style with something of a mini-Amarone finish. He also uses the high-altitude Pedro Jimenez in a seventy/thirty per cent blend with Sauvignon Blanc and labels it as such. "Everyone has Merlot, Chardonnay, and Sauvignon in three levels, but few have Pedro Jimenez," he told me. "We are one of 250 wineries in Chile. We have to invent something different."

Innovation for innovation's sake, especially when it is market-driven, rarely makes for fine wine. However, in this case, Flessati's wines are far from being gimmicks. Although Falernia is still an incipient project, many of its wines already exhibit an exciting level of quality and character. More flesh still needs to be put around the bones, more concentration and finesse imbued in the wines, but for now, Flessati's challenging attitude remains refreshing in a country crying out for pioneering spirits.

1b

Limarí

BRIEF FACTS

Vineyard: 1,632ha (90% red)
Main grape varieties (ha): Cabernet Sauvignon (725), Merlot (190), Carmenère (125), Chardonnay (117), Syrah (110)
Climate: warm, dry, temperate with 80–100mm (3.2–4 inches) annual rainfall and high sunshine levels
Soils: variety of clays and loams on flat land, with lighter granitic-based sand soils on hillsides

INTRODUCTION

Induced inspiration has come in many forms in Limarí since it was first inhabited. Hallucinogens such as the peyote cactus (*Lophophora williamsii*) were used in ritual ceremonies as well as home life – and still are. Then, with the advent of grapes came pisco, the powerful brandy that marries so well with the small, toothsome Pica lemons also grown in Chile's desert north. Finally came wine, though at the outset few would have even charitably predicted much of a future for the region's efforts beyond the most basic brews.

Francisco de Aguirre was the first winery to be set up in the region, founded in 1993 by the pisco cooperative Capel in conjunction with private growers. It was to remain Limarí's principal wine producer for around a decade, significant in volume terms though its wines rarely rated above average quality. In latter years, however, it was afflicted by a combination of financial difficulties and a lack of strategic direction.

A long period of speculation ended in 2005 when Concha y Toro bought Aguirre's winery and vineyards.

The story of Francisco de Aguirre is pertinent to the history of wine in Limarí because much of what is now good in the region was a by-product of this initial venture. For example, what is now Tabalí's vineyard used to be one of many grape sources for Aguirre. The same was true of Casa Tamaya, whose winemaker from 2001 to 2005 was Carlos Andrade, previously Aguirre's winemaker between 1994 and 2001. In addition, Concha y Toro's takeover and now permanent presence brings further credibility and ambition to Limarí.

Over a decade after wine appeared in Limarí, the region is now making excellent progress. It took a while but now pisco and peyote are no longer the region's most vaunted intoxicants; wine is on the up and is being met with increasing critical acclaim. It is true to say that, of the total vineyard of 14,810 hectares, nearly half is still used for table grapes and another forty per cent is destined for pisco, but a definite shift in emphasis has taken place.

A PICTURE OF LIMARI

It was a cloudless spring day, the sun showboating in its lonely cerulean heights. A warm wind whipped across the land and rattled our car windows as we travelled in desert convoy, first along flat, palm-lined dirt roads, and then down into the ravine, one of many that constitute the secretive relief of Limarí. Here, the air was still, the sun more savage than before. Looks of concern for the diaphanous English skin flickered across our hosts' faces; eyes narrowed in the glare.

It was the rocks that took centre stage. Cyclopean slabs and boulders, but not the silent type: these had art and life. Chiselled lines, hammered out hundreds of years ago, revealed petrified faces with staring eyes and curious headgear. A series of patiently worn holes, their meaning impenetrable. We strolled down the valley to see a boulder known as the devil's face and on the way we crossed the ravine's apologetic little watercourse. Though diminutive, it seemed to have remarkable life-sustaining powers: its banks revealed a parallel universe, where, in the shade of trees, the most enormous butterflies teemed, filling the air with colour and fragility, and birds chattered in rich, guttural tones.

This was the Enchanted Valley, a place of travel, rest, and ritual in ancient times. For thousands of years, people had trod this land and gazed upon these skies when it had been a highway from mountains to coast. Inca; Diaguita; Molle; their nameless precursors. It was a rare glimpse into Chile's distant history.

THE NATURE OF LIMARI

Two Andean rivers congregate to form the river Limarí. They are the Hurtado and Grande, which have their confluence three kilometres (1.9 miles) east of Ovalle, Limarí's capital. The river Limarí then flows west for some sixty kilometres (thirty-seven miles), sinking a relatively broad depression beneath a flat plateau on which much of the region's agriculture takes place, before emptying into the Pacific, having passed through the coastal range of the Talinay Hills.

The key to understanding Limarí's climate lies in the low profile of these hills and also the fact that, directly to the north on the coast at Tongoy Bay, there are no hills whatsoever between the ocean and land. This is an unusual occurrence in Chile, where there is generally a substantial coastal range bordering the seafront which minimizes the oceanic influence in inland areas. This is not the case in Limarí, a situation that gives rise to a complex interaction between a cool, humid maritime influence, and the hotter, dryer land zone. The main points of entry for the sea influence as temperature charts clearly show, are Tongoy Bay, and also the aperture that the Limarí River has forged in the Talinay Hills.

In effect, there are three main climatic zones in Limarí. The first is the most seaward and westerly, a strip some twenty to thirty kilometres (twelve to nineteen miles) wide, starting ten kilometres (six miles) inland, which includes Tamaya and Tabalí. This is a climate with significant maritime influence. Early morning conditions are often misty or hazy, though this would be more pronounced were it not for the Talinay Hills, which to a certain extent block these *camanchaca* fogs on their coastal side. As the land heats up inland and hot air rises, cool air is drawn relatively freely off the ocean to scour the land with its winds and mollify temperatures. Summer temperatures in the hottest month (January) thus have notably moderate averages: 24–27°C (75–81°F) in the daytime and 12–13°C (54–55°F) at night.

Farther inland, the intermediary zone around Ovalle and Punitaqui eastward, is generally warmer and less moderate: hot during the day with a summer average of 27–29°C (81–84°F) and cooler at night (10–12°C (50–54°F)). The third band, which extends into the Andes in the east, shows a more extreme climate in which daytime summer temperatures can soar into the high thirties (over a hundred degrees Fahrenheit), though tempered by cool nights.

Rainfall is very low, at around 80–100mm (three to four inches) per year, and skies are generally clear, allowing for good levels of sunlight for photosynthesis. Winters are mild.

Soils are varied, the product of volcanic activity followed by glacial and river movements. In general, heavy clay and clay-based loam appear on much of the flatter land, with some limestone in the sub-soil profile in areas. The presence of minerals such as quartz is common. Sandy soils of predominantly granitic make-up can be found in the hilly areas.

VITICULTURE AND WINES

Limarí's coastal strip is the best-suited area to fine wine production in this region. The more inland parts, often warm and planted to high-yielding pergola vines of indifferent stock, are in general better suited to table grapes or pisco production. This is not to say there is not potential in the area, but it will take experience, the right varieties (perhaps more heat-resistant vines such as Grenache or Mourvèdre might be considered), and careful management if good results are to be produced.

It is a different situation over toward the coast. Here, Limarí has a moderate climate with a long season. Mild winters ensure a relatively early start to the season – for example, in 2004, bud-break at Tabalí started during the third week of August, around a month before parts of the hotter Central Valley. Flowering and fruit set are unhindered by frosts or rains. Harvest times tend to be similar or slightly later than in Chile's hotter areas. What this means is that, owing to the early start and moderate summer temperatures, Limarí enjoys a longer growing season than much of Chile's traditional viticultural areas. For example, Concha y Toro winemaker Marcelo Papa notes that in the 2005 vintage he brought in his Syrah on May 13, whereas the same variety was harvested in Colchagua on April 5 and Maipo on April 10.

Tabalí winemaker Yanira Maldonado sees the results of this long growing season manifested in the wines. She likens the effect to "cooking on a slow fire", in a process that gives the wines "complexity and a sense of terroir". Carlos Andrade points to the wines' "impressive aromatic intensity, steering toward floral notes", as well as their balance and "appreciable natural freshness". (Acidification, the norm in Chilean winemaking, is less prevalent in coastal Limarí due to natural acid retention.)

Limarí's coastal area also presents challenges for its winemakers. One is oidium, caused by humidity from the morning *camanchaca* mists, which needs careful monitoring and localized treatments of sulphur where necessary. Another is the nematode roundworm, which eats new roots and has also caused severe problems in Casablanca. These can be treated by chemical products, though Tabalí is conducting trials with more eco-friendly methods involving natural predators. (In general, Limarí's benign conditions mean that producers are often working at near-organic levels, even though few have so far gained accreditation in this regard.)

By far the most significant challenge, however, is that of the soil. Much of Limarí's flat plateau land is heavy clay, which is easily compacted and saturated and means vine roots not only have difficulty penetrating the soil but can also be starved of oxygen during irrigation or rain. As one winemaker quipped darkly to me, "In the Central Valley, this type of soil would be used for rice." Work to counter these problems includes regular breaking up of the topsoil, clipping surface roots to encourage deeper penetration, and adapting irrigation techniques – for example, Tabalí is now irrigating less often but in longer bursts to enable the soil to dry and break up between drenchings. "We have a wonderful climate – it's the soils that are our limiting factor," concedes Maldonado.

Irrigation seems to be both a challenge and a boon. In a region that receives negligible rain during the growing period (2004 being an exception) but whose soils can easily saturate, the question is how best to fine tune the irrigation in any given year. "We're working on finding the perfect level of hydric stress for each variety, but I've been in the region since 1994 and, frankly, we don't know yet so we're still learning," comments Andrade. There is also the issue of restricted access to water, which in some cases can lead to people irrigating not when they want but when they can. On the plus side, no rain means in theory that the winemaker has total control over his vines' water intake – something many European vintners can only dream of. "That's a big advantage in this region," notes Tamaya's viticulturist Lisardo Alvarez, "We can turn the tap on or off; we have control."

With regard to grape varieties, a consistent theme among producers is the potential for Chardonnay and Syrah in this coastal zone. For example, Concha y Toro recently conducted a detailed survey of climate and soils in a wide variety of sites across Chile, many of which have no vineyard at all, and one of the best matches for Chardonnay was found in Limarí. The ultimate proof is, however, only ever in the wines and on the basis of this evidence it does seem that both Chardonnay and Syrah have great potential.

However, if any of Chile's wine regions can be generalist, it seems Limarí can. Apart from those already mentioned, a range of varieties seem to do well here, including Sauvignon Blanc, Viognier, Cabernet Sauvignon, and Merlot. Even Carmenère is promising, though its style can be somewhat pyrazinic (green), so it needs careful viticultural management and attentive winemaking for best results. It is still too early to tell for Pinot Noir, though some winemakers are backing it.

Even sweet wines could be part of the portfolio: old-vine Moscatel de Alejandría, previously used for pisco production, is now being turned to fine wine purposes. However, as most pisco grapes are planted in the warmer areas, winemakers struggle to obtain the high acidity levels needed to match the sugar and make truly concentrated stickies, which means that, for the moment at least, these remain pleasant though lightweight styles of sweet wine.

CASE STUDY: LIQUID GOLD IN LIMARI

"Water is a key factor in the Limarí Valley." So says the region's most experienced winemaker Carlos Andrade, one of whose former colleagues at Casa Tamaya put it in more vivid terms: "Water is like gold up here." It is a telling turn of phrase.

Limarí is a semi-desert climate and receives less than 100mm (four inches) of rain in an average year, almost none of which falls during the growing season. The region's agriculture simply would not exist without regular water, with the result that this resource is both scarce and highly sought after. As Tabalí winemaker Yanira Maldonado comments, "Without water here, there's nothing," and it's easy to see what she means. Beyond the clearly defined perimeters of the irrigated land there is little save dust, wind, and only the hardiest of scrub.

However, Limarí does boast an efficient water distribution system (in fact the largest existing irrigation infrastructure in South America), fed by three large man-made reservoirs: Recoleta, Cogotí, and La Paloma. La Paloma is the largest irrigation reservoir in Chile and the second largest in South America, with capacity for 750 million cubic metres of water. Each reservoir is fed by Andean rivers and their extensive catchment areas stretch down to the Choapa Valley. They effectively ensure the region's water supply. Nonetheless, water is a finite resource with an inevitable supply and demand dynamic to reconcile, which brings us onto the real heart of the matter. Cost.

Water rights are an expensive business in this kind of agricultural land – in fact, according to Casa Tamaya's executive director René Merino, the water rights can in extreme cases cost more than the land itself. He puts the figure at around two million pesos (US$3,950/£2,100) for a hectare of land without water rights, but some 3.2 million pesos (US$6,400, £3,400) with water rights. (Though he adds that this is still cheaper than Casablanca or Colchagua, where land prices with water rights can be as high as twelve million and eight million pesos (US$22,600/ £12,000 and US$15,000/£8,000) respectively.) Drilling wells is an option, though aquifers are under strain in the north largely due to the demand from the mining sector, and this also implies considerable expense in both installation and prior studies: Merino puts the cost of a 100-metre (328-foot) well giving enough water (around seventy to eighty litres per second) for around 150 hectares at US$28,000–38,000 (£15,000–20,000).

Merino's conclusion is that the water issue will ultimately restrict wine development in Limarí. But does this imply a fundamental lack of water, or simply a lack of desire to invest the money to obtain it? Both, I would suggest. There can be no doubt that water is a limiting factor in Limarí: this is an extensive semi-desert region and it is simply not feasible or financially viable to irrigate the whole area. Nevertheless, it would be a great shame if a highly promising wine region has its development stunted not just by a simple water shortage but also by a lack of will to invest in building wells, obtaining water rights, implementing sound water management, or generally ensuring an adequate water supply. This gold is surely a worthwhile investment.

Noteworthy

Proof that Limarí has convinced Chile's wine industry of its potential for fine wine comes in the list of influential producers that are actively involved in the area. As one of the region's winemakers told me, "Let the big boys come and make their premium wines – it means we're no longer just pioneers, we now have a solid reputation. If you have good neighbours, the neighbourhood improves."

One such neighbour is Concha y Toro, which now has a major presence in the region, having bought Francisco de Aguirre in 2005 for US$17 million (£9 million) in a package that included the winery and 320 hectares of vineyard. Although this was partly to ensure grape supplies in an era of fluctuating prices, it was still interesting to hear

Concha's vice-president Rafael Guilisasti call Limarí "one of the most attractive areas of recent years".

Concha y Toro previously bought grapes from the region – its Marqués de Casa Concha Chardonnay contains a small percentage of Limarí fruit – but now it has a permanent base it is beginning to plant vineyards in the coastal strip, having bought 300 hectares over three separate sites, and will look for more. (Of the 320 hectares inherited from Aguirre, 270 are pergola vines and will be used only for basic wine.) Plantings started in 2005 and are mainly Chardonnay and Syrah, along with some Sauvignon Blanc, Viognier, and Petite Sirah. Winemaker Marcelo Papa is clearly a great admirer of Limarí and, whilst he has already made some excellent wines from the region, urges patience while the young vines mature to give even better results. "The future", he once told me conspiratorially, "is here."

De Martino has a long-term contract to source fruit from a vineyard in Quebrada Seca that lies nineteen kilometres (twelve miles) from the ocean. Winemaker Felipe Müller comments that while Sauvignon Blanc, Cabernet Sauvignon, and Merlot have so far not performed well, Chardonnay is outstripping expectations.

> We have maximum temperatures of 25.5°C [78°F] in January and February (similar to the mid-low part of Casablanca) and when you study the geology, this is an old alluvial terrace and in the sub-soil profile there is a great accumulation of calcium carbonates that give a nice minerality and freshness to the wine as well as great volume. This makes it something completely different from what Chile has been producing, and is only true of a few places in Quebrada Seca – the soil profile can change within metres.

De Martino's first Chardonnays from Limarí were produced in the 2004 vintage and the deft combination of structure and freshness is already impressive.

Other notable producers linked to Limarí include Maule-based winery Calina, which has sourced Chardonnay here since 1995 from the relatively warm site of Camarico, just south of Ovalle. Cono Sur is testing the water. Santa Rita, which had been interested in the purchase of Francisco de Aguirre, bought 600 hectares close to Tabalí at the end of 2005 and plans to plant around 480 hectares, mainly with Sauvignon Blanc, Chardonnay, Carmenère, and Syrah.

Producer profiles

AGUA TIERRA
Casilla 40, Ovalle. Tel: +56 51 550355. Email: jmpryor@aguatierra.cl.
Website: www.aguatierra.cl
Established: 1999. Vineyard: 33ha (Syrah, Cabernet Sauvignon, Carmenère, Pedro Jimenez). Production: 20,000 litres.

Agua Tierra specializes in producing organic grapes, used to make red and rosé wines. The project was started in late 1999 by Jim Pryor, a Texan by birth, whose previous business interests had been in television and boating, and by 2006 was in something of a transitional phase.

Pryor owns a 120-hectare estate northwest of Punitaqui planted to a variety of crops, including thirty-three hectares of pergola vineyard for wine made up exclusively of red varieties. The wines are made elsewhere, an arrangement which has led to variable quality since the first vintage in 2002. Pryor is consequently working on cementing a more permanent relationship with another winery whereby he would sell all the grapes to the partner and have a small quantity of his own wine produced, probably an organic red blend. As Pryor comments, "The idea would be to make one wine that best represents our terroir."

If this situation arises, then Pryor plans to plant up to twenty-five hectares more in a simple wire-trained system. While pergola does have its advantages in this kind of area – minimizing sunburn for the grapes and maximizing photosynthetic capacity – it has yet to prove capable of producing more complex styles of wine. The plan is to remain organic (the vineyard has been certified by IMO Switzerland since the 2004 harvest) while introducing Biodynamic practices.

Improvements need to be made in both the vineyard (especially attention to harvesting times and more sensitive management of the training systems) as well as winemaking if Agua Tierra is to be successful. Currently, the rosé is its best product, showing earthy, peppery, and leafy notes with slightly jammy fruit and warming alcohol. Syrah and Carmenère demonstrate some earthy, spicy promise, though Cabernet Sauvignon is less convincing. Late-ripening, Mediterranean-type varieties would be suited to this hot, dry area.

CASA TAMAYA

Av Nueva Tajamar 481, Torre Sur, Of. 1002, Las Condes, Santiago. Tel: +56 2 6585040. Email: vina@tamaya.cl. Website: www.tamaya.cl

Established: 2001. Vineyard: 163ha (Chardonnay, Cabernet Sauvignon, Sauvignon Blanc, Merlot, Syrah). Production: 750,000 litres.

Tamaya is still a winery getting to grips with its vineyards and wine-making. Progress is undoubtedly being made and, with time and a sus-tained focus on wine quality, there is no reason why the considerable potential in this project should not eventually be realized.

Tamaya started out life as a fruit farm and diversified into wine-growing on the advice of Carlos Andrade, who was working as wine-maker for Francisco de Aguirre at the time and also owned the property opposite Tamaya. Both sold their grapes to Aguirre but, when grape prices plummeted and Aguirre could not honour its contracts during the 2000 harvest, the five owning partners decided to set up their own winery and ushered Andrade into the fold. The first vines were planted in 1997 and the winery was finished in time for the 2002 vintage.

Both Tamaya and Tabalí (*see below*) are located in Limarí's cool mar-itime strip, but where Tabalí is situated in the southern part of the Limarí plateau on flat land tousled by stiff breezes, Tamaya is set to the north of the river, adjacent to hills that not only afford some protection from the winds but also present viticultural opportunities for different microclimates, exposures, and soils such as the granitic sand identified by Andrade as especially promising for Viognier. In 2005, Tamaya planted fifty-three hectares of hillside vineyard with Syrah, Viognier, Chardonnay, Sauvignon Blanc, and Gewurztraminer.

The Tamaya team are getting to know the vines. Studies and trials of rootstocks and plant material (including different clones) are under-way. In addition, there is a detailed focus on each variety – take

Sangiovese, a recalcitrant vine that demands careful canopy management and low yields. On a recent visit, viticultural manager Lisardo Alvarez explained in detail just how he was going about adjusting the leaf-to-fruit ratio to ensure proper ripening, and that in doing so he had halved the yield – adding that it would need to be halved again if real quality were to be obtained. "These are long-term trials to get to know our vines," Alvarez noted. "It isn't something you can just achieve from one year to the next."

On the winemaking side, early on in its existence Tamaya adopted a policy of creating blends, often quite unusual in their make-up, such as Viognier/Chardonnay/Sauvignon Blanc. This was a winemaking decision that ended up helping Tamaya create an identity for itself and open new markets. Some of these blends work better than others and this particular part of the winemaking policy will need modifying as the project matures. As of 2005 some of Chile's top consultants have been brought in to advise, and after Carlos Andrade left in 2005, José Pablo Martín became winemaker from the 2006 vintage.

TABALI

Vitacura 4380, Piso 3, Santiago. Tel: +56 2 4775394. Email: info@tabali.com.
Website: www.tabali.com
Established: 2003. Vineyard: 180ha (Cabernet Sauvignon, Syrah, Chardonnay, Sauvignon Blanc, Pinot Noir). Production: 650,000 litres.

Tabalí's has been a debut to die for: the winery received critical acclaim for its very first wines – and rightly so. It has established Limarí's credentials for fine winemaking and it continues to improve.

Tabalí is a joint venture between the giant San Pedro winery and Agrícola y Ganadera Río Negro, the company that originally planted the vineyard in 1993. The owner of Río Negro is Guillermo Luksic, whose family business is the Luksic Group, which, through its controlling stakes in the holding company Quiñenco and, by extension, brewing firm CCU, effectively owns San Pedro, Guillermo Luksic sits on the boards of CCU, San Pedro and Quiñenco (the latter two as chairman) – though not that of Tabalí, for reasons of propriety. It is a highly self-involved situation.

Not that this has harmed the winemaking – in fact, quite the opposite. One major advantage that Tabalí has over many other recently established projects is vine age: the majority of the plantings (150 hectares) took place between 1993 and 1998 and benefited from the input of French consultant Jacques Lurton, who was consulting for San Pedro at the time. This meant that when San Pedro's considerable technical expertise and experience were introduced and the first wines were made in 2002, it was already a maturing prospect. (Although the joint venture wasn't officially established until 2003, the 2002 wines were made by San Pedro and were received so well that they were then later bottled as the first wines of the Tabalí project.)

Since then, further progress has been made. A new winery completed in 2005 will inevitably mean a step up in quality, given that previous vintages had to be trucked some 400 kilometres (248 miles) to another facility in Santiago, with consequent pressures on picking times and risks of spoilages such as oxidation. The winery also now has a dedicated live-in winemaker in the talented Yanira Maldonado, who is advised by San Pedro head winemaker Irene Paiva.

The hallmark of Tabalí's wines at this early stage seems to be a marriage of vibrant character and finesse, wherein a vivid New World flavour profile is underpinned by an integration and subtlety that imbue the wines with sophistication. Whites and reds impress across the board and look to be improving by the vintage.

2

Aconcagua

BRIEF FACTS
Vineyard: 1,052ha (87% reds)
Main grape varieties (ha): Cabernet Sauvignon (476), Merlot (155), Syrah (93.5),
Carmenère (58), País (51)
Climate: warm temperate with annual rainfall of 150–250mm (6–10 inches);
cooler and wetter near the coast
Soils: clay-based loams on the valley floor with more sand and rock near the river
and hills; granitic sands and stones on the hillsides

INTRODUCTION
In Chilean wine law, the Aconcagua Region is that which coincides
with political Region V (Valparaíso), so officially it also includes
Casablanca and San Antonio as "sub-regions". It is a good example of
how wine denominations drawn up along political or administrative
lines are not only ill-suited to charting wine's complexity, but can lead
to faintly absurd situations. Because, if we follow the logic that all of
Chile's political Region V be lumped together in one demarcated wine
region, then if wine were made on Easter Island or the Juan Fernández
archipelago, these too could use the Aconcagua appellation, because
they are officially classed as part of Chilean Region V.

The truth, of course, is that the Aconcagua Valley is very different to
Casablanca, which is again different to San Antonio. This is why I treat
these areas according to their own merits in different chapters in this
book. In this regard, it is worth making a point about terminology.
When I use the term Aconcagua it signifies the Aconcagua Valley itself
(i.e. that defined by the Aconcagua River) and has no relevance to

Casablanca or San Antonio and the wider Aconcagua Region, unless this is made explicit. In doing so I hope to avoid the ambiguities of the official system.

The Aconcagua Valley denomination is broader in scope than many realize, stretching from some 900 metres (2,900 feet) altitude in its eastern Andean extremity down, almost, to Viña del Mar on the coast. (It also includes a small outpost in Petorca, around fifty kilometres (thirty-one miles) to the north). Despite this, its vineyard is by no means extensive (Casablanca is nearly four times bigger), principally because the valley's benign climate has also proved popular for other crops, mainly citrus fruits, avocados, and table grapes, as well as the very Chilean fruits *lúcuma* and *chirimoya* (custard apple). For example, the table grape vineyard outweighs the wine vineyard by a factor of more than eleven to one (12,172 hectares versus 1,052).

Aconcagua's warm climate and lack of frosts mean that fruit growers here can get their produce onto markets early and reliably, and as such it can make better financial sense than wine. It also means that land is in great demand, often to the detriment of the wine vineyard. Horacio Vicente, whose San Esteban winery also owns twenty hectares of table grapes, explains how:

> Fruit tends to be a faster and better return because there's no investment in building a winery or marketing a brand, and as a result this is some of the most sought-after and expensive land in Chile. However, one benefit for wine is that fruit uses the fertile land; the poorer soils on riverbanks and hillsides that are naturally better terrain for vineyards are then left over.

But this is true only to a certain extent, as anyone who has seen the extensive terraces of avocado plantations being established on the lower hills can attest. This is a growing cause of concern for the region's viticulturists. "I'm sure all these new avocado plantations are disrupting the local ecosystem," frowns Von Siebenthal's Ireneo Nicora as he gazes up at just such an installation above his vineyard.

> I believe it makes the microclimate more humid from the frequent irrigation. The trees also introduce pests, though some of these are beneficial. In general, I consider the avocado trade to be the main threat to wine in Aconcagua simply because it's so profitable.

Nonetheless, the region's few wine producers have stuck to their guns and Aconcagua now seems to be entering a new phase in its vinous development. It would be good to see them making more of a concerted effort to develop wine tourism too. Aconcagua is situated on the main route into Argentina (with 1,300 vehicles passing per day) and to the El Portillo ski resort; it is also close to both Santiago (Chile's capital) and the coastal cities of Valparaíso and Viña del Mar; La Campana National Park with its hot springs and Inca petroglyphs is also nearby; all these are factors contributing to a huge tourist appeal.

A PICTURE OF ACONCAGUA

The insistent beeping had been going on for some time, and our pilot Ricardo had become increasingly agitated, before he finally leaned over to me and said, "I need you to find a switch."

Ricardo had briefed us before setting out in our state-of-the-art, dual-engine, German-manufactured Aerocopter. Do not pull or push anything that looks like it might do something. Ricardo was a former Chilean Air Force pilot and had flown hellish chopper missions over burning oil wells in Kuwait and sub-zero sorties in the South Pole. He had proudly shown me the photos earlier. This had boosted my confidence in him, and while I was touched that he trusted me to help him sort out the problem, I did not have the same faith in my ability to find the right switch. The drawn faces of my colleagues in the back confirmed my instinct. We were going to have to put down and Ricardo could sort it out on the ground.

As it happened, we touched down right in the middle of the Aconcagua Valley, where we had a broad and verdant valley floor to cushion us.

Our pit stop was brief and worry-free. It turned out to be a false alarm – another helicopter's emergency signal broadcast by mistake. That was not the memorable thing about this interlude. Instead, what sticks in the mind is the subsequent dramatic vertical ascent. Neat vineyards, olive groves, and citrus plantations stretched as far as the eye could see at first; then, with more height, the valley shrank into perspective, framed by hulking brown-skinned hills whose skirts were laden with orderly lines of eucalyptus and avocado trees. One big, sprawling garden beneath a clear blue sky.

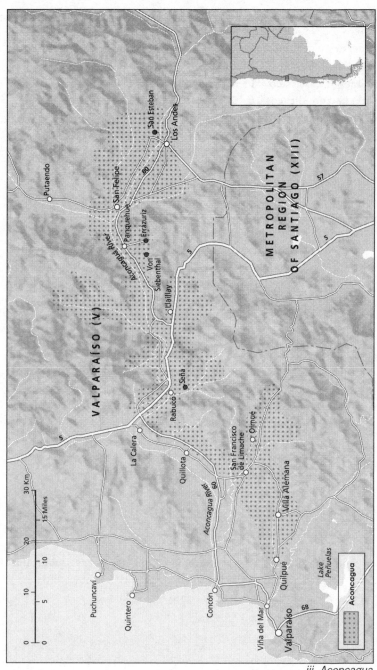

iii Aconcagua

THE NATURE OF ACONCAGUA

Aconcagua is a steep-sided, flat-floored valley that winds a sinuous path west from the Andes to the ocean around Viña del Mar. The terrain is relatively mountainous here, in what is essentially a transitional zone between the broad, flat expanses of the central valley depression to the south and more inaccessible areas to the north, where the Andes bustle across the country, fusing with the coastal range in an inhospitably rugged landscape.

The valley takes its name from Mount Aconcagua, the highest mountain peak outside Asia, at 6,962 metres (22,835 feet), which lies across the border in Argentina. The main route into Argentina, which passes through the valley, follows the course of the Juncal River, which flows down from high in the Andes and is the major initial tributary of the river Aconcagua. The river Aconcagua then flows northwest from Los Andes to just past San Felipe, where it is joined by the Putaendo River and changes course southwest, past Panquehue and Llaillay. At this point the river swings round to the northwest again before colliding with coastal hills at La Calera and abruptly deviating directly south past Quillota before finally making its path directly westward and emptying into the ocean at Concón.

Aconcagua can be broadly divided into three main climatic sectors. The first is the far eastern end, from San Felipe toward the Andes, where temperatures tend to be hot in summer, with a daytime January average of 30–31°C (86–88°F), making it one of the warmest viticultural zones in Chile. However, this area is at relatively high altitude (800–900 metres (2,600–2,900 feet)) and does benefit from the cooling night-time air that descends from the Andes and whose influence also affects areas farther to the west. This cool night air, and the day–night temperature fluctuation in this inland part of Aconcagua, is one of the valley's most salient climatic features. (The night-time temperature average in January is remarkably similar for most of the valley at around 10–12°C (50–54°F), but temperatures in the day can be over 20°C (36°F) higher in the warmer eastern parts.)

This temperature fluctuation is also compounded by the influence of cool coastal winds which are sucked in from the Pacific by the hot air rising off the land in the afternoon and whose main influence is felt from La Calera to San Felipe in what is effectively one big wind tunnel. (The name of the town Llaillay, which lies in the middle of this wind path, translates as "big wind".) This section constitutes Aconcagua's second main climatic zone, which is also characterized by warm conditions (daytime January average of 27–30°C (81–86°F)) but tempered by the afternoon breezes and cool nights. Even within this small sector there is significant climatic variation, however, and the western extremes are generally cooler and more humid than the eastern parts.

The third climatic area is that which lies at the coastal extreme of Aconcagua, roughly from La Calera to the south and west, where the cooling, humid influence of the Pacific Ocean is relatively unimpeded by hills and thus more keenly felt. Average daytime January temperatures can reach as low as 21°C (70°F) in the more coastal parts, though for the main the mercury moves between 24 and 27°C (75–81°F). (As a point of reference, these conditions are broadly similar to those experienced in Casablanca and San Antonio to the south.) The day–night temperature fluctuation is less marked here and rainfall averages some 450mm (eighteen inches).

Aconcagua's soils are varied. On the valley floor, the common soil profile is clay-based loams of alluvial origin which tend to be deep, with good water retention and medium fertility. Near to the river, these loams tend to be sandier in texture and with a high content of alluvial rocks, making for lower fertility and water retention. The hillsides are generally characterized by sands of granitic origin, often in a shallow soil with rocky sub-soils, good drainage, and low fertility.

Rainfall can be variable, ranging from 50mm to 800mm (two to thirty-two inches) in recent years according to Errázuriz viticulturist Cristián Marchant, but averages around 150–200mm (six to eight inches) per year in the dryer parts and up to 450mm (eighteen inches) per year in the more humid coastal reaches. Precipitation is usually confined to the winter months. In general, Aconcagua benefits from a consistent climate characterized by high levels of light and a long, dry, warm growing season.

VITICULTURE AND WINES

Being a warm, sunny, dry climate in its traditional heartland around Panquehue, the Aconcagua Valley has naturally tended toward the production of a certain style of red wine: ripe fruit, low acid, warming alcohol with soft but firm tannins. Cabernet Sauvignon has been the pre-eminent player in this vinous tableau, which could be described as classic Chile writ large.

However, things have been progressing. Following the national planting boom from 1995 to 2000, both viticulturists and winemakers at the better producers have been questioning their methods and aims in an attempt to move Aconcagua onto the next level. This has led to a re-evaluation of the vineyards and winemaking as well as the development of new areas within the valley (*see* Case Study, p. 82).

I talked to Errázuriz viticulturist Pedro Izquierdo back in 2002, when this rethink was already underway, and he put his finger on a number of key issues in this regard:

> *We've gone overboard in the past in adopting a French mentality to wine, which in Chile means overripeness, because ripeness is what they crave in France. But now we've reached a mature stage as an industry and we're looking to rein in the alcohol and recognize that not all herbaceousness or minerality is bad. They may be essential ageing components. Also, extraction is no longer the prime issue, nor is using the most efficient commercial yeasts. We want personality in our wines – Chilean personality.*

It was a point that Errázuriz president Eduardo Chadwick would later take up with me in 2004. "What is Aconcagua today in wine terms?" he questioned.

> *In the past we've looked elsewhere to define the answer to this – Bordeaux, the Rhône – but now the key question in Chilean viticulture is to define what is best for us in our individual Chilean terroirs. Perhaps a blend of Cabernet Sauvignon, Shiraz, and even Carmenère would represent us best here. It's early days, but we now need to do some fine tuning.*

Since then, Errázuriz has indeed started adding a percentage of

Syrah to its iconic Don Max Cabernet Sauvignon – a notable statement of intent. In addition, a new release from Errázuriz called The Blend has impressed with its vibrant combination of Cabernet Sauvignon with some Syrah, Sangiovese, and Carmenère. As winemaker Francisco Baettig states, "It represents what I want to produce with the fruit from Aconcagua." Vineyards have been developed in the cooler westerly reaches of the valley to give wines with more balance and freshness as well as establishing a broader varietal base. All in the drive to expand Aconcagua's vinous palette.

It's not just Errázuriz, either. At Von Siebenthal there has been a notable focus on matching each vine variety to the different soil types in its heterogeneous twenty-five hectare parcel – Carmenère and Merlot on the lower ground where the heavier, more water-retentive clays prevent dehydration, Cabernet and Syrah on the poorer, rockier slopes. As the vines age, there has been an increasingly selective and parcelized harvest, aiming at obtaining ripe but not overripe fruit. Similarly, farther up the valley at San Esteban, Horacio Vicente explains how he increasingly prefers the fruit from the easterly exposures of his hills, which give a better balance of acidity and ripeness than those that receive the stronger afternoon and evening sun from the west.

Hillside planting is an aspect of Aconcagua's viticulture worth mentioning. While such a phenomenon is a relatively common sight in Europe – the Douro, Mosel, and Northern Rhône spring to mind – in Chile traditional flood irrigation, restricted largely to the flat land, precluded it. So, when in 1992 Errázuriz began planting its steeper Don Max 1 hillsides (at thirty-five to forty-five per cent incline) with Cabernet Sauvignon installed with modern drip irrigation, these were some of the first such plantings in Chile.

Hillsides are sought after because they offer poorer, less fertile, and often better-drained soils than the flat valley floors, as well as a range of exposures. Being able to exploit these kinds of soils and move away from the often fertile, humid soils of the flat lands has proved immensely beneficial to both Aconcagua and Chile's viticulture. Selecting the ideal exposure has been more problematic: it would seem natural in a warm climate like Aconcagua's to seek out the cooler, south-facing aspects, but in fact almost none of the valley's traditional vineyards are to be found with this feature. North-facing is common, as are east and west, but south is an aspect that has been relatively under-exploited in Aconcagua, although this is now changing with the emergence of new vineyards such as Errázuriz's Las Vertientes and Llay Llay.

Certified organic and Biodynamic viticulture is now becoming a reality in the valley, perhaps somewhat overdue given the region's natural propensity for eco-friendly methods of cultivation (dry, warm, bright, and windy conditions naturally control many vine diseases).

Red grapes in Aconcagua can acquire a hefty phenolic and alcoholic charge due to the long growing season and sunny conditions; the challenge is to retain elegance and not go over the top. For example, Izquierdo notes that flowering occurs in mid-September and harvest does not take place until early April, a long season that permits a high accumulation of polyphenols in the grapes. Scrupulous canopy management can act as a necessary brake in this regard because, as he comments, "the dark berry can be up to 10°C (18°F) warmer than the ambient air, so at temperatures of 30°C (86°F) it's easy for the organic compounds to get burnt off. So shade needs to be well managed."

To reprise on the varietal topic, it should be noted that this region has probably the longest commercial growing history of Syrah in Chile. Errázuriz's first plantings were established in 1995 after vine stock was imported from France, so it has not only some of the oldest vines but also a good experience of working with what is fast becoming Chile's star variety. It certainly looks to be well suited to Aconcagua's warm climate and granitic hillside soils, and it will also be interesting to see how it fares in the valley's cooler areas such as Chilhué.

Petit Verdot is enjoying something of a boom, being used to add tannin, colour, and spicy aromatics to red blends, most notably at Von Siebenthal. Carmenère is well suited to the warm climate and long growing season of Aconcagua though when harvested too late can easily become jammy and insipid. Other long-cycle varieties could prosper here, such as Mourvèdre and Grenache, both of which Errázuriz is looking to plant at Las Vertientes, where Viognier is also going in. In addition, Errázuriz's new Llay Llay vineyard could even see some

Touriga Nacional on steep terraced slopes. Experimentation, development, and fine tuning are the order of the day in Aconcagua.

CASE STUDY: ACONCAGUA ON THE MOVE

A subtle but substantial change has been taking place in the tectonics of Aconcagua's wine landscape. Its beginnings have passed largely unnoticed because these are changes that have been taking place at ground level, the foundations for a vinous renaissance rather than transformation of the wines themselves just yet. But the implications are at once far-reaching and also symptomatic of the wider Chilean renaissance in the vineyard.

Aconcagua's best wines have traditionally been reliable, warm-climate reds showing ripe fruit, warming alcohol, and often a tell-tale smidgen of minty, eucalyptus character. Consistent and heart-warming though perhaps lacking somewhat in elegance, ambition, and yes, let's admit it, real excitement at the top end.

Now this may all be about to change. What could be described as a one-dimensional offering is in the process of being expanded and broadened. At the forefront of this move is the ever-progressive Errázuriz, a winery that has dominated Aconcagua's wine scene since its inception and yet continues an impressively forward-looking trajectory. And the first step has been to diversify the valley's viticultural territory away from its traditional epicentre at Panquehue.

The most extreme example of this is at Errázuriz's new Chilhué estate, a 1,000-hectare formerly virgin property which lies on rolling hillsides just thirteen kilometres (eight miles) from the Pacific Ocean near Concón. Although this is uncharted territory for the Aconcagua Valley's fine wine lands, it is worth remembering that San Antonio is in a similar position not far south, so the precedent exists, although this is still a bold move. "It's a risk," admits Errázuriz president Eduardo Chadwick, an opinion seconded by head viticulturist Raul Baumann, who commented to me during a visit in early 2006, "It's a new area for cool-climate viticulture but we're absolutely convinced it's the right place to produce very special Sauvignon, Chardonnay, and Pinot Noir."

According to Errázuriz, Chilhué is slightly cooler in climate than

Casablanca, with a mean January temperature of 17.6°C (64°F). Soils are a thin layer (40–60cm/sixteen to twenty-four inches) of loam over clay and granite rocky strata, and the first varieties to go in have included mainly Sauvignon Blanc along with Chardonnay, Pinot Noir, Merlot, and Syrah – the latter in the warmer, more wind-protected sites. Vineyards began to be planted in 2005 and results are keenly anticipated. Wind is expected to be an issue here, with average speeds of around twenty kilometres (twelve miles) an hour at the end of the growing season, so windbreaks have been installed and vigorous Sauvignon Blanc has been planted in the most exposed parts – the orientation of the rows of vines will also be studied in this regard. Exposures are varied and slopes can be steep, though thirty per cent is a maximum incline for planting.

Errázuriz is also developing sites in the mid-valley toward the coast. The farthest west of these is the Seña vineyard, which, since the split with Californian partner Mondavi, has undergone something of a facelift. Conversion to Biodynamic viticulture is now in full swing and twenty-six hectares (Merlot, Malbec, Petit Verdot, Cabernet Franc, Cabernet Sauvignon, Carmenère) have been added to the existing sixteen of Cabernet Sauvignon and Merlot. Much of the new development is on the higher hillsides, the cost of which has been around US$50,000 (£27,000) per hectare, according to Eduardo Chadwick. Why Biodynamics and the new varieties? Chadwick sees it as a step forward in his search for a sense of place in the wine. "I want Seña to be a 'unique terroir' wine that tastes of where it is grown," he asserts, "and I am convinced that moving into Biodynamic viticulture will get us there."

Nearby, new and promising sites at Las Vertientes and Llay Llay are also being developed. Las Vertientes is an 850-hectare estate set in its own amphitheatre of hills some forty-one kilometres (twenty-five miles) from the Pacific. New vineyards have been going in since 1999, and this is Errázuriz's coolest site in the mid-valley, according to estate manager Cristián Marchant, rarely exceeding 26°C (79°F) in summer, and with frequent coastal mists. Soils range from very stony with some sand content ("basket") to deeper, clay-rich soils ("pot") – the best being shallow loam over a basket sub-soil ("little basket"). Pot soils are planted to Merlot; basket soils to Syrah, Sangiovese, and Cabernet Sauvignon; little basket soils to Cabernet Sauvignon, Cabernet Franc, and Petit Verdot. Grenache, Mourvèdre, Viognier, Carmenère, Marsanne, and Roussanne are also set to be planted, taking advantage of slopes and steeper, rockier soils in the property. The focus on terroir and cooler climate in this area is already giving good results, in balanced, complex wines.

As a visibly enthused Eduardo Chadwick informed me in 2005, "It's great to be able to develop new properties, it's energizing. In a viticultural sense, it's like being back in 1995 in top gear of planting and expansion. This is a really exciting time." Exciting, Aconcagua? It's ground-breaking news.

Noteworthy

One major viticultural presence in the region is that of the Córpora group (see Cachapoal p. 200), which has just over 100 hectares of vineyards in six properties in the Panquehue area and close to the Aconcagua River. The majority (seventy-five hectares) is planted to Cabernet Sauvignon, which, along with a small amount of Cabernet Franc and Carmenère, is planted in loamy soils of sand and clay. Twenty-eight hectares of Syrah, meanwhile, are planted in poorer soils nearer the river comprising mainly sandy and alluvial rocks. In 2006 and 2007, the Syrah plantations are being bolstered by a further fifteen hectares of new vine clones on rootstocks. Both Córpora's vineyards on the south side of the river, totalling seventeen hectares, are being organically managed and certification was achieved in 2005.

Córpora's best wines from Aconcagua are currently its Gracia brand's two top Cabernet Sauvignons, Porquenó and Caminante, both big styles majoring on ripe fruit, big mouthfeel, and simmering power.

Maule-based winery Carta Vieja is sourcing fruit for its organic Chardonnay and Pinot Noir near Olmué, which is south of Quillota and in the coastal end of Aconcagua.

Producer profiles

ERRAZURIZ

Av Nueva Tajamar 481, Of 503, Torre Sur, Las Condes, Santiago. Tel: +56 2 3399100. Email: wine.report@errazuriz.cl. Website: www.errazuriz.com Established: 1870. Vineyard: 745ha (Cabernet Sauvignon, Merlot, Syrah, Carmenère, Sangiovese). Production: 6.5 million litres. *See also*: Seña, Viñedo Chadwick, Caliterra.

Significant changes have been taking place at Aconcagua's most venerable producer, affecting all levels of the company, from the vineyards to the personnel and the products, all of which look set to herald an exciting new era for Errázuriz. To put the winery in context, it is one of Chile's most significant exporters and forms part of the Chadwick family group of drinks companies, which has interests in beer (Malterías Unidas), bottling (Coca-Cola Polar), and distribution (Distribuidora Errázuriz), as well as the wineries, including Caliterra, Seña, and Viñedo Chadwick.

In 2004, Errázuriz split from California winery Robert Mondavi, with which it had developed not only the icon Seña wine but also the Caliterra winery and its premium Arboleda range, based in Colchagua. The same year, head winemaker Ed Flaherty left, followed by viticulturist Pedro Izquierdo, who retained a consulting role. Flaherty was replaced by the Chilean Francisco Baettig, a former protégé of Michel Rolland at Casa Lapostolle, with New Zealander Nick Goldschmidt drafted in to consult. Raul Baumann is now head viticulturist. The Seña project underwent a radical overhaul in the vineyard (*see below*) and the Arboleda project was changed wholesale, with its fruit source moved from Colchagua to the new vineyards in Aconcagua, specifically, the newly developed Las Vertientes and Chilhué vineyards, where both white and red premium fruit will be sourced. (While these vineyards mature, some fruit is being sourced from producers elsewhere, such as the excellent 2005 Sauvignon Blanc from Leyda.)

These modifications have cemented Errázuriz's commitment to the Aconcagua Valley, most notably in its willingness to invest in order to broaden the region's repertoire of wine styles by developing the vineyards in the mid and westerly sectors of the valley (Seña, Las Vertientes, Llay Llay, Chilhué – see Case Study, p. 82). The winery retains its focus on its older vineyards around Panquehue with El Ceibo and the four Max plots, where hillside Syrah and Cabernet habitually perform well.

Farther afield, the winery's seventy-five-hectare La Escultura estate in Casablanca continues to provide the backbone of the premium Sauvignon Blanc, Chardonnay, and Pinot Noir fruit, and the winery is also looking to develop a sixty-hectare parcel of land also in Casablanca, though in cooler territory farther to the south and west. It will be interesting to see how Chilhué matches up to both of these. El Descanso's 147 hectares are located in Curicó and mainly used for basic varietal wines including Merlot.

Errázuriz's wines generally offer excellent quality across the range. Wines and lines such as the Organic, Single Vineyard, Wild Ferment, and The Blend all show good quality as well as a desire to develop new niches for Chilean wine. The Wild Ferment Chardonnay works particularly well because the wild yeast fermentation imbues the wine with a sort of depth and dimension of flavour that many Casablanca Chardonnays struggle to attain. The Blend 2003 seems to fuse the virtues of all the component grapes (Cabernet, Syrah, Sangiovese, and Carmenère) as well as remaining faithful to the Panquehue terroir.

Top wines Don Max, Seña, and Viñedo Chadwick are all good quality and are undoubtedly improving. However, I would question Errázuriz's pricing policy with regard to the latter two. It may well be that these wines take on and beat the best Bordeaux and Tuscan wines in comparative tastings (see Winemaking p. 40), but these are wines that are still evolving, still in their vinous adolescence – both Chadwick and Seña's vineyard have been undergoing changes of late. Although I take Eduardo Chadwick's point that the wines have shown well in blind tastings and the country needs to set a precedent at this level, it still seems that the winery might have won more friends by reflecting this process of improvement and refinement in a more gradual build-up of prices rather than setting the bar so high so soon.

In the meantime, the process of improving these wines continues, and, for example, Don Max will certainly benefit from the recent decision, from 2003, to blend in Syrah and flesh out what was previously a fine if somewhat linear and one-dimensional style of classic, mint-tinged and ripe, cassis-fruited Chilean Cabernet. Both Seña and Chadwick are works in progress – *see* individual profiles for more details.

SAN ESTEBAN

La Florida 2074, Casilla 326, Los Andes. Tel: +56 34 481050. Email: sanesteban@vse.cl. Website: www.vse.cl

Established: 1974. Vineyard: 97ha (Cabernet Sauvignon, Merlot, Chardonnay, Syrah, Carmenère). Production: 1.2 million litres.

San Esteban started out life as a bulk and own-label provider for other packagers, and moved into marketing its own brand in 2001 after these businesses became less profitable in the late nineties with the global wine glut, which also affected Chile. "It's a flooded market," says owner and manager Horacio Vicente. "We just can't compete, so that means we have to explore other niches. We must promote Chile as premium wine."

The winery sits in the warm easterly extreme of the Aconcagua Valley at around 870 metres (2,900 feet) altitude, one of the highest in Chile (its highest vines are at 920 metres (3,000 feet)). Around thirty-six hectares out of the winery's ninety-seven are planted on hillsides, the rest are from riverside areas on the valley floor. Fruit is also sourced from a further fifty-two hectares, including Chardonnay from Maipo. Former Errázuriz head winemaker Ed Flaherty consults and most of the wine is sold in the USA, a market in which San Esteban cut its teeth with own-label produce. The most successful wine so far has been the Laguna del Inca, a blend of Cabernet Sauvignon, Syrah, and Carmenère, and the top-level reds do show some promise in what is an interesting terroir for the late-ripening varieties. However, in general more work is needed in the vineyards to develop a basic balance and rein in alcohol levels.

SENA

See Errázuriz for contact details. Website: www.sena.cl

Established: 1995. Vineyard: 42.5ha (Cabernet Sauvignon, Merlot, Carmenère, Malbec, Petit Verdot, Cabernet Franc). Production: 112,000 litres.

Seña, like all of Errázuriz's projects, has undergone something of a sea-change recently. It started out life as a joint venture between California winery Robert Mondavi and Errázuriz. Initially, the wine was sourced from selected sites around Aconcagua and occasionally Maipo while a search was mounted for a vineyard site to call its own. The process took four years and involved detailed climatic and soil studies throughout the Aconcagua Valley.

Eventually, in 1999 a 350-hectare hillside site near Rabuco with fifty plantable hectares was chosen and installed with sixteen hectares of Cabernet Sauvignon and Merlot in 2000. The plot is around thirty-five kilometres (twenty-two miles) from the Pacific, sited in the mid-west part of the valley on east-facing slopes. The vineyard enjoys well-drained soils of rocky gravel and loam content as well as a breezier, slightly cooler growing season than Panquehue, with temperatures rarely exceeding 26–28°C (79–82°F) according to viticulturist Cristián Marchant.

Following Errázuriz's split with Mondavi, in 2005 the project was put into Biodynamic conversion and twenty-six hectares of additional plantings went in, boosting the Cabernet Sauvignon and Merlot and adding Carmenère, Malbec, Petit Verdot, and Cabernet Franc. Syrah may also join the mix in the future. Californian Biodynamic guru Alan York consults and a new winery is planned for the site in 2007, while Biodynamic certification is expected in 2009. Meanwhile, the first Seña to be sourced solely from its own vineyard is the 2003.

The wine itself is still a work in progress. It has shown glimpses of real quality but too often just seems to be lacking a certain something, call it integration or vibrancy, to sew it together and make it a truly premium wine to justify its intended stature. A settled vineyard base, new varieties, and Biodynamic viticulture are certain to help in this regard. That said, to my mind, the 2001 has been the best Seña so far, marrying a yeasty, earthy, bay leaf complexity with dried fruit and a dense, ripe, spicy palate. Ultimately, Eduardo Chadwick's stated aim to make this a "unique terroir" wine is to be congratulated.

VON SIEBENTHAL

O'Higgins S/N, Panquehue, San Felipe. Tel: +56 34 591827. Email: info@vinavonsiebenthal.com. Website: www.vinavonsiebenthal.com Established: 1998. Vineyard: 25ha (Cabernet Sauvignon, Merlot, Carmenère, Syrah, Petit Verdot, Cabernet Franc). Production: 80,000 litres.

New kid on the block Von Siebenthal came to Aconcagua courtesy of Swiss lawyer Mauro Von Siebenthal in conjunction with four investors, and proceeded, in impish fashion, to set up shop on the south side of the valley right next to the headquarters of regional stalwart Errázuriz. "They gave us a good precedent," explains managing director Ireneo Nicora, simply.

The land was bought in 1998 and twenty-five hectares of vineyard were planted in 1999 on a mixture of slopes and flat land in one contiguous block. The first vintage was 2002. Although a further ten hectares are scheduled to be planted, the project remains small-scale and entirely focused on reds from this area of Panquehue. (The first Montelig was sourced mainly from Colchagua for commercial reasons.) Only four wines are currently made, all of which are barrel-aged red blends. Terra Andina (see p. 336) winemaker Stefano Gandolini consults while the splendidly named Darwin Oyarce acts as day-to-day winemaker.

Early wines have shown considerable promise and things look set to improve as the vineyard matures. The style tends to the broad, round, and ripe end of the spectrum, with a pleasant savoury edge and hints of eucalyptus. More structure and definition would benefit the wines, though a barrel tasting at the winery in 2004 saw the Carmenère, Syrah, and Petit Verdot shaping up nicely in this regard. Low yields, sensitive extractions, and a well-thought-out planting plan all bode well, but given the current trend in Aconcagua away from Panquehue and into terroirs that give more diverse, cool-climate styles of wine, it will be interesting to see how, and perhaps where, Von Siebenthal develops.

3

Casablanca

BRIEF FACTS

Vineyard: 3,829 ha (69% whites)
Main grape varieties (ha): Chardonnay (1,773), Sauvignon Blanc (756), Pinot
Noir (475), Merlot (434), Cabernet Sauvignon (107)
Climate: temperate, moderated by maritime influence, with annual rainfall of
250–500mm (10–20 inches)
Soils: clays and sands over weathered granite

INTRODUCTION

Located between Chile's capital, Santiago, and its second city,
Valparaíso, Casablanca has for much of its history been little more than
just another stretch of land on the way to somewhere else. Its fog-
bound, flat confines were used in desultory fashion for livestock and
crops such as alfalfa and wheat; other than that, this was a fallow sort
of land.

Then, in 1982, winemaker Pablo Morandé was working for national
winemaking giant Concha y Toro and, inspired by similarities between
this area's maritime-affected climate and that of California's coastal territory, he decided to undertake an experimental planting of twenty
hectares of Chardonnay, Sauvignon Blanc, and Riesling.

This was the not the very first vineyard to go into the valley. In fact,
some low-grade viticulture was already taking place in Casablanca –
Morandé visited a small País vineyard in Tapihue before taking the
plunge, to convince himself that it could be done. He had also considered other areas – Mulchén (Bío Bío) was discarded because of its dis-

tance from Santiago and the work entailed in its rainy climate, while Leyda's problem was the lack of easily accessible irrigation water. Casablanca it was; more specifically, the area of Vinilla in the mid-valley. The first wines were made in 1986.

Success was not immediate but soon the area's accessibility and potential for developing fine white wine, not traditionally a speciality in Chile, attracted other producers. The biggest growth was in the nineties – at the start of the decade Casablanca's vineyard covered little more than 100 hectares; by 2000, this total was 3,578 – but given high land prices and water shortages this has now slowed. More recent development has focused on fine tuning existing plantings. Nonetheless, Casablanca had finally made its name.

Wine is now the only real tourist attraction in the region and, given the amount of traffic that passes through the area on a daily basis, the wineries have sensibly been proactive in developing this aspect of their business. The region was recently twinned with California's famous wine and tourism centre, Napa Valley, and now, as well as individual wineries offering visitor facilities, Casablanca has its own wine route, which includes restaurants such as House of Morandé. *See* www.casablancavalley.cl for more details.

As the capital of Region V, in which Casablanca as well as San Antonio and Aconcagua are located, the coastal city of Valparaíso is an important nearby presence. Valpo, as its residents call it, is an intriguing mix of the dilapidated and ultra-modern, the picturesque and the industrial. It is a spectacular tableau if seen in its entirety, with a jumbled mass of colourful buildings tumbling down the many hillsides that crowd around the bay and port. In 2003, its historic centre was named a UNESCO world heritage site. Valparaíso is also a major commercial port and naval base, in addition housing Chile's national congress, which was inaugurated in 1990 after being moved by Pinochet from Santiago to his home town in a somewhat unpopular move with the politicians. It looks likely that it will return to the capital at some point.

A point of terminology to note in this chapter – Chilean wine law refers to the Casablanca winemaking region as the Casablanca Valley.

Like San Antonio, however, Casablanca is not in actual fact a valley but instead a broader region spread over the western side of the coastal hills. Nonetheless, it does have at its centre and as its main focus of plantings a depression or plain surrounded by hills which, for concision's sake, I will refer to as the valley, in lower case.

A PICTURE OF CASABLANCA

The day had been spent talking to producers in Casablanca. Tasting, chatting, discussing maritime influence while gazing squinted-eyed over flat plains toward distant, grey-green hills. It was time for a break.

So we went to see the ocean. Earlier that morning we'd driven through the Zapata tunnel, an anxious ride through fumes and blurry lights under thousands of tons of Chile's most ancient rock, before emerging, blinking, into Casablanca's piercing light. Now we took up the same road, past Casablanca's diffident main town and up a slow rise out of the valley. The undulating motorway carried us past woodland and Lake Peñuelas before revealing its most spectacular panorama: the mighty Pacific, with Valparaíso at its shore.

We drove slowly through the city. Sights seeped in through our dusty windows: a monument to Lord Cochrane, ancient-looking trolley buses filled with blank faces, the despotic square arch of the National Congress building. A donkey tethered to a lamppost calmly eating from a rubbish bag; behind it, the shell of a three-storey building with beautiful stucco design on the remaining exterior. The face of Jesus on the back of a fast-moving micro bus.

We parked and gazed out over the harbour. Sinister grey frigates were moored to a long jetty. Fishing boats tethered in lines rocked against each other; unused cranes hung listlessly. And in the distance, beyond all the human endeavour, the glinting granite waters of the Pacific lay calm and immense. Somewhere in the distance, invisible beneath the broad ocean swells, an icy current was wending its way north: the Humboldt, Chile's secret air conditioner, a regular provider of cool, humid air to the country's coastal reaches. As we strolled back to the car, its cool afternoon wind gently buffeted our backs and ruffled our hair as it journeyed inland, toward Casablanca.

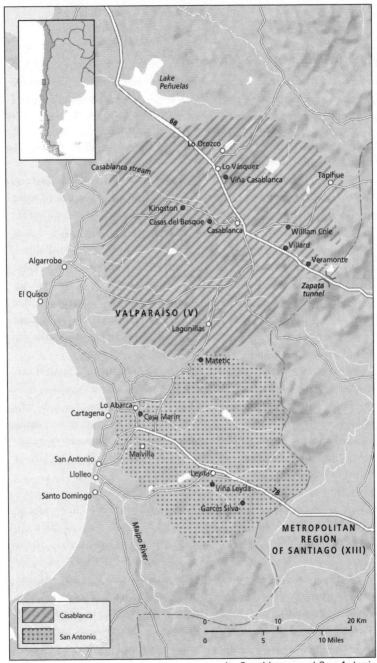

iv Casablanca and San Antonio

THE NATURE OF CASABLANCA

Casablanca is a broader, more complex wine region than it may at first seem. It is far from being a homogeneous cool-climate region; its range of microclimates, soils, exposures, and altitudes make it a varied and challenging winemaking prospect. All of which is good news for the diversity of Chilean wine; less so for wine writers who like things to be neat and tidy.

The winemaking region of Casablanca is a broad area spread over the western side of Chile's coastal range whose major focus is a plain or depression surrounded by hills. It contains no major watercourse, and certainly no gushing river fed by Andean snow melt; instead several meagre *quebradas* and *esteros* (streams and brooks) run off the hills or down from reservoirs, some of which merge into the Estero Casablanca, which flows west past Manzano to the coast at Tunquén. Rainfall is generally low, at around 250–500mm (ten to twenty inches) per year, but most of this falls from May to October, with the growing season months of November to April usually very dry, although occasional spring and autumn rains do occur. Irrigation is thus the norm.

The key to understanding Casablanca's somewhat peculiar climate lies in its relief and position – and the relationship of these factors to the ocean. The main Casablanca depression lies around twenty kilometres (twelve miles) inland from the Pacific coast and runs southeast to northwest, with hills to all sides but the steepest ones, the coastal range summits, lying in the east and north. This creates a sort of catchment pool, into which the cool, dense ocean air flows from the west. As a result, it is the most westerly and also low-lying areas that tend to be the most affected by the maritime influence, while the hillsides (especially those on northern exposures), sheltered sites, and especially the more easterly parts, remain warmer, less humid, and with greater sun exposure.

It is precisely this maritime effect that gives Casablanca its moderate climate. During the growing season, mornings are often characterized by sea-sent fog, which is then burnt off and, as hot air rises off the land, fresh air is drawn in from the ocean in the form of afternoon winds, again moderating temperatures. The result is sunny but moderate conditions (Cono Sur winemaker Adolfo Hurtado explains how he often gets sunburn working in Casablanca because he rarely feels it's hot enough to put on sun-cream). This has the effect of increasing the length of the growing season – up to 150 days from flowering to harvest, according to former Viña Casablanca winemaker Joseba Altuna.

These days, it is common to hear producers talking with reference to three discrete parts of Casablanca: upper, middle, and lower. Upper Casablanca refers to the easterly, landward end, where conditions are generally the warmest and most continental in the region, with January temperatures in daytime averaging up to 27–29°C (80–84°F) and at night 10–11°C (50–52°F). Middle Casablanca denotes much of the central section of the region, in which temperatures are generally in the mid range, around 24–27°C (75–80°F) on summer days, while Lower Casablanca is that part in the west of the region that receives the most marked oceanic influence and where average January daytime temperatures can be as low as 21–24°C (70–75°F). Within all of this, exposures and altitude modify conditions, with lower altitudes generally experiencing lower temperatures, and northern exposures offering the greatest sunlight. (The difference is such that harvests for the same variety can be up to two or even three weeks apart from different ends of the region.)

It is also interesting to note that, while Casablanca clearly benefits from maritime influence, the temperature variation between day and night gives a more extreme and less moderate climate, especially in those parts where daytime temperatures are highest, in the east. Overall night-time temperatures are regularly cooler than, for example, San Antonio, which has a more direct maritime influence and hence a more regularized climate. The reason for this is, again, Casablanca's unique situation: close enough to the sea to draw in its cooling influence but not close or low enough in altitude to be moderated at night.

One major challenge posed by these low night-time temperatures is frost. In winter and spring (June to October, roughly speaking), the risk of frost is high, especially in the lower-lying vineyards, exacerbated by the low night time temperatures, clear skies, and the way the air is easily trapped by the hills. Evidence of how seriously producers take the risk can be seen just by looking around the valley, where huge windmills have been installed to circulate air. They also use heating pots, micro-aspersion (not the favourite option because water is scarce; *see* Glossary p. 343), and even helicopters to counter the threat. Although frosts do not usually occur every year, they hit in 2003, 2004, and 2005.

The underlying geology of the region is relatively uniform, largely being made up of the decomposed granite which forms the common parent material in the coastal range. Clays and sands dominate the soils, with the heavier clays widespread on the flatter ground while purer, sandier decomposed granite (often known as maicillo) is commonly found on the hills. Some producers prize the more humid black soils (*see* Casas del Bosque), but the redder decomposed granite on the slopes is also popular, for example with De Martino, whose winemaker Felipe Müller explains why:

> These are really old soils with high weathering and chemical alteration, allowing the rock to disintegrate and giving to the rooting system the possibility to penetrate more easily the sub-soil profile. The roots explore 2.5 to 3.5 metres [eight to eleven feet] deep, giving an elegant minerality in the wines, plus an excellent balance of acidity and sugar content.

It is also worth noting that sandy soils are particularly susceptible to infestation by nematodes, microscopic roundworms that feed on vine roots. This is a major problem in Casablanca, especially for the more fragile vines like Chardonnay and Pinot Noir.

The boundaries of Casablanca are currently being expanded by producers planting outside what has been known as the traditional valley but still within the broader Casablanca appellation. Such developments are most notably taking place to the south and west, for example by Matetic on the border with San Antonio (*see* p. 129), and are having the effect of expanding the Casablanca net to include an even wider variety of winemaking conditions.

VITICULTURE AND WINES
When Casablanca's modern viticultural development began with an

experimental twenty-hectare plot in 1982, the first varieties to go in were Chardonnay, Riesling, and Sauvignon Blanc. Since then, producers have flocked to the area to get a piece of the cool-climate action, swelling the region's plantings to 3,829 hectares and bringing with them a range of grape varieties. There are currently twenty-two varieties registered in the region.

Casablanca's evolution (*see* Case Study, p. 99) is continuing, though it is now more a question of re-evaluation and fine tuning than outright expansion. The region's growth has slowed dramatically since 2000, with a mere 250 hectares added since then (compared to 1,858 hectares between 1997 and 2000), due to the rising cost of land and also shortage of water.

The issue of water is important in Casablanca, where the lack of a major watercourse means that much of the necessary irrigation water is sourced from underground aquifers via deep wells. However, with the region's rapid expansion these subterranean water resources have been extensively tapped, which has led the local authorities to issue a blanket ban on issuing any new water rights from wells. This has inevitably slowed new plantings, which are allowed but the water for which must come from existing water rights (which can be purchased with land if not already owned). Pablo Morandé estimates that the valley has the potential for 5,000 hectares but is already topped out in terms of water. Much of the region's irrigation water is distributed via modern drip-fed systems, preferred over the traditional Chilean flood method for its greater control over water usage as well as vine vigour and yield.

The cooling, humid ocean influence in the region has inevitably led to a predominance of white varieties, with Chardonnay and Sauvignon Blanc alone representing two-thirds of plantings. The fact that many of these grapes are used to make relatively simple, crisp, and commercial styles of wine is good for business but does little to reveal the area's true potential. Nevertheless, more ambitious wines are increasingly appearing, to prove that both red and white varieties can work to a commendably high level.

The key with Chardonnay seems to lie in finding sites that have sufficiently cool conditions to retain natural acidity and allow a long development. (Overly cold sites, meanwhile, can mean spring frost damage, and the variety is also sensitive to nematodes, so in some areas protective rootstocks need to be factored into the equation.) Cono Sur, for example, sources the Chardonnay for its 20 Barrels from the El Centinela vineyard, located around eight kilometres (five miles) from the coast in what is decidedly cool, westerly Casablanca, and then matures the wine in new barrels for thirteen months without allowing any soften- ing malolactic to take place in order to preserve the steely structure. The resulting wine is immensely impressive, fresh, and complex.

Sauvignon Blanc, meanwhile, seems to thrive in Casablanca's coolest and most maritime sites and, being a vigorous and later- budding vine, is less susceptible to nematodes and spring frosts than Chardonnay. It seems no coincidence that the Sauvignons from both Kingston and Casas del Bosque, located not far apart in the far western extremity of the region, offer excellent balance and depth in their own ways. Casablanca's Sauvignons have seemed to lack the sheer thrill and palate breadth of those from San Antonio, though this is changing as Casablanca ups its game with this variety and explores more extreme maritime territory (both Kingston's Cariblanco and Cono Sur's 20 Barrels are interesting to try in this regard).

Other whites such as Riesling and Gewurztraminer look promising, and proof that more exotic varieties can fare well here comes in the form of Emiliana Orgánico's Chardonnay/Viognier/Marsanne blend, a wonderfully vibrant tropical and floral white with density and zing on the palate. Sparkling wine is also made in the region, though on a lesser scale since the withdrawal of Mumm, whose winemaker once complained to me that his fizz wasn't as good as he'd hoped because "the base wines are just too fruity here".

Top-quality Pinot Noir still remains elusive, though Kingston is having a creditable go with Alazan as well as Cono Sur with Ocio. Generally speaking, however, it still seems as if more clonal diversity is needed, as well as vine age, and simply more experience in working with the variety. Too often the fruit is either lightweight or lacks vari- etal character, and the winemaking clumsy or formulaic.

Among the other reds, Syrah has become the region's most recent star, showing sleek fruit and plenty of spicy, herbal complexity from the likes of Kingston and Casas del Bosque. Given the success of this variety in San Antonio to the south, as well as Casablanca's promising elevations with granite-based soils, it looks as if we will see more of this style of Syrah (Veramonte also has high hopes in the east). Merlot has as yet failed to impress on a consistent basis, largely due to its persistent tendency to dehydrate, though winemakers such as Veramonte's Rafael Tirado remain convinced that Casablanca has both the climate and water-retentive clay soils for it to prosper in the long term. Cabernet can produce well in the very warmest areas, though Carmenère is more questionable, often giving virulently green-pepper aromas due to being harvested underripe. It is crucial for the quality of reds in Casablanca that yields are scrupulously low; otherwise the plants simply cannot mature the fruit given the testing conditions.

There is undoubtedly more to come from Casablanca in terms of both white and red wines.

CASE STUDY: CASABLANCA – CHILE'S GUINEA PIG

Before the concerted expansion of Chile's vineyard in the nineties and the subsequent influx of wines from new and often cool-climate areas in the early twenty-first century, Casablanca was, for a decade and a half, the country's viticultural darling. First developed in 1982, it offered new and exciting winemaking prospects, its maritime-influenced climate giving crisp acidities and intense aromatics, especially for whites, in a way the traditional areas had struggled to do. In a country of mostly easy-going reds made in warm climates and flood-irrigated, fertile soils, this was marginal, edgy, thrilling.

But Casablanca's development has not been straightforward. It has followed a learning curve in which mistakes have been made and lessons learned. So what exactly have been the ups and downs in Casablanca's evolution?

First, the blunders. The gravest of these relate to the vines, including use of poor plant material, making ill-conceived site selections, and taking a blinkered, old-school approach to planting and vineyard management. Grave because these are the errors that are the costliest to remedy and, with any planting requiring at least two or three years before giving viable fruit, such change is hard to stomach for any winery. And change has been needed.

Poor plant material means the likes of Sauvignonasse, Carmenère, and unresearched Chilean selections of Pinot Noir being planted when Sauvignon Blanc, Merlot, and carefully sourced clones of Pinot were what was required. As one grower commented to me, "We didn't know much at the time; we just went to our friends' nurseries, tasted the grapes, and they supplied us vine stock of whatever tasted the nicest." In addition, early-budding varieties like Chardonnay were planted in low-lying sites where spring frosts often proved devastating. Rows were planted wide apart for mechanization with little regard to quality, and rootstocks were considered only once the nematodes had infested the sandy soils and had begun to kill off the less vigorous vines, a situation that may have been aggravated by the use of chemical fertilizers. Many of these problems continue.

Despite all this, Casablanca has proved remarkably resilient and successful, often due to the work of a small elite of conscientious producers. Its first major achievement was to prove that Chile is more than capable of making serious white wine – firstly, with Sauvignon Blanc and Chardonnay, and latterly with Riesling, Gewurztraminer, Viognier, and even Marsanne. Reds have also proved successful, made in a fresher, sleeker style than those from the warmer areas: Veramonte's Primus and Kingston's Syrah are two cases in point, from very different terroirs. In short, Casablanca spread the message of potential diversity and quality in Chilean wine in a highly effective way, just when the country needed it. Other new cool-climate regions, such as Malleco, Bío Bío, San Antonio, Limarí, and Elqui are in its debt.

Noteworthy

Since its modest beginnings in the early eighties, Casablanca has attracted many growers – in fact, official figures now show seventy-nine wine-growing properties in the area. Many of these are private growers who sell to wineries or, alternatively, vineyards established and owned by wineries based outside Casablanca.

Among those owning their own vineyards in Casablanca but based elsewhere are Morandé, Emiliana, Casa Lapostolle, Errázuriz, Santa Rita, and Carmen. Emiliana, for instance, owns some 228 hectares in two different properties in Casablanca, which include 117 hectares set aside for organic and Biodynamic production for Emiliana Orgánico. As one of these properties is at the warmer, easterly end of the valley, winemaker Alvaro Espinoza is keen to develop the potential of Merlot and Syrah. Near to this vineyard is Morandé's 133-hectare vineyard, where he has also built a restaurant.

Casa Lapostolle's Atalayas property is located in the hills to the south of the valley floor and is planted mostly to Chardonnay and Pinot Noir. Errázuriz has a new property close by as well as its La Escultura estate in the northeastern sector of the valley. Santa Rita sources mainly Sauvignon Blanc, Chardonnay, and Merlot from its sizeable Casablanca vineyards as well as spot purchases. Carmen buys grapes but also owns three properties, two in Vinilla in the upper valley and one near Lo Ovalle, with a range of varieties including Merlot. Matetic, a winery based in San Antonio but close to the border with Casablanca, has been planting in the latter and in doing so effectively expanding Casablanca's southern limits.

Concha y Toro, meanwhile, both owns vineyards in Casablanca and sources fruit (mainly Chardonnay and Sauvignon Blanc) from different growers. It owns around 350 hectares in three estates: Lo Ovalle is the most westerly and coolest, with varieties including Gewurztraminer, Pinot Blanc, and Viognier planted on east-facing shallow slopes. The intermediate in terms of temperature is El Triangulo, the oldest and most easterly vineyard, near Veramonte in Vinilla, and the warmest site is Los Perales, in the mid-north of the valley and sheltered behind a ridge of hills, on loam and granite soils.

For the winery's Sauvignon Blancs, the Trio is a blend of the three sites, whereas Terrunyo is sourced from a single block in El Triangulo. The Amelia Chardonnay is another notable Concha wine from Casablanca. Winemakers Ignacio Recabarren and Marcelo Papa pride themselves on having set new trends in both these grape varieties in Chile. (Indeed, Recabarren was one of the key developers of the Casablanca region, along with Pablo Morandé, largely due to his work with Viña Casablanca in the mid-nineties.)

Other wineries sourcing fruit from growers, often with long-term contracts, include Montes, Cono Sur, and De Martino. Montes buys Sauvignon Blanc, Chardonnay, and Pinot Noir from areas both in the western part of the valley (Lo Orozco) and the centre, from both sandy and clay soils. De Martino also sources Sauvignon Blanc and Pinot Noir from north-facing slopes in the lower part of the western valley in a site with decomposed reddish granite soils.

Cono Sur's is a special case, given that El Centinela (*see* p. 98) belongs to winemaker Adolfo Hurtado's uncle, Leonardo Marchant. Hurtado likes the red clay in this vineyard due to the way in which it retains water and then releases it to the plants in regular, small doses, allowing for better retention of acidity and a fresh, mineral character in the wine. Cono Sur is already doing excellent things with Chardonnay and Sauvignon Blanc in El Centinela, and also sources fruit from Concha y Toro's vineyards, a privilege of being part of the same wine-making group. For example, in 2003 the winery's highest-level Pinot Noir, Ocio, came entirely from vines planted in 1990 in the El Triangulo vineyard.

Producer profiles

CASAS DEL BOSQUE

Alonso de Córdova 5151, Of 1501, Las Condes, Santiago. Tel: +56 2 3785544. Email: info_cdb@casasdelbosque.cl. Website: www.casasdelbosque.cl
Established: 1993. Vineyard: 200ha (Merlot, Sauvignon Blanc, Chardonnay, Pinot Noir, Carmenère, Syrah). Production: 600,000 litres.

Casas del Bosque has improved immensely since its first wines were released in 1998. It has an excellent site at the far western end of the main Casablanca depression, some twenty kilometres (twelve miles) from the coast, with vines on the north-facing hillside as well as flatter land, which make for an intriguing range of wines from Sauvignon to

Syrah but which at their best major on bold flavours underpinned by a fresh, balancing acidity.

The winery is owned by the Cuneo family, major shareholders in the Falabella retail group. The first vines were planted in 1993 (Chardonnay, Sauvignon Blanc, Merlot) and since then have evolved in significant fashion – for example, Syrah was first planted in 1999, and trials are ongoing with recent plantings comprising new rootstocks (101-14 and SO4) and clones (Pinot Noir 777, Chardonnay 70). New plantings have mainly been Merlot, Sauvignon Blanc, and Chardonnay.

Perhaps the winery's most successful variety to date has been Sauvignon Blanc, which is mainly planted on the flat land and currently occupies fifty-five hectares, though there are plans to arrive at eighty. The best fruit comes from vines planted in black clay soil, which the winemakers say gives the best concentration and power, even though it can be difficult to manage due to compaction and water saturation when it rains (the winery has installed drainage systems). The wines are impressive, all showing admirable concentration, zingy freshness, and palate presence, from the simple freshness of the Casa Viva to the more restrained, subtle tones of the Reserve, which has more skin and lees contact as well as some old oak maturation.

The hillside sites become warmer with altitude, which on this property ranges from 250 to 325 metres (820 to 1,070 feet). Temperature monitoring has shown a simultaneous difference of up to 2°C (4°F) between high and low sites due to the fog lifting earlier on the higher slopes as well as greater sunlight exposure and the fact that cool air mainly rests on the valley floor. Pinot Noir, Merlot, Syrah, and Carmenère are all planted on the hillside, the latter two in the highest parts to attract the greatest warmth, with Pinot and Syrah in red clay and Merlot in more loamy soils.

The Syrah is harvested in mid-May, very late in the season but necessarily so for ripening in this cool site, and is currently the winery's most impressive red, deliberately made with the Rhône in mind, a spicy, sexy wine that manages to carry its full flavours in stylish fashion. Carmenère is often harvested at the same time as the Syrah but still tends to lack proper ripeness, so the winery is looking to plant even higher – for the moment, this fruit is blended into the Estate Selection, an eclectic mix of this variety plus Merlot, Syrah, and Pinot that actually makes for a pleasantly full, fleshy, peppery red with plenty of grip and fresh acid to balance it out.

A recent change in the winemaking team saw long-term winemaker Camilo Viani leave in 2005, to be replaced by to be replaced by former Calina winemaker Felipe García, one of Chile's bright new talents. Australian consultant David Morrison has been advising since 1997. Casas del Bosque also makes Cabernet Sauvignon wines from fruit sourced in Rengo (Cachapoal), though these tend to lack the interest and elegance of the Casablanca wines. In general, the different lines from Casa Viva to Reserve present a soundly graded commercial range with some superb value for money. Prices are more ambitious at the very top end.

KINGSTON

520 La Mesa Drive, Portola Valley, CA 94028, USA. Tel: +1 650 599 5812. Email: info@kingstonvineyards.com. Website: www.kingstonvineyards.com Established: 1998. Vineyard: 100ha (Pinot Noir, Syrah, Sauvignon Blanc). Production: 18,000 litres.

As the contact address indicates, there's an American connection here. Michigan-born Carl John Kingston came to Chile in the early nineties in search of precious metals and acquired a 3,000-hectare estate in coastal Casablanca, which has remained a family property ever since, although most of the family are now based back in the USA. Winemaker Byron Kosuge, a Californian Pinot Noir specialist, flies in from Napa to make the wine with Evelyn Vidal, the locally based day-to-day winemaker. Expert viticulturists Anne Kraemer and Yerko Moreno consult. A small winery was completed in 2006 and the business also includes a successful vine nursery.

Vines were planted in 1998 on north-facing hillsides in what is the far western end of the valley, around fifteen kilometres (nine miles) from the coast, on well-drained soils of red clay loam and decomposed granite. Kosuge likens the vineyard's microclimate to the Sonoma

Coast but at a higher elevation, giving better aromatics, and with stronger sunlight, meaning thicker grape skins and more naturally concentrated wines as a result. He sees the mild temperatures, long season, and intense sun as "almost ideal for the growing of cool-climate red wine grapes like Pinot Noir".

Kingston sells ninety per cent of its fruit (which also includes Merlot, Chardonnay, Riesling, and Gewurztraminer) to other wineries but it made its first wines in 2003, partly as a way of advertising the quality of its wares to grape buyers. These have set an audaciously high standard, already making Kingston one of Chile's winemaking gems. The plan is to expand slowly but only to use a maximum of ten to fifteen per cent of the vineyard fruit for the estate wines.

For the Pinot Noir, four selections of plant material were used: 777, 115, and two Chilean field clones, which are largely planted in decomposed granite soils. After the first two vintages, Kosuge favours the Burgundian 777 clone for its "sweet core of black fruit", while the others lend colour and structure to the blend. The 2003 is an expansive style of New World Pinot but one that wears its brawn well, even if more structure and delicacy would become it better in the long term. Kosuge is commendably frank in admitting that he has yet to produce Pinot of the level he is seeking, but is working on remedying this. It is nonetheless a very encouraging debut.

Syrah clones 300 and 174 are planted in the steepest, highest, and most exposed sectors of the property in poor soils. Syrah is normally harvested in May, at which point Kosuge notes that the fruit is ripe but with a character more akin to Rhône Syrah than super-ripe New World versions. He is also keen to avoid over-extracting or "blurring" the fruit with oak, so the Syrah undergoes a similar gentle vinification to the Pinot and ends up, in his words, as an "edgy" style. I can see what he means. His risk-taking style is something that I commend and encourage, because the wine ends up with a vibrant, meaty, earthy, peppery, and bright fruit character supported by a delicious underlying acidity and firm, round tannins.

Three clones of Sauvignon Blanc are used: 242, 107, and 1, and in

2004 the fruit was picked at two different maturities five days apart and blended for complexity. The wine was then vinified in stainless steel "barrels", designed to encourage temperature fluctuations during fermentation for broader flavour profiles as well as to increase lees contact for added body. Only native yeasts were used and the wine was stirred for its three months' ageing. The 2004 vintage is an intriguing blend of fleshy, rich, creamy white fruit with vegetal and mineral traits and a taut, lemony acidity that is quite exuberant in character and works well with food. The lees contact is evident, as is a touch of residual sugar from the native yeasts not quite finishing fermentation. As excellent and, perhaps, edgy as it is, it would benefit from more focus and definition.

Tobiano is the second label.

LAROCHE CHILE

Santa Lucía 330, Of 71, Santiago. Tel: +56 2 2166550. Email: julian@larochewines.cl. Website: www.larochewines.cl

Established: 2004. Vineyard: 55ha (Sauvignon Blanc, Chardonnay, Pinot Noir, Merlot, Carmenère, Cabernet Sauvignon). Production: 220,000 litres.

The initial venture made by French winemaker Michel Laroche in Chile was a joint one with Jorge Coderch of Valdivieso that consisted of sourcing fruit from different areas to make premium wines under the Laroche-Coderch label. This relationship came to an abrupt end in 2004, at which point Laroche set up an independent winemaking operation, though still under the stewardship of English winemaker Julian Grubb.

The new-look Laroche Chile operation is based out of Casablanca and, with the purchase of land in Tapihue, aims to eventually reach a balance of around thirty per cent own fruit and seventy per cent contract fruit, the origin of which could vary between years. Two lines are produced: Punto Niño at the lower end, and the higher-priced Punto Alto, which includes Chardonnay, Pinot Noir, and Cabernet Sauvignon.

As of the 2004 vintage, the wines are much the same as they were under the Laroche-Coderch label: acceptable and sometimes with glimpses of quality though too often formulaic and lacking in complexity, especially for the price. There is great room for improvement in the Chardonnays, which tend to lack ambition as well as balance in the top line – sensitive oak handling and an emphasis on freshness should surely not be beyond a Chablis producer. The Pinot Noir is better but the clear challenge is still to introduce more complexity without losing the restraint and delicacy that can make this variety so compelling. For now, it is the Cabernet Sauvignon that proves the best of both lines – for example, the 2004 Punto Alto is a pleasant, warm, spicy blend of Alto Maipo fruit of which ten per cent is Carmenère from Colchagua.

Grubb is confident that improvements are being made and that the transition will end up in better wines. For example, a potentially new source of red varieties from coastal Maipo, including Cabernets Sauvignon and Franc, Merlot, Syrah, and Petit Verdot, could eventually lead to a new top-level Bordeaux blend, as well as lending freshness and structure to other reds in the range. Colchagua will increasingly be the source of Carmenère. It would be good to see the winery focusing on several key contracts as well as its own vineyards to stabilize production and introduce some consistency and complexity to the range.

QUINTAY

Nuestra Señora de los Angeles #179, Las Condes, Santiago. Tel: +56 2
2077363. Email: czunigac@zr.cl.

Established: 2005. Vineyard: 150ha (Sauvignon Blanc). Production: 15,000 litres.
Quintay is an ambitious new project in Casablanca dedicated to the production of one top-end Sauvignon Blanc. Eight partners, many of whom are independent grape producers in Casablanca, clubbed together in 2004 and their first wine was produced in 2005. By 2006 the group had some 400 hectares of vineyard to work with (though not all in production), sixty of which are in Leyda. A Chardonnay is planned for the 2007 harvest.

The 2005 Sauvignon – the only wine I have tried from this property at the time of writing – was made mainly from grapes grown in Tapihue, in the mid-north of Casablanca, principally from clones 242 and 5, as well as fifteen per cent of fruit from Leyda. It shows an overtly herbaceous, citrus character with a somewhat aggressive, racy acidity – attractive in its own way, though it cries out for breadth and complexity to make it the really interesting wine the project is aiming for.

Nonetheless, Quintay looks to be a producer to watch in the years ahead. It has sound backing and an interesting concept, described by its winemaker as "multi-zonal and multi-clonal: it's the blend of different things that makes the most interesting wine". In other words, blending fruit from a range of sites in Casablanca as well as Leyda, in addition to working with several different clones of Sauvignon Blanc (242, 1, 5, 107, 297). This is just the kind of focused, detailed work needed to improve Sauvignon Blanc in Chile.

VERAMONTE

Ruta 68, km 66, Casablanca Valley. Tel: +56 32 329924. Email: calvarez@veramonte.cl. Website: www.veramonte.com
Established: 1990. Vineyard: 400ha (Sauvignon Blanc, Chardonnay, Pinot Noir, Carmenère, Merlot). Production: 2.8 million litres.

Another American connection within Casablanca's borders, Veramonte is owned seventy per cent by the giant Constellation Brands group as part of its Icon Estates portfolio and thirty per cent by the Huneeus family, whose patriarch Agustín is a Chilean businessman based in the USA with wine investments there including Quintessa in the Napa Valley. The winery is largely focused on the US market, which accounts for eighty per cent of its sales, though this is slowly changing as Veramonte takes advantage of Constellation's huge distribution network.

Veramonte occupies the extreme eastern, or landward, end of the Casablanca valley. Its vineyards spill down from the skirts of the steep coastal rises over a range of exposures, predominantly west-facing but also north and south. This is Casablanca's warmest territory and also some of its highest – the winery is at 300 metres (980 feet), the top vineyards at 400 metres (1,300 feet). The coolest sites – on lower ground, southern exposures, or near a creek that runs through the property – are planted to Chardonnay, Pinot Noir, and Sauvignon Blanc, while land higher up is reserved for the likes of Merlot,

Carmenère, as well as a new five-hectare plot of Syrah that may well expand in the future. The soils are mainly red clays, with sandier textures on lower ground.

Although the winery has developed a following for its reliable, crisp (though often quite short) Sauvignon Blanc, to my mind it is the reds that increasingly offer the most interest here, with the elegant, complex Primus blend (Merlot, Cabernet Sauvignon, Carmenère) a regular case in point. Although the winery has steadily been reducing its Carmenère and Cabernet in Casablanca (the last of the latter was grubbed up in 2005), winemaker Rafael Tirado is convinced that Merlot has found a good match in the climate and red clay hillside soils. My tastings would bear him out, especially when the Merlot is pepped up by a smidgen of Cabernet or Carmenère. Tirado also has high expectations for his new Syrah, first harvested in 2005, which may also eventually be used in the Primus blend.

Although changes are still taking place in Casablanca, Veramonte has reached near-capacity in its vineyards here and is now looking to develop elsewhere. It already sources fruit from Maipo, but is now turning its eye to Marchihue in coastal Colchagua, where it recently bought 140 hectares and plans to plant Cabernets Sauvignon and Franc, Merlot, Carmenère, Syrah, and Petit Verdot as part of a top-end red project. From 2006 it is buying Cabernet Sauvignon from the area, as well as dabbling in fruit from Maule and Leyda.

It will be interesting to see how Veramonte develops over the coming years. It would be good to see the Primus reaching new heights and further improvements made in Chardonnay and Pinot Noir. Tirado is honest about current shortcomings with the latter, saying Pinot has proved "very testing", and even after extensive trials with rootstocks and clones, "we still need time to get to know it better". He is realistic, saying that Pinot is like Sauvignon Blanc in that any shortcomings in the vineyard are exposed in the wine, so more work is needed in the vineyard.

VILLARD

La Concepción 165, Of 507, Providencia 664 1780, Santiago. Tel: +56 2
2357857. Email: info@villard.cl. Website: www.villard.cl
Established: 1989. Vineyard: 23ha (Sauvignon Blanc, Chardonnay, Pinot Noir).
Production: 200,000 litres.

Thierry Villard's engaging dark Gallic humour and direct, sometimes
caustic commentary are very much part of the personality of his small
winery. Originally from France, though partly educated in England, he
established the business in the nineties after spending fifteen years
working for Orlando in Australia, developing Jacob's Creek among
other things. He now runs the winery in conjunction with two other
related businesses: a cooperage for French barrels (Nadalie Chile) and
wine consultancy for other Chilean producers, though it is his winery
that has increasingly become his principal focus.

Villard bought land in the flat area of the middle-eastern section of
the valley in 1990 and planted twenty-three hectares of Sauvignon
Blanc, Chardonnay, and Pinot Noir in 1992 without rootstock at low
density. Now Villard is looking to introduce better clonal material, on
rootstocks and at higher density – for example, 2.6 hectares of mainly
Pinot Noir was replanted in 2005 with clone 262 Sauvignon on rootstocks at higher density (5,600 plants per hectare instead of 4,000).
This replanting is also the result of nematode infestations, a particular
problem here. Frost is also a constant threat in this low-lying area – for
example, in 2004 Villard lost half his Chardonnay crop to spring frost.

Ana María Pacheco is Villard's long-term winemaker. The wines,
though generally consistent and sound, tend to be made in a self-
consciously Old World, lightweight style and, to my mind, often lack
the necessary concentration and personality to make them truly enjoyable. This is especially the case with Pinot Noir and, while I would
applaud Villard's aim to place the emphasis on delicacy in the wines, it
is a fine balance to strike without falling into austerity. Both the dry
and sweet Sauvignon Blancs are pleasant. From 2003 Villard switched
his customary strategy of sourcing red grapes from eastern Maipo
(which often made for an old-school style of dried cassis with strong

notes of eucalyptus) to sourcing Cabernet from Melipilla and Merlot from a grower in Casablanca. The 2003 version of the latter is promising, showing good freshness and berry juice. Esencia is the top line; Expresión the tier below.

VINA CASABLANCA
Rodrigo de Araya 1431, Macul, Santiago. Tel: +56 2 4503000. Email: info@casablancawinery.com. Website: www.casablancawinery.com
Established: 1991. Vineyard: 50ha (Sauvignon Blanc, Chardonnay, Chenin Blanc, Gewurztraminer, Cabernet Sauvignon). Production: 1 million litres.

Significant changes have been taking place at both Viña Casablanca and its parent winery Santa Carolina, including an overhaul of wines and winemakers. As a result, Viña Casablanca's new chief winemaker is Andrés Caballero, who came from Rosemount (Australia) via Montes to replace Joseba Altuna in 2005. Altuna remains as external consultant to the group, while former Errázuriz viticulturist Pedro Izquierdo is also now advising in the vineyard.

Viña Casablanca was one of the first and foremost exponents of Casablanca's excellent potential for white wines in the nineties, most notably under the winemaking guidance of Ignacio Recabarren, who initially convinced Santa Carolina to invest in the land and made wine between 1993 and 1999. It has since lost something of that pioneering buzz about it, having not developed as fast or as meaningfully as most of its competitors. That said, the recent changes do seem to have reintroduced a certain dynamism to the project.

The Santa Isabel estate is planted with fifty hectares of vines in mainly sandy soils on sloping ground in the northwestern extreme of the Casablanca valley, an east-facing site that receives a strong maritime influence being some twenty kilometres (twelve miles) from the coast. Plantings are a mixture of reds and whites, with Chardonnay on the lowest ground. Poorer soils on the slopes are used to reduce Sauvignon Blanc's natural vigour, while higher up in the property warmer temperatures and greater sun exposure mean reds are planted: Merlot, Carmenère, and Cabernet Sauvignon. Fruit is also sourced from other growers in Casablanca, an activity that has increased under

Caballero with a view to initiating changes in the Santa Isabel vineyard. Such modifications could see Cabernet and Carmenère replaced by grafting to Syrah, Cabernet Franc, or Riesling.

The winery made its name with the Santa Isabel Estate Sauvignon Blanc, and this continues to be a highlight of the range, with pleasant intensity and lean varietal character. The Santa Isabel Gewurztraminer also offers some good character. Commercial is perhaps the best way to describe the Colección Privada wines as well as the El Bosque reds, which tend to be ripe but lacking in real presence. The El Bosque and Colección Privada reds are made from Maipo and Rapel fruit. (As an addendum, the Santa Isabel brand was re-launched in 2006 as Nimbus after trademark issues; there will be some cross-over in the meantime.)

The Santa Isabel reds have traditionally run an altogether more compelling gauntlet, with the likes of the Merlot and Neblus regularly polarizing opinion with their edgy Casablanca style. I have always found much to like in both, especially the attractive freshness and spice as well as sleek fruit and smooth tannin, though many drinkers are put off by the inclusion in both blends of Carmenère, which in Casablanca inevitably gives vivid vegetal, green bean aromas. Caballero's aim is to soften this green character in the reds and make them more approachable. This is probably a positive move in the long run, though it is critical that within this broader shift the reds are not simply dumbed down but retain the characteristic freshness and verve that has made them so engaging until now. The Santa Isabel Cabernet Sauvignon 2004 looks promising in this regard, a fresh yet broad blend of Casablanca Cabernet fleshed out with Petit Verdot from Cachapoal.

Winemaking takes place in Miraflores (Colchagua) which, over a decade after the vineyard was first established in Casablanca, represents a serious failure of investment by the group – trucking the grapes this distance is inevitably detrimental to quality, especially to delicate whites. A new winery is, however, envisaged under Santa Carolina's new investment plan. It would be good to see Viña Casablanca ushering in a new era with its recent changes, consolidating the range as well as injecting some new interest, and placing more of an emphasis on the top-level Casablanca wines – white and red.

WILLIAM COLE

Casilla 76, Casablanca. Tel: +56 32 754444. Email:
wcv@williamcolevineyards.cl. Website: www.williamcolevineyards.cl
Established: 1998. Vineyard: 130ha (Chardonnay, Sauvignon Blanc, Pinot Noir, Merlot, Carmenère). Production: 1.7 million litres.

"The first olive out of the jar hasn't been the best," comments a ruminative Bill Cole, a Wyoming native who sold his software business in Denver to fund a venture south of the equator, originally a fruit farm. His eponymous Casablanca wine operation was established in 1998 and it swiftly became clear, after a series of setbacks, that hands-on management was needed. "So I've ended up spending ninety per cent of my time here, instead of the ten per cent I'd planned," he smiles.

Such setbacks included planting thirty hectares of the late-ripening Carmenère in this cool, low mid-valley site where even some Pinot Noir struggles to ripen properly. As a result, two-thirds of the Carmenère has now been replaced – ten hectares have been grafted to Sauvignon Blanc, managed in a dual-cordon TK2T training system designed to curb this vine's vigour. In addition, eighteen hectares of Chilean field selection Pinot Noir have been grubbed up, to be replaced largely by Sauvignon Blanc (clones 242, 107) with some Pinot Noir (clone 777). Specialists Yerko Moreno and Ignacio Recabarren have been drafted in to advise on this operational reconfiguration.

The winery makes a variety of lines, some from fruit sourced in other regions, but it is the Casablanca whites that are the best in the range, with the Sauvignons and Chardonnays generally pleasant and with some signs of ambition. This is a property with significant financial clout behind it and could, and should, improve in time.

4

San Antonio

BRIEF FACTS

Vineyard: 289ha (60% whites)

Main grape varieties (ha): Chardonnay (116), Pinot Noir (98), Sauvignon Blanc (53), Merlot (5.5), Syrah (4.5)

Climate: temperate, with strong maritime influence and annual rainfall of 400–500mm (16–20 inches)

Soils: clay-loams with gravels and decomposed granite in depth

INTRODUCTION

Wine is a new enterprise for the San Antonio region. Its breezy, humid hillsides and invigorating coastline, within easy striking distance of the capital, traditionally found better service as a holiday-home destination for wealthy Santiago dwellers. Forestry, fishing, cattle farming, and the odd bit of cereal, fruit, and vegetable cultivation have been the typical activities here. For a long time, San Antonio was a modest, pleasantly backward sort of place, hardly a destination in itself.

The region's fortunes began to change, ironically enough, when a serious earthquake hit the area in 1985. In the subsequent reconstruction, the foundations were laid for the city of San Antonio to become Chile's largest container port, which it did in 2002 by overtaking Valparaíso. It is now one of the busiest ports on South America's western coastline, handling over nine million tons of cargo every year. The modern Autopista del Sol toll motorway was also installed between Santiago and San Antonio to facilitate the area's development and underlined its importance as a commercial hub.

The area had also begun to attract the attention of Chile's more forward-looking viticulturists, tempted by its long, moderate growing season yet also proximity to major logistical and population centres. When Chile underwent a period of massive vineyard expansion in the late nineties, fuelled by high grape prices and booming export markets, the time was finally right and San Antonio's first wine vines were planted in 1998. This was a pioneering move. Inevitably there have been challenges along the way.

Since the first wines were released in 2001, San Antonio has enjoyed a rapid emergence and success that has been little short of phenomenal. Although this is primarily due to the high quality of the wines, a significant part of this achievement has been built on the sound planning, hard work, and commitment to investment of the region's original wineries: Viña Leyda, Casa Marín, Garcés Silva (Amayna), and Matetic. As a result, the region has become one of the hottest names in Chilean wine both at home and abroad, and investors have flocked in.

Geographically speaking, San Antonio is like a westerly extension of the Maipo Valley, although officially – and nonsensically – it falls under the Aconcagua Region wine denomination. (Before San Antonio acquired its own wine appellation in May 2002, its first wines from the 2001 vintage had to be released under the Aconcagua appellation.) San Antonio currently has only one officially recognized sub-denomination, Leyda, though others may well follow, such as Cartagena.

Wine is already proving a major regional boon for San Antonio in aiding its attempts to shed its industrial backwater image in favour of something more up-market and tourist-friendly. The coastline has already earned the nickname El Litoral de los Poetas because of its connections with poets (Pablo Neruda's eclectic seaside residence is at Isla Negra, Vicente Huidobro's family property is in Cartagena, and Nicanor Parra has connections with Las Cruces). El Litoral del Vino also has a nice ring to it.

A PICTURE OF SAN ANTONIO

We are standing on top of a hill, chatting. In the distance, the ocean is covered by a fine mist. It is framed by two spurs of hills whose brown flanks converge in a gentle V. The dark greens and silvers of eucalyptus trees mark the landscape, though in our immediate vicinity there is little save a multitude of young vines, their spindly trunks still wrapped in polythene nappies, spilling down the hillside like a close-cropped haircut. It is a bright, breezy day full of fresh aromas.

María Luz Marín is telling me her story. "I spent a lot of my childhood in this area," she recounts.

> When I was young my father owned land nearby and we could come every summer and winter holidays. I loved riding and exploring. My three elder siblings weren't interested but I was. I remember my father tried to plant fruit but there was too little water and the rabbits ate it all anyway, so we just kept with a eucalyptus forest and our holidays.
>
> I became a winemaker and, in the mid-nineties, I spotted an opening in the market and went into bulk wine broking. I saw it as a means to an end, to build up the funds to have my own winery. When I was in a position to do that, I came back here. Why? Instinct and intuition. And because I've always felt that there's something here you don't find elsewhere. You can see this in the local produce – look at the lettuces from this area, which are bigger, crunchier, and more flavoursome than those from Casablanca. Everything that grows here is good, even roses, so I thought, why not wine? I remember the first thing my teacher in university taught us was that the vine is the most loyal plant because it adapts to so many different climates and soils. So I was confident.
>
> I looked for a partner for four years, but people were scared by the area – with its steep slopes, winds, and cool humid ocean climate, they feared the grapes wouldn't ripen. Plus, the investment costs were very high, perhaps four times that of the Central Valley. Even the old lady I was buying the land from tried to stop me – I'd known her since I was young – because she was convinced I was going to lose all my money. So I went it alone.
>
> The other big problem was that this was all eucalyptus forest and CONAF [the state forestry board] said it couldn't be changed due to ero-

sion risks. I said I knew what I was doing, that I would be cultivating veg-
etation in the rows to prevent run-off, and I did a study for them to prove
it. They still forbade it, which meant I'd lost a whole year to bureaucracy!
So in the end I just went ahead and did it. Since then, they've threatened
fines but nothing's come of it.

I've put everything into this project – passion, effort, work, and money.
I've thought about giving up many times, especially when it's got me
down. Nothing has been easy, I've had to learn everything myself, the
hard way.

THE NATURE OF SAN ANTONIO

San Antonio is all about the ocean. Its breezy, humid, moderating presence is pervasive and it is precisely because of this that wine-growers
have been drawn to the area in their search for more challenging and
potentially rewarding terroirs away from the consistently warm and
productive Central Valley. It is even more extreme in this sense than
Casablanca, for example, which prior to San Antonio's arrival on the
scene was Chile's quintessential cool-climate region in the coastal hills.
No longer.

All the same, the temptation to think of San Antonio as one homogeneous cool-climate zone should be resisted. Small it may be but even
within its relatively petite confines this region contains a range of soils
and climates, the effects of which are already being demonstrated in
notably different styles of wine. And it looks certain that more such
diversity is to come as the focus on premium wines remains and new
areas are developed by the recent influx of site-conscious producers.

San Antonio is not a valley so it makes little sense to refer to it in
this way, as is the case in official Chilean wine law. It is a broad area
that covers several minor watersheds and is located on the western
slopes of Chile's coastal hills roughly on a level with Santiago. It is predominantly hilly in nature, with slopes ranging from steep to gently
undulating. Most importantly, however, it is these jumbled hills that
are the prime shapers of the region's diversity, determining the nature

and extent of the marine influence as well as providing a range of different exposures, soil types, and drainage profiles.

Perhaps the most instructive way to approach San Antonio, then, is by adopting a relatively small-scale focus and considering the key areas that have been developed to date. These are Leyda, Rosario, and Lo Abarca. Of these, Leyda is the most extensive: it is the most southerly of the three and is set on rolling hills around fifteen kilometres (nine miles) from the Pacific but with relatively unhindered access for the oceanic influence, meaning morning mists, afternoon winds, and a generally moderate climate. Average summer maximum temperatures rarely exceed 27°C (81°F) and rainfall is around 400–500mm (sixteen to twenty inches). Soils are predominantly slow-draining, shallow clay over decomposed granite. Organic matter is low and soils are slightly acidic.

Rosario is San Antonio's northernmost wine area and borders Casablanca. Its vineyards are marginally farther from the coast than Leyda (at eighteen kilometres/eleven miles) but its conditions are different due to the bowl-like shape of its self-contained valley. This formation means that the seaward rises impede the oceanic influence somewhat, making the area slightly warmer, less moderate, less wind affected, and also more prone to frost due to the enclosed valley trapping any cool air. (This is a somewhat analogous situation to that experienced by Casablanca, to the north.) Soils are varied but decomposed granite is common on the hillsides with deeper clay soils on the flat land. The region's sole producer, Matetic, is now looking to plant both to the north and west where the marine influence is more marked.

Lo Abarca is the most extreme of the three viticultural zones. Located just four kilometres (two miles) inland from Cartagena on the coast, it is accordingly maritime. Average summer daytime temperatures are around 24–27°C (75–81°F) and the area often receives morning mists and stiff afternoon breezes. The vines here grow on a variety of terrains, many of these being precipitous hillsides and windy hilltops – those on the flatter ground can be affected by frost. Soils are relatively rich clays with some calcareous content as well as poorer, granite-based soils on the steeper slopes.

That San Antonio is a cooler-climate area than many traditional Chilean winemaking regions is due entirely to the moderating influence of the cool Pacific Ocean. It generates morning cloud cover and afternoon breezes and generally means that otherwise warm, dry conditions are tempered, and that grapes can mature slowly while still developing full flavours and relatively high alcohol levels.

VITICULTURE AND WINES

San Antonio is a young wine region. Its first vines were planted as recently as 1998 and its producers are only just beginning to appreciate the intricacies of its nature. Nonetheless, it is already clear from the quality of the wines being produced that this is a potentially great wine terroir.

There are several reasons why San Antonio has got off to such a flying start. The first is experience – by the time the area came to be developed for wine from 1998 onward, Chile's viticulturists were savvier than they had been due to increasing international exposure and also knowledge gained from the planting boom. Specifically, lessons had been learned from what had worked in Casablanca, itself a maritime-influenced region to the northeast of San Antonio. The effects of the climate and soils were better understood, so proper consideration was paid to issues such as varietal selection, training methods, exposures, densities, and irrigation. On a basic level, the materials were also better – sound clonal material was used for Sauvignon Blanc, for instance, and not Sauvignonasse.

In addition, San Antonio has benefited from the kind of producers it has initially attracted. The focus has been almost exclusively on premium wine, with low yields and meticulous management – in other words exactly the kind of wines guaranteed to invite attention. There is no doubt that the investments have, as a result, been considerable, both in terms of finances and the hard graft needed to get such projects off the ground.

San Antonio was considered for wine before 1997, but investors had been put off by the water situation and associated costs. (Perhaps the most notable of these was Pablo Morandé in the early eighties, who then went on to develop Casablanca instead.) As with many areas on the westerly side of Chile's coastal range, water is not freely available for irrigation, meaning either that wells have to be sunk, or alternative solutions found. However, in 1997, a group came together – initially comprising the four partners of Viña Leyda but which subsequently grew to include several other growers – to invest in an eight-kilometre (five-mile) pipeline bringing water from the Maipo River. This got things off the ground.

Even now, a shortage of water for the necessary irrigation during the dry growing season remains an issue and it is clear that the region's viticultural development is being slowed as a result. Nonetheless, it hasn't troubled a producer like Cono Sur, whose new 160-hectare vineyard in Leyda will be supplied by two wells, providing fifty-eight litres of water per second. Winemaker Adolfo Hurtado is of the opinion that water is available if people are prepared to make the necessary investment.

> We brought an irrigation expert over from Israel and he just laughed at us. It is true that [San Antonio] is difficult to develop, but you just have to think round it and manage the water well, such as building up reservoir stock in winter. Leyda is limited not in terms of water but in terms of the money people are prepared to invest to make it available.

Another water-related issue is botrytis. Due to the ocean's humidity, and spring and summer morning fogs followed by warm days, rot is an ever-present challenge, particularly in vintages such as 2004 (when, for example, about a quarter of Casa Marín's fruit was affected). Growers try to open the vine canopy up to encourage ventilation, as well as spraying with sulphur, and selecting unaffected grape bunches at harvest. In addition, Casa Marín is experimenting with a cannibal fungus, *Thrichoderma*, a measure also being used elsewhere in Chile. Oidium (powdery mildew) is another threat. Rootstocks are not widespread, though producers are now beginning to experiment in this regard.

Vintage differences are a significant factor due to the marginal nature of the climate. For example, the differences between 2003, 2004, and 2005 Sauvignons are marked – the first tending to be ripe and full, the second more variable with more vegetal notes and often some botrytis, and the latter having complexity and restraint.

San Antonio's maritime climate gives a long, moderate growing season and seems ideal for varieties such as Sauvignon Blanc (*see* Case Study, p. 122). And though Sauvignon has been the stand-out variety initially, Syrah has also shown very well, adapting well to the granitic soils to make expressive, sleek reds that differ markedly from the riper styles.

Chardonnay was one of the first varieties to be planted, along with Pinot Noir. The former has so far shown the best results, although it seems there is still a way to go with both grapes in the search for real quality. Chardonnay often has good, broad natural acidity, but it can lack elegance and harmony on the palate. Growers also struggle sometimes with irregular yields though it is not yet clear why.

Similarly, Pinot Noir is making some good, solid wines – some of the best so far in Chile – but it often lacks the necessary complexity on the palate and majors instead too much on punchy, oaky power. This may well change with experience, vine age, and choice of plant material – traditional Chilean field selections of Pinot Noir tend to give big but one-dimensional wines so other clonal material is needed to introduce delicacy and depth, but growers are only just starting to get to grips with these alternatives. Producers remain convinced that they will prevail with Pinot, however – take Cono Sur, which has already initiated a plan to plant sixty-five hectares of Pinot Noir in Leyda using Burgundian clones 777, 667, 115, and 113 as well as Chilean field selections. Viña Leyda and Garcés Silva, both of whom started out just with field selections, have planted modern clones of Pinot from 2003 onward in their search for more complex wines.

Other varieties currently planted in San Antonio include Cabernet Sauvignon, Malbec, Merlot, Gewurztraminer, Sauvignon Gris, and, inevitably if not advisedly, Carmenère. It is clear from the early Syrahs that San Antonio has the potential to make good reds, so it will be interesting to see how these varieties perform. Cabernet Franc and

Merlot could be two good bets as relatively early ripeners that thrive in maritime climates.

CASE STUDY: A PASSIONATE AFFAIR – SAN ANTONIO AND SAUVIGNON BLANC

A commonly held view on Chile is that it produces good, though not exceptional wines, with better reds than whites, and little in the way of real complexity or what might be termed the expression of terroir. But Chile has an answer to this, as strident as it is compelling. It is Sauvignon Blanc from San Antonio.

The essence of a terroir wine is that it transcends the basic characteristics of the variety or varieties from which it is made and expresses a character unique to the particular winegrowing area in which it is created. I remember my first experiences tasting San Antonio Sauvignon Blanc because it was precisely this that I kept returning to: it was Sauvignon but then again it wasn't, and the more I tasted across the region the more I became aware that there was a recognizably San Antonio character here, typified by aromas of nettles, roasted grapefruit, fennel, and wet stone underpinned by a tell-tale broad, food-friendly palate full of vibrant acidity, spicy structure, and warming alcohol. It was as if, at once, a new dimension in Sauvignon Blanc had been created.

I visited San Antonio to investigate further and what I found was a passionate quest to make top-quality, terroir-based Sauvignon Blanc. Take Casa Marín's María Luz Marín:

> I was asked by my consultant what style of Sauvignon Blanc I wanted to make here, New Zealand or French. I couldn't answer. I wanted a style that was adequate to this site. I don't know if that's more New Zealand or France, the only thing I want is for it to reflect our terroir, if indeed we have one. We must let the grapes speak for themselves.

At Garcés Silva, the winery that makes Amayna, I received a similar response from the winemaker of the time Alejandro Galaz.

> I'm looking for an expression of terroir in my wine. Yes, you can harvest Sauvignon early and ferment it cool with special yeasts to keep it varietal

and easy to sell, but you can do that anywhere. I, on the other hand, want the wine to speak for itself. I want personality and individuality. I try to express what this area gives us, which is why I harvest ripe. My grapes are the best expression of the local soil, weather, and plant that I can manage.

The secret of San Antonio's success with Sauvignon Blanc is founded upon three fundamentals: the microclimate, the clones, and harvesting practices. Firstly, and most importantly, there is the area's microclimate, in which warm days are moderated by morning mists and cool, humid afternoon winds. This has the effect of lengthening the hang time of the grapes, enabling the development of complex and delicate aromas as well as the retention of natural acidity, all of which tend to give the aromas and the broad, spicy palate expression so typical of the region. It seems an ideal climate for Sauvignon Blanc, for which slow and moderate maturation is the key to ensuring complex character.

Then there are the clones. Sound clonal selection has been fundamental to San Antonio's success with this variety, whose development in Chile has been gravely retarded by plant material issues. The two major clones used in San Antonio are 242 and Davis 1 – the former is from Sancerre in the Loire Valley and can give a more tropical, ripe fruit character, whereas the latter majors more on structure and citrus fruits. Amayna, for example, blends the two for complexity (the 2005 is fifty/fifty), as does Viña Leyda. Casa Marín started out just with Davis 1 but as of the 2005 vintage has 242 to hand. Matetic has been the opposite, majoring on 242.

Finally, the harvest: a critical issue with Sauvignon Blanc because, as one winemaker told me, "It's like Pinot Noir – you know by the time you arrive at the winery with the grapes if you have a good wine or not." The best Sauvignon needs a small-scale approach to harvesting, taking in different blocks and clones at different times, in order to ensure complexity in the final wine. Most San Antonio practitioners prefer to harvest ripe in order to express the area's character fully, confident that the resulting high alcohols (often around 14.5% ABV) will be balanced by the full-bodied style of the wine. Nonetheless, the harvest is still a lengthy affair – as María Luz Marín comments, "Our Sauvignon harvest lasts at least two weeks, bringing in different parcels at different times. It's because picking is one of the most important quality issues for the variety."

Noteworthy

The list of wineries that have flocked to share a piece of the action in San Antonio is evidence of its burgeoning reputation on the Chilean wine scene. Producers that have bought land in the area to develop vineyards include Cono Sur, Anakena, Chocalán, Luis Felipe Edwards, and MontGras. Others are sourcing fruit from the region to make wine, including Santa Rita, Concha y Toro, San Pedro, Errázuriz, and Veramonte.

Cono Sur bought a 160-hectare plot in 2005 in an undulating area called Las Palmas, a short distance south of Rosario and around twenty kilometres (twelve miles) inland from Lo Abarca, where Casa Marín is located. There are around 130 hectares of plantable land; the first seventy hectares were installed in 2005 and the plan is to finish up with sixty-five of Pinot Noir, forty of Sauvignon Blanc and thirty of Chardonnay. Cono Sur is one of Chile's leading Pinot Noir specialists (Burgundian producer Martin Prieur has been consulting for several years) so it comes as no surprise that a special emphasis is being placed on this variety in the area. A new winery is also planned for the site to vinify Cono Sur's top lines.

Cachapoal-based winery Anakena bought 150 hectares in Leyda in 2005, planting eighty the same year and a further forty hectares in 2006. Also investing in Leyda was Colchagua winery Luis Felipe Edwards, which bought 162 hectares around ten kilometres (six miles) from the Pacific, with the first sixty hectares planned for planting in 2006. Chocalán, a winery based in Maipo but located very close to the border with San Antonio, planted twenty hectares some five kilometres (three miles) from the coast in the Malvilla area in 2005 on a 340-hectare estate, including some Riesling and Gewurztraminer. MontGras is looking to develop its premium whites range with the purchase of an estate in Leyda around eleven kilometres (seven miles) from the sea beside the Maipo River in the south of the region. The aim is to have 300 hectares planted by 2009, mainly with Sauvignon Blanc as well as some Pinot Noir, Chardonnay, and Syrah.

Producer profiles

CASA MARIN

Las Peñas 3101, Las Condes, Santiago. Tel: +56 02 657 1530. Email: info@casamarin.cl. Website: www.casamarin.cl
Established: 2000. Vineyard: 40ha (Sauvignon Blanc, Pinot Noir, Syrah, Gewurztraminer, Pinot Gris). Production: 50,000 litres.

Extreme is a good word to describe Casa Marín. It conveys something of the nature of the wines themselves as well as the grand ambition of this pioneering wine project and the force of personality of its owner, María Luz Marín.

Casa Marín's vineyards are located in Lo Abarca just four kilometres (two miles) from the Pacific Ocean over a mixed terrain of flat valley floor, steep hillsides, and blustery hilltops with a range of soils and climatic conditions. They result in some very individual styles of wine that vary subtly even with the same variety – for example, a comparative tasting of Sauvignon Blancs from 2003, 2004, and 2005 is a revelation in terroir and vintage variation from a country that has traditionally majored on neither. (In general, the 2004s are more subdued and less impressive than the punchy 2003s and the considered 2005s.)

The winery's focus is on Sauvignon Blanc (twenty hectares) and Pinot Noir (ten hectares): two versions of each variety are produced, with notably different characters. Both Sauvignon Blancs show nettle and anis aromas with broad, structured, spicy palates, though the Laurel comes from a wider hillside area and tends to give slightly less youthful austerity and edgy mineral power than the Cipreses, which is sourced from a windier, low-yielding hilltop site. Similarly, with the Pinot Noirs it is the fruit from the west-facing Lo Abarca hillside site made purely from the Burgundian 777 clone that seems to offer more class and harmony over Litoral, sourced from flatter land and a mixture of the 777 and national Chilean field selection.

Casa Marín's first vines were planted in 1999; now there are forty hectares and Marín plans for ten more in the future. It seems logical to expect the wines to improve as the vines age and experience is gained – for now, however, it is the Sauvignon Blancs that are proving the most successful of the winery's output, and indeed are already impressively complex examples of this variety. Pinot, though promising, needs more work on promoting delicacy and complexity with less reliance on toasty oak and power. Gewurztraminer and Sauvignon Gris are also made; Riesling was planted in 2003. Syrah could also prove a hit at Casa Marín. In late 2005, I tasted the first vintage (2004) of Syrah made from an initial planting of three hectares, a production of one barrel – it was scented, floral, and fresh, with outstanding definition, complexity, and juicy fruit on the palate. "It's the next thing for us," Marín told me.

Marín also produces two other labels. Cartagena started out life as a Cabernet Sauvignon from Rapel and a Chardonnay from Casablanca, but is now being converted into Casa Marín's second brand, for which it will be switched to Sauvignon Blanc and Pinot Noir from Lo Abarca. Matisses is an entry-level varietal line, bought and vinified in other areas across the country. She also continues her bulk wine business, although on a smaller basis than before.

An experienced winemaker and saleswoman, Marín has been accused by her detractors of setting her prices too high. She replies that her wines are expensive because not only are her costs high, due to a range of factors including very low yields (Sauvignon typically gives eighteen to twenty-four hectolitres per hectare), frost, botrytis selection, and high winds. There is no doubt that these are ground-breaking wines for Chile and as such deserve to command higher prices than the norm, though I would reiterate my opinion that it is better to start low and rise slowly, winning admirers along the way, than set the bar very high very early.

A new winery was inaugurated in 2005 and Marín is keen to set up a local tourism trail, promoting the local artisan handicrafts of Lo

Abarca and its rustic cuisine specializing in spicy hot roast pork and goats' cheese. A wine spa is also now installed amid the vineyards.

GARCES SILVA (AMAYNA)

Avda El Golf 99, Of 81, Las Condes, Santiago. Tel: +56 2 4288080. Email: mgarces@vgs.cl. Website: www.vgs.cl
Established: 2003. Vineyard: 120ha (Sauvignon Blanc, Chardonnay, Pinot Noir). Production: 100,000 litres.

First, an introduction to the names here: this winery is owned by the Garcés Silva family, and produces just one line of wines under the Amayna brand. This affluent family has traditionally focused on the agriculture business, though also has interests in insurance and soft drink distribution. Indeed, this 700-hectare estate in Leyda was originally bought in 1996 for livestock but, after seeking advice and ensuring water was available, they began planting vineyards in 1999. The family also bought an eighteen per cent holding in Montes (see p. 241) the same year.

Although the winery has 120 hectares planted, it uses only around a quarter of its fruit for its own wines and sells the rest to producers such as Montes and Concha y Toro. Its first commercial release was from the 2003 vintage and my attention was immediately drawn to the straight Sauvignon Blanc, whose complex, ripe aromas and towering, thrilling structure won me over immediately. I spoke to winemaker at the time Alejandro Galaz (since replaced by Francisco Ponce) who stressed that the search for and expression of terroir were central to the concept of Amayna, hence the decision to harvest late in the search for complex, broad, food-friendly wine (*see* Case Study, p. 122).

Since the debut 2003 vintage, the wines have shown some variation in their character, for example in the Sauvignon Blanc the 2004 was markedly more vegetal, and the 2005 a more restrained blend of ripeness and herbaceousness. Swiss consultant winemaker Jean-Michel Novelle is unrepentant, stressing the inherent vintage variation in terroir wine, which does not aim for a standardized product. It's hard to argue with this reasoning, especially as the wines consistently show an admirable underlying structure. The formula still needs refining, but the initial evidence suggests excellent things to come.

Currently, the Amayna line comprises five wines: two Sauvignon Blancs (one unwooded, one wooded), a rosé Pinot Noir, a straight Pinot Noir, and a Chardonnay. The wooded Sauvignon has raised many eyebrows but I believe this is a tremendous wine in a somewhat Bordelais mould that delivers both the character and unity to make it a classic in the long run; it is certainly a bold wine to make. The Chardonnay has not yet managed to reach the heights achieved by the Sauvignons and needs a better marriage between steely freshness and warm figgy presence as well as a longer finish. The winery's hopes are high for its Pinot Noir in the long term but the vineyard still needs time and increased clonal diversity before what is an attractive wine can attain real complexity and elegance.

It is clear that a lot of thought and investment have gone into this operation, from the immaculate vineyards to the stunning wooden design of the winery and the elegant bottle designs. Much of this credit is down to the hard work of the congenial Matías Garcés Silva, who runs the winery. "We saw a space in the Chilean category for a project focused specifically on one terroir," he relates. "As a result we have been keen to differentiate ourselves. We're not contaminated by Chilean winemaking history; we've had a fresh start."

There is the possibility that the family will also develop its land in Marchihue (Colchagua) alongside the Leyda project, though the latter remains the sole focus for now. The aim in Leyda is to arrive at an annual production of around 200,000 litres (20,000–25,000 cases).

MATETIC

Hernando de Aguirre 430, Providencia, Santiago. Tel: +56 2 2323134. Email: info@mateticvineyards.cl. Website: www.mateticvineyards.com
Established: 1999. Vineyard: 90ha (Syrah, Pinot Noir, Sauvignon Blanc, Merlot, Chardonnay). Production: 90,000 litres.

The Matetic family, one of Chile's largest landowners, made their money in livestock, forestry, and steel. In 1999 they decided to diversify into wine and set up their eponymous winery in the idyllic, self-contained Rosario Valley, which is spread over 9,000 hectares in an east–west line. The vineyards are located around eighteen kilometres (eleven miles) from the coast in a slightly warmer climate than San Antonio's more maritime areas.

The first thirty hectares were planted in 1999 and by 2004 were certified organic, with Biodynamic certification pending. Since then, a further thirty hectares of organically managed vineyard have been added. An increasingly detailed focus on the specifics of site location and fruit quality has led Matetic to enlist the services of Pedro Parra, a specialist in terroir, and to pursue a considered improvement and expansion programme. For example, twenty hectares have been planted on north-facing slopes beyond the northern rim of the Rosario property in what is a cooler, more maritime-affected climate and which actually falls within the Casablanca appellation. Here, Matetic is studying several different clones of Syrah (174, 300, 470) on different rootstocks (101-14, 3309) with different irrigation patterns and five discrete soil profiles identified. There are seventeen individual parcels under cultivation and whose results are being monitored.

The winery is also diversifying its sites nearer the coast. Four hectares of Sauvignon Blanc have gone in at the westerly end of Rosario around eight kilometres (five miles) from the coast – a site that was initially considered unsuitable due to frost risk, lack of water, and restrictions imposed by forestry authorities. In addition, a new planting project is planned for Sauvignon Blanc and Pinot Noir in a location known as Valle Hermoso, near Lagunillas and around ten kilometres (six miles) from the Pacific in what is also officially part of the Casablanca appellation.

This re-evaluation and expansion are the right course of action for Matetic, whose wines have proved somewhat one-dimensional and imbalanced during its formative years. From my tastings, this was due to inappropriate sites and plant material (for example, the EQ Sauvignon Blanc was too often flabby and hot, likely due to an overly warm site in Rosario and a predominance of the 242 clone) as well as heavy-handed winemaking (too much malolactic, lees stirring, and new oak on the EQ Chardonnay).

It does appear, however, that the winery is looking to introduce more elegance and restraint to the wines, and a broader range of fruit can only promote complexity. The plan is to grow mainly Syrah, Pinot Noir, and Sauvignon Blanc. The winery already makes two different styles of Chardonnay (EQ made with oak and Coralillo without) and the idea is to develop this concept of giving the consumer an option by offering two different styles of Syrah and Sauvignon Blanc. It is worth noting in this regard that Matetic's main consumer is North American (sixty per cent of sales are in the USA), so it comes as no surprise that its consultants are also American: Ken Bernards and Anne Kraemer.

Of Matetic's two lines, Coralillo and EQ, the latter is the more prestigious, and within it the Syrah is by far the best bottling – it is this wine that has made Matetic's name. Grown in the decomposed granite of Rosario's hillsides, its dense black fruit is elegantly married with a spicy, floral complexity, and a grippy but smooth palate – this was one of the first examples of Chile's new style of cooler-climate Syrah and it deserves to be feted for reflecting its origins so lucidly. First made in 2001, it has evolved subtly, in different ways, every year, and should continue to do so, with ever more interesting results. This is still the benchmark for the rest of Matetic's portfolio to live up to.

Wine tourism is being developed on the Rosario estate, with a new restaurant installed and a beautiful guest house on site. The sensitively constructed, modern winery is well worth a tour, as are the blueberry plantation and cheese factory.

VINA LEYDA

Av Apoquindo 3401, Of 32, Las Condes, Santiago. Tel: +56 2 2340002. Email: gllona@leyda.cl. Website: www.leyda.cl
Established: 1997. Vineyard: 216ha (Sauvignon Blanc, Chardonnay, Pinot Noir, Merlot, Syrah). Production: 530,000 litres.

That this winery was able to co-opt the name of the local area is evidence of the fact that Viña Leyda was the first wine property to arrive on the scene, investing in the eight-kilometre (five-mile) pipeline from the Maipo River in 1997 and planting in 1998. The winery is owned by four partners, three members of the Fernández family and Gustavo Llona, former commercial director of Santa Rita. At the winemaking helm is the young and talented Rafael Urrejola, whose work experience at Saintsbury and Jacques Prieur provides a clue as to his Burgundian inclinations.

In fact, the first varieties to be planted by Viña Leyda were Chardonnay and Pinot Noir, and it has managed admirably with both. In particular, the Lot 5 Wild Yeasts Chardonnay, grown on south-facing slopes to retain acidity and given only thirty per cent malolactic, has emerged as an eminently successful, grown-up style of Chardonnay, structured and layered. Similarly, the Lot 21 Pinot Noir works very well and, while there is still room for improvement, it is one of the better Chilean Pinots for my money, with a savoury delicacy to its smoky red fruit character.

The laid-back, rangy Urrejola is explicit about his desire to promote elegance over power in his wines. "Sometimes it seems as if there's a competition to make the biggest, most extracted wine," he comments, "but I want to make wines of complexity and elegance, which invite you to have another glass." To this end, Urrejola has adopted a more oxidative approach to his Chardonnay winemaking since 2002, which together with a lack of acidification means he expects them to develop better in bottle. He is relaxed about making Sauvignon Blanc with high alcohol levels because he believes the full flavours and racy acidity can match it, "even though the numbers can sometimes be scary". As for Pinot Noir, "it needs a completely different mindset to what we're used to in Chile", in other words low yields and gentle winemaking are the order of the day. In addition, new clones of Pinot were planted in 2003 to introduce more complexity to the blends.

While Viña Leyda is making some excellent wines at the top end, it is a winery with a forthright commercial approach and as a result tends to cover its bases, sometimes to its detriment. For example, its cheaper San Antonio wines can lack concentration and therein the essence of this wonderful terroir in what seems an attempt to fulfil commercial requirements. Likewise, it makes wines sourced from other valleys such as Colchagua and Maipo but still sells them under the Viña Leyda label, which surely dilutes the brand and could risk confusing consumers. (As a further string to its bow, the winery sells the fruit and some bulk wine from around 150 hectares of its 200 hectares to third parties.)

Nonetheless, Viña Leyda should be congratulated for its good work to date. It continues to experiment, planting new clones and varieties and trialling new wines and blends. A winery is planned for the Leyda site in 2007 and the ambition is to increase the vineyard to 300 hectares by 2010. There is a focus and energy about this winery that bode well.

5

Maipo

BRIEF FACTS

Vineyard: 10,680ha (84% reds)

Main grape varieties (ha): Cabernet Sauvignon (6,320), Merlot (1,140), Chardonnay (953), Carmenère (536), Sauvignon Blanc (415)

Climate: warm temperate with annual rainfall of 300–450mm (12–18 inches)

Soils: deep, varied alluvium on the flat land with gravel and rock content near rivers and shallow soils on hillsides

INTRODUCTION

The Maipo winemaking region corresponds to the administrative oddity that is the Metropolitan Region. It is counted as the country's thirteenth region even though it sits between numbers five (Valparaíso in political terms, Aconcagua for wine) and six (O'Higgins and Rapel). It is the only Chilean administrative, and hence winemaking, region without a coastline. It is also home to the country's capital, Santiago.

Maipo is one of Chile's best-known wine regions, mainly because this was where the majority of the country's big wineries were established in the mid-nineteenth century. Proximity to Santiago meant ease of access to logistical hubs as well as a ready market. However, by the start of the twenty-first century the city was swallowing up vineyards as it expanded relentlessly (*see* Case Study, p. 143). As a result, many new vineyards have been established in the region's south and west.

This is Chile's smallest yet most densely populated region. It has a population of over six million, virtually all in Santiago, which is equivalent to well over a third of the Chilean total. Yet it covers a trifling 2.1 per cent of national territory. What is more, Chile's centre-heavy profile is becoming more and more exaggerated. The government is attempting to reverse this trend though there has as yet been little in the way of tangible results.

Santiago has been undergoing substantial changes of late as a result of massive investments aimed at improving transport, infrastructure, and living conditions. Efficient new toll roads have appeared, largely the result of private concessionary investment. The old, thundering, polluting yellow buses (known locally as *micros*) are being replaced by more environmentally friendly green versions in an attempt to reduce the city's notorious smog. The airport is being extended and improved. Affordable housing projects are being developed in the suburbs in an attempt to reduce the visible poverty in some outlying areas.

Although the Metropolitan Region is comparatively small in Chile, around eighty per cent of its land is earmarked for agricultural production. Wine is one element within this; wheat, maize, and potatoes are others. The Maipo region has 10,680 hectares of wine vineyard, the majority of which is planted to red grapes. Many wine producers are easily accessible from central Santiago and a day trip to visit a few makes for an excellent way to get to know the region.

A PICTURE OF MAIPO

The first time I arrived in Chile I was nervous and tired. Not much stuck in the mind other than lots of people, lots of noise, and having to leave an apple on the plane, such was the severity of the warnings about importing such things.

Now the same journey is like returning to a second home, an arrival in a place charged with memories, associations, and vivid pictures.

The Andes, imperious even from above, slowly give way to valleys and the country's central plain. Green rectangles of crops are bordered by eucalyptus and cypress trees; some of these are vineyards. Hyena-skin hillsides rise abruptly from this tranquil plain, a small hint of the power of the climate and the tectonic forces that have shaped this land.

Santiago airport is busy but orderly. Fur-coated ladies sip coffee while baggage handlers and taxi runners mill around. Out into the open and there are the first wafts of warm concrete and dusty earth. The mountains loom large in the east.

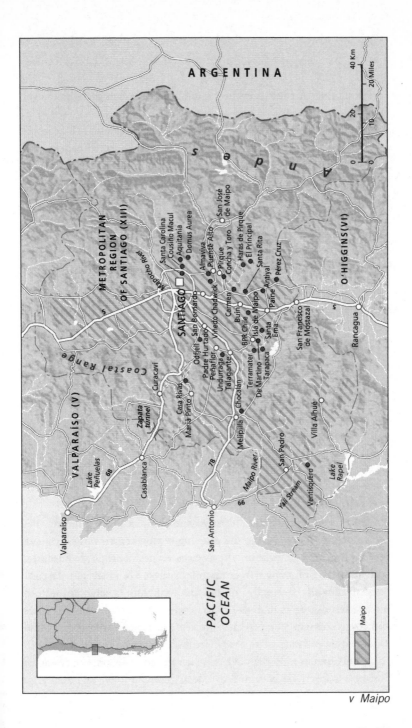

ARGENTINA

40 Km
20 Miles
20
10
0
0

Andes

San José de Maipo

METROPOLITAN REGION OF SANTIAGO (XIII)

O'HIGGINS (VI)

Santa Carolina
Cousiño Macul
Aquitania
Domus Aurea
Almaviva
Puente Alto
Pirque
Concha y Toro
Haras de Pirque
El Principal
Santa Rita
Carmen
Antiyal
Pérez Cruz
Vinedo Chadwick
Buin
Paine
BPR Chile
Isla de Maipo
Santa Ema
San Bernardo
San Francisco de Mostazal
Odfjell
Padre Hurtado
Peñaflor
Undurraga
Talagante
De Martino
Tarapacá
Terramater
Chocalán
Rancagua

Mapocho River

SANTIAGO

Coastal Range

Curacaví

Casa Rivas
María Pinto

Zapata tunnel

Melipilla

Maipo River

San Pedro

Villa Alhué

VALPARAÍSO (V)

Lake Peñuelas

Casablanca

Yali Stream

Ventisquero

Lake Rapel

Valparaíso

San Antonio

PACIFIC OCEAN

Maipo

v Maipo

MAIPO 135

Taking the old route into the capital, the car moves through dense, vociferous traffic. Past the Mercado Central, where weekend lunchtimes are a riot of noise, fresh fish, and vegetables, with a host of restaurants touting for business. Jugglers, windscreen washers, and newspaper sellers spill onto the streets at traffic lights. Rising soberly above central Santiago is the Santa Lucía hill, once known as Huelén until conquistador Pedro de Valdivia founded a new city on this spot in 1541 and called it Santiago de la Nueva Extremadura. Farther on, we skirt the river Mapocho, whose muddy waters have flowed down past ski resorts and wildlife reserves and now move through the heart of a growing, changing city. It is always a pleasure to arrive.

THE NATURE OF MAIPO

Maipo is a land-locked wine region. Its borders correspond to those of the administrative Metropolitan Region, which stops short of the coast. To put the region in context, San Antonio and Casablanca should logically be part of coastal Maipo but political divisions dictate otherwise (officially, they fall within Aconcagua's confines).

Hills and mountains form Maipo's borders on all sides. The Andes and its foothills rise in the east; the Chacabuco range forms the border with Aconcagua in the north; Maipo's western border is the coastal range, and in the south the Paine range of hills crosses the country, almost colliding with the Andes at Angostura, separating Maipo from Cachapoal. Most of the main roads that leave the region do so via tunnels under these substantial hill formations.

This lack of prime coastal territory and enclosure by hills mean that conditions in Maipo during the growing season are of warm days and cool nights. Around eight to nine months of the year are dry and warm, with a short, cool, rainy winter taking place between June and August. Annual rainfall is usually around 300–400mm (twelve to sixteen inches) but can be as high as 750mm (thirty inches) toward the Andes and coast; some of Maipo's driest areas are those in the eastern lee and rain shadow of the coastal range. Rainfall varies partly due to the El Niño phenomenon (*see* p. 18), which can cause heavy precipitation due to a superficial warming of ocean temperatures, or equally its converse La Niña, which causes drought. El Niño years can experience up to ten times the rainfall of La Niña (1,000mm versus 100mm (thirty-nine versus four inches) in Santiago, for example).

Relief is significant in Maipo because it is a major factor in determining local climatic conditions. For example, Maipo's far eastern piedmont experiences cooling breezes that descend along the hillsides at night, which as well as extending the growing season also gives a marked continental effect to the climate, a factor compounded by altitude. (Winds in this part can also be warm, however – the Puelche or Raco wind is one example, which mainly blows in winter and spring and can cause early bud-break.) The predominantly west-facing nature of this gentle slope also has the effect of increasing sun exposure, especially when the sunlight is at its strongest in the late afternoons.

The region's more central areas tend to be consistently warmer by contrast, though still with a notable day–night temperature differential due to the height of the coastal range (which can reach over 2,000 metres/6,600 feet) impeding the moderating maritime influence. Some of Maipo's consistently warmest areas are those situated just to the east of coastal hills, which act as a shelter and retainer of the sun's heat.

The part of Maipo that does receive some maritime influence lies to the west and southwest, especially around the river Maipo and where viticultural territory reaches closest to the coast. Although this is still a warm area (average January daytime temperatures are over 30°C (86°F) around San Pedro, some of the warmest in the region), the influence of morning cloud cover and sea breezes in the afternoons moderates these highs. (In some ways, this is a similar climatic pattern to that of Marchihue, to the south in Colchagua.) This is one of Maipo's newest areas for viticulture.

Because, broadly speaking, Maipo sits on a gentle slope that runs down from east to west, it is common to hear the terms Alto (upper), Medio (central), and Bajo/Costa (lower or coastal) used to differentiate vineyards in the respective areas. It is important to note that, as yet, these are still relatively imprecise definitions. For example, some sources refer to Alto Maipo as being that area above 600–650 metres altitude (2,000–2,100 feet) (including Peñalolén, Pirque, Puente Alto, etc.),

Medio Maipo as being at 350–600/650 metres (1,100–2,100 feet) (Buin, Paine, etc.), and Maipo Costa as being land below this at 100–350 metres (300–1,100 feet) (Isla de Maipo, María Pinto, etc.). The downsides to this system, however, include the facts that Isla de Maipo is generally accepted to be in central Maipo as opposed to the coastal area, and Alto Maipo's territory is widely considered to include land over 400 metres (1,300 feet) in the east of the region (thus including the likes of Alto Jahuel, Huelquén, and the higher parts of Buin and Paine).

No doubt the system will be refined but in the meantime it is helpful to think in general terms of Alto Maipo as occupying the region's sub-Andean territory, as distinct from the flatter, warmer central parts of the region and the more moderate coastal reaches in the west. This issue and what it means for the wines is a topic explored in Viticulture and Wines (*see* p. 140).

Maipo's soils do not offer great diversity in terms of parent material – most are derived from the granites (diorites, granodiorites, etc.), other igneous rocks, and material typical of the volcanic activity common in central and eastern Chile. These are young soils in geological terms. Where they do differ is in terms of texture, fertility, and depth, all of which can affect water retention and root development significantly between areas even in relative proximity.

Over the millennia, tectonic, volcanic, glacial, and river action has meant that Chile's central trench or depression has been filled with deep soils, fine-textured clays, and loams often of high fertility. Exceptions to this rule are found near river courses, such as in Puente Alto or Isla de Maipo, where a higher percentage of coarse alluvial material such as stones and gravels has accumulated, giving good drainage and lower fertility. Hillsides or slopes, both in Alto Maipo and elsewhere in the region, are also distinct in their soil profile, often loose-textured and poor, composed of a sandy or loam layer over decomposed granite. Alluvial and colluvial soils with a mixture of clay, sand, gravel, and stones are also common in Alto Maipo in areas such as Peñalolén, Puente Alto, and Pirque.

Maipo's principal watercourse is a river of the same name that descends from the Andes and crosses the region in a westerly direction. It is a broad and diffuse river whose rate of flow naturally varies according to the season – its volume increases both in winter (from rain) and summer (from melt water coming off the mountains). However, this flow suffers substantial interruption due to man-made interventions such as the many hydroelectric stations that feed off its upper reaches as well as water for Santiago and irrigation. As a result, it is often a fairly apologetic river that ends up emptying into the Pacific at Llolleo, near San Antonio, after flowing down the Maipo Canyon, past Puente Alto, Pirque, Buin, Isla de Maipo, and Melipilla. The river Maipo's main tributary is the Mapocho, which cuts through the north of Santiago before turning south past Talagante to the confluence.

VITICULTURE AND WINES

Maipo is not Chile's biggest winemaking region nor its oldest. It contains 8,999 hectares of red grapes and 1,681 hectares of white, a total that represents under ten per cent of the national vineyard. So why is Maipo Chile's most recognized wine region?

To put it simply, Maipo has been at the centre of things. It is where the Chilean fine wine industry first began in earnest; it is home to the majority of the country's largest and most established producers; it lies in and around Santiago, the nation's capital, home to over a third of the country's sixteen-million population. What is more, Maipo has consistently delivered a recognizable style of wine to the world – earthy Cabernet Sauvignon with notes of dried fruit and eucalyptus oil. Maipo Cabernet has been the Chilean equivalent of Barossa Shiraz or Marlborough Sauvignon.

But things are changing. No longer is Maipo simply a handful of traditional producers making simple though striking Cabernet. Improvements in the vineyard have meant increasing variety in the field (Syrah, Carmenère, and Malbec are performing well) and a growing awareness of the diversity of Maipo's terroirs. The direct result of this is that Maipo's wine map is being re-written in ever-greater detail.

It therefore makes sense to try to explore the difference between areas as a means of understanding the wines.

The logical place to start is in Maipo's easterly piedmont at the foot of the Andes in what is known as Alto (high) Maipo. The first axis within this area is the north–south line that runs along the southeast of Santiago from Peñalolén to Puente Alto to Pirque.

The viticultural area of Peñalolén, which includes Macul, is located on a sloping plateau over 600 metres (2,000 feet) above sea level in the eastern suburbs of Santiago, pressed up against the steep rises of the Andean foothills. This is where Cousiño Macul, Aquitania, and Domus Aurea are located. It is a historic winemaking area whose viticulture stretches back to the 1560s and both Cousiño and Domus have old vineyards. However, the increasing pressure of Santiago's urban sprawl and rising land prices has already seen a gradual move away from the area: Cousiño is selling most of its land and buying farther south; Aquitania has also bought land in southeast Maipo. It looks likely that further moves will happen (*see* Case Study, p. 143).

Soils in Peñalolén are generally well drained with sandy loams and notable alluvial gravel and rock content on the higher slopes (which reach up to 700 metres/2,300 feet), with more clay on the flat land. Soil pests such as nematodes and margarodes are common; replanting on rootstocks is one solution being employed to avoid them. The local climate is generally one of warm days and cool nights, with a marked day–night temperature flux caused by the cool breezes that descend from the hills (the San Ramón foothill that rises directly above the area is 3,250 metres/10,600 feet high). The wines tend to be fresh, structured, and often understated in style, with old vines giving some good concentration.

Puente Alto is at Santiago's southeastern tip, some ten kilometres (six miles) south of Peñalolén but at comparable altitude. Vineyards here tend to be slightly farther away from the mountains so this is a marginally warmer climate though still moderated by cool air that spills down the Maipo Canyon. Another significant difference is the soils: Puente Alto is on the northern bank of the river Maipo and as a result the soils have a high content of alluvial gravels and stones that lie under well-mixed loams of moderate fertility. The resulting soil profile is well balanced, well drained, and makes for good root penetration and even canopy growth. Cabernet Sauvignon has shown itself to be well suited to these soils, making concentrated but elegant wines such as Almaviva and Viñedo Chadwick. This is one of Chile's oldest and finest terroirs for Cabernet.

Pirque is south of Puente Alto across the river Maipo. It is a broad area, essentially a massive horseshoe of hills formed by the Andean foothills to the south and east and a hilly spur in the west, with an expansive plain in the middle that opens out to the north. At its northern limit are Concha y Toro's Pirque Viejo vineyards, a series of terraces that become progressively rockier down toward the river Maipo, and from which the winery sources its savoury, dense Terrunyo Cabernet from old vines. Farther south on the plain are William Fèvre and Santa Alicia. Haras de Pirque is located on the western side of this U-shaped bowl up against the east-facing hills, while El Principal is at the far southeastern end of the Pirque basin. Concha y Toro's Santa Isabel vineyard is at 730 metres (2,400 feet) in the eastern hills.

The warmest sites in Pirque are the lower, north-facing hills and the sheltered flat land that can warm up and trap heat in the summer sun. However, both altitude and proximity to the Andes result in cool nighttime temperatures here – it is a continental-style climate in the summer and frosts are common especially on the flatter land in winter and spring. The area can be particularly breezy, especially in those parts close to the mouth of the Maipo Canyon, which is at Pirque's northeast end and tends to funnel mountain winds down along its path and out over Pirque and Puente Alto. The cooling influence is such that white grapes can perform decently here and reds tend to show a characteristic freshness and herbal, savoury nature.

Just over the other side of the Pirque basin's western rim of hills and extending to the south is an area that lies above the main viticultural centres of Buin and Paine. This is where the likes of Carmen, Santa Rita, Antiyal, and Pérez Cruz are located and could be considered the last bastion of Alto Maipo, before altitude drops toward the west in Buin and Paine proper. The best vineyards are located in the contact zone between the Andes foothills and the plain, on stony alluvial and colluvial soils that moderate vigour and give good drainage. Altitude is slightly lower here than in Pirque and conditions less extreme, with warmer daytimes and cool nights. The best wines are reds that show good ripeness but also balance and depth of character – Santa Rita's Casa Real is a good example.

What could be termed central or middle Maipo is an ill-defined area that essentially consists of land that is neither part of Alto Maipo to the east nor coastal Maipo to the west. As a general rule, conditions here are consistently warmer than in either of Maipo's two other areas, particularly in sites located in the eastern lee of hills, and soils can be deep and fertile in the flat land away from river courses. These areas give ripe fruit that usually lacks concentration but gives decent basic wine.

By contrast, where central Maipo does offer quality is in those specific areas that have poorer, better-drained soils and sites or exposures that benefit from some kind of cooling or moderating influence. A good example of this is Isla de Maipo, where the river Maipo has deposited significant amounts of alluvial stones and gravels, giving a varied soil matrix but which in certain areas, where the stones mix with sandy loams and clays, makes good ground for late-maturing red varieties such as Carmenère and Cabernet Sauvignon. More exposed vineyards also benefit from breezes that travel along the river and offset temperature spikes in the summer. One of the most notable producers in this area is De Martino, whose best Carmenère from a former river-bed site has a tremendous depth of flavour, with heady, ripe cherry fruit and a broad, layered palate with round tannin.

Another area worth mentioning in central Maipo is Alhué, surrounded by the hills that occupy Maipo's south-central area and form the border with Cachapoal to the south. This is a relatively recent area to be developed for wine but the likes of Córpora and Carmen/Santa Rita both have significant vineyard holdings here. The land is higher than areas around the river Maipo and, though soils can be rich in the flat parts, the hillsides can offer promising viticultural territory. The local climate is warm.

Perhaps the least explored part of Maipo for wine is the area in its western reaches, sometimes referred to as Maipo Costa. The term is somewhat confusing given that Maipo has no coast. Nonetheless, some vineyards situated in exposed sites toward the west of the region do receive maritime influence, with foggy mornings, warm days, and breezy afternoons. The moderating maritime influence mitigates the extremes of day-night temperature fluctuations although their effects are still felt here, especially at higher altitudes in the hills.

The coastal influence in western Maipo prolongs the growing season and tends to give a fresh edge to the wines, with reds such as Cabernet Sauvignon, Syrah, and Carmenère often showing juicy fruit and spicy, peppery notes. Soils are poor and well drained on the contact-zone slopes above the plain and on the granitic hillsides, which seem to offer the best viticultural promise in the area. Wineries in this part of the region include Casa Rivas, Chocalán, Tres Palacios, and Ventisquero, and other producers are starting to source fruit from here as interest grows. Most vineyards are still young, though some good diversity is to be found in the range of varieties planted.

One final issue worthy of note relates to the style of wine I described in the second paragraph, and more specifically the topic of eucalyptus. This minty, sometimes medicinal aroma has traditionally been a hallmark of Maipo's reds. There is still no unanimous consensus on what causes it – theories range from heat stress to cool nights and soil compaction. However, it seems clear to me (and the majority of Chile's winemakers) that this aroma and flavour are direct results of vineyards being planted next to eucalyptus trees, whose volatile oils are transferred onto grape skins by wind. The resulting aromas have sometimes proved overly dominant, rendering the wines out of balance. The better winemakers are now working to reduce the dominance of eucalyptus either by cutting down trees or employing other methods so that, even if the aroma is present, it is part of the complexity rather than the overriding element.

CASE STUDY: THE LOST VINEYARDS – A CLOUD WITH A SILVER LINING?

When I visited Santiago zoo I was surprised to find a giraffe there. It was standing in magnificent other-worldly fashion, gazing disconsolately from its cramped pen on the steep slopes of the San Cristóbal Hill over Santiago's sprawling rooftops. It was an arresting sight, but one that will hopefully not be seen for too much longer. The zoo is scheduled for relocation, moving to a far larger site in western Santiago where space is at less of a premium, smog is less invasive, and Santiago's pulsing pressure of people, cars, and buildings is altogether less intense.

The capital's voracious urban sprawl is having a similar effect on vineyards. It is both an inevitable and disturbing trend, the way in which houses, airports, shopping malls, and other urban development are slowly paving over some of the country's most prized vineyards, many with old vines, a rare and precious commodity in Chile. The pressing issues are: where will it end, and what kind of an effect is this having on Chilean wine in general?

First, the evidence. Wine estates are still common to the east and south of Santiago, established before the city expanded but now under increasing pressure to move. Some have already gone: Tarapacá upped sticks and left Santiago completely in the nineties, relocating to Isla de Maipo. The old Planella winery in La Florida has given up the ghost and is now houses. Others have sold the vineyards but kept the wineries, often historic landmarks: Santa Carolina is a case in point, Santa Catalina y Algarrobal another. Cousiño Macul is located in one of Chile's longest-standing vineyard areas but in 1996 it began to sell off its estate and old vines to develop houses and shops. Canepa, a winery already hemmed in by gigantic shopping malls, is also contemplating selling up and simply retaining the winery as a logistical base.

Others are standing firm. Both Aquitania and Domus Aurea, located up the hill from Cousiño Macul in Peñalolén, are resisting the urge to sell up and move on, although to be fair their respective vineyard holdings are small. Concha y Toro is loath to consider the idea of giving up its prime seventy-hectare vineyard (*see* Producer entry, p. 158) in Puente Alto, the source of prestigious wines such as Don Melchor and Almaviva, even though land prices have gone through the roof in the last decade.

Nonetheless, it seems reasonable to expect that in the short to mid term, more vineyards will be lost beneath Santiago's concrete sprawl. Once the land value reaches a certain point it simply makes good business sense to sell, and Chileans tend to be pragmatic businessmen before staunch defenders of the wine cause.

It would be good to be proved wrong. I hope to see certain producers resisting the urban expansion because the loss of the fine slopes of Macul or prime gravels of Puente Alto would be a blow for Chilean wine in terms of its diversity as well as its history and legacy. Giving in to the developing urge means a quick buck in the short term but a decision that may ultimately be regretted.

On the other hand, this process could prove beneficial for Chilean wine, especially if it provides the impetus for improvement and innovation with a view to long-term success. Grubbing up established vineyards and planting new ones elsewhere may impact negatively on quality in the short term, but if those changes are undertaken with a responsible, forward-looking attitude and investment, there is no reason why in time it cannot ultimately match or even improve overall quality. Chile boasts a multitude of diverse and quality sites for winemaking, some very similar to the land currently being lost. If producers can spot the right opportunities and develop good vineyards with sound stock then this might prove a cloud with a silver lining after all.

Noteworthy

In other regions, it tends to be wineries based in Maipo that are the interlopers. However, there are a fair number of wineries based outside Maipo that source fruit from this area. Most come for the Cabernet Sauvignon.

Some wineries that use Maipo fruit are located in cooler climates where Cabernet struggles to reach consistent ripeness. One example is Viña Leyda, which sources Cabernet from Alto Jahuel for its Single Vineyard line. Others simply prefer the style of Cabernet produced by the soils and climate in certain Maipo sites: this is the reason that Colchagua winery MontGras acquired a 270-hectare estate in Linderos as part of its recent expansion drive.

Certain producers prefer to use Maipo Cabernet as the dominant element in a wine but supplemented by fruit from elsewhere. Valdivieso winemaker Brett Jackson, whose winery sources its Single Vineyard Cabernet Sauvignon from Alto Jahuel, thinks Alto Maipo Cabernet is improved by an injection of freshness. "The style from these areas is dried fruits, round and soft tannin, and lazy acidity, which means it benefits from some fresh fruit and lifted acidity from Curicó or Maule." Emiliana Orgánico farms around fifty hectares organically in Los Morros, north of Alto Jahuel, and winemaker Alvaro Espinoza blends Cabernet from here with Merlot from Colchagua. He comments, "Alto Maipo has high pH soils and the fruit is generally low in acidity, though with good tannin, volume, and body."

Cono Sur uses its connections at Concha y Toro to source the Cabernet Sauvignon that lends some structure to its 20 Barrels Merlot as well as providing the majority of its 20 Barrels Cabernet Sauvignon, which is a mixture of Puente Alto and Pirque fruit together with a dash of Carmenère from Colchagua. Hard by Concha y Toro's Puente Alto vineyard is the twenty-five-hectare site owned by Aconcagua-based Errázuriz and used for its Viñedo Chadwick wine (see p. 183).

San Pedro uses Cabernet Sauvignon from Buin for its 1865 line. The same variety for Morandé's top-of-the-line House of Morandé is grown in San Bernardo in southern Santiago. A short distance north of here is the site of Canepa's Maipo winery and twenty-three-hectare vineyard in Cerrillos that is used for its Finísimo Cabernet, though there is a possibility this land may be sold before too long.

Exceptions to the Cabernet rule include Maule-based Terranoble, which buys Carmenère and Syrah from Puangue, an area just over the hills from Leyda that, according to winemaker Ignacio Conca, gives "good acidity and structure". Its regional stable mate Botalcura sources Malbec for its La Porfia line from the region. The Córpora group, meanwhile, has a range of varieties planted in Alhué in Maipo's southern hills, an area that winemaker Ana Salomó praises for its "expressive, spicy fruit".

Producer profiles

ALMAVIVA

Av Santa Rosa 0821, Puente Alto, Santiago. Tel: +56 2 8529300. Email: info@almavivawinery.com. Website: www.almavivawinery.com
Established: 1996. Vineyard: 70ha (Cabernet Sauvignon, Carmenère, Cabernet Franc, Petit Verdot, Merlot). Production: 100,000 litres. *See also*: Concha y Toro, Baron Philippe de Rothschild Maipo Chile.

Both controversial and iconic, Almaviva is one of Chile's leading wineries, making its wine in a very particular style and pricing it formidably high. It is keen to challenge preconceptions about Chilean wine.

Almaviva was officially formed in 1997 when an agreement was signed between Chilean winemaking behemoth Concha y Toro and Baron Philippe de Rothschild SA, the French winemaking group that controls wineries in Bordeaux (Château Mouton Rothschild) and California (Opus One) as well as elsewhere. The first wine was made from the 1996 vintage and released in 1998.

The concept at Almaviva is for the winery to produce one red blend made from a single vineyard in Puente Alto. The winery was essentially built around the vineyard – Concha hived off a section of its best-quality Tocornal estate in Puente Alto for the project. The reasons behind its quality are partly climatic – the warm but moderate conditions of Alto Maipo give a long growing season – but largely it's the nature of the soil that is the issue here. It is a well-drained, well-balanced soil with sand, clay, and silt loams intermixed with a high percentage of alluvial stones and gravels that are particularly suited to Cabernet. A mature forty-two-hectare vineyard, planted in 1978 to Cabernet Sauvignon, Carmenère, and Cabernet Franc, forms the heart of the project.

Significant changes have taken place at Almaviva since its inception. Some twenty hectares of new vines have been added, including a small percentage of Merlot and Petit Verdot. Experiments with rootstocks are underway, as are tests with a new underground irrigation system to encourage deeper root growth. More significantly, in 2003/4 the winery gained newfound commercial and winemaking independence from its parent companies, giving it the vital capability to make independent decisions (before, the policy of joint decision-making had proved strained at times). American winemaker Tod Mostero, who had experience of working with BPDR in France, was brought in as head winemaker in 2004.

Mostero defines his task as one of fine tuning and observation: adopting a detailed focus in the vineyard in order to identify individual parcels by quality and improving on this basis (via yield control, canopy management, and irrigation) as well as tweaking the winemaking in such areas as cooperage selection and fermentation temperatures (generally, slower and cooler). He is easy-going on the subject of brettanomyces, the yeast that can give notably feral, animal aromas in the wine, maintaining that it can be controlled by strict cellar hygiene and adds complexity in moderation, albeit with the risk of bottle variation. His aim is for the wine to be "intense, harmonious and elegant".

One of Almaviva's strengths is its consistency of character. It is not a heavyweight wine, instead majoring on elegant balance and complex, tight-knit flavours with silky tannin, good though lowish acidity, and a gently warming edge to the finish. Typical aromas include ripe dark berry fruits with spicy, meaty elements that can develop into cumin, ginger, or oriental spice with age, as well as a savoury pepper and dark chocolate character. It is both food-friendly and ageworthy.

Of the eight vintages that I have tasted (1996–2003), Almaviva's best wines to date are the 1999, 2001, and 2003. These are the vintages that continue to develop well and show the greatest complexity and balance within the parameters of the style described above. To have made eight wines of this calibre makes for a fine track record of the kind that few Chilean wineries can boast. Even lesser vintages such as 2000 can show a stylish, multifaceted character albeit in a lighter style.

One criticism often levelled at Almaviva is that of over-pricing. The winery's standard responses are that in comparative tastings it fares well against more expensive wines from Bordeaux or California; it sells its stock; it has a proven track record; it is important for Chile to compete with and rank alongside the world's most prestigious wines. In my opinion the jury is still out on this issue. I believe Almaviva's quality does justify a premium price and it is indeed one of the most established and proven of Chile's top order. However, it is a steep price and one that few can afford. It remains to be seen if this wine's commercial success is guaranteed over time. For those who prefer a less pricey drop, Almaviva occasionally makes an excellent second label, Epu, which can be bought at the winery.

ANTIYAL

Casilla 191, Paine. Tel: +56 2 8214224. Email: marina@antiyal.com. Website: www.antiyal.com

Established: 1998. Vineyard: 6ha (Cabernet Sauvignon, Carmenère, Syrah). Production: 10,000 litres.

There are few wineries in Chile like Antiyal. It started out life as the pet project of winemaker Alvaro Espinoza: one red wine made from one hectare of Cabernet Sauvignon planted around the family home near Alto Jahuel as well as some Carmenère and Syrah from his parents' property in Isla de Maipo. A tiny winery was installed next to the house and Espinoza made the wine in his time off from Carmen, where he worked until 2000. The first production run was 1998 and comprised 3,000 bottles.

Since then the project has grown but it has remained faithful to Espinoza's original goal. That is, to make wine on a small-scale basis from grapes grown following organic and Biodynamic principles. Two wines are now made, Antiyal (a blend of Carmenère, Cabernet Sauvignon, and Syrah) and, from 2001, Kuyen (Syrah and Cabernet Sauvignon). Two other vineyards have been added to the supply chain. The first was Los Morros, a vineyard north of Alto Jahuel owned by Emiliana (for whom Espinoza consults – see Colchagua p. 233) from where Cabernet is sourced. More significantly, in 2003 Espinoza also planted a new six-hectare vineyard up toward the Andean foothills near Huelquén at around 500 metres (1,600 feet), which will form the project's main base for future vintages. Organic certification from IMO was achieved from the 2005 vintage.

Espinoza has been at the forefront of developing organic and Biodynamic viticulture in Chile, virtually introducing the latter single-handedly after being influenced by Fetzer consultant Alan York while working in California. He launched the organic Nativa line at Carmen in the late nineties but perhaps his greatest initial success was at Emiliana Orgánica (formerly VOE, *see* p. 233) where, from 2000, he introduced Biodynamic practices on a large scale (over 224 hectares) with such good results that substantially more vineyard has been put over to the project since. It proved to be a welcome synergy for Antiyal, because Espinoza has been sourcing Biodynamic preparations from Emiliana to use at his private project.

Espinoza's attitude toward his eco-friendly farming methods is a mixture of wholesome positivism and down-to-earth practicality. "My approach to Biodynamics is practical," he explains.

> *It's a good way to organize a farm and it's also good for the environment. I do happen to believe in the influence of the cosmic bodies, but I'm not a fundamentalist. Does it affect the fruit? Well, there are other practices like irrigation and canopy management that are clearly more immediately important, but if it ultimately helps the vines find a healthy balance then it will affect the fruit and give better results.*

As regards his signature style of wine, he describes it as "Mediterranean", although California would be another point of reference. The accent is firmly on ripe but not overripe fruit, heady spice, and herbs on the nose together with a broad, warming palate with lowish acidity, plenty of volume, and smooth tannins. It is a style that finds full expression in both Antiyal and Kuyen, and one whose appeal is fundamentally visceral rather than cerebral (in contrast, say, to Almaviva), seemingly able to tap into a powerful gut instinct in the drinker with the compelling sunny, wild, expansive character of the wines.

Both Antiyal and Kuyen have improved steadily since their respective debuts in 1998 and 2001, gaining in elegance and integration. Antiyal is the bigger, fleshier, and generally more complex of the two, while Kuyen tends toward a more peppery, fresh, and meaty fruit character. Both are very approachable young.

AQUITANIA

Av Consistorial 5090, Peñalolén, Santiago. Tel: +56 2 2988000. Email: info@aquitania.cl. Website: www.aquitania.cl

Established: 1990. Vineyard: 18ha (Cabernet Sauvignon, Carmenère).

Production: 150,000 litres. *See also*: SoldeSol (Malleco).

Aquitania was one of Chile's first stand-alone terroir wine projects, established by reputable French investors in 1990 with the aim of making just one red wine from a single site in Macul. That goal has proved elusive so, a decade after it was founded, the winery made significant changes, welcoming a further investor and starting to source grapes from elsewhere in Maipo. While it is a pity that the original project has in effect failed, Aquitania's wines are improving as a result of the changes and it seems there will be more developments to come in the future.

Aquitania's initial partnership was between Bordelais winemakers Bruno Prats, formerly of Château Cos d'Estournel, and Paul Pontallier of Château Margaux, along with experienced Chilean winemaker Felipe de Solminihac. Both Prats and Pontallier had come to Chile in the eighties and were looking to set up a wine project there; when de Solminihac finished working for Cousiño Macul they established Aquitania on the slopes above Cousiño's vineyards in Macul. Planting of the Cabernet Sauvignon and Merlot vineyard (which inevitably included some Carmenère) began in 1991 though the initial vintages, 1993 to 1995, were made with grapes bought from neighbour Domus Aurea – 1996 was the first vintage made entirely with fruit from the property. Just one wine was made, a Cabernet-Sauvignon-dominated blend named Domaine Paul Bruno.

But the project never quite took off in the way its partners had hoped. Sales were much slower than anticipated and the wine was not living up to expectations. A change of policy was implemented and the winery started sourcing fruit from other areas of Maipo such as Pirque and Isla de Maipo in order to increase volumes and attain the complexity it was struggling to achieve solely in its Macul vineyard. The underperforming Merlot was grafted to Cabernet. The last Domaine Paul Bruno was made in 2000 and all wine from the 2001 vintage was sold as bulk. From 2002 onward, two Cabernet-based reds were made, Agapanto (which sometimes includes a touch of Carmenère) and Lazuli (a more ambitious blend of 100 per cent Cabernet from Peñalolén, Isla de Maipo, Pirque, and Buin). In 2003, a fourth investor joined, Ghislain de Montgolfier of Champagne Bollinger, who lived and worked in Chile in the late sixties.

Aquitania's owners are refreshingly open about their shortcomings and ongoing search for quality. "We planted in 1990 and the first wine to meet our expectations was made in 2002; we are conscious there is still lots of room for improvement," comments Prats. Pontallier and Prats admit that their Bordelais preconceptions may have impeded development, especially in areas such as harvest timings (in general Chile has a much longer growing season than Bordeaux) and irrigation (banned in Bordeaux and an imprecise science in Chile in the nineties).

"We were taught an important lesson that we should have known from the beginning: terroir matters," says Pontallier.

We are now focusing on the soils and climate, we've learned a lot about when and how much to irrigate, and we're finding that blending across terroirs gives greater complexity, like the way in which [Château] Margaux's complexity comes from a range of different soils.

The winery currently sources around forty per cent of its production from other producers in Maipo. It has also bought forty hectares farther south in Alto Maipo near Huelquén, which may be planted in the future to red varieties including Cabernet, Syrah, and Carmenère. Further developments are expected. As Pontallier comments, "We're still not yet totally satisfied with what we've got; we need more time."

The style of Aquitania's wine has undoubtedly changed as a result of its moves, generally for the better. There is still a notable emphasis on a restrained, elegant, structured style of wine overall, but, where Domaine Paul Bruno could often be angular and lack weight, its successor Lazuli shows more peppery, savoury, spicy fruit with better breadth and vibrancy – altogether a more successful wine. Agapanto, meanwhile, is similar in style to Paul Bruno (fresh red fruit with minty notes and silky tannin, somewhat one-dimensional) but works better in the more basic price range as a simple, fresh Cabernet for everyday drinking.

SoldeSol is a parallel project for Aquitania. The estate, located in the southerly Malleco region, is owned by de Solminihac's in-laws, who sell the grapes to Aquitania. The steely, structured Chardonnay has enjoyed well-deserved success and there are plans for expansion (*see* Malleco).

BARON PHILIPPE DE ROTHSCHILD MAIPO CHILE

Casilla 253, Buin, Santiago. Tel: +56 2 8216200. Email: fdegeloes@bphr.cl. Website: www.bpdr.cl

Established: 1997. Vineyard: 0ha. Production: 1.3 million litres. *See also*: Almaviva.

When, in 1997, the French-based winemaking group Baron Philippe de Rothschild embarked on a high-profile and ambitious joint venture with Concha y Toro in the form of Almaviva (*see* p. 147), it did not stake all its money on one horse. As is BPDR's wont, it developed a parallel, more commercial project – in comparable fashion to the way Mouton Rothschild sits alongside Mouton Cadet in Bordeaux. BPDR Chile is the result.

The winery owns no vineyards and instead sources all its fruit from around 100 hectares of growers. BPDR's strategic alliance with Concha y Toro means that it has access to the Chilean group's fruit – for example, the Sauvignon Blanc from Mulchén is sourced from the Guilisasti farm in Bío Bío. At the lower end the wines have tended to be decidedly commercial in style with little to recommend them, although improvements have been made since 2004, giving the wines more concentration and character. Escudo Rojo is the winery's most interesting product, a blend of mainly Cabernet Sauvignon with Carmenère, Cabernet Franc, Syrah, and occasionally Malbec.

CARMEN

Apoquindo 3669, Piso 16, Las Condes, Santiago. Tel: +56 2 3622122. Email: info@carmen.cl. Website: www.carmen.com

Established: 1850. Vineyard: 600ha (Cabernet Sauvignon, Sauvignon Blanc, Merlot, Chardonnay, Carmenère). Production: 1 million litres. *See also*: Santa Rita.

At the end of the nineties, Carmen was one of Chile's more innovative, forward-looking wineries. That momentum has slowed now and its wines tend to be solid rather than ground-breaking. However, the combination of significant investment (around US$6 million/£3 million) and progress in the vineyard since 2000 has already resulted in improvements in the wines and could see Carmen's fortunes improve in the near future.

Carmen is one of Chile's oldest wine brands, traditionally focusing on the national market. It was bought in 1987 by the Claro group, owner of Santa Rita, and was revamped and re-launched in the nineties as an innovative, export-focused winery under the winemaking auspices of Alvaro Espinoza. An organic project began in 1994 that resulted in the Nativa line. The winery was one of the first to identify and acknowledge the existence of Carmenère in its vineyards and market it as a variety in its own right (also in 1994) – albeit under its Bordelais name Grande Vidure. It was the first in Chile to launch a straight Petite Sirah (no relation to Syrah) besides using it to blend into its top Gold Reserve red.

Rapid growth and innovation in the nineties were followed by a period of consolidation at the start of the twenty-first century. However, Carmen has continued to expand its operations, purchasing and planting land in Alhué (a secluded, warm area in Maipo's south-central hills) as well as developing its vineyards in Casablanca and Apalta (Colchagua). The winery's other vineyards are in Palmilla (Colchagua), Molina (Curicó), and at its base in Alto Jahuel. Nativa is sourced from a twenty-five-hectare organic Cabernet Sauvignon and Chardonnay vineyard near Villaseca (Buin).

Work in the vineyard has focused on improving the quality of vine stock by planting clones and also using rootstocks in all new plantings since 2000 to improve consistency in the vineyard and better match vines to different soil types. Viticultural methods are also being refined. For example, in Apalta, where Merlot was planted from 2000 onward, temperatures and humidity levels have been carefully monitored, with canopy management, yield policy, and harvest times adapted accordingly – as well as subsequent vinification. Winemaker Pilar González says, "From 2004 it was as if we were working with a different variety."

There is still further progress to be made at Carmen. Its more commercial wines can be insipid and need work to give them greater character and vibrancy to compete with Chile's best wineries at this level. In the mid ranges the wines can often fall into the category of solid but unexciting, while at the top end a wine like the Gold Reserve is undoubtedly a quality old-vine Maipo Cabernet but one made in a decidedly traditional and rather linear style that in my opinion would benefit from work to imbue it with more breadth and depth of flavour.

On the flip side, there is much to be positive about in Carmen's portfolio. The standard of its Sauvignon Blanc is steadily improving as greater attention is paid to clonal selection and blending. Gewurztraminer offers a sound element of diversity to its whites, a category in which Chardonnay generally performs well (Winemaker's Reserve and Nativa are usually ripe but balanced and structured wines in their different styles). Nativa Cabernet Sauvignon is a traditional but consistent style of Maipo Cabernet, chunky and warming with ripe dried fruit and eucalyptus notes. Significant progress has been made with Merlot, with an interesting comparison to be made between its versions from Casablanca (fresh, vibrant fruit) and Apalta (ripe dried red and black fruit), though most importantly both show good balance on the palate. Petite Sirah makes for a heady, fleshy wine in the reserve range that is worth trying.

It is in a wine like the Winemaker's Reserve red that Carmen has a great opportunity to stand out from the crowd. This blend of around half Cabernet Sauvignon with Carmenère, Merlot, Syrah, and Petite Sirah can show exciting complexity though in the past has been a bit overdone, becoming extracted and alcoholic with age. However, more recent vintages have shown a better balance between freshness and ripeness, breadth and structure, with the 2001 the best vintage to date and made in a style that promises better things to come.

CASA RIVAS

Los Conquistadores 1700, Piso 16, Providencia, Santiago. Tel: +56 2 7076288. Email: mlamunategui@sswg.cl. Website: www.casarivas.cl

Established: 1993. Vineyard: 217ha (Merlot, Cabernet Sauvignon, Chardonnay, Sauvignon Blanc, Carmenère). Production: 1.4 million litres. *See also*: Tarapacá, Misiones de Rengo.

Casa Rivas is located in the María Pinto area that lies between Santiago and Casablanca. This broad area of central-western Maipo can be very warm and arid, especially in sites sheltered from the coastal influence by hills; Casa Rivas occupies a more exposed site that is warm in the daytime but receives afternoon breezes from the ocean, cooling the vineyards and extending the growing season (Carmenère is harvested around mid-May here). The wines reflect this climatic reality, showing fresh and ripe characters in both whites and reds.

The winery was originally set up by agronomist Mariano Salas together with his brother-in-law Patricio Browne. The first vines were planted in 1993, with further additions made between 1999 and 2002, including plantings farther up the slopes on the estate's southern and eastern sides. A nursery was set up in order to ensure sound plant material for the new vineyards and research was conducted into rootstocks and clones with a view to achieving greater consistency of maturity in the vineyard as well as protecting vine health. Soils are granitic in origin with sandy-loam textures, well drained and low in fertility. White wines are mainly planted on the lower ground, which is the area most influenced by the cooling sea breezes.

In 2005, the winery was acquired by the Southern Sun Wine Group, a consortium of wineries owned by the Fósforos group and including Tarapacá, Viña Mar, and Misiones de Rengo. At the time of writing it is unclear what the long-term effects of this will be on the wines, though the new owners have stressed that Casa Rivas will continue to develop in independent fashion and there are plans for further planting.

Former Casas del Bosque winemaker Camilo Viani became the first head winemaker under the new ownership.

I can comment only on wines made before the takeover. In this regard, the whites include a solid, zippy Sauvignon Blanc and a very creditable Chardonnay Reserva made in a restrained and structured style. Among the reds, Merlot and Carmenère have traditionally been Casa Rivas' forte, both made in a ripe but sleek-fruit style often with bitter chocolate and leafy, peppery notes, especially in the Carmenère. The two most successful examples of this style are the Merlot Reserva and the Carmenère Gran Reserva, in which the added concentration and attention to detail in the viticulture and winemaking give excellent results. There is more yet to be done but much good work has already taken place at Casa Rivas and it would be good to see this trend consolidated and developed by the new owners.

CHOCALAN

Cruz del Sur 133, Of 901, Las Condes, Santiago. Tel: +56 2 2087401. Email: wines@chocalanwines.com. Website: www.chocalanwines.com
Established: 1998. Vineyard: 125ha (Cabernet Sauvignon, Syrah, Carmenère, Sauvignon Blanc, Merlot). Production: 550,000 litres.

Chocalán is one of Maipo's most promising newcomers. Although its wines are as yet at an early stage in their development (the first vintage was 2002 from vineyards planted in 1999), the overriding impression here is one of sound viticulture, attention to detail, and potential for the future.

The winery is owned by the bottle-making Toro family, who bought the Chocalán estate in 1998. The property is set into hills south of Melipilla overlooking the Maipo river plain to the west and with the Pacific shoreline at a distance of about thirty-five kilometres (twenty-two miles), from which some humid, cooling maritime influence is evident in the otherwise warm local climate. Some eighty hectares were planted in 1999 and 2000, with a further 25 added in 2005 mainly to bolster the Syrah contingent as well as adding Viognier. Around a third of the vines have been planted on northwest-facing hillsides with the remainder on gentle inclines at the foot of the hills. There is good diversity in the plantings, which include Malbec, Syrah, Cabernet Franc, Pinot Noir, and Petit Verdot.

In 2005, Chocalán added San Antonio to its portfolio, planting a small part of a 340-hectare estate near Malvilla just five kilometres (three miles) from the coast. A total of twenty hectares went in, half of which is Sauvignon Blanc and the rest split between Riesling, Chardonnay, Pinot Noir, and Gewurztraminer. The first vintage from this estate will be the 2007.

From the beginning, Chocalán has sought the advice of some of Chile's most experienced winemakers and viticulturists, a strategy that has served it well in the initial process of setting up the winery and vineyard. What it now needs to do is focus on getting the best out of its vineyards and forge an identity for itself on this basis. Initial signs are positive. In the basic Selection line, the wines are fresh and balanced with good varietal differentiation and soft fruit flavours. The Reserva range has more concentration, with Syrah, Cabernet Franc, and Cabernet Sauvignon all showing impressive character. It would be good to see Chocalán continuing a policy of measured progress to give the wines ever-greater structure and complexity over time.

CONCHA Y TORO

Av Nueva Tajamar 481, Torre Norte, Piso 15, Las Condes, Santiago. Tel: +56 2 4765000. Email: webmaster@conchaytoro.cl. Website: www.conchaytoro.cl
Established: 1883. Vineyard: 5,700ha (Cabernet Sauvignon, Carmenère, Merlot, Chardonnay, Sauvignon Blanc). Production: 165 million litres. *See also*: Cono Sur, Emiliana, Almaviva.

Concha y Toro is not only Chile's largest winery; it is also one of its best. Consistency, value for money, diversity, and ambition are notable features of this producer. This success has partly been built around an aggressive policy of expansion and consolidation that the winery has been pursuing since the fifties. Mostly, however, it is down to the sound viticulture and winemaking that have been evident since the late nineties.

The winery was founded in Pirque in 1883 by politician and entrepreneur Melchor Concha y Toro. In the thirties the winery was listed on the Santiago stock exchange and dispatched its first exports. From the fifties onward the company expanded significantly, upgrading its technology in the eighties and nineties and later founding subsidiary wineries: Emiliana (1986), Cono Sur (1993), Trivento (1996, in Argentina), and Almaviva (1997, a joint venture with Baron Philippe de Rothschild SA).

Concha y Toro continues to grow at the start of the twenty-first century. In 2004, it posted strong results with net revenues of US$381 million (£202 million), a rise of 19.5 per cent on 2003. In the same year it exported some 9.4 million cases at a value of US$192 million (£102 million). By 2005, total production was 165 million litres (roughly twenty per cent of the national output, though this figure does include subsidiary winery production), sourced from around 18,000 hectares of vines, of which 5,700 were under Concha's direct ownership. This total had been boosted in 2005 by the US$17 million (£9 million) acquisition of Limarí producer Francisco de Aguirre's assets and further purchases in the area, part of a wider US$150 million (£80 million) investment programme running between 2005 and 2008 that includes securing ever-greater control over its grape supply. Concha continues to plan for growth, eyeing Argentina in particular as a likely source of future growth via its rapidly expanding Trivento operation, which in 2004 was Argentina's second-largest brand in exports.

Concha is a ubiquitous presence across Chile's wine lands. It owns nine wineries (capacity: 170 million litres) and sources fruit from Limarí to Bío Bío. What is impressive is the way it manages to pursue such a widespread grape sourcing policy and yet maintain such a high level of quality even in its more basic, volume-driven lines such as Frontera, Sunrise, and Casillero del Diablo. This is the direct result of a change in strategy that took place after the 2000 vintage, when winemaking and viticultural activities were brought closer together within the company in a drive to improve wine quality by placing more of an emphasis on the vineyard. Around the same time the winery acquired two talented and ambitious winemakers, Ignacio Recabarren and Marcelo Papa, who have been instrumental in building Concha's reputation for quality, diversity, and value.

Being able to source fruit from some of Chile's best winemaking areas as well as having the winemaking skill to take good advantage of this is the secret of Concha's success. There is also an element of sound forward planning and financial muscle to back it up. Concha's move from 2005 to set up a significant base in Limarí is one example of this. Another is the recent development of land in coastal Colchagua near Navidad, not far south of San Antonio, where in maritime conditions just twelve kilometres (seven miles) from the coast a 350-hectare vineyard named Ucuquer is being planted mainly with Sauvignon Blanc and Chardonnay. Both of these projects came about as a result of a detailed climatic and soil study carried out across the country in 2002.

Other notable vineyards in Concha's portfolio include the Peumo site in Cachapoal, the source of its Terrunyo Carmenère. It sources whites such as Riesling and Gewurztraminer from Bío Bío (a farm that belongs to the Guilisasti family, Concha's largest shareholders), and also has three estates in Casablanca, which produce Amelia Chardonnay and Terrunyo Sauvignon Blanc among other wines. Closer to home, it has four vineyards in and around its base in Pirque. Notable among them are Puente Alto (Don Melchor, Marqués Cabernet), the riverside old vines and terraces of Pirque Viejo (Terrunyo Cabernet), and Santa Isabel (Marqués Chardonnay), a cooler site high in the Pirque basin at around 730 metres (2,400 feet) with notable day–night temperature fluctuations.

Concha's portfolio is generally reliable, outstanding in places, and with good diversity and quality in both reds and whites. Of the basic wines, Frontera and Sunrise offer simple pleasures at a good level for the price, while Casillero del Diablo regularly delivers commendable character and value for money across twelve wines. The Cabernet Sauvignon and Syrah are particular highlights. Trio is a line in which three elements are blended to good effect, such as the Cabernet Sauvignon/Syrah/Cabernet Franc, or the Sauvignon Blanc from three sites in Casablanca.

Marqués de Casa Concha is a reliable line in which the wines generally show plenty of ripeness and character. Terrunyo is a more recent innovation and its concept is to focus on a specific terroir and variety, such as Sauvignon Blanc from hillside vines in El Triángulo (Casablanca) or Carmenère from block 27 in Peumo. It is an admirable project already producing good wines but should improve over time. At the top end, Amelia is a Casablanca Chardonnay that exhibits sensitive oak handling and well-integrated acidity, making for a balanced though ripe style of this variety. Don Melchor, meanwhile, is a well-structured Maipo Cabernet whose character is built around minty dark fruit, sweet oak spice, and some elegant, savoury notes of olives and grilled almonds.

COUSINO MACUL

Av Quilin 7100, Peñalolén, Santiago. Tel: +56 2 3514100. Email: maria@cousinomacul.cl. Website: www.cousinomacul.cl

Established: 1856. Vineyard: 420ha (Cabernet Sauvignon, Merlot, Chardonnay, Riesling, Sauvignon Blanc). Production: 2.5 million litres.

A new era in Cousiño's long history began in 1996 when the company bought land in Buin and started to sell off its historic vineyard in Macul. The winery has since been undergoing a testing period of transition that has resulted in notable changes in the wines.

Cousiño Macul was founded by industrialist Matías Cousiño in 1856 in Macul, around three centuries after the land in this area was first planted to vines and other agriculture by conquistador Juan Jufré. French vine stock was introduced, principally from Bordeaux and Burgundy, and French winemakers plied their trade here from the 1880s onward, in the process perhaps helping to institute what was to become Cousiño's hallmark style of wine: structured though restrained, often austere, and earthy wines made from white and red fruit grown exclusively on this estate at the foothills of the Andes to the east of Santiago.

By the late 1990s, however, Santiago's urban sprawl had all but overrun the Cousiño estate and so the family, now in its sixth generation of ownership, decided to cash in on rising land prices by developing and selling off much of its property in the area. The family home and magnificent fifty-hectare park were retained from the original 1,100-hectare estate. A decision had to be made whether or not to stay in the wine business – they opted to carry on and bought 330 hectares in Buin (in an area known as El Tránsito).

As regards the wine estate in Macul, the historic wine cellar was kept along with 120 hectares of vines although this is planned to be reduced to around twenty-five hectares, all under organic management. By 2006, the new vineyard in Buin covered 275 hectares, planted to a mixture of reds and whites using vine stock purely from Cousiño's plants and nurseries in Macul. Plantings include less common varieties such as Riesling, Sauvignon Gris, Syrah, Malbec, and Cabernet Franc. A new winery in Buin was built and Matías Rivera replaced winemaker-of-thirty-years Jaime Ríos.

Cousiño's decision to move on in such decisive fashion represents both an opportunity lost and an opportunity gained. The former because losing much of its old vineyard in Macul means losing much of the identity on which Cousiño built its success, and old vineyards are scarce and valuable assets in Chile. On the other hand, it was time for Cousiño to change. Once an industry leader, by the late 1990s and early 2000s the winery had somewhat lost its direction, its wines were often tired and overly traditional, its vineyard was not performing to the best of its ability, and it was struggling to compete in a more dynamic, diverse Chilean wine scene. A new focus and drive were needed, especially in the vineyard – this is an aspect that the winemakers have been working hard on.

It is the wines that will be the ultimate proof of how successful Cousiño's bold decision has been. There is no doubt that the overall style has changed. Taking Cabernet Sauvignon as an example, where Macul offers finesse, balance, and structure, Buin tends to give riper, bolder fruit with a broader palate expression and somewhat looser framework. The Buin vineyard is younger and, although essentially still in Alto Maipo territory some thirty kilometres (nineteen miles) southwest of Macul, is farther from the Andes foothills than Macul, with the inevitable difference in soils and climate that this entails.

The wines show a more overtly New World character as a result, a welcome development in some ways although it would be good to see the winemakers working toward ever-greater structure and complexity in the wines. Overall wine quality at Cousiño still needs improving as the wines can lack balance and certainly do not yet exhibit the kind of unique character the winery is keen to achieve. For now its best results are coming from unassuming styles of Merlot and Cabernet Sauvignon. Finis Terrae is a blend of the two, as is the new icon wine launched in 2006 to commemorate the winery's 150th anniversary.

Cousiño's whites have traditionally been its weakness, although a pleasant mid-weight Riesling and an earthy Sauvignon Gris make for interesting points of difference. If the winery is to improve this it needs to look beyond its Macul or Buin vineyards for inspiration (the company has always been opposed to this idea even though there has been a suggestion of late that it may be looking to Chile's far south in this regard).

DE MARTINO (SANTA INES)

416 V Correo 21, Santiago. Tel: +56 2 8192959. Email: office@demartino.cl. Website: www.demartino.cl

Established: 1934. Vineyard: 280ha (Cabernet Sauvignon, Carmenère, Sauvignon Blanc, Malbec, Merlot). Production: 1.7 million litres.

As a direct result of a good deal of excellent, even pioneering work in the vineyard in recent years, De Martino has transformed itself from a reliable Maipo producer into one of Chile's most interesting and promising wineries.

By way of context, the winery is part of a larger operation whose most significant commercial activities are the production of bulk wine (five to six million litres per year) and both juice and juice concentrate. This part of the business in effect gives the bottled wine division the freedom to develop its more niche products, a strategy that is beginning to pay dividends. De Martino is the brand used for this higher-end segment of wines, while Santa Inés is used for the lower end – there can be overlaps between the lines.

De Martino's base is in Isla de Maipo. It owns 280 hectares of vineyard, all of which is organically managed and certified (BCS Germany, see p. 15) but only around a third of which is used for bottled wine, the rest going for bulk. It was this need to segment the vineyard on a purely qualitative basis that led to the genesis of what has become a major ongoing focus at De Martino: the drive to research, document, and better exploit Chile's terroir. In this regard De Martino, and more specifically its dynamic winemaking team of Marcelo Retamal and Felipe Müller, has been at the forefront of activities in documenting soil types, climatic conditions, vine behaviour, and wine results across the country, vinifying up to 400 different vineyard lots from Elqui to Bío Bío in the process.

As a result, De Martino's winemaking horizons have expanded far beyond Isla de Maipo. For example, the winery's top Chardonnay used to be sourced from Maipo but from 2004 the fruit has come from Limarí, a vineyard nineteen kilometres (twelve miles) from the sea chosen for its soil profile and distinctive style of structured, understated fruit. The winery has pioneered production in Choapa, a new viticultural region between Aconcagua and Limarí, from where it produces a spicy, fleshy Syrah. Pinot Noir from San Antonio, old-vine Malbec from Maule, and Sauvignon Blanc from coastal Casablanca are further instances of this ongoing search for Chile's best terroirs. "We used to make lots of wines from just one estate," comments Müller, "but to get quality that way is impossible, so now we go and find where the best places are and we focus on improving it."

Isla de Maipo remains an important terroir within the winery's ever-expanding line-up, however. This is largely down to the performance of Carmenère in specific sites within the vineyard. Much of central Maipo is hot and fertile but parts of Isla de Maipo benefit from cool and humid air that travels up the river Maipo from the coast, prolonging the growing season, as well as stony alluvial soils left behind by parts of the river that have dried up. It is from this kind of site that De Martino's best Carmenère is sourced, in warm but not too warm conditions over a mix of clay, gravel, and sandy soils. The first pure Carmenère block was planted in 1992 on this soil matrix and has since provided the winery's best fruit from this variety.

Carmenère has an important place within De Martino's history because it was one of the first wineries, along with Carmen, to champion the variety in its own right. The Santa Inés Carmenère 1996 was the first of its kind (Carmen's was called Grande Vidure), released at a time when the variety was not officially recognized by Chilean or other wine authorities around the world. This wine was produced from the 1992 parcel, fruit from which is now more regularly used for the winery's top Gran Familia line as well as the very impressive Single Vineyard version. De Martino's style of Carmenère is typically ripe and intense with layered flavours of dark cherry, damson fruit, and sweet spices together with soft tannin and good length.

If I had one criticism of De Martino it would be for its occasional tendency to overdo things, in which cases its wines can veer into not just ripe but overripe territory, with extraction, oak, and alcohol levels uncomfortably high. It would be a great pity if the excellent progress being made in the vineyard aimed at expressing different nuances in Chile's terroir were then to be stifled in the winery by regimented vinification policies. It does seem, however, as if this is being taken into account. Retamal notes that his style of Carmenère has evolved from green and lean in the early days (the 1996 was only 12.8% ABV) toward ripeness (the 2002 was 14.6%), but now the challenge is to reduce the alcohol without losing the maturity and complexity. Attention is also being paid to maceration times, both pre and post fermentation. This is, inevitably, the beginning of a long and arduous process involving very detailed work.

We can expect more and greater things to come from De Martino. For now its range offers generally good quality across the board, especially in the Legado and Single Vineyard ranges, with the latter of particular interest due to the ongoing terroir work.

DOMUS AUREA (QUEBRADA DE MACUL)

Av Consistorial 5900, Peñalolén, Santiago. Tel: +56 2 2848271. Email: isabellezaeta@domusaurea.cl. Website: www.domusaurea.cl
Established: 1970. Vineyard: 26.5ha (Cabernet Sauvignon, Merlot, Petit Verdot, Cabernet Franc). Production: 50,000 litres.

Domus Aurea is a small-scale, terroir-focused wine project situated on sloping land set hard against the Andean foothills at Santiago's eastern limit in Peñalolén. A change of winemaking direction in 2001/2 has led to an improvement in the wines.

At the heart of Domus is the sixteen-hectare vineyard of predominantly Cabernet Sauvignon with some Cabernet Franc that was planted in 1970. Initially, the fruit was sold but in 1995 its owners, the Peña family, decided to launch a bottled wine project; the first vintage released was 1996. The initial winemaker was Ignacio Recabarren but he was replaced by Patrick Valette in 2002, with Jean-Pascal Lacaze as day-to-day winemaker. The vineyard has also been supplemented by a further ten hectares of Cabernets Sauvignon and Franc, Merlot, and Petit Verdot, planted in 1990 and located around 500 metres (a third of a mile) from the original vineyard slightly farther down the slope. Replanting continues in the old, wide-spaced vineyard; selected clones and rootstocks are being used.

Soils in the area are predominantly loose-knit sandy loams with a significant gravel and stony content; as a result roots can penetrate deep underground, with some old vines delving down up to five metres (sixteen feet). Being close to the hills means that conditions are frequently breezy and slightly cooler than the lower-lying areas to the west, especially at night when temperatures are regularly 20°C (36°F) lower than daytime during the growing season.

A range of wines is made at the property: Domus Aurea and Stella Aurea are the most prestigious, supposedly made in "masculine" and "feminine" styles respectively. (I have found that both wines offer a similar character though Stella tends to be more immediate in its appeal and a touch less concentrated.) Peñalolén (aka Alba) is a more basic range in which the concept is to use different regions for different varieties – the Cabernet is from Macul but a Sauvignon Blanc from Limarí is also made, and further wines may be included in the future, such as Syrah and Carmenère.

Domus Aurea has many admirers but I have never been totally convinced by it as a top-quality wine. It has many good features, including a notable freshness and refined palate profile, as well as a typically earthy fruit character, but my criticism is that the wine is often too dominated by eucalyptus flavours (the result of the eucalyptus trees that surround the old vineyard) and all too often lacks real complexity and depth on the palate. Forceful though relatively linear Cabernet flavours with heavy overtones of eucalyptus do not make for a truly complex wine even if it has other redeeming features.

However, things have been changing since 2002. There has been a drive to tone down the eucalyptus notes by working on promoting the fruit character of the wine (as well as cutting down some of the trees). Increased complexity is now the aim and as a result more Cabernet Franc is being introduced as well as Merlot and, in the 2004, Petit Verdot makes its debut. Slightly higher-toast barrels are being used to sweeten the tannins and introduce more complex aromatics.

The results are promising, with Domus Aurea 2003 a clear step up in quality, with a better balance of eucalyptus, dried red and black fruit, dark chocolate, and earthy, herbal notes. There is still more to be done but the new winemaking approach is encouraging, focusing on retaining Domus's hallmark character but imbuing it with greater complexity and depth. As Lacaze comments, "A great wine is a blend of perfection and imperfection; this terroir is fabulous so we don't try too hard to intervene and improve it beyond ensuring a good balance."

EL PRINCIPAL

El Principal de Pirque, Calle la Escuela S/N. Tel: +56 2 7074592. Website: www.elprincipal.cl

It hasn't been an easy ride for El Principal in the first years of its existence. The lack of precise details above reflects the fact that, in mid-2006 at the time of writing, the winery was still undergoing significant changes and exact details were unavailable. Nonetheless, this winery has proved capable of producing quality and as such merits attention.

El Principal was established in 1998 when the landowning Fontaine family signed up for a joint venture with Bordelais winemaker and former owner of Château Pavie, Jean Paul Valette. The first vines on the property had been planted in 1993 but the majority were added from 1998 onward, taking the total to fifty-six hectares of Cabernet Sauvignon, Carmenère, Merlot, and Cabernet Franc. The estate is located on foothill slopes in a self-enclosed area at the far southeastern limit of the Pirque basin. Its sheltered nature and north-facing aspect mean that this is a warmer area than some of the more exposed land in Pirque, though the altitude (700–800 metres/2,300–2,600 feet) and generally cool nights offset the heat during the growing season.

Just two wines were made in the first three vintages: El Principal and second wine Memorias. The aim was to convey a sense of terroir and the wines were well received initially, especially the 1999 El Principal, which showed excellent potential in its fresh, savoury character with charred pepper, juicy fruit, and spicy, bitter dark chocolate flavours with elegant tannins. Initial results suggested this was a winery at the start of something special that, with time and experience, would achieve great things.

However, in 2000 Jean Paul Valette died. An irreparable schism rendered the joint venture dead in the water after the 2001 vintage and the situation was not resolved until mid-2005 when the property was bought by German shipping magnate Jochen Dohle, former partner at Botalcura (see p. 283). The interim vintages have almost entirely been lost as a result. A further fifty hectares of hillside plantings are planned, including Syrah and Petit Verdot. As of early 2006, Gillmore winemaker Andrés Sánchez was being announced as the new consultant winemaker.

HARAS DE PIRQUE

Camino San Vicente S/N, Casilla 247-Correo Pirque, Santiago. Tel: +56 2 8547910. Email: contact@harasdepirque.com. Website: www.harasdepirque.com Established: 2000. Vineyard: 143ha (Cabernet Sauvignon, Carmenère, Chardonnay, Sauvignon Blanc, Merlot). Production: 700,000 litres.

Haras made its first wines in the 2000 vintage and since then has established itself as one of Maipo's most promising wineries. Its wines are made exclusively from its Pirque estate.

Haras began life in 1991 when businessman Eduardo Matte bought an estate including a thoroughbred horse stud on the western rim of the Pirque basin. Some 120 hectares of vines were planted in 1992/3 on gentle east-facing slopes at the foot of hills at the western end of the estate; the remaining land was used for horses and for fruit plantations.

The vineyard rises from 550 to 660 metres above sea level (1,800 to 2,200 feet) and local conditions are warm during summer daytimes though temperatures drop off fast in the afternoons due to strong downdraughts from the mountains that funnel out of the Maipo Canyon. Harvests are relatively late as a result, extending into late May for Carmenère.

The project sprang into life at the start of the century when Haras started bottling its own wine (initial vintages were sold off to third parties; the first reds were produced in 2000, whites in 2001). A further twenty-five hectares were planted in 1999/2000, some of which went onto steeper hillsides. New varieties such as Syrah, Viognier, and Petit Verdot were added. Since then, further modifications have been made, for example Merlot has been grafted to Sauvignon Blanc and some Chardonnay in warm north-facing sites has been switched to Cabernets Franc and Sauvignon.

It is clear that significant time and resources have been invested in developing the vineyard at Haras and that this is an ongoing process. Such evolution is natural in a terroir-focused project such as this and it is good to see the winemakers and viticulturists making progress in this regard and focusing on creating wines with a sense of identity. There seem to be some excellent raw materials here and it would be good to see an increasing integration, complexity, and harmony in the wines that come with diversity in the vineyard, experience of the same, and vine age.

The wines tend to be restrained in style and with a pleasant food-friendly aspect to them. Cabernet Sauvignon accounts for over half of the plantings and has so far proved the winery's most successful variety, making wines in a fresh, savoury style with herbal, black olive, and warming fruit characteristics. Chardonnay has also given some promising results in the cooler sites within this continental climate, making for a ripe but understated style. I have yet to try the Syrah or Viognier though would expect interesting wines in time from both.

Haras produces wines under the Equus, Character, and Elegance labels, in ascending order of price. In 2003, it entered into a joint venture with Italian wine producer Antinori, producing two wines: a

Sauvignon Blanc (Albaclara) and a top-end red, Albis (an impressively peppery, savoury Cabernet Sauvignon/Carmenère blend whose component parts may change over time). The concept is for a Chilean red made with Italian input.

ODFJELL

Camino Viejo a Valparaiso 7000, Santiago. Tel: +56 2 8111530. Email: info@odfjellvineyards.cl. Website: www.odfjellvineyards.cl
Established: 1998. Vineyard: 100ha (Cabernet Sauvignon, Malbec, Merlot, Carignan, Carmenère). Production: 800,000 litres.

"A cake maker should stick to making cakes" was the answer I was given when I asked why Odfjell produces only red wine. The reasoning being that Chile's speciality is reds, so the winery focuses entirely on that. It is an admirable strategy and Odfjell deserves credit for specializing in the way it has and developing some excellent diversity within this red wine niche.

The winery is owned by Norwegian shipping magnate Dan Odfjell, who initially came to Chile on business and ended up buying land in the hills west of Santiago suburb Padre Hurtado. The farm, located in warm central Maipo on an east-facing slope and flat land, was initially planted to fruit orchards but in 1992 the conversion to vineyards began; the first wines for release were made in the 1999 vintage.

In its short existence so far, Odfjell has worked hard on improving the level of its viticulture and searching out diversity within Chile's red wine vineyard. The winery is now vinifying around seven different red varieties, including Malbec from Curicó and Carignan from Maule. Around thirty-five per cent of production is currently sourced from producers, though the winery is looking to increase its ownership in time. For example, in 2004 Odfjell purchased sixty-five hectares of land south of Cauquenes in Maule just to secure access to a four-hectare plot of very old, dry-farmed, bush-trained Carignan it had previously been purchasing. The plan is to plant more Carignan, Cabernet Sauvignon, Syrah, and Malbec here. Plus, the winery now owns the small Malbec vineyard near Molina in Curicó. Further land purchases are planned – mostly in areas south of Maipo. Progressive changes to

Odfjell's sourcing programme can be expected as this process continues.

In the Maipo vineyard, Merlot has not been performing well so it is being grafted to Cabernet Sauvignon, while experiments are being conducted with free-standing Cabernet Franc planted at the highest part of the vineyard (around 500 metres/1,600 feet). French winemaker Arnaud Hereu sees the project as a work in progress:

We're making good wine but we're just starting. In Chile it's not difficult to make good, fruity wine – but in the next twenty years we'll be making great wine. And how we do this is by planting on hillsides, going down south, improving our viticulture, and knowledge, working for low yields and careful winemaking.

Armador is the winery's basic varietal line, with Orzada a step up in concentration and diversity, while Aliara is the top wine. Orzada is consistently the most exciting and successful range, with highlights including the bright, blue-fruited Carignan from Maule, the wild, inky, and punchy Malbec from Curicó, as well as a well-judged blend of Carmenère that combines the fresh pepper and fruit of Maule with a riper, broader character from warmer areas farther north.

Armador is generally consistent though Aliara, while it shows undoubted quality, was affected in its early vintages by cellar hygiene issues (between 2000 and 2002 the winery had a brettanomyces infestation that has, since the 2003 vintage, been brought under control). This meant the wine showed notably animal, earthy, and slightly dry-tannin characteristics in its debut vintages of 2000 and 2001; this style is set to change from 2003 onward with a greater emphasis on purity of fruit. In addition, the wine itself has been evolving, from a blend of mainly Cabernet with some Carmenère from Maipo in 2000, to a mix of Colchagua and Maule fruit in 2002 with the same varieties supplemented by Cabernet Franc and Malbec.

PEREZ CRUZ

Estado 337 of 825, Santiago. Tel: +56 2 6323964. Email: wines@perezcruz.com. Website: www.perezcruz.com

Established: 2001. Vineyard: 140ha (Cabernet Sauvignon, Merlot, Carmenère, Syrah, Malbec, Petit Verdot). Production: 800,000 litres.

Pérez Cruz is a red wine specialist located in Maipo's southeastern extreme, tucked into the Andean foothills near Huelquén. Despite being a relative newcomer to the Maipo scene it has already gained a deserved reputation for complex, characterful wines and should continue to improve.

The 550-hectare Liguai estate was bought by the Pérez family in 1963 and used initially for cattle and crops such as alfalfa and almonds. The first twenty-seven hectares of vines were planted in 1994 (Cabernet Sauvignon, Carmenère, and Merlot) with a further 113 hectares added in 1998, including Syrah, Malbec, and Petit Verdot. Initial plans were simply to sell the fruit but, as the Chilean wine industry took off in the late nineties, the family decided to build a brand, and so began the construction of an elegant, curvaceous winery in 2001, and the subsequent bottling of wines in 2002.

The estate sits on a shallow slope at an average altitude of 450 metres (1,500 feet) in the contact zone between the Andean foothills and the plains to the west. Soils are both colluvial and alluvial in origin, formed by glaciers and rivers bringing material down from the hills, with the rock and gravel content giving good drainage and low fertility. Summer temperatures are warm but moderated by cooling mountain downdraughts in the afternoons and at night.

Pérez Cruz currently produces only reds and it is heartening to see this sort of specialization in a country where wineries have traditionally been generalists. The vineyard is worked on a parcel-by-parcel basis (around sixty parcels have been identified so far) with an emphasis on localized treatments for minimal environmental impact. Pérez Cruz's overall style is for wines that tend to show a ripe but also fresh and savoury character with good complexity and weight. Winemaker Germán Lyon explains that the house style is one of "ripeness and concentration with soft tannins".

Around eighty-five per cent of production is accounted for by the Cabernet Sauvignon Reserva, which includes small amounts of Merlot,

Carmenère, and Malbec (all the wines are blended to varying extents). It is an elegantly constructed mid-weight wine, in a pleasant, leafy red-and-black-fruit style with notes of tobacco and pepper, and a fresh undercurrent of acidity to match the warming alcohol. Above this is the Limited Edition line, comprising a sturdy Syrah, a perfumed and robust Malbec, and a ripe, earthy style of Carmenère. The top wine is called Liguai, a blend of Cabernet, Syrah, and Carmenère in roughly equal proportions, a juicy, peppery wine with plenty of dark fruit and hints of dried mint.

SANTA CAROLINA

Til Til 2228, Macul, Santiago. Tel: +56 2 4503000. Email: malvarez@santacarolina.com. Website: www.santacarolina.com
Established: 1875. Vineyard: 825ha (Cabernet Sauvignon, Chardonnay, Merlot, Sauvignon Blanc, Carmenère). Production: 20 million litres. *See also*: Viña Casablanca.

One of Maipo's historic producers, Santa Carolina lost its way during the nineties and by the start of the twenty-first century was in dejected shape, producing wines of decidedly indifferent quality, and generally in need of a radical overhaul. This process was belatedly begun in 2004 with wholesale personnel changes, modifications in ownership, funding, and logistical structure, as well as a profound re-evaluation of the viticulture and winemaking.

Santa Carolina was founded in 1875 by Luis Pereira Cotapos in Macul but as Santiago expanded the firm gradually sold off its vineyard in the vicinity – first in Macul, then later in Puente Alto (the last vintage from its Santa Rosa estate was 2003). This left the winery with one Maipo estate in Buin and the majority of its owned vineyards in Cachapoal and Colchagua, with a presence in Casablanca in the form of its subsidiary Viña Casablanca as well as a large contract grower base. Its headquarters remain in downtown Santiago though the majority of its vinification now takes place in Colchagua and Curicó, where it owns wineries. The firm is owned by food and drink group Empresas Watts, formerly Empresas Santa Carolina. It also owns an Argentine operation, Finca el Origen, which is reflected in the fact that Santa

Carolina's Antares brand includes wines from both Chile and Argentina.

The fundamental problems with Santa Carolina's wines have stemmed from a lack of investment in vineyards and infrastructure, not enough hands-on viticultural work on the part of the winemakers, a formulaic approach to basic issues such as irrigation and harvesting, as well as old-fashioned winemaking, and poor oak handling. As a result, the wines have lacked fruit, varietal character, balance, and complexity, most notably in the upper price ranges.

The long-term process of change began in 2004 with new management and an investment plan. In 2005, new head winemakers were installed at both Santa Carolina (Sven Bruchfeld) and Viña Casablanca (Andrés Caballero), with viticultural consultant Pedro Izquierdo brought in to advise. Immediately after taking on what he termed "a big professional challenge" and obtaining the necessary backing for reform, Bruchfeld wasted no time in implementing sweeping changes in both wineries and vineyards.

The initial task was to taste all the wines in the cellar, mainly from the 2002–5 vintages. ("There was some decent stuff in there but most of it was downgraded in quality – very little went up," comments Bruchfeld. "It was a costly exercise.") Blends were redone. Winemaking policies were substantially revised, coopers changed, unused small vinification tanks were brought into service and installed with temperature control. The vineyards also came under scrutiny. "We have beautiful red vineyards in Cachapoal and Colchagua but it was clear they were being managed ineffectively and harvested too early," says Bruchfeld, who has also instigated a policy of purchasing grapes for upper levels of wine. The 2006 vintage is the first under his mandate and he estimates that three to five years are necessary before the winery is back at the top of its game.

At the time of writing it is still too early to comment on the effect of these changes on the finished wines. But necessary changes they were for Santa Carolina (as well as Viña Casablanca) and it does seem from the initial blends made since that there is a greater emphasis on cleaner, fresher fruit and more palate presence in the wines. By far the biggest challenge for Santa Carolina is to get its premium wine project back on track, from its Reservas up to its top wine, Viña Santa Carolina (VSC), in order to regain lost ground. Its whites also need significant improvement. In the meantime, the winery's best value is to be found in its basic ranges.

SANTA EMA

Izaga 1096, Casilla 17, Isla de Maipo. Tel: +56 2 8192996. Email: santaema@entelchile.net. Website: www.santaema.cl
Established: 1956. Vineyard: 270ha (Cabernet Sauvignon, Merlot, Carmenère, Cabernet Franc, Syrah). Production: 4 million litres.

Santa Ema is a solid, traditional Maipo winery. Based in Isla de Maipo, it sources around sixty per cent of its fruit from growers in the region, with the supply balance made up with fruit from its own 270-hectare Rosario vineyard near Peumo in Cachapoal. This vineyard was originally planted in 1935 after the Pavone family, which still owns the winery, had arrived from Italy and was setting up a wine grape-selling business that would later become Santa Ema in 1956.

It is no surprise, then, that most of Santa Ema's best wines come from this old-vine vineyard in Cachapoal. Catalina is a case in point: it is the winery's top red blend (Cabernet Sauvignon with Merlot and Cabernet Franc) and shows a dense tobacco and spicy fruit character with ripe, tight-knit flavours. The Barrel Select is an increasingly interesting line, with both the Syrah and the Carmenère showing commendable savoury complexity for the price.

SANTA RITA

Apoquindo 3669, Piso 7, Las Condes, Santiago. Tel: +56 2 3622000. Email: info@santarita.com. Website: www.santarita.com
Established: 1880. Vineyard: 1,723ha (Cabernet Sauvignon, Merlot, Sauvignon Blanc, Chardonnay, Cabernet Franc). Production: 40 million litres. *See also:* Carmen, Los Vascos.

Santa Rita is one of Chile's largest wine producers and it continues to grow. (As an overall group, including subsidiary wineries, it vies with

San Pedro for second spot behind Concha y Toro and has a sizeable share of the domestic as well as the export market, like both these producers.)

The winery was established in 1880 at its present site in Alto Jahuel. A century later it was acquired by Chilean businessman Ricardo Claro, one of the country's foremost entrepreneurs with interests in fields as diverse as television, shipping, and bottle-making. By 2006 it was producing around forty million litres per year, with three vinification facilities, the country's third largest exporter, and with one of the highest average export prices of the big volume producers. It had also acquired Carmen (1987), Terra Andina (2001), and a forty-three per cent share in Los Vascos in 1996 as well as establishing Doña Paula in Argentina in 1998.

Claro's desire for expansion and consolidation remains undiminished at the start of the twenty-first century. In 2005, the group was foiled in both its bid for Limarí producer Francisco de Aguirre and an ambitious takeover of Undurraga. Further developments are expected in this regard. Meanwhile, the wine group's commercial structure was overhauled and Santa Rita acquired a total of 1,800 hectares of new land in 2005 – 1,200 hectares in coastal Colchagua (Pumanque) and 600 hectares in coastal Limarí, near Tabalí. This adds to the winery's vineyards in Casablanca, Maipo (Buin, Alhué), Curicó (Molina), and Colchagua (Palmilla). In 2006, consultant Patrick Valette was drafted in alongside Santa Rita's long-standing winemaking team of Cecilia Torres and Andrés Ilabaca.

Santa Rita has a sound portfolio of wines that is slowly growing in diversity. At its lower end, the 120 line is made in significant volume (it accounts for around half of total production in any given year) but generally offers good consistency and easy-going character for the price. Highlights include the Syrah, the Cabernet Sauvignon rosé, and the Petite Sirah. At the Reserva level both reds and whites show more concentration though not diversity – things can be a little predictable in this range.

The winery's best results are to be found in its upper-level wines such as Medalla Real, Floresta, Triple C, and Casa Real Reserva

Especial (note that this is different from the Casa Real domestic label). These seem to fall into two broad stylistic camps: traditional (Medalla, Casa Real) and modern (Floresta, Triple C). Although this distinction is simplistic and increasingly blurred as the wines evolve over time, it is worth mentioning as a broad categorization because, at this level, Santa Rita's portfolio can be confusing in terms of what it offers.

Take three top reds made from the Alto Jahuel vineyard. Medalla Real Cabernet Sauvignon is made from vines planted in the mid-eighties, with a touch of Cabernet Franc and fourteen months in oak. Its style is classic Cabernet, with fresh, peppery black fruit and a structured palate. Triple C is sourced from the same plot of Cabernet Sauvignon and has a slightly longer period of oak ageing but around seventy per cent of the blend is Cabernet Franc (grafted in 1990 onto twenty-year-old Cabernet Sauvignon) and Carmenère. In this case, the wine is more concentrated and multifaceted, with vibrant, ripe, complex aromas, and a warming, broad palate. Finally, Casa Real is a supremely ageworthy, traditional style of Maipo Cabernet, a pure varietal sourced from vines planted in the sixties and cropped at the lowest yields of the three, around three tonnes per hectare. Its style is of vanilla and ripe dark fruit with herbal and mint notes when young, developing into yeasty, sweet spice and dried flowers with age. Tasting in 2005, the 1990 was still vibrant and structured; in 2006 the 1995 was drinking well, while the 2001 was well integrated, young, and impressive.

Floresta is a more flexible concept all round, the idea being that the wines change every year according to which varieties and areas perform best. It was introduced around the same time as Triple C, in the late nineties, and has since provided some of Santa Rita's most appealing wines, made in a concentrated, complex style. The Sauvignon Blanc from Leyda and Cabernet Sauvignon from Apalta have both performed well in the line; it will be interesting to see which grape varieties and areas become regular fixtures as Santa Rita homes in on its best terroirs.

TARAPACA

Los Conquistadores 1700, Piso 15, Providencia, Santiago. Tel: +56 2 7076288.
Email: vinos@tarapaca.cl. Website: www.tarapaca.cl
Established: 1874. Vineyard: 605ha (Cabernet Sauvignon, Merlot, Sauvignon
Blanc, Chardonnay, Syrah). Production: 4.5 million litres. *See also*: Misiones de
Rengo, Casa Rivas.

Many Maipo wineries have plenty of history behind them, Tarapacá
included. But history in Chilean winemaking terms is no guarantee of
quality – it is those wineries that have combined a shrewd moderniz-
ing instinct with the benefits of tradition that have made the best
progress. On the evidence of its wines, Tarapacá has been lagging
behind the field in this fundamental regard.

The winery was founded in 1874 as Viña de Rojas; after over a hundred years of cultivating noble vine stock in Maipo, as well as a few
name changes, the winery was acquired by the Fósforos group in 1992.
Shortly afterward an ambitious relocation plan was put into action,
transferring the winery from the Santiago suburb of La Florida to a
stunning new home in the 2,600-hectare Rosario de Naltagua estate, a
self-enclosed natural amphitheatre in central Maipo with hills on three
sides and the river Maipo at its eastern border. The first 420 hectares
were planted between 1992 and 1997; a further 185 were subsequently
added, including around seventy hectares on hillsides, and less
traditional varieties such as Viognier, Malbec, Syrah, Gewurztraminer,
Mourvèdre, and Cabernet Franc.

Given the range of varieties, exposures, soils, and local mesoclimates that exists within this estate, which supplies the majority of
Tarapacá's fruit, the lack of diversity and quality in the final wines is
disappointing. It often seems as if there are good elements in the wines
but these are too often overshadowed by tired fruit characteristics and
over-extracted tannins, and undermined by a lack of palate structure.
Many wines cry out for an injection of freshness, roundness, and concentration to fill out what is often an interesting but angular character.

Changes in the winemaking structure in 2006, including the depar-
ture of long-term chief winemaker Sergio Correa, may presage a
change of direction in the wines in this regard. There does seem to be

a real desire among the new winemakers to improve quality, primarily by focusing on the vineyard and aiming for wines that major more on fresh fruit and terroir qualities than on oak and overripeness. For now, Syrah, Carmenère, and Viognier currently show the best potential within the range.

Tarapacá is part of the Southern Sun Wine Group, a subsidiary of Fósforos, which also includes Misiones de Rengo, Viña Mar, Casa Rivas (acquired in 2005 for US$8 million/£4 million), and Argentine brand Tamarí.

TERRAMATER

Luis Thayer Ojeda 236, Piso 6, Providencia, Santiago. Tel: +56 2 4380000.
Email: terramater@terramater.cl. Website: www.terramater.cl
Established: 1996. Vineyard: 607ha (Cabernet Sauvignon, Carmenère, Merlot, Chardonnay, Sauvignon Blanc). Production: 4.1 million litres.

TerraMater has three main arms to its business: fresh fruit, wine, and olive oil. Of these, wine is the dominant element, with around half of the annual four-million-litre production sold in bulk. Its bottled wine range is patchy but shows some interesting diversity and has been improving of late.

TerraMater was created in 1996 when the Canepa winery was split up and the Canepa sisters retained the winery's former estates, including vineyards, olive groves, and orchards. Its associate winery is Millaman (Hacienda el Condor), based in Curicó. TerraMater has three main vineyards, located in Maule (San Clemente), Curicó (Los Niches), and Isla de Maipo. The winery's potential lies in the combination of age and diversity in its vineyard. Some plantings date back to 1945 – its Cabernet Sauvignon in Curicó, for example – and in addition the winery can draw on the likes of Zinfandel, Sangiovese, and Malbec. It is also purchasing fruit from Casablanca and Limarí.

The aptly named Unusual range has proved to be a welcome recent addition to the portfolio. Its straight Zinfandel is a powerful but charming wine with plenty of rustic, Italianate appeal, showing dried cherries, leather, and woody notes with good grip and acidity. Another highlight of the same range is the Cabernet/Shiraz/Zinfandel blend, another expansive wine made from the Maipo vineyard with dried herbs and fruit with leather and minty notes and a food-friendly palate.

The Altum range, essentially a collection of single-vineyard wines, still needs work as the wines often show good character initially, only to be undermined by a lack of balance or integration. The one notable exception to this general rule is the Cabernet Sauvignon made from old vines situated near the Andean foothills in Curicó, a typically under-stated version of the variety from this area with an agreeably taut, fresh character.

UNDURRAGA

Av Vitacura 2939, Piso 21, Las Condes, Santiago. Tel: +56 2 3722932. Email: info@undurraga.cl. Website: www.undurraga.cl

Established: 1885. Vineyard: 1,000ha (Cabernet Sauvignon, Carmenère, Merlot, Chardonnay, Sauvignon Blanc). Production: 13.5 million litres.

After over a century of involvement in its eponymous winery, the Undurraga family left the business in 2006 after a protracted dispute with their business partners, the Colombian Picciotto family. The latter took control of the winery and, at the time of writing, appeared to have secured a new Chilean partner in the form of businessman José Yuraszeck. It is to be hoped that the new owners implement a wide-reaching programme of improvement in the wines, which is sorely needed.

Undurraga is one of Chile's largest and most historic producers. Expansion in the eighties and nineties saw its vineyard base grow to around 2,000 hectares, around half of which is owned and spread over four estates: two in central Colchagua and two in Maipo (Codigua, south of Melipilla, and Santa Ana, in Talagante where the winery is based). There is potential in these areas but it seems that more focus is needed in the vineyard as well as a rethink on the winemaking policy.

Positive signs at the winery include the introduction of new line Aliwen as well as some good quality in the two top wines, Altazor and Founder's Collection, both single-varietal Cabernet Sauvignons made from old vines in Santa Ana that show decent, earthy, elegant spice and some concentrated dried fruit. All the Aliwen wines, however, need altogether more character than the 2004 whites and 2003 reds were showing in 2006 when I visited the winery; they were formulaic and bland, a criticism that could also be levelled at many of the other wines in the range, both reds and whites. This is something that the winery is apparently working on. It will be interesting to see how the range evolves under the new regime.

VENTISQUERO

Camino La Estrella 401, Of 5, Sector Punta de Cortés, Rancagua. Tel: +56 72 201240. Email: info@ventisquero.com. Website: www.ventisquero.com
Established: 1998. Vineyard: 1,600ha (Cabernet Sauvignon, Merlot, Syrah, Carmenère, Chardonnay). Production: 14 million litres.

Ventisquero is a young winery that has grown at a prodigious rate since its creation in 1998. However, it has managed its growth well and its early wines have been generally consistent and commercially sound. Its next challenge is to introduce better quality at the top end and raise the standard across the board in what is a crowded portfolio, an achievement that should not be beyond this talented team of wine-makers with some good-quality vineyards at their disposal.

The winery was created by Agrosuper, a large Chilean company specializing in the production of white meats, salmon, and fruit. Initial plantings began in 1998 and by 2006 the company had 1,500 hectares of vineyard across five different estates in Casablanca (Tapihue), Colchagua (Peralillo, Apalta), and Maipo (Tantehue and Trinidad). Further plantings are being added in Colchagua (Ránguil, southwest of Lolol) for Sauvignon Blanc, Chardonnay, and Carmenère. The wine-makers also have their eyes on land in Huasco, the region to the north of Elqui, where Agrosuper has extensive land holdings, as well as coastal territory such as that around Navidad just over the border in Colchagua. The total investment bill by 2006 was running at US$60 million (£32 million).

Ventisquero's policy is to be self-sufficient in grape supply, hence its aggressive early expansion. The Trinidad estate, where the winery is based and the first to be planted, is in far southwestern Maipo. This is one of Maipo's more maritime winemaking climates at around thirty-five kilometres (twenty-two miles) from the shoreline, with cloudy and foggy mornings followed by warm days and breezy afternoons. Soils on the flat land are clay loams, becoming sandier with decomposed granite content on the hillsides.

Winemaker Felipe Tosso defines the challenges in the area as reducing herbaceousness in the fruit and finding the right balance for each variety in its respective soil and site, with neither too much stress nor excess vigour. The learning process has involved adjusting irrigation methods, canopy and yield work, and even changing some varieties around (for example grafting Merlot to Syrah and replacing Malbec with Chardonnay). Rootstocks are also being trialled. Plans for future development include planting Viognier, Grenache, Mourvèdre, and Pinot Gris. The wines from here tend to have good natural acidity and fresh fruit character.

Ventisquero's first wines for release were made in 2001. In the early wines, reds have been notably more consistent and impressive than the whites, which is an aspect the winery needs to improve. Its Tapihue site in Casablanca is not the coolest and Sauvignon Blanc, for example, can lack definition. Pinot Noir is also a weakness. Both issues may be improved if new coastal plantings including those in Lolol (near Ránguil, around twenty-five kilometres (sixteen miles) from the coast) prove successful. Ventisquero's initial strengths have been its Carmenère, Cabernet Sauvignon, and Syrah in styles that range from fresh and spicy from Trinidad to broader and riper from Colchagua. It is no coincidence that the top Grey line includes these three varieties and, in 2006, Ventisquero also launched a new top-of-the-line Syrah from Apalta named Pangea, made in association with former Penfolds and Grange winemaker John Duval.

The winemaking policy at Ventisquero has been under review and the new direction is toward balance and finesse. The winemakers are making a conscious effort to move away from overripeness and overly high alcohol and tannin levels. To this end, trials have been conducted to compare different methods, such as lower fermentation temperatures and more cold pre-fermentation maceration. All of this is to be applauded and, having tasted the results in a series of mini-vertical tastings of Grey Carmenère and Syrah from 2001 to 2004, it is starting to have a good effect, making for better-integrated and more balanced wines. As Tosso puts it, "In Chile we've been too macho in our wine-making in the past; now we want balance without forcing things."

Ventisquero has evolved at a breakneck speed during its early existence; it would be good to see the wines being refined and consolidated. Brands include Ventisquero, Yali, Ramirana, Chileno, and Yelcho.

VINEDO CHADWICK

Av Nueva Tajamar 481, Of 503, Torre Sur, Las Condes, Santiago. Tel: +56 2 3393100. Email: wine.report@errazuriz.cl. Website: www.vinedochadwick.com
Established: 1999. Vineyard: 16ha (Cabernet Sauvignon, Carmenère, Merlot, Cabernet Franc). Production: 13,500 litres. *See also*: Errázuriz.

Viñedo Chadwick forms part of the diverse portfolio of the Aconcagua-based Errázuriz winery. The property produces one red wine from a sixteen-hectare vineyard in Puente Alto planted in 1992 over an old polo field. The first wine was made in 1999 and released in 2002; the style is elegant and impressive though could yet benefit from improvement.

Viñedo Chadwick is a new concept but it has an interesting history. Entrepreneur and avid polo player Alfonso Chadwick Errázuriz bought the 300-hectare property known as Viña San José de Tocornal in 1945. As a result of Chile's agrarian reforms, aimed at redistributing land ownership, he sold the majority of the estate in 1967 to Concha y Toro, which would later go on to produce top reds such as Don Melchor and Almaviva from this vineyard (the latter is now located cheek by jowl with this estate). Chadwick retained twenty-five hectares that were the family home and polo field. This field was planted to vines in 1992; the polo goals and tree-lined borders remain.

The vineyard is typical Puente Alto: a warm but moderate climate with alluvial soils composed of a 60cm (two-foot) topsoil layer of well-mixed loams over a deep stratum of river-bed stones. Well aerated and drained, with moderate fertility and good potential for root penetration, the soil is ideally suited to Cabernet Sauvignon, which covers fourteen hectares here. A small amount of Cabernet Franc, Merlot, and Carmenère is also present, though small modifications are taking place. Errázuriz winemaker Francisco Baettig is keen to increase the quantity of Cabernet Franc and Merlot and is not so fond of Carmenère. "It just doesn't ripen every year as much as we would like; it can be quite cool in May here but Carmenère works best when it is fully ripe and not herbaceous," he comments.

Carmenère was included in Viñedo Chadwick's first vintage, 1999, but its four subsequent vintages are 100 per cent Cabernet Sauvignon. The wine is developing a recognizable style. On the nose it tends to show pressed black fruit with herbal and leafy notes, graphite and mocha with some dark chocolate and tobacco that develop with age. The palate is well integrated and commendably elegant, although would benefit from more breadth and complexity – these could be achieved, for example, with increased vine age or judicious blending. Tasting the five initial vintages in 2006, the 2001 showed the finest all-round expression, with the 2003 – the first wine made under Baettig's control – generally warmer and more powerful than its precursors.

6

Cachapoal

BRIEF FACTS
Vineyard: 9,591ha (87% reds)
Main grape varieties (ha): Cabernet Sauvignon (4,757), Merlot (1,786),
Carmenère (702), Sauvignon Blanc (612), Chardonnay (483)
Climate: warm temperate with annual rainfall 350–650mm (14–26 inches)
Soils: alluvial loams and clays with poorer, larger-textured soils close to the Andes
and rivers

INTRODUCTION

Agriculture and mining are at the heart of the economy in Region VI, which incorporates the winemaking regions of Cachapoal in the north and Colchagua in the south. Indeed, Cachapoal has almost as many table grapes as wine grapes (7,873 hectares versus 9,591) and the road that runs from Pelequén in the south of the region to San Antonio on the coast is known as the Fruit Road, such is the volume of fresh goods exported via this route. (Several of Cachapoal's wineries are also connected to fruit companies – La Rosa and La Roncière are examples.) Corn, apples, pears, watermelon, cereals, peaches, kiwis, avocados, and wheat can all be found growing here.

Cachapoal's mining activity is largely centred on the cavernous El Teniente, Chile's second-biggest mine after Chuquicamata, and one of the world's largest underground mines. It is located to the east of Rancagua in the Andes and such was its importance that an entire town, known as Sewell, was built to house the mine's workers complete with police station, hospital, swimming pool, and church. In the sixties, for practicality, Sewell's inhabitants were transferred to

Rancagua and it is now a ghost town. The mine remains a highly productive source of copper, however, contributing around eight per cent of the national total, as well as by-products including molybdenum and silver.

Rancagua is the capital of Region VI and lies at the heart of Cachapoal. It is an unremarkable though relatively cosmopolitan town, perhaps most renowned for being the location of a crucial battle in the Chilean wars of independence. In 1814, Bernardo O'Higgins found himself trapped by royalist forces in the town. He staged a desperate bid for safety, fleeing with his troops across the Andes where he met the Argentine General San Martín. Although the battle is traditionally known in Chile as "the disaster of Rancagua", it ultimately led to the country's independence from Spain – San Martín and O'Higgins later crossed back into Chile and inflicted a definitive defeat on the royalists following the battles of Chacabuco (1817) and Maipú (1818).

One notable historical legacy in the region is that of the Chilean cowboy (*huaso*). Horses are still commonly used for transport and agricultural labour, and are only slowly being replaced by machinery. What continue are the rodeos – trials of horsemen's skill and determination in which they have to pin heifers up against the padded walls of a round paddock. Rancagua holds the national championships every year in late March. On special occasions it is common to see men dressed in the traditional *huaso* outfit of flat-brimmed hats and ponchos, known here as *chamantos*. The town of Doñihue in Cachapoal is known for its handcrafted garments, including *chamantos*.

In the west of the region is the Rapel reservoir, one of Chile's largest man-made lakes, formed in 1968 to serve the Rapel hydroelectric plant. The reservoir has capacity for some 700 million cubic metres; the hydroelectric facility generates an average of 575 gigawatts per hour. Rapel is the name of a town near the coast and also the river that runs from the reservoir to the Pacific. It is also the title of the broad denomination that includes both Colchagua and Cachapoal – wines from either area, or blends between them, can use this appellation.

Wine has been an important part of Cachapoal's regional make-up since the Jesuits helped establish vineyards in the late sixteenth century. However, it has never reached the same level of prominence as, say, in Colchagua or Maipo. The reasons for this are discussed in the Viticulture section, but things are now beginning to change as

Cachapoal stakes a claim to its place among Chile's better-known wine regions. At the heart of this drive are, quite simply, better quality and more ambitious wines, as well as a growing will to promote Cachapoal in its own right as distinct from Colchagua and Rapel. Moving vineyards out of the warm, fertile lands of the central depression – ideal for fruit but not so good for wine production – has been an important part of this process.

As of 2003 the region has a wine route to coordinate tours to the area (www.cachapoalwineroute.com). One wine-related sight not to be missed is that of La Rosa's La Palmería vineyard, where, in an isolated valley in the coastal range, hundreds of soaring palms (*Jubaea chilensis*) tower above the vines in wizened, statuesque majesty.

A PICTURE OF CACHAPOAL

There is a single-carriageway road that runs eastward from the muted bustle and sprawling industry of Rancagua. It disappears into the mountains and, before reaching a dead end, arrives at a small thermal baths complex and hotel called Termas de Cauquenes.

We arrived at the Termas after a long day. It was dark and bitterly cold; the high-ceilinged rooms struggled to hold the biting July temperatures at bay. The other rooms were unoccupied; we ate quickly and alone. Small noises were amplified by the emptiness and cold; dripping melt water punctuated our conversation. The waiter's footsteps echoed around the dining room.

I thought it would be a shame to come to the Termas and not try a hot bath. Early the next day, with an icy blue sky hanging over the steep valley, I gingerly crossed the courtyard and descended a flight of steps, arriving in a damp corridor with individual bath rooms. My breath ballooned around me. I waited; the place seemed deserted. It was only when I called out that a face appeared round the door, a woolly hat pulled hard down over the eyes. He looked me up and down. A puzzled look gave way to amusement as he ambled out with a large spanner and began to crank open the tap over one of the baths. The water was remarkably clear.

I remember the bath because it was profoundly relaxing, clearing a racing mind in minutes, and inducing a state of deep calm. It was as if this water, sent up warm and charged with minerals from the millennia-old bedrock, was like an ancient remedy for the stress and strain of the modern world. Charles Darwin and Chile's liberator Bernardo O'Higgins had soaked their skins here; I wondered if they had felt the same way.

It was a struggle getting out, drying and dressing in the cold, damp air. As I left, I shouted a loud goodbye. It was a muffled voice that replied – it came from the bath room next door. My attendant had clearly decided that sitting around in the cold wasn't for him. He was taking his own bath; his woolly hat hung cheerfully on the door handle.

THE NATURE OF CACHAPOAL

Cachapoal is a wine region that sits sandwiched between Maipo and Colchagua. At its westerly tip is the Rapel reservoir; its southern apex is the bowl of land around San Vicente. The majority of its wine producers are located in the eastern side of the region, in the central north–south depression and sub-Andean territory.

On the map, Cachapoal is a U-shaped region. The indent in this U shape is a range of hills, the kind of which litters the centre of the country at this latitude. These hills almost meet the Andes foothills at Angostura (literally "narrow passage"), where the border between Cachapoal and Maipo is located. These central hills run to a point near the town of Peumo, where a narrow corridor of flat land has formed along the path of the river Cachapoal. The hills on the southern side of this feature, which extend to the south and east, are those that form Colchagua's northern rim (Apalta, for example, lies on the south-facing side of these peaks).

The major watercourse in the region is the river Cachapoal, which rises in the Andes and flows down west, passing just to the south of Rancagua, at which point it turns southwest toward Peumo. At this juncture it is met by the river Claro, which crosses the region's southeast territory. The river's course then swings round to the northwest and it empties into the Rapel reservoir. From the western end of the reservoir to the coast the river is called Rapel; on its northern side is Maipo, to its south Colchagua.

As discussed in the Colchagua section, by a curious quirk of Chile's appellation system, what should logically be coastal Cachapoal has

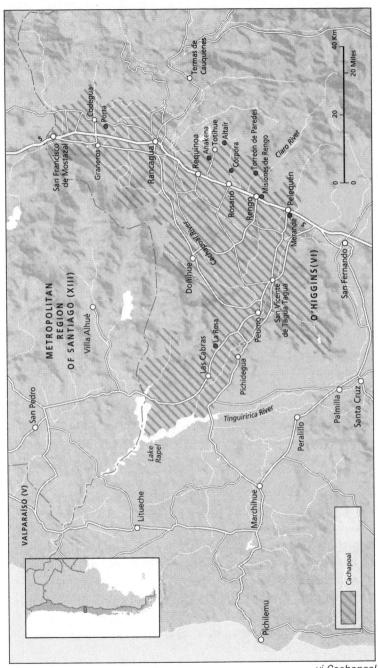

vi Cachapoal

been bundled into Colchagua's broad territory. In reality, all this land along the coast from southwestern Colchagua up to Navidad at the border with Maipo forms part of an anomaly classified as the Cardenal Caro denomination. Until recently this small and insignificant area has been largely overlooked – until, that is, serious wine development started taking place in Marchihue. As Marchihue is clearly part of Colchagua, Cardenal Caro has been lumped in with Colchagua, though it may well be that, with new developments in Navidad, and possibly Litueche, Cachapoal will reassert its claim over these coastal areas.

Historically, however, almost all Cachapoal's wine activity has taken place in its central and eastern territory. (This constitutes the principal difference between Cachapoal and Colchagua: the latter's wine producers are mainly to be found in an east–west depression that opens out toward the coast.) The general climatic pattern is one of warm summers and cold, damp winters, with a well-defined dry season lasting six to eight months of the year. Being largely isolated from maritime influence, temperatures during the growing season in the central and eastern territory are hot in the day and cool at night, with low relative humidity.

Within this overall pattern, individual areas show localized variations. The region's far eastern, sub-Andean territory is known as Alto Cachapoal. Here, average daytime summer temperatures are similar to elsewhere in the central depression (27–29°C/81–84°F) but exposure to fresh winds from the south and southwest, as well as cool air descending from the mountains to the east, moderates conditions later in the day. This is especially marked at night, when temperatures drop to around 10°C (50°F). Slopes are shallow in incline until the first, steep rises of the Andean foothills begin in the east. The soils are well suited to viticulture, with a good alluvial and colluvial mix of stones and gravels together with sandy clay loams. As a general rule, closer to the Andes means a more marginal climate and soils – and, as a frequent result, more interesting wines.

The region's central territory is generally warmer and dryer than

Alto Cachapoal. This is most notable in sites sheltered from southerly and westerly breezes by hilly ground, such as some areas around Graneros, Doñihue, San Vicente, Peumo, Las Cabras, and Pichidegua. These last three areas fall within the corridor of land between the Rapel reservoir and the central depression, though, and as such often attract coastal breezes which moderate temperatures.

Chile's central depression, running north–south from Santiago, is a trench caused by land sinking between the area's two major geological driving forces: the coastal range and the Andes. Its soils were formed after glaciers and rivers moved material (mainly volcanic in origin) down from the mountains. Soils in the central depression are thus fluvio-glacial sediments principally of volcanic origin and mainly consist of clays and loams of varying development, with rocky content nearer the rivers. The hills in the central area are the typical mix of intrusive diorites, granodiorites, and basalts of the central granite batholith, the massive body of igneous rock that runs down Chile's spine.

VITICULTURE AND WINES

Despite being located between Maipo and Colchagua, two of Chile's most recognized wine regions, Cachapoal is one of the country's lesser-known appellations.

There are several reasons for this. One is that its wine producers have tended to be less ambitious and less unified than elsewhere. Another is that the wines simply have not been good or terroir-focused enough to draw attention to the region. What is more, much of the wine has been sold under the Rapel denomination, a catch-all term that covers both Colchagua and Cachapoal (this would be like calling a wine "Médoc" when it could be sold as Pauillac or St-Julien). Some of these wines are blends of Colchagua and Cachapoal fruit (therefore earning the catch-all name), often made by large producers based outside the region; but others are not. The wineries simply prefer the association with Colchagua or appreciate "Rapel" as an easily-pronounceable regional name. As a result, Cachapoal has become the wallflower of Chilean wine.

But although Cachapoal's development has lagged somewhat behind its neighbours', it is now finally starting to assert its identity. A wine route was formed in 2003 partly to encourage visits to the area but also to act as a sort of regional winemaking association to foster region-wide cooperation and promotion (*see* www.cachapoalwineroute.com for more details). Through this organization, a detailed study of the region's soils, climate, and vineyards was carried out and the findings were reported in early 2006. The report, compiled in association with Talca University's CTVV (Centro Tecnológico de la Vid y el Vino) wine research department, is just the kind of focused analytical approach that can help Chile's wine producers improve. Among other things, the study noted the relatively low use of clones and rootstocks in the region and encouraged more detailed soil analysis. It recommended further studies "to allow the evaluation in site-specific fashion of the winemaking potential of different sectors of the region and to permit decisions to be made in an informed and opportune manner".

Progress hasn't just been happening behind the scenes, however. Cachapoal's wines have improved noticeably in recent years as the region has gained in experience and there has been a growing focus on making wines from the better individual sites. This, in turn, has meant a more prominent use of the Cachapoal appellation on labels, hence greater visibility to wine consumers. Two examples of this are Concha y Toro's Terrunyo Carmenère, which is labelled as coming from Peumo, and Altaïr from Cachapoal. It is a trend that should be encouraged both in the winemaking and labelling; Cachapoal does have the ability to craft excellent regional wines and it should increasingly exploit this potential and identity.

The major concentrations of vineyards in Cachapoal are in the Rancagua, Requínoa, Rengo, San Vicente, and Peumo areas. As the region has historically lacked developments in more coastal territory, the main differences in the wines are between those vineyards located in the slightly cooler, more continental conditions toward the Andes (an area generally known as Alto Cachapoal, and which includes Requínoa and Rengo), and those in the warmer mid-valley sites such as

San Vicente and Peumo. Red wines have always been Cachapoal's strongest suit.

However, there are qualifications to be made to this broad definition. Firstly, vineyards are starting to appear in what is, too all intents and purposes, coastal Cachapoal – Concha y Toro's new vineyard near Navidad is one example (*see* Noteworthy). This should provide a new style and standard of whites which has, until now, largely eluded the region, although recent efforts with Viognier in Alto Cachapoal (Anakena, Torreón de Paredes) have also shown promise. Chardonnay and Sauvignon Blanc will remain mediocre until new vineyards are developed nearer the coast or higher into the Andes.

In addition, experimentation and research are beginning to show the suitability of certain varieties to specific areas. Syrah, for example, tends to make good wine all over Cachapoal but particularly in the well-drained, granitic stone soils and continental-style climate of Alto Cachapoal. Fruit from Casa Lapostolle, Anakena, and also Altaïr's vineyards is starting to demonstrate this potential for ripe but savoury and characterful wines, although in general the vines need to mature for better results.

Carmenère, on the other hand, seems more at home in the warmer sites around Peumo. This is a variety that needs a long, even season in order to mature properly, good sun exposure, and deep but well-drained soils of moderate fertility (it struggles in poor soils) to keep the vine going late in the season. Peumo has deep alluvial soils, rarely attracts late-season rains, and its conditions are warm but moderated by sea breezes, meaning less extremes of temperature than other areas. This makes for a long season, with early flowering and late harvests in May. Concha y Toro's Terrunyo Carmenère is a good example of the style and quality emerging from this area; in addition, Anakena uses a portion of Peumo Carmenère to blend with its fresher Alto Cachapoal fruit in a successful combination.

Merlot has in the past been one of Cachapoal's most celebrated varieties. It is increasingly clear that a good deal of this success has in fact been due to Carmenère, as many wines labelled Merlot (a practice that continues) include a percentage, if not a majority, of the Carmenère grape. The truth is that Merlot continues to struggle with problems of poor root development and dehydration in Chile, and Cachapoal is no exception. More work is needed on this front. In the meantime, producers need to face up to their responsibilities and label wines in the correct manner: either Carmenère or Carmenère/Merlot. It is, after all, in their long-term interests to do so.

It is good to see wine diversity beginning to emerge from Cachapoal between sites as well as varieties. More needs to be done to foster the region's individual character and quality, but the emergence of varieties like Cabernet Franc, Malbec, and Syrah alongside the more traditional Cabernet Sauvignon gives grounds for optimism.

CASE STUDY: GETTING DOWN TO THE NITTY GRITTY

In July 2004, I spent a week travelling around Alto Cachapoal, the far easterly part of the region. I was given a series of presentations by the local winemakers on soils, climates, and varieties. The following is an edited, bullet-point version relating to three vineyards located in a line between Requínoa in the central depression and the foothills of the Andes in the east. My tasting notes of relevant wines are included.

Merlot in Requínoa: Stephane Geneste (Chateau Los Boldos). "Skeletal" soils with good drainage comprising sixty per cent river stones, fifteen per cent gravel and the rest loose clay and sand. Low in nitrogen, high in potassium due to stones and phosphates; pH around seven, low organic material. Merlot plantings have both young and old vines (from 1959). In Chile the variety tends to dehydrate, resulting in tart, unripe, alcoholic wines; flood irrigation is used to increase soil humidity and the soils are broken up to encourage root growth at depth. Soils with higher clay content are targeted for new Merlot plantings. Wine: Merlot Vieilles Vignes 1998 – very ripe plum and prune fruit, leather notes and fresh herbs, dried sweet fruit palate.

Syrah in the Las Kuras vineyard (east of Requínoa): Jorge Castillo (Casa Lapostolle). Well-drained soils of alluvial origin with sand, stones, and gravel underlying a 30–50cm (12–20-inch) layer of clay-silt loam. Marked day–night temperature oscillation, 410-metre (1,300- feet) altitude, harvest early April. Clones 100 and 174, grafted onto existing vine roots and rootstocks since 2000. Ditch irrigation, six bunches per vine (twenty-six hectolitres per hectare). The aim is for ripe, concentrated, fine fruit. Wine: Cuvée Alexandre Syrah 2003 – toasty, meaty aromas with charred black fruit, ripe style with a warm finish though with attractive savoury elements.

Cabernet Sauvignon in the Altaïr vineyard: Ana María Cumsille (Altaïr). Pre-Andean slopes at around 650 metres (2,100 feet) altitude with four main types of soil, the principal one being alluvial in origin with abundant stones both on the surface and in depth. The top layer is 0–40cm (zero to sixteen inches) of clay-sand loams with gravel content; 40–80cm (sixteen to thrity-two inches) is a stratum of gravels, stones, and boulders, with loam filling; below 80cm (thirty-two inches) the quantity of stones increases within a clay-loam matrix; pH 6.2, 1.6 per cent organic material. Drip irrigation. Average January temperatures: day 30–32°C (86–90°F), night 10–12°C (50–54°F). Budbreak from September 15; flowering December 15; fruit set December 28; veraison January 10; harvest April 15 (120-day growing season). The aim is for concentrated but elegant wines with fresh fruit and good natural acidity. Wine: Cabernet Sauvignon 2004 (barrel sample) – fresh pressed cassis juice with spicy notes and a bay leaf, bell pepper edge; elegant, firm tannin, fresh acidity, and good persistence.

Noteworthy

Cachapoal's stature is rising among the wineries based outside its borders and fruit from the region is increasingly being used in up-market ranges.

Concha y Toro and its associated wineries are notably active in Cachapoal, using the fruit for some prestigious lines. Emiliana uses Cabernet Sauvignon and Syrah from the region in its Reserve and Special Reserve lines. Cono Sur sources Carmenère and Merlot from Peumo, and Syrah from the Totihue area both for the Visión and 20 Barrels ranges. Concha, meanwhile, has its main base in the region in Peumo, from where it sources its Terrunyo Carmenère and Syrah, Marqués de Casa Concha Merlot and Syrah, as well as the majority of the fruit for wines like the Casillero del Diablo Merlot and Carmenère.

The oldest vines in the Peumo vineyard date back to 1983; it also lays claim to some good Malbec.

Concha also buys Syrah from Totihue and is in the process of developing a new 350-hectare vineyard near Navidad some twelve kilometres (seven miles) from the coast for Sauvignon Blanc, Chardonnay, Pinot Noir, Pinot Gris and Syrah.

Santa Carolina has a 260-hectare vineyard known as La Rinconada near Pichidegua on the flat land and north-facing slopes not far from the Rapel reservoir. It was first planted in 1997 and is mainly for reds (Cabernet Sauvignon, Merlot, Carmenère) though there is some Sauvignon Blanc and Chardonnay here. Much of the latter was taken out and replanted to Syrah in 2000 and 2001. It has also bought another property nearby called Llallauquén in which plantings began in 2005 to varieties such as Carmenère, Sauvignon Blanc, Malbec, Syrah, and Chardonnay. The winery tends to blend Cachapoal fruit with that of Colchagua, although a new Petit Verdot from Cachapoal is an exception. Its sister winery Viña Casablanca also uses fruit from here for its reds.

San Pedro owns around 200 hectares near Totihue, part of which vineyard was hived off to become Altaïr in 2001. This vineyard dates back to 1991 and is planted to Cabernet Sauvignon, Merlot, Syrah, and Chardonnay. Perhaps the winery's most high-profile wine from this property is its organic Harmonia Cabernet/Merlot blend, a herby, spicy berry fruit wine with a smooth, juicy texture. Not far from here is Casa Lapostolle's Las Kuras vineyard: 120 hectares planted in stony soils, which used to include Merlot, Carmenère, and Chardonnay, but it is mostly now planted to Syrah and Sauvignon Blanc.

Another notable producer in the region is Maipo-based Santa Ema, whose Rosario vineyard near Peumo was first planted in 1935. The winery now sources around forty per cent of its fruit from Cachapoal, including Cabernet, Syrah, Carmenère, and Merlot. Wines such as Catalina and the Barrel Select Syrah are worth trying as good examples of reds from this area.

Producer profiles

ALTAIR

Av Vitacura 4380, Piso 3, Vitacura, Santiago. Tel: +56 2 4775394. Email:
info@altairwines.com. Website: www.altairwines.com
Established: 2001. Vineyard: 72ha (Cabernet Sauvignon, Merlot, Carmenère,
Syrah, Cabernet Franc, Petit Verdot). Production: 180,000 litres. *See also*: San
Pedro.

Altaïr represents a step up in Cachapoal's vinous ambitions. It is a
niche project with substantial financial backing which produces just
two wines, both costly red blends. Although its early years have
inevitably been surrounded by much hype, this winery does not lack
for substance or potential and is already producing some first-rate
wines.

Altaïr is a joint venture between San Pedro and Château Dassault of
St-Emilion. Laurent Dassault was already involved in the Clos de los
Siete project in Argentina when the opportunity arose to develop a pre-
mium project in Chile. San Pedro split its Totihue estate in two, donat-
ing the better half, situated on slopes at the farm's eastern end and
planted with mature vines, to the project that would become Altaïr.
Chilean winemaker Ana María Cumsille and French consultant Pascal
Chatonnet were brought on board along with viticulturist Yerko
Moreno.

The vineyard at Altaïr covers seventy-two hectares, with little room
left to exploit. All are on hillsides of varying gradients and a range of
exposures (westerly, northerly, and southerly). Temperatures in summer and autumn are warm but night times tend to be cooler than lower
in the valley, giving significant day–night fluctuations. Soils on these
slopes are also poorer than on the flat land, mainly comprising gravels
and sandy loams. Vines are planted in a range of different densities,
from 4,000 to over 10,000 plants per hectare (the latter is for Syrah and
Carmenère on the higher slopes). Yields are kept low but not fanati-
cally so, as Cumsille comments, "We're looking for balance above all
and overly low yields can be too much in the wine." Planted varieties

include Cabernets Sauvignon and Franc, Carmenère, Merlot, Syrah (planted in 2000), and Petit Verdot (planted in 2004).

Cabernet Sauvignon accounts for nearly eighty per cent of plantings so it is no surprise that it forms the backbone of both wines. Altaïr is the more expensive of the two and is sourced exclusively from this vineyard; Sideral contains around twenty per cent of fruit from Maipo and Colchagua. The concept is to focus on blends but vary the constituent parts between vintages. Cumsille comments:

> The idea is we get to know our terroir better and change the ingredients while maintaining a consistent style. The base for the wines will always be Cabernet, though, because the climate and soil here give concentrated fruit but with very elegant tannins and good freshness.

The first wines were made in 2002 and it was clear from the start that the winery was aiming for a concentrated but structured, complex, and ageworthy style. The 2003 vintage represented a step up in quality in both wines. This was partly a vintage issue – 2003 was warmer, which suited this cooler site better – but was also down to other factors. These include more experience and control of the vineyard after it passed from San Pedro to Altaïr's management in mid-season in 2002. Having a new winery also meant more control over the winemaking (in 2002 all the barrels used were new, but by 2003 this was reduced to a judicious fifty per cent for Sideral – and for the 2004 onward this level will be nearer twenty per cent).

Considering the 2002s were launched at stellar prices, the same as the (better-quality) 2003s, Altaïr was wrong to go in so high so fast; much better to launch at a more modest price level and build from there. This is often a problem with new Chilean icon launches, when producers attempt to run before they can walk. This strategy may have been influenced by the decision – later reversed – to market the initial vintage through Bordeaux merchants (négociants).

However, it is clear from both vintages and especially the 2003s that these are serious wines that show excellent structure, concentration, and ability to age and develop. Both seem to show a characteristic mix of fresh and dried fruit, herbal notes, and cedary, bay leaf character along with good acidity and a layered, well-integrated, and complex palate. Sideral is generally a more open, approachable style whereas Altaïr takes time to open up; both benefit from time in the bottle.

ANAKENA

Av Alonso de Cordova 5151, Of 1103, Las Condes, Santiago. Tel: +56 2 4260608. Email: info@anakenawines.cl. Website: www.anakenawines.cl
Established: 1999. Vineyard: 335ha (Cabernet Sauvignon, Carmenère, Merlot, Sauvignon Blanc, Chardonnay). Production: 1.9 million litres.

Anakena's evolution has been a rapid and largely successful one since its beginnings in 1999. There is still room for improvement in the wines but there is great potential here given the positive, go-ahead attitude at this young winery and the willingness on the part of the owners to invest in its future.

Anakena was set up by school friends Jorge Gutierrez, former owner of Porta (*see next entry*) and businessman Felipe Ibáñez. Planting began in 1999 in land close to the Andes foothills to the east of Requínoa, reaching 150 hectares by 2005 with the possibility of more on the hillsides to come. In 2004, Anakena expanded its operation by buying two more sites, 150 hectares in Leyda for whites and Pinot Noir, and 110 hectares on the Ninquén hill in Colchagua for reds, including Syrah and Carmenère. Fruit from these new vineyards comes online from 2007. The winery also purchases grapes from contract growers, for example sourcing Merlot and Syrah from Marchihue, Riesling from Lolol, Carmenère from Peumo, and whites from Casablanca.

The philosophy at Anakena in its early years has been one of expansion and experimentation, trying out new varieties and areas as well as blends. Such an approach bodes well for the future, although it has tended to mean some variability in the quality of the wines in the interim – not all its experiments have worked. (My personal doubts are over wines such as the multi-varietal white blends like Viognier/Riesling/Chardonnay from Rapel as well as the Sauvignon Blanc and Merlot from Requínoa.)

It has also seemed as if the winery has in some cases been trying to run before it can walk, launching new wines at startlingly regular intervals and also attempting to squeeze too much out of young vines too early. Nonetheless, it is clear that Anakena's vineyards do have good potential, which will improve as the vines mature, and make for naturally more complex, concentrated wines. What is more, the wines will only be improved by the access to fruit from Ninquén and Leyda as well as more experience in the winemaking.

Anakena should continue its policy of purchasing fruit, which broadens the range (the Ona Sauvignon Blanc from Casablanca is an example) as well as giving the winemakers the ability to use complementary blends. For instance, some of its best Carmenère wines are the product of well-judged blends between Requínoa fruit, which gives a fresh, peppery, red fruit character, and Peumo's, which is riper and broader on the palate.

CORPORA

Av Andrés Bello 2777, 28th floor, office 2801, Santiago. Tel: +56 2 2407600.
Email: info@gracia.cl. Websites: www.gracia.cl www.agustinos.cl
www.portawinery.cl www.verandawinery.com
Established: 1989. Vineyard: 810ha (Cabernet Sauvignon, Chardonnay,
Sauvignon Blanc, Merlot, Pinot Noir). Production: 5.5 million litres. Includes:
Gracia, Porta, Agustinos, Veranda.

Córpora is a company owned by the Ibáñez family which has interests in diverse fields such as hotels and tourism, agro-industrial products, fresh fruit, and farming. It also has ambitious plans for its wine enterprise, which comprises the Gracia, Porta, Agustinos, and Veranda brands. It is a broad portfolio that has its ups and downs but is improving with time.

Within Córpora's extensive land holdings, which amount to nearly 4,000 hectares, wine accounts for over 800 hectares. The main centres of production are Aconcagua (Panquehue), Cachapoal (Requínoa/Totihue), Maipo (Alhué), Casablanca (Las Dichas), Curicó, and Bío Bío (Negrete).

Each brand uses fruit from a variety of locations and each has its own range of wines within the brand umbrella. This tends to mean that, although each brand supposedly has a distinct identity and emphasis, they often overlap. For example, the concept for Gracia is unconventional, modern, New World wines; the emphasis at Porta is on terroir; Agustinos sits somewhere between the two, and Veranda's focus, being a joint venture with Burgundian producer Boisset, is Chardonnay and Pinot Noir. And yet Veranda also produces Syrah and Cabernet/Carmenère, Porta makes basic wines from broad appellations like Central Valley, and Gracia's top two wines are single-vineyard Cabernets.

In truth, such overlaps matter little and are more testaments to the close cooperation at work within Córpora's youthful winemaking team, a mixture of Americans and Chileans that has been in place since a programme of restructuring was carried out in 2004. These changes seem to have reinvigorated Córpora's wine operation and a more hands-on approach in the vineyard is having tangible results. Experimentation is taking place, to good effect.

One of Córpora's most exciting developments is in Bío Bío, where the company has an extensive nursery including over 700,000 plants as well as a growing vineyard and plans for a new winery. It epitomizes the company's ambitions for its wines, with an emphasis on developing varietal diversity (Córpora's Grenache, Malbec, Mourvèdre, Viognier, and Gewurztraminer plantings are propagated from this base) through clonal selection and also development of rootstocks. It is an ongoing project and one whose results will take time to appear in the wines, but this is an important initiative both for Córpora and Chile. Sauvignon Blanc, Chardonnay, and Pinot Noir are the focus here and all are showing some good initial results.

One of Córpora's aims is to become a leading Pinot Noir specialist in Chile. Its extensive plantings of this variety in Bío Bío demonstrate their commitment to the cause and the association with Boisset may also provide some useful perspective. Although the results in the final wines are still not what they should or could be, it is heartening to see Córpora's winemakers working toward a consciously more delicate and complex style of Pinot achieved through careful site selection, diverse clonal plantings (mainly 777 and 115), and considered blending and vinification.

There are notable trends of coincidence in quality between the ranges in terms of varieties and regions. Bío Bío is making for some interesting Chardonnays with restrained aromatics but broad, structured palates – Gracia's Ilusión Lo Mejor or Porta's Grand Reserve are good examples. This area is also producing some sleek, perfumed styles of Merlot and Malbec – Agustinos' Winemaker Selection and Grand Reserve are worth trying in this regard. At the other end of the spectrum, ripe, heady styles of Syrah and Cabernet are being made in Aconcagua (Gracia and Porta's top wines are from here). Syrah is also working increasingly well near the group's winemaking headquarters in Requínoa, Alto Cachapoal, giving a meaty, savoury style of red. More work is needed on Pinot Noir and other minority grape varieties.

Gracia's wines have tended to be over-commercial and insipid in the past. Among its basic lines, the Central Valley whites remain uninspiring while the reds are slightly better. Carmenère and Merlot could do with more character and concentration across the board. Pinot Noir and Syrah offer more interest while Cabernet remains a reliable bet, especially in the two top wines Porquenó and Caminante, both from Aconcagua and made in a heady, warm-climate style.

Porta has had a new winemaking team and base near Rancagua since 2004. In the past the wines have commonly come across as overdone: over-oaked, over-extracted, with just too much heady ripe fruit and alcohol, hardly the stuff of top terroir wines – and with a high price tag to boot. A shift in emphasis was needed, toward a more elegant, understated style of wine achieved simply by choosing better sites for each variety. This does seem to be starting to happen under the new direction: Merlot from Casablanca, Syrah from Totihue, Chardonnay and Pinot Noir from Bío Bío, Carmenère from Alhué are all making for more interesting and rounded wines, which is exactly what Porta needs to be doing.

As regards the other two brands, Veranda is a work in progress, having started in 2002. It has lofty ambitions and rightly so, but striking the right balance with Pinot Noir and Chardonnay between delicacy and complexity is a tough one in Chile and will take time. (And until it is achieved, the wines remain over-priced.) Agustinos tends to be more experimental, often with very creditable results – its Merlot and Malbec from Bío Bío are sleek and toothsome examples of what these varieties can do in more marginal areas, while Sauvignon Blanc from the same area is made in an unassuming but fleshy style.

LA ROSA

Of 602, Edificio Paseo Las Palmas, Coyancura 2283, Providencia, Santiago. Tel: +56 2 6700600. Email: wines@larosa.cl. Website: www.larosa.cl
Established: 1824. Vineyard: 749ha (Cabernet Sauvignon, Merlot, Chardonnay, Carmenère, Syrah). Production: 5 million litres.

La Rosa's principal virtues are its reliability and consistency. It is far from being Chile's most dynamic winery – its winemaking policy veers more toward safe, measured progress than outright risk-taking. In my opinion it would be good to see a little more innovative zeal at work in the vineyards and wines, though in general the winery deserves credit for its sound line-up and determined commercial attitude.

The winery was founded in 1824 with money earned from the mining business by the Ossa family, which still retains majority control. The parent company is La Rosa Sofruco, whose earnings are split roughly half-and-half between wine and fruit (fresh and dried). The company owns around 13,700 hectares, of which 745 are dedicated to wine and around double that to fruit.

The original vineyard, known as La Rosa-Peumo, is located between Peumo and Las Cabras in what is the corridor of land that leads toward the Rapel reservoir. The river Cachapoal runs along this corridor, often carrying fresh breezes, which is why the winery has planted whites including Sauvignon Blanc and Chardonnay here. This vineyard also has warmer sites due to the south-facing hilly bowl that acts as a partial shelter for the estate. La Rosa's oldest vines are located here, mainly Merlot and Carmenère planted in 1960.

In the 1990s, La Rosa expanded its winemaking vineyard by planting two other areas, both warm sites tucked away in isolated valleys in the coastal range of hills. The first was La Palmería, famous for its soaring, ancient palms, which was planted purely to reds. The second, planted in 1999, was La Cornellana, described by winemaker José Ignacio Cancino as "the warmest estate we have, and one of the warmest in all Cachapoal". In both vineyards it is mainly Cabernet Sauvignon, Merlot, Carmenère, and Syrah that have been planted – although La Palmería has some Cabernet Franc and La Cornellana, oddly, includes Chardonnay.

La Rosa would do well to focus on diversifying its vineyard. As of 2005, over ninety per cent of its vine area was accounted for by just four varieties: Cabernet Sauvignon, Merlot, Carmenère, and Chardonnay. Its predominantly warm-climate vineyards have little in the way of real diversity in terms of climate or soil, but increasing its range would be beneficial nonetheless. A good but belated example can be seen in the winery's results with Syrah, which was first planted in 2000 but has shown itself to be well adapted to the warm, continental-style climate and poor, granite-derived soils of the coastal range. The winery has plans to add a further 250 hectares, including the likes of Syrah, Sangiovese, and Viognier.

It is reds that La Rosa does best and its hallmark style is fresh but ripe fruit with good concentration and balance. Its more commercial wines are well-made and successful examples of a varietal style. Carmenère and Merlot still tend to be somewhat interchangeable in the range – the best of both are those wines that show ripe, dark fruit with tarry, peppery hints and a fleshy, broad palate. Blending is a common feature of the whole range and in general is handled successfully. Cabernet Sauvignon and Syrah are two of the winery's strongest suits, and it will be interesting to see how the latter develops in particular. A new top-line wine is also planned for release in 2009, a multi-varietal red blend sourced from all three vineyards.

MISIONES DE RENGO

Los Conquistadores 1700, Piso 16, Providencia, Santiago. Tel: +56 2 7076288. Email: mlamunategui@sswg.cl. Website: www.misionesderengo.cl
Established: 2000. Vineyard: 120ha (Cabernet Sauvignon, Syrah, Carmenère).
Production: 5 million litres. *See also*: Tarapacá, Casa Rivas.

Misiones de Rengo is a welcome new addition to the Chilean wine scene. Commercial to a fault but in an affirmative and ambitious way, it is, for my money, the best-performing element within the Southern Sun Wine Group (which includes Tarapacá and Viña Mar, among others).

Misiones is a modern Chilean winemaking phenomenon. It was set up to be a fast-growing brand sourcing fruit from growers and taking advantage of SSWG's infrastructure and distribution to target both domestic and export markets. By 2005 it was producing some 400,000 cases with a turnover of US$13 million (£7 million). The plan is to grow the pool of producers and reach the one-million case mark by 2010.

Much of the credit for this good work should go to the talented winemaker who has steered Misiones through its early years in such skilful fashion, Sebastián Ruiz. His ability to source quality fruit and coax the best out of it in the wines has been impressive. It would be good to see this commendably quality-orientated winemaking maintained as Misiones continues to expand at a heady rate.

Misiones sources over eighty per cent of its fruit from contract growers. Its own vineyards are located in Requínoa (Cachapoal) and María Pinto (Maipo), and they supply Cabernet, Syrah, and Carmenère, while its growers are located mainly in Cachapoal and Colchagua, but also in Maipo, Casablanca, Curicó, and Maule. This system gives the winery good flexibility as well as potential for experimenting with newer wine areas such as Lolol and Marchihue.

There are three main lines of wine – the basic varietal range, Reserva, and the confusingly titled Cuvée (which is simply the name of the top line). A new organic Carmenère is being produced from the 2005 vintage and the idea is to expand this range. In addition, somewhat controversially, from the 2006 vintage the winery is including a Malbec from Argentina in its range (using fruit from the group's Tamarí operation across the Andes).

At the lower levels, Misiones' wines conform to a sound commercial style. In the Reserva and Cuvée ranges, however, the standard rises noticeably and the wines regularly offer good quality and outstanding value for money. Though there is still room for more complexity and finesse in the wines, from Chardonnay to Carmenère, Cabernet, Merlot, and Syrah, the wines show admirable concentration and character. Ruiz prefers Cabernet Sauvignon from fresher, more marginal areas such as Totihue to avoid overripe fruit and encourage structure and complexity. For Carmenère and Syrah, on the other hand, the style tends to be riper without falling into over-maturity – Carmenère has been the star performer of the top ranges. The reds are often blended – for example, the Cuvée Carmenère benefits from a significant portion of Cabernet for structure and acidity while the Cuvée Cabernet has small amounts of Carmenère and Syrah to flesh it out.

MORANDE

Alcántara 971, Las Condes, Santiago. Tel: +56 2 2708900. Email: morande@morande.cl. Website: www.morande.cl

Established: 1996. Vineyard: 309ha (Cabernet Sauvignon, Merlot, Carmenère, Chardonnay, Sauvignon Blanc). Production: 4 million litres.

Considerable growth and change have been the main features of Morandé's first decade of existence after being founded in 1996 by well-known Chilean winemaker Pablo Morandé. As a result, the wines have tended to reflect this reality of a winery in a state of flux.

Morandé was founded in 1996 when Empresas Lourdes, a massive producer of bulk wine and grape juice concentrate both in Chile and Argentina, formed a venture with Pablo Morandé, who had just left Concha y Toro after twenty years. Lourdes, the majority stakeholder, was keen to enter the growing trade in export wines. However, by 2000 the firm was struggling and, citing high operating costs and faster-than-expected growth, moved to raise US$15 million (£8 million) largely by selling thirty-six per cent of the company to Empresas Juan Yarur, which also controls Chile's BCI bank.

By 2005, Yarur had acquired over ninety per cent of Lourdes, which continued to post overall financial losses. In 2004, an aggressive restructuring plan was implemented aimed at cutting costs and also maximizing profits by focusing on premium bottled wine, both increasing prices and upping sales. At the same time, via its subsidiary

AgroMorandé the company expanded its vineyard holdings in Casablanca and Maipo.

Amidst all this frantic growth and financial instability it is perhaps not surprising that the wines have been inconsistent. A sustained period of consolidation and attention to detail in the vineyard is called for if Morandé is to cement its credibility as a quality wine producer. This will inevitably be helped by controlling more of its own vineyards, a process already in hand, and working more closely with the contract growers who supply a large proportion of the winery's fruit. A positive example of the latter is the development of organic wines within the Edición Limitada line – the Cabernet/Merlot/Carmenère blend from Maipo is one of Morandé's better wines.

Morandé's principal brands are Pionero, Terrarum, Vitisterra, Edición Limitada, and House of Morandé. Vistamar is a parallel brand under Morandé's control though with a separate winemaking structure, a modern image, and fresh, simple wines. In general, Morandé's range offers good diversity, including Carignan from Maule, Malbec from Maipo, and Gewurztraminer from Casablanca, all of which is to be encouraged. It is simply the quality that needs working on.

TORREON DE PAREDES

Apoquindo 5490, Of 203, Las Condes, Santiago. Tel: +56 2 2115323. Email: torreon@torreon.cl. Website: www.torreondeparedes.cl

Established: 1979. Vineyard: 150ha (Cabernet Sauvignon, Merlot, Chardonnay, Sauvignon Blanc, Syrah). Production: 700,000 litres.

Torreón de Paredes is a small-scale family wine producer located to the east of Rengo in sub-Andean territory. After over twenty years of producing solid if unexceptional wines, the winery is looking to make improvements in its vineyard in a drive for better quality and more diversity in its portfolio.

Such developments include working with satellite mapping to monitor vigour, working toward sustainable viticulture via integrated pest management techniques, developing a nursery and rootstock programme, as well as re-assessing planting densities, fertilization, irrigation, and canopy management. The winery should also look to improve its cellar hygiene in order to avoid undermining the freshness of fruit and easy-going structure that is an attractive feature of the wines. Part-owner and viticulturist Alvaro Paredes comments:

> We're heading in the right direction, but there's a lot more work to be done. In the past, we've been listening to too many voices; what we need to do is focus on our own land and move forward from there. But these things don't happen fast.

Slow it might be, but progress is undoubtedly needed if Rengo is to reveal its true potential for wine. Veteran winemaker Yves Pouzet is enthused by the prospects for Syrah and Viognier in Torreón's vineyards, noting the area's climatic similarity to the Northern Rhône due to the marked day–night temperature fluctuations. These varieties were first planted in 2000 and, though the fruit lacks the concentration of mature vines, the aromatic potential is promising. Pinot Noir, meanwhile, hasn't worked. The winery is considering buying land elsewhere to develop diversity and improve its whites, which is a good idea.

Older vines at the property include Cabernet Sauvignon and Merlot. It is these varieties, along with Syrah, that have shown the best results at Torreón. One good example is the winery's top line, Don Amado, a blend of Cabernet and Merlot from twenty-five-year-old vines made in a typically traditional, concentrated, earthy-fruit style. It is a pity that the winery is pursuing a programme of replacing its older vines, due to nematode infestations and a desire to renew plantations to ensure "commercial viability", when it is clear that these give good quality in the area.

7

Colchagua

BRIEF FACTS

Vineyard: 22,225ha (90% reds)

Main grape varieties (ha): Cabernet Sauvignon (11,113), Merlot (3,334), Carmenère (2,308), Chardonnay (1,163), Syrah (1,305)

Climate: warm temperate with annual rainfall of 500–800mm (20–32 inches)

Soils: fertile conglomerate soils on much of the flat land; weathered granites on hillsides with sedimentary and metamorphic intrusions in the west

INTRODUCTION

The political divisions of Chilean Region VI (Libertador Bernardo O'Higgins) define the limits of the Cachapoal and Colchagua wine-making regions, which are collectively known as Rapel. Cachapoal is the northernmost of the two, mainly covering land in the north–south central depression and west to the Rapel reservoir; Colchagua sits in the south, bordering Curicó but also covering a swathe of coastal terri-tory that reaches up to the Rapel River, which borders Maipo.

These are Chile's traditional agricultural heartlands. Dated colonial-style architecture abounds, as can be seen by driving through Lolol and Marchihue or visiting Hacienda Los Lingues or the San José del Carmen el Huique museum. Farming and mining are what most people are busying themselves with here and, as almost all mining takes place in Colchagua's mountainous parts, it is agriculture that is the most vis-ible emblem of the region's endeavours as well as being the source of nearly one-third of its revenue. These are fertile soils, which is good news for fruit growers but less so for wine producers – the ins and outs of this are discussed below.

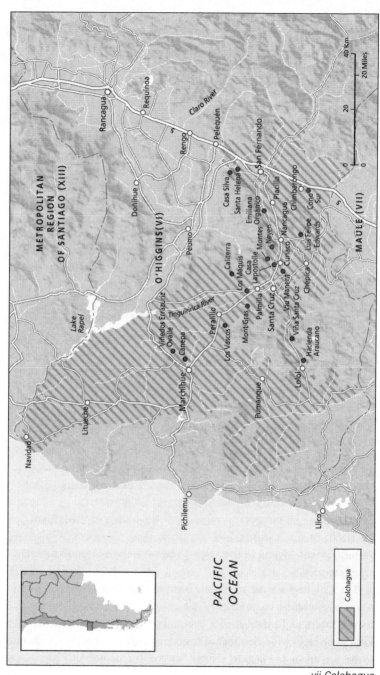

vii Colchagua

One in every four hectares of Chile's fruit orchards are found in Region VI, the main crops being apples and pears, followed by table grapes, plums, kiwis, and nectarines. The quality of the fruit here is a delight to experience. As most of Chile's best fruit is packed straight off to export, bypassing the majority of Santiago's outlets, it is only by visiting these production areas that you can get a chance to taste the properly ripe, achingly gorgeous seasonal produce – an experience that those of us from limper climates very rarely enjoy. On a recent visit I was chatting to local chef Pilar Rodriguez, whose cooking is based around local ingredients (I made sure to sample her scallop and coconut ceviche as well as the delicious *lúcuma* crème brûlée with fresh fruit). "Having such fresh and varied local ingredients makes me feel proud and lucky to work here," she said, simply.

This industry is served by a large and skilled agricultural work-force in the area, which also benefits the wine business. Flying winemaker Hugh Ryman works in the region with VEO and he has been struck by the standard of quality of the work in the vineyard. He told me:

> It's one of Chile's strongest assets, having all these skilled technicians who understand the plants from their experience working in the fruit industry. I noticed it immediately in the vineyards, which are unlike any other country's due to the care, attention, and sheer understanding they clearly benefit from.

Despite its tradition and air of tranquil torpor, Colchagua has been remarkably proactive in forming commercial bonds between its producers, investing in research and development, promoting itself and its wines, setting up visitor attractions, and generally creating an identity for itself. In the last decade it has without doubt been Chile's most ambitious wine region in this regard and continues with its commendable activities.

The Colchagua wine route has been a notable success, not just in terms of attracting visitors to the region but it has also united many of its producers and established a common set of commercial aims, as a kind of de facto wine chamber of commerce. Quality hotels have begun to be set up in the region (Hotel Santa Cruz, Hotel La Playa, Casa

Silva's guest house) where none existed in the late nineties. The valley's old railway has been renovated and now runs the "wine train" at weekends, an antique steam engine that plies the track between San Fernando and Santa Cruz. The wineries have thrown open their doors and many now incorporate shops – others are more ambitious: when finished, the new Viña Santa Cruz (*see below*) is set to have a wine spa, hotel and convention centre, fairground, restaurant, and astronomical observatory, among other things.

On the subject of Viña Santa Cruz, it would be remiss to discuss Colchagua without mentioning Carlos Cardoen. A wealthy businessman and former arms manufacturer, Cardoen was born in Santa Cruz and in later life decided to invest in the area, becoming something akin to Colchagua's fairy godmother in the process. His investments, which have served the region extremely well, include the Hotel Santa Cruz and its adjoining museum, the Viña Santa Cruz winery, and joint initiatives such as the wine train and the new Colchagua Technological Institute. "To change the course of things you have to give things a push, an investment," he told me during a visit to the winery in 2006. "It's a risk, but this is where my heart is."

A PICTURE OF COLCHAGUA

This time, instead of taking the usual bumpy drive around the vineyard, we walk. It's mid-morning and the moisture is still lingering in the air – there is a smell of damp earth and wispy clouds are clinging to the upper slopes of the hillsides. Other than that, it's a fine day.

Miguel begins to explain about the vineyard and his concept of sustainable farming. He's a statuesque man with firm features and a gentle manner. He also has a long stride; I struggle to write my notes while keeping up. I'd read up about Emiliana's organic winery so I knew to expect the eco-friendly approach, although the attention to detail is impressive. We talk about mealybugs, miniature wasps, and covercrops. We peruse redeveloped water courses, vine stems, and habitat breaks. At one point, he delves into a compost pile and rubs the dark matter thoughtfully between his thumb and forefinger.

On the upper hillsides of the estate is a nature reserve – the slopes are a mottled green mass of vegetation. Standing on the flat land, the hills lend a sense of isolation and enclosure to the vineyard. We turn away from the horseshoe of hills and gaze over the flat, hazy valley. In the foreground, the attractive winery and assorted buildings make little impact on the surroundings. We move back down toward them, into the building where I assume we are having the tasting.

But it isn't. Immediately on entering I am hit with a disorientating smell of dried herbs and earth. A woman in a lab coat is patiently de-leafing what looks like mint into a jar. She doesn't look up as we file down a narrow flight of steps toward the source of the aromas. It is a small, half-lit room like a cocoon in appearance and filled with ceramic jars and barrels cut in half. Each of the jars has a number on the lid, a few have labels: yarrow, camomile, nettle, dandelion. Some contents look earthy; others, like dried herbs, have simply been stuffed in. They are used for composting or homeopathic sprays, I learn. The odd, vaguely medicinal odour follows us back upstairs and out into the fresh air – next stop, the alpaca enclosure.

THE NATURE OF COLCHAGUA

Colchagua is not defined by one major geographical or climatic feature. It is a large region – much larger than is often credited – and it contains the inevitable range of natural diversity that such expanses demonstrate in Chile. While this makes generalizations difficult, it has added to the interest of the region as wine styles have developed and diversified.

Colchagua occupies a relatively short stretch of Andean territory in its eastern end before funnelling westward along a narrow corridor that opens out around the town of Santa Cruz and then fans out to encompass a very broad area in its westerly reaches. (A curious oddity to point out here is that Colchagua's western extensions effectively cover what would be coastal Cachapoal and thus it actually borders Maipo near the coast around Navidad – *see* the Cachapoal chapter for more details.) In its central and eastern parts, the valley follows the path of the tongue-tying river Tinguiririca, which flows from the Andes into the Rapel reservoir, the border with Cachapoal.

Generalizations about Colchagua tend to take the region's central heartlands, around the town of Santa Cruz, as a standard reference point. Here, conditions are generally warm (average January temperatures of 29–30°C (84–86°F) during the day and 12–13°C (54–55°F) at night) and vines are planted on flat land in fertile alluvial soils beneath which the water table, or humidity level, can be as high as one metre (three feet). The broader reality, however, is more diverse than this.

The easternmost section of Colchagua runs like a narrow north–south valley between the Andes and interior hills thrown up by volcanic upheaval. Although protected from the ocean's influence and thus relatively warm during the daytime (27–29°C/81–84°F in summer), cool night-time breezes mean that this area receives the largest temperature fluctuation (over 20°C/36°F) of the region during the growing season. This effect is somewhat moderated in the southern end of this stretch of land, around Chimbarongo (home to Cono Sur), which tends to be cooler due to the common morning mists in the area. Soils in the flat valley floor are mainly clays and sands that vary in fertility and depth.

What might be termed central Colchagua is defined not just by the course of the river Tinguiririca and the flat valley floor but also the significant presence of several ranges of high hills. While some of the reality of winemaking in the flatter areas has been mentioned above, the hills are of increasing relevance as producers have begun to plant on the slopes with the advent of drip instead of traditional flood irrigation and the lure of no shallow water table, less fertile soils, and a range of different exposures. Apalta is a notable example (*see* Case Study). The ocean's influence can often be felt in this central part of the region, especially in more westerly parts, with days starting foggy or with low cloud that is quickly burned off, and winds noticeable, especially on the high ground in the afternoons.

Western Colchagua is an altogether broader proposition, where much depends on local conditions. Two current major centres of production are Marchihue (also spelt Marchigüe, pronounced mar-chi-way), on the open rolling hills in the northwestern extension of the valley, and Lolol, a narrower valley that starts to the southwest of Santa

Cruz and extends out toward the coast. One relative constant is the coastal wind: the zone around these two areas, though protected by farther hills toward the coast, is more exposed to the oceanic effect than the interior reaches of Colchagua – which has the effect of lowering yields and vigour as well as moderating temperatures and extending maturation. Though these are both fundamentally warm climate zones, especially in the more wind-protected sites, temperature peaks are short-lived and nights are relatively cool, so grapes tend to mature up to a week later here than in more inland zones.

Areas like Marchihue and Lolol are also proving attractive in terms of their soils, which are less subject to the fertility and humidity problems encountered farther east, meaning it is easier for vines to find a natural, de-vigorized state. Fine volcanic sands can be found in Marchihue as well as a more common shallow clay-loam over decomposed granite material, the product of long-term weathering in the area. What is more, geological surveys indicate that in the hitherto little-explored far west of the region, between Marchihue and the coast around Pichilemu, there is a fan of Carboniferous slate that could provide the basis for further vineyard developments. Indeed, some hillside vineyards at Montes' Marchihue estate contain elements of mica and schist: further rock and mineral types known for yielding quality vines. (*See* p. 217 for further explanation.)

Water is an issue in Colchagua. In the west, it is problematic in its absence – there being no major water course in the area, so almost all irrigation must by necessity come from underground aquifers. Water rights in Marchihue have already been frozen by the authorities for fear of depleting these reserves in what is naturally a dry area even in winter (it sits in the rain shadow of the coastal range, with annual rainfall of around 400–500mm (sixteen to twenty inches) compared to Apalta's 600mm (twenty-four inches) plus). This will inevitably slow development of the area. By contrast, in the flat land in the central and eastern parts of the region, water can be problematic in its abundance due to a high-lying humidity level. Though this does vary significantly between sites and fluctuates between seasons (lower in summer, higher in winter), it can prove detrimental to vine health and vigour as well, ultimately, as wine quality.

VITICULTURE AND WINES

Colchagua is growing, both in size and stature. It has been at the centre of the country's wine boom, its total vineyard area having nearly trebled in size since 1997, when plantings were just over 8,000 hectares. A burgeoning number of wine producers (thirty-four at the last count, with many others sourcing fruit in the region) have been attracted to the area. This growth has pushed back the traditional limits of the region, notably in the west and into the hillsides. This, added to a growing experience and confidence in the region, is starting to produce wines of diverse styles and increasing quality.

Owing to its predominantly warm climate, Colchagua is fundamentally a red wine region. The classic Colchagua red wine profile is one of dark colour, ripe, sweet fruit, and a sturdy palate showing lowish acidity and fleshy tannins, topped off by a warming alcohol kick on the finish. The main challenge for producers is achieving a successful balance between concentration and elegance – what Cono Sur winemaker Adolfo Hurtado terms "drinkability" – within a broad Colchagua mould.

"Our biggest challenge in Colchagua is getting ripeness and complexity without too much alcohol, dry tannin, or over-maturity," comments MontGras winemaker Santiago Margozzini. It is a point on which all the region's better winemakers now concur, and which most are starting to address both in the vineyard and winery. Combative techniques include working the canopy to provide adequate but not excessive shading, with the aim of retaining acidity and freshness, as well as re-evaluating irrigation patterns, yield requirements, and harvest dates between sites. Such practices are a minimum requirement in Colchagua and can avoid many subsequent problems in the winery. On the vinification front, it is encouraging to hear how many winemakers are refining their methods of extraction, conducting trials as well as adapting to the requirements of each vintage, using cold soaks and lower fermentation temperatures as well as softer pressings. Some, including MontGras and Casa Lapostolle, are also using wild yeast fermentation, one by-product of which tends to be less alcohol in the final wine.

Another, perhaps more fundamental means of addressing the same issue has been for producers to search out vineyard sites that are naturally better for producing balanced wines. Balance is difficult to establish in what might be termed the traditional Colchagua vineyard, where the combination of a fiercely warm climate, deep fertile soils, and a high water table can make vines difficult to control, leading to excessive vigour and high sugar levels without proper phenological maturity. Hence the development of new areas toward Colchagua's fringes, such as Apalta, Marchihue, and Lolol, where soils are generally poorer so more control can be established over vine nourishment and irrigation. Marchihue, for example, is already giving a notably sleeker, fine-grained fruit than, say, more traditional areas in Palmilla or Nancagua.

These new areas, which have only really begun to emerge since the late nineties, are already delivering very promising results. Winemaker Aurelio Montes described his feeling at the initial results of planting Syrah in Apalta as "a 'bingo' feeling: the right variety in the right terroir". Patrick Valette describes the same area as "a gem, with a real sense of identity". And where Apalta has led, other new areas are following – not just the likes of Marchihue, Lolol, and Pumanque but also farther afield. New white wine projects, for example, are being trialled in several virgin sites along the Colchagua coastline, from Navidad in the north (Concha y Toro), to around Pichilemu (VEO), and near San Pedro de Alcántara in the south (Viña Santa Cruz). This could yet usher in an even newer and more exciting era – that of successful Colchagua whites.

White wine has never been Colchagua's forte. However, it has achieved notable success of late with Viognier, a grape described in admiring terms by Viu Manent's winemaker Grant Phelps as "a red wine masquerading as a white". Although Chilean winemakers are still struggling to find the right balance with this variety, which can be mean and tannic if harvested too early, or over-alcoholic if picked too late, a range of successful styles is now starting to emerge from the region, hinting that this kind of Mediterranean white variety could provide an interesting option for Colchagua's slightly cooler sites.

Among the reds, Cabernet Sauvignon is still by far the most planted variety. When handled well and in the right sites it can produce excellent top-level wines (Montes Alpha and M as well as Le Dix de Los Vascos are examples) as well as sound commercial styles, though its naturally firm tannic structure can easily descend into tough chewiness in the wrong hands. Gentle extraction and blending are both sound options for Cabernet in Colchagua.

Merlot remains problematic due to its tendency to develop weak root systems and dehydrate; conversely in sites where the water table is too high it is overly vigorous. This is being addressed by improved site selection as well as replanting on rootstocks. Nonetheless, some good Merlot is produced in the region, mainly from older vines (*see* Casa Silva, Casa Lapostolle) and in newer areas such as Marchihue.

It is varieties like Syrah, Carmenère, Petit Verdot, and Malbec that are currently proving Colchagua's brightest stars, especially when planted in low-vigour sites. Syrah has taken to Colchagua's granitic hillside soils and significant day–night temperature fluctuations like a duck to water, while Carmenère is working well in warm, breezy areas with well-drained soils. Petit Verdot is finding favour as an increasingly prominent blending ingredient, adding a welcome dose of structure, tannin, and warm black fruit to varieties such as Carmenère and Merlot. Malbec, meanwhile, is making some increasingly successful wines that stand out for their individuality and freshness. Other long-cycle varieties like Grenache and Mourvèdre are currently being planted and could work well in this region.

Blending should be mentioned as a positive trend in Colchagua, especially for the reds, in the move toward achieving balance and complexity in the wines. Successful producers such as Emiliana Orgánico, Montes, Cono Sur, and others are all employing this technique to a greater or lesser extent. And not just between varieties, but also areas and regions – for example, Casa Silva is blending fruit from Lolol and Los Lingues, Montes is using Marchihue fruit to complement its Apalta wines, and Emiliana Orgánico is blending Maipo with Colchagua. Especially now that different areas in Colchagua are starting to give different fruit profiles, it makes sense to blend in the search for complexity.

Additional note should be made of several studies that are currently underway, aimed at researching Colchagua's soils, climates, and vineyards in order to provide workable results for the region's viticulturists. The most prominent is that undertaken by Casa Silva in conjunction with Talca University's CTVV (Centro Tecnológico de la Vid y el Vino) wine department under the leadership of agronomist Yerko Moreno. The focus is on five different varieties (Cabernet, Syrah, Carmenère, Petit Verdot, and Viognier) in two areas (Los Lingues and Lolol) over nine separate sites, giving a total of 90 different micro-vinifications every year. Detailed information on climate, viticulture, and soils is then compared with results in the wines.

"It's about making sense of the vineyard, challenging preconceptions and accepted truths, asking why certain sites make better wine, and then using that as a basis for further development," comments Moreno. Initial results are demonstrating that it is those vines whose local conditions enable them to establish a natural balance between vigour and stress that provide the best results in the wines, with Syrah working well in Lolol and Carmenère in Los Lingues, at the foothills of the Andes.

CASE STUDY: APALTA

It is heartening to see how fast Apalta is becoming established as a recognized individual terroir within a Chilean wine industry whose traditional appellations are decidedly broad-brush. But what exactly lies behind this name and what is the emerging reality of its so-called terroir?

First, a bit of geography and history. Apalta lies just north of the town of Cunaco and resembles an amphitheatre in shape, with steep hills rising in the west, north, and east from flatter land that slopes gently down to the area's southern limit, the Tinguiririca River. Within this amphitheatre of hills, several hilly fingers extrude from the northern wall, creating a further variety of exposures and mini-crescent shapes.

Despite its newfound-ness, vines are a historic fixture in the area, indeed some are thought to be over 100 years old, having survived land reforms and wine crises in part simply due to their natural affinity with the area. This is immediately visible in the fact that the old vines here are dry farmed (not irrigated), a practice that is made possible by Apalta's specific topography and hydrogeology: in winter the water level rises to within one metre (three feet) of the surface on the flatter land, swelled by the river and run-off from the hills. Come summer, this humidity level drops (the exact depth depends on individual sites, soil profile, and relative height of the land), encouraging the vine roots to penetrate deep but also allowing the vines to establish a natural balance and source of nourishment.

It was precisely these dry-farmed old vines that initially attracted the likes of Aurelio Montes, Alexandra Marnier Lapostolle, and others to the area in the early nineties. But it was also clear that Apalta held another appeal for the braver winegrowers: its hillsides. This was perhaps not so self-evident at the time, when hillside vineyard plantations were almost unknown in Chile because the traditional system of flood irrigation was not feasible on such slopes. However, in the mid-nineties, Chile was ripe for viticultural expansion and modern systems of drip irrigation were becoming more commonplace, so it was only a matter of time before Apalta's hillsides were developed. Aurelio Montes began planting on the lower slopes in 1993; his Montes M wine (first vintage 1998) was the result.

Apalta's hillsides have many attractions for wine-growers. They have a range of exposures (which is good for variety) but mainly Apalta's slopes face south: in Chile this is the coolest exposure, and in an otherwise warm region this has the effect of lengthening the growing season and hence, in theory, the quality of the fruit. This cooling effect is compounded by the breezes that sweep up the valley and are caught in this natural catchment area of hills, as well as the slight elevations involved (currently the highest vineyards are at 370 metres/1,200 feet), and the late-afternoon shadow thrown by the high ridge in the west. Then there are the poor soils: their main profile is a thin layer of topsoil (30–50cm/twelve to twenty inches) on top of decomposed granite of a texture between gravel and sand, and they are well drained and lightly acidic, with rocky content. (A similar profile occurs on the flatter land, though generally with a deeper layer (one metre/three feet) of sandy-loam topsoil and fewer rocks.)

Although Apalta's hillside vines are still young, it is clear that red varieties like Syrah, Carmenère, and Petit Verdot have great potential here. The nature of the wines is somewhat different from those of the flatter land, giving more raw power, structure, and grip. And while it is still premature to generalize about wine styles as a whole in the area, it is notable how Apalta's better wines tend to show ripe, heady fruit characters together with an expansive yet seldom imbalanced or tiring palate. Indeed, on the basis of wines it has hitherto produced, such as Purple Angel, Clos Apalta, Montes Folly, and Neyen, it is difficult not to be tremendously positive about Apalta's future and the important precedent it has set within Chilean viticulture.

To finish on a note of caution, it is important to realize that, at the time of writing, Apalta is still not officially delimited as an appellation within Chilean wine law. Unofficially, its borders are well defined, but this could be open to liberal interpretation by growers keen to cash in on the Apalta name, for example by planting in the more fertile, humid soils near the river in the future. It would be wise to close the stable door before this valuable horse bolts.

Noteworthy

Many Chilean wineries source fruit from Colchagua, attracted by its extensive vineyard, reliably warm climate, and ripe style of red wine.

Some of these wineries are based in cooler areas where late-season reds are not ideal – Viña Leyda and Viña Casablanca are two examples of this. Laroche Chile is also now sourcing its Carmenère from Peralillo rather than Elqui in order to have better ripeness in its fruit. Maule-based Calina and Terranoble have similar views, though more in relation to Cabernet Sauvignon. As former Calina winemaker Felipe García says, "Colchagua may be hot but it gives very smooth wines." Terranoble winemaker Ignacio Conca is quick to point out that

Colchagua is not just about easy grape growing in beneficent conditions, however.

You have to get your harvest date and vinification right in Colchagua. The big mistake that's been committed in the past is overripening and over-extraction; we need to rein all this back and aim for juicier, fresher wines, though of course with the region's characteristic ripeness.

Though it continues to produce successful reds from its base in eastern Casablanca, Veramonte has also come to Colchagua. More specifically, it has set up just north of the town of Marchihue, with plans for a 140-hectare vineyard devoted exclusively to reds, including Cabernets Sauvignon and Franc, Carmenère, Syrah, and Petit Verdot. "We're thinking top-end wines here," says winemaker Rafael Tirado. "Its particular climate and soils make for very individual wines." Leyda-based Garcés Silva also owns land in this area that it may look to develop in the future.

Apalta is another area attracting outside interest, to such an extent that its grape and land prices now are enough to make potential purchasers think twice. Von Siebenthal made its attractive Montelig 2002 from mainly Apalta fruit while its Aconcagua vineyards were being developed, while Odfjell has also bought from here in the past. "Not any more," says winemaker Arnaud Hereu, wincing. Now the Maipo-based winery sources Cabernet and Malbec from around Cunaco. Meanwhile, on the south side of the valley, Cachapoal-based Anakena is developing a 110-hectare plot on the Ninquén hill with mainly Cabernet, Syrah, and Carmenère. It also buys Riesling from old, dry-farmed and head-pruned vines around fifteen kilometres (nine miles) from the Pacific.

The large, Maipo-based Ventisquero owns a vineyard in Apalta which was planted in 1999 and 2000 and from which the winery is starting to produce a new top-level Syrah called Pangea. More recently, it has also bought land in southerly Lolol, near the border with Curicó around Ránguil, where at a distance of twenty-five kilometres (sixteen miles) from the coast it has planted Sauvignon Blanc and Chardonnay as well as high-density Carmenère on a hilltop.

Santa Rita is also in the process of developing its Colchagua connections, sourcing fruit from Apalta (from its subsidiary Carmen's vineyard as well as contract growers, some with old vines) and recently buying a 1,200-hectare estate in Pumanque, where it is planting Sauvignon Blanc, Syrah, and Cabernet Sauvignon. "It could be an interesting new style of Cabernet to complement our Maipo fruit," comments winemaker Andrés Ilabaca.

Finally, Chile's largest wine producer is rarely absent from the action and Concha y Toro is also looking to expand in Colchagua. Although it already has a strong presence in the area via its subsidiaries Viñedos Emiliana and Cono Sur, recently the winery purchased 350 hectares in Marchihue, where it is focusing on Merlot, Carmenère, and Cabernet Sauvignon. More interestingly, it has also bought land right in the far northwestern tip of Colchagua – in what should by rights be coastal Cachapoal – for an estate called Ucuquer. Here, just twelve kilometres (seven miles) from the coast in stony red clay soils near the Rapel River, plans are to plant around 350 hectares of mainly Sauvignon Blanc and Chardonnay, together with a little Pinot Noir, Pinot Gris, and Syrah. The land was discovered after a long and detailed survey of climates and soils around Chile; its first fruit is expected for 2008.

Other notable wineries also sourcing fruit from Colchagua include Botalcura, GEO (Rayun and Cucao brands), Santa Carolina, San Pedro, J Bouchon, Valdivieso, and the Spanish winery Guelbenzu.

Producer profiles

CALITERRA
Av Nueva Tajamar 481, Of 503, Torre Sur, Las Condes, Santiago. Tel: +56 2 3399100. Email: wine.report@errazuriz.cl. Website: www.caliterra.com
Established: 1989. Vineyard: 245ha (Cabernet Sauvignon, Carmenère, Merlot, Syrah, Malbec). Production: 3.5 million litres. *See also*: Errázuriz.

Just like its parent company Errázuriz, changes have been taking place at Caliterra. Necessary and welcome changes, too, because Caliterra had for some time been the weak link in the otherwise impressive Errázuriz portfolio, providing uncomplicated but often underwhelming wines. While it is still too early to judge the results of these changes, these are positive moves for Caliterra.

Caliterra started out life in 1989 as a joint venture between Errázuriz and Agustín Huneeus, current part-owner of Veramonte, as an entry-level brand aimed at targeting the US market. A similar philosophy was kept in place when, in 1995, Mondavi replaced Huneeus and in 1996 the winery bought an attractive, self-contained estate in the hills around Palmilla. Nevertheless, the winery never really took off, so in 2004, when Errázuriz split with Mondavi and took sole control of Caliterra, it began to instigate a series of changes aimed at improving the wines and revamping the range.

What had been Caliterra's premium line, Arboleda, was split from Caliterra entirely and moved into Aconcagua. (Before, it was a somewhat confused concept, in theory an estate-grown premium line but in reality rarely so.) As well as now benefiting from what had previously been fruit for Arboleda, Caliterra production was slashed from 600,000 cases per year to 350,000. Henceforth all reds would be Colchagua sourced, mainly from the Caliterra estate, with whites bought from Casablanca and Curicó.

A new hillside planting project began in 2005 and is set to add a further seventy-two hectares; the total plantable land in the 1,032-hectare estate is 415 hectares. Kiwi winemaker Kym Milne was drafted in to consult on the whites from 2004 and a fully finished winery and cellar-door sales area are slated for completion by 2007.

CANEPA

Camino Lo Sierra 1500, Cerrillos, Santiago. Tel: +56 2 8707100. Email: josecanepa@canepa.cl. Website: www.canepa.cl

Established: 1930. Vineyard: 400ha (Cabernet Sauvignon, Merlot, Carmenère, Syrah, Chardonnay). Production: 6 million litres.

Although it is traditionally associated with Maipo, Canepa has now switched its focus to Colchagua, hence its inclusion in this chapter.

This process has been part of a transition that has not been wholly positive for the winery.

Canepa was originally established in 1930 but in 1996 the family feuded and the company was split. The vineyards were hived off and became TerraMater; the brands, producer contracts, the eleven million-litre winery in Maipo and its immediately surrounding vineyard were retained by José Canepa's widow, Luciana Garibaldi, under the original name. New vineyards were needed with some urgency so, in 1997, Canepa purchased 500 hectares in Marchihue (Trinidad estate), 300 hectares in Lolol, and 150 hectares in Apalta. Planting in Marchihue began the same year, reaching 350 hectares by 2005, with development in Lolol and Apalta planned to start in 2007.

What this has effectively meant is that much of Canepa's fruit is now from young vines (for example, Marchihue fruit was rushed into production in its first year of crop in 1999). What is more, the company adopted something of a scatter-gun approach to plantings in the area, putting in seventeen different varieties – from Sauvignon Blanc to Sangiovese and Zinfandel – not all of which have worked (Carignan and Pinot Noir were two early casualties; some of the whites are also proving challenging). Though there is something to be said for giving things a go to discover what works and what doesn't, it has meant that wine quality has suffered in the interim.

Trinidad lies around thirty-five kilometres (twenty-two miles) from the coast and is characterized by a warm daytime climate, regularly reaching 34°C (93°F) in summer time, though cooling off in the late afternoons and at night. Conditions are windy on the rolling shallow hillsides and the soils, especially near surface level, are predominantly fine-grained white volcanic pumice, with weathered volcanic rock, sand, and clay at depth. Tasting wines at the property in 2006, it looked as if Syrah, Malbec, and Viognier were proving well adapted, with Sangiovese and Tempranillo also showing some glimpses of quality, though all were in need of more palate presence and depth. The new premium Genovino blend from Trinidad is a case of premature ambition.

Ironically, for now it is the winery's more traditional lines that show best, such as the earthy, traditional style of Finísmo Cabernet Sauvignon, sourced from thirty-year-old vines around the winery in Maipo. (A wine, incidentally, that has aged gracefully in its past vintages, with the 1978, 1982, and 1985 holding up well in 2005.) Ironic also because it may well be that this Maipo vineyard will soon disappear – indications from Canepa are that this land could be sold within the next decade to accommodate Santiago's ongoing urban sprawl, with the winery retained as a logistical base.

CASA LAPOSTOLLE

Av Vitacura 5250, Of 901, Vitacura, Santiago. Tel: +41 22 900 07 01 (Geneva).
Email: marnier@marnier-ge.ch. Website: www.casalapostolle.com
Established: 1994. Vineyard: 350ha (Merlot, Cabernet Sauvignon, Sauvignon
Blanc, Chardonnay, Syrah). Production: 1.8 million litres.

There is a certain obsession with purity that lies at the heart of Lapostolle. What this tends to mean is that the wines, and the people, can polarize opinion. And for a winery that courts headlines like few others in Chile, it is difficult not to take notice.

The winery was established in 1994 in a joint venture between the Chilean Rabat family and Alexandra Marnier Lapostolle, whose family owns the Grand Marnier liqueur operation as well as Château de Sancerre in the Loire; the Rabats were later bought out of the project in 2003. From the beginning, the services of French consultant winemaker Michel Rolland were obtained with exclusive rights in Chile. The debut wines were made in 1994; the first vintage of the icon Clos Apalta from old, dry-farmed vines was 1997; and in 2006 a stunning new US$6 million (£3 million) winery was inaugurated in Apalta, solely to vinify Clos Apalta (maximum annual production: 5,500 cases). So far, the total investment bill is running at US$25 million (£13 million).

It is hard not to have an opinion about Lapostolle – such is the fate of industry leaders, who by their very nature generate debate. For my part, I firmly believe that Lapostolle continues to prove a positive influence within the Chilean wine scene. To justify this I would point to Lapostolle's steadfast faith in the potential of terroirs such as Apalta as well as varieties like Carmenère and Syrah, and its investments to back this up. Much of the vineyard (two-thirds and increasing) is managed organically, though the wines are not labelled as such. The emphasis is firmly on natural winemaking, a particular focus of Rolland's, involving using natural yeasts, a reticence to acidify, and even hand-destemming – all of which demand scrupulous cellar hygiene to avoid spoilage. In addition, both Marnier Lapostolle and Rolland, while occasionally bullish in their beliefs, are both candid in their respective admissions that they have much more to learn and achieve as regards their wines.

Needless to say, while there is much to respect about Lapostolle, there are also shortcomings I would criticize. For example, the white wines are too often below par – the Sauvignon Blanc from Requínoa (Cachapoal) tends to be inexpressive and short, while more work is needed on the Casablanca Chardonnay to introduce length and structure to the wine. In addition, alcohol levels in the reds can be high which, while not necessarily making for wines that are out of balance, is an issue that needs addressing in the coming years.

There also seems to be an endemic over-ambition at the winery, mainly relating to pricing policy though also to wine styles. Take Borobo 2001, a wine priced above Clos Apalta on its release in 2005 despite being an entirely unsuccessful blend of Pinot Noir, Merlot, Syrah, Carmenère, and Cabernet Sauvignon (the Pinot tends to dominate though not in a pleasant way and the palate is inelegant and disjointed – the basic elements are not of sufficient quality for this level nor apt for blending in this manner). While innovation is to be encouraged in Chile, launching a wine like Borobo at such a high price smacks of over-ambition and almost proving a wine theorist's point at the expense of consumers.

More successful are Lapostolle's endeavours with its individual Merlot, Cabernet Sauvignon, and Syrah wines. The latter has done well in the winery's Las Kuras vineyard in the well-drained stony soils and moderate climate of Alto Cachapoal, giving a wine of vibrant spicy, meaty, floral character in the Cuvée Alexandre range, though its power could benefit from more restraint and structure. Syrah is now also being planted on Apalta's steeper slopes – which, if it turns out like other Syrahs from the area, could prove an ideal foil for the Requínoa fruit (though current plans are for a single-vineyard Apalta Syrah).

Clos Apalta is where Lapostolle's focus on purity reaches its maximum expression. Tasting through the vintages since its debut from 1997, it is clear that this Merlot/Carmenère/Cabernet blend is a wine driven by several key elements, all of which have been refined and accentuated over the years. The essence of Clos Apalta is the conjunction of heady ripe fruit, plenty of integrated oak spice, warming alcohol, and low acidity. It is not a wine built around a steely structure (few of Lapostolle's wines are); its effect relies more on its fine-grained tannin and sweet fruit and spice to fill the palate. Nevertheless, the wine still ages pleasantly in the mid-term (long-term is less certain) – tasting in 2006, the 1997 remained buoyant (and, at 13% ABV, a good match with food). Both the 2001 and 2003 demonstrated great quality, with the latter perhaps the most impressive by a shade.

One point to add is that the winery has now adopted a policy of hand-destemming for Clos Apalta (i.e. removing all the individual berries from the bunch by hand, a process that requires eighty people and some 1,000 man-hours during the harvest). Trials began in 2001 and by 2005 the wine was all hand-destemmed, a technique that looks set to further increase the intense purity of the wine. In addition, hillside Apalta Petit Verdot may be included in the 2005 blend or later, and Rolland has also declared himself open to other ingredients. "We're still in development," he comments.

CASA SILVA

Hijuela Norte, Casilla 97, San Fernando. Tel: +56 72 716519. Email: casasilva@casasilva.cl. Website: www.casasilva.cl
Established: 1892. Vineyard: 800ha (Cabernet Sauvignon, Carmenère, Chardonnay, Merlot, Syrah). Production: 4.5 million litres.

For a company that started selling bottled wine only in 1997, Casa Silva has made commendable progress, working hard to improve its wines as well as undertaking a ground-breaking micro-terroir study between 2004 and 2008. This willingness to examine and learn from its vineyards should lead to further improvements in the wines, which still need more work if they are to match the winery's lofty ambitions.

Casa Silva is based in Angostura, in the northwest part of Colchagua's eastern corridor. This was the original family estate, divided over the years but which Mario Silva Cifuentes began to piece back together in the seventies, in doing so creating a successful bulk wine enterprise. In 1997, the family began commercializing its own wine and at the same time bought and began to plant two more estates, one in Los Lingues, northeast of Angostura at the foothills of the Andes, and one in western Lolol around fifteen kilometres (nine miles) from the coast.

As these sizeable vineyards matured, it became clear that certain varieties were adapting better in certain areas than others. For example, Los Lingues has a warm climate with a significant day–night temperature flux as well as frequent breezes from the southeast, its terrain is undulating, and soils are a mixture of stones, sands, and clays of alluvial and colluvial origin. Carmenère seems to work best here, as well as Cabernet Sauvignon and Petit Verdot, due to the low incidence of autumn rain as well as the deep soils with good drainage and low fertility that allow good control over vigour. The Lolol vineyard has more maritime influence in its winds and morning fogs but is nonetheless a warm climate with notable day–night temperature fluctuations (over 20°C (36°F) in the growing season according to the winery's figures). This tends to give a long season with low rainfall, and soils are decomposed granite with red clay, quartz gravel, and low fertility. Syrah has so far given the best results here.

This learning process is typical of any new viticultural enterprise, but Casa Silva has gone one step further. Having also noticed that differences in fruit quality came not simply from broad sites but also within vineyards on a much smaller, parcelized basis, the winery decided to instigate a three-year micro-terroir study aimed at discovering why such differences existed and as a result established a system, known as an Integrated Site Index, that can be used to ensure consistent quality in the vineyard as well as being a tool for developing new plantings. In part government funded, the study is being headed up by

Talca University's CTVV wine research facility under the leadership of agronomist Yerko Moreno, in conjunction with Casa Silva's winemaking team. (*See* Viticulture, p. 15, for more details.)

An improved understanding of its terroirs will no doubt prove highly beneficial for the wines, which have tended to struggle with Colchagua's main problems: too much alcohol, ripeness, and coarse extraction. However, it is fair to say that, in general, they have improved in the last few years, moving gradually away from an overly tannic and alcoholic style toward a better overall balance of fruit and extraction, albeit within a relatively commercial formula. It is to be hoped that the progress made to date is further developed and refined in the coming years, because it would be a great shame if good work in the vineyard is obscured by a heavy-handed or formulaic approach to the winemaking.

Syrah from Lolol and Carmenère from Los Lingues provide the winery's best results. The reds in general seem to work best in the middle and upper ranges, while the top levels (Quinta Generación, Altura) require more elegance and integration to justify their high price tags. Whites are not the winery's forte but Viognier is giving good almond and apricot character in Lolol even if the alcohol needs to be brought into line. (Cooler sites will be needed if the winery is to make real improvements in its whites, a move that is under consideration.)

CONO SUR

Av Nueva Tajamar 481, Torre Sur, Of 1602, Las Condes, Santiago. Tel: +56 2 4765090. Email: query@conosur.com. Website: www.conosur.com
Established: 1993. Vineyard: 940ha (Pinot Noir, Cabernet Sauvignon, Merlot, Chardonnay, Sauvignon Blanc). Production: 14.4 million litres.

Cono Sur is, for my money, one of Chile's best wine producers, exemplary not only in its quality but also value, diversity, and ambition.

Cono Sur is part of the Concha y Toro group and was set up in 1993 with the brief to do something different and focus on export markets. It immediately adopted an irreverent, modern approach in its image and winemaking, a trend that continues today albeit in more mature fashion. In 1998, it adopted integrated pest management practices (*see*

Emiliana Orgánico), also undertaking a small organic project in 2000, with the result that by 2005 some sixty per cent of its vineyard was under these management systems. It was the first winery in Chile to use screwcaps in export wines – in its Visión Riesling 2002 – also adopting synthetic closures early on.

One of Cono Sur's most successful developments has been the Isla Negra brand, which has grown to account for over half of the winery's sales by volume (nearly eight million litres) and with plans to grow further. It constitutes the financial anchor that allows the winery to develop its other, more premium, projects. Such success has helped fund a US$10 million (£5 million) investment programme that began in 2005 to improve infrastructure and, more significantly, acquire new land for vineyards.

These new vineyards are in Peralillo (western Colchagua, mainly for Merlot, Carmenère, Malbec, and Syrah) and Leyda (San Antonio, principally Pinot Noir, with Sauvignon Blanc and Chardonnay), with Elqui or Limarí also likely to be added. "It's an exciting time for us and for Chilean viticulture in general," comments Adolfo Hurtado, head winemaker and also general manager, noting that the winery is now sourcing fruit from Elqui in the north, right down to Bío Bío in the south. Cono Sur owns nearly 1,000 hectares of vineyard, which supplies around half its fruit, with a further thirty per cent supplied by vineyards under Concha y Toro's control though with Cono Sur managing, and the remaining twenty per cent sourced from growers. It is a balance Hurtado is happy with, asserting that small independent growers can provide niche elements to complement his overall fruit portfolio.

Hurtado has been central to Cono Sur's success, the reason being not only his considerable winemaking talents but also his character, which marries a frank readiness to learn and improve with a stubborn and restless nature. This is a winemaker who has consistently pushed Chile's limits of diversity, both in terms of regions and varieties – his work with Pinot Noir, Chardonnay, Riesling, Viognier, and Gewurztraminer has been exemplary.

Hurtado has worked on Pinot Noir from Bío Bío to Casablanca with Burgundian Martin Prieur since 1999 and comments, "The biggest lesson we learned from Burgundy was that to make good Pinot Noir in Chile we had to do everything differently from how we'd done it until then." Pinot represents perhaps the ultimate challenge for winemakers, one which Hurtado has gamely taken on, radically revising his vinification methods, working with new clones (including 777, 115, 667, 113), and now planting sixty-five hectares of the variety in Leyda, a bold move for a country that still has much to prove in this regard.

Hurtado describes his winemaking style as one that seeks to promote elegance, food-friendliness, and "drinkability" in his wines above extraction and alcohol. It is a style that generally holds true across the range, from the sound Isla Negra up to the more prestigious lines, though perhaps finds its best expression in the mid-ranges where the sheer value, character, and diversity are hard to fault.

Perhaps Cono Sur's strongest, most dynamic offering is in its whites. Its basic Viognier is a striking statement of intent, great value for money, and with excellent varietal character in a balanced and moreish package. Gewurztraminer and Riesling also work well at this level, though the latter especially is more successful in the Visión line from Bío Bío: a masterful wine full of elegant apple fruit and mineral, honeycomb structure. Another outstanding white is the 20 Barrels Chardonnay from coastal Casablanca just eight kilometres (five miles) from the ocean: to my mind one of Chile's best examples of this variety, showing an enviable marriage of vibrant structure and oaky density, though it would benefit from more layers of complexity being added to the profile, perhaps something that will come with time (the vines were planted in 1998). This vineyard is also being used for the exciting new 20 Barrels Sauvignon, another structured and characterful white.

If I had one criticism of Cono Sur it would be that I would like to see as much diversity and excitement in its reds as is currently the case with its whites. It is fair to say that the winery produces some good-quality reds from the likes of Cabernet, Carmenère, and Syrah, as well as making creditable headway with Pinot Noir, but it would be good to see some more happening on this front in keeping with the winery's adventurous spirit. It seems that, for now, Pinot Noir remains Hurtado's primary focus. His basic varietal is a delight – sourced from cool-climate sites around the country including Bío Bío, it is balanced, fresh, and with good varietal character, proving that Chile can do good basic Pinot as well as anyone. What remains a more elusive goal is wringing complexity as well as delicacy from the variety at the top end – while Ocio is undoubtedly one of Chile's best Pinots, with its hints of violets and earthy red and black fruit, it still tends to be a touch one-dimensional and chunky. More work and time are needed, a point that Hurtado readily concedes.

EMILIANA ORGANICO (FORMERLY VINEDOS ORGANICOS EMILIANA, VOE)

Av Nueva Tajamar 481, Of 701, Torre Sur, Las Condes, Santiago. Tel: +56 2 3539130. Email: info@voe.cl. Website: www.voe.cl

Established: 1998. Vineyard: 448ha (Cabernet Sauvignon, Merlot, Syrah, Carmenère, Chardonnay). Production: 1.3 million litres. *See also*: Viñedos Emiliana.

It would not be an understatement to describe Emiliana Orgánico's success as phenomenal in its relatively short existence until now. And the reason for this success is simple – the quality of the wine has been exemplary from the outset. Is this the direct result of its organic and Biodynamic practices? It's impossible to say and, to a certain extent, irrelevant: each winery has its own approach to viticulture, some are better than others, and the results are best judged in the glass. On this basis, this winery is doing excellent work and improving every year.

Emiliana Orgánico's existence began in 1998 when Viñedos Emiliana set aside 224 hectares of its vineyards in Casablanca, Maipo, and Rapel for organic production. (Viñedos Emiliana, *see* p. 248, is a large-scale producer and itself an offshoot of Concha y Toro (p. 158), so all effectively form part of the same group.) Critics may argue that it's easy to undertake a venture like this when you have such solid backing including established vineyards and commercial structures, though the fact remains that Emiliana Orgánico is the first large-scale organic project to have been established in Chile, a country whose nat-ural propensity toward such methods of cultivation is clear cut. As such, it is very welcome.

The inspiration for the project came from José Guilisasti, managing director of Emiliana, who was initially helped by consultant agronomist Miguel Elissalt and also, from 2000, winemaker and organic specialist Alvaro Espinoza (who was appointed head winemaker in 2005). Elissalt and Espinoza persuaded Guilisasti to incorporate Biodynamic practices into the organic methods, with the result that all organic vineyards are now also under Biodynamic management. (The IMO and Demeter are the respective certifying bodies; the vineyards are certified but often not the final wines, as this would incur an additional cost per bottle.)

In 2004, a further 224 hectares were ceded from Viñedos Emiliana, meaning that by 2007 the winery will have some 450 hectares of certified organic vineyard. Such has been Emiliana Orgánico's success that future plans involve converting over half of Viñedo Emiliana's 1,500-hectare vineyard to organics.

The winery's base is in Los Robles, a 750-hectare estate set within a southeast-facing bowl of hills that lies to the north of Placilla and the Tinguiririca River in the warm mid-eastern section of Colchagua. Its isolation and the established quality of its 145-hectare vineyard (planted entirely to red grapes) made it ideal for a project like this. It has since been developed into a fully fledged Biodynamic farm, complete with habitat breaks ("biological corridors" as Elissalt terms them, to encourage beneficial insect life as well as biodiversity), composting areas, and production centres for Biodynamic preparations and infusions, as well as animals such as geese and alpacas to control pests and fertilize the vineyard. "The most important thing with Biodynamics is the organization of the farm as a self-sustaining unit of production," explains Espinoza. "But at its core is sound viticulture, because no amount of Biodynamics can make good fruit from poor management." (For more details on Biodynamics, see Viticulture, p.16.)

The wines are made in a bold style though with a roundness and complexity that imbue them with a raw, instinctive appeal. Adobe is a first-rate entry-level line, while Novas offers excellent character and complexity across the range. The Syrah/Mourvèdre and Chardonnay/Viognier/Marsanne blends are prime examples of this as well as being wines that typify Espinoza's propensity for using unusual varieties and blending. (He comments, "We don't want to make traditional Chilean varietal wines, we want to experiment with blends, create wines more related to the place than the varieties, in a Mediterranean style.") The wines are very approachable when young.

The winery has two top wines, Coyam and a new release entitled G, both of which are blends from Los Robles. Coyam is a blend of Merlot, Carmenère, Cabernet Sauvignon, Syrah, and Mourvèdre and its style offers plenty of vibrant, ripe red and black fruit with integrated oak spice and roasted herbal notes together with a sinewy, juicy palate. It has consistently improved from the 2001 to 2003 vintages and is an excellent wine, although the alcohol could do with being reined in. The new wine G is predominantly Syrah with smaller amounts of Carmenère, Cabernet Sauvignon and Merlot. A sneak preview of the debut 2003 vintage showed it to be dense and spicy with silky tannin and an excellent structure.

HACIENDA ARAUCANO (JACQUES & FRANCOIS LURTON)

Km 29, Ruta I-72, Colchagua, Lolol. Tel: +56 2 1966631. Email: hacienda.araucano@jflurton.cl. Website: www.jflurton.com
Established: 2000. Vineyard: 20ha (Cabernet Sauvignon, Carmenère, Syrah, Chardonnay). Production: 800,000 litres.

Jacques and François Lurton are widely acknowledged to be producers of quality-orientated, ambitious wines. It has always been something of a disappointment to me, then, that their Chilean range is not better. This may be an issue of personal taste, or indeed of high expectations, but I have consistently struggled to understand or admire their Chilean output. The wines seem to veer between a self-consciously Old World mould (green-pepper Carmenère or light, zingy Sauvignon Blanc) and a super-ripe New World style, especially in the reds. Nonetheless, their recent endeavours with Carmenère in particular have been encouraging and I hope this signals a move towards a greater emphasis on balance and a more identifiably Chilean character in the wines in future.

Jacques and François Lurton are brothers from Bordeaux who have set up a successful business both consulting and establishing their own wineries in countries such as Spain, France, Argentina, and Uruguay. Hacienda Araucano was established in Chile in 2000 after Jacques finished a seven-year stint consulting for San Pedro (*see* p. 265); the first wines were vinified from bought fruit in rented winery space – both practices they still continue although they now have a small winery along with 200 hectares of land in a warm, windy site on the southern rim of Lolol around forty kilometres (twenty-five miles) from the ocean.

Some twenty hectares of young vines are planted around the winery – Cabernet Sauvignon, Carmenère, Syrah, and Chardonnay – but the majority of the fruit is sourced from producers in Casablanca, Curicó, and Colchagua. Purchases in Colchagua are from Lolol and Apalta. In addition, the brothers may plant a new Pinot Noir and Sauvignon Blanc vineyard in Lolol but higher on the hills in what are thought to be cooler conditions.

The wines are made in two main ranges: Hacienda Araucano and Gran Araucano. The whites are generally weaker than the reds, with the Gran Araucano Sauvignon Blanc from Casablanca perhaps the most interesting in its tangy, sweaty style. Both Chardonnays tend to be tropical and somewhat simple, a result of the puzzling decision to source them in the warm areas. Both Cabernet Sauvignons are pleasant, offering sweet, ripe fruit in a traditional Colchagua style, with the Gran Araucano giving more tight structure on the palate.

Carmenère is proving to be the most interesting variety at Hacienda Araucano. The straight Hacienda version tends toward a slightly underripe, fresh green-pepper style of the variety (which may appeal to more Euro-centric palates). More interesting is Alka, a new top-of-the-range (with an ambitious price tag to match) 100 per cent Carmenère made with a blend of fruit from Apalta and Lolol, which shows a dark fruit, tea-leaf, ginger, and tarry complexity with a grippy, fleshy palate. Somewhere in between these two lies what is for my money their most successful wine to date, the Clos de Lolol, a blend of Cabernet Sauvignon and Carmenère from Lolol that marries fresh berry fruit with herbal, oaky complexity in an unassuming but appealing way.

LOS MAQUIS

Fundo Los Maquis, Palmilla, Santa Cruz. Tel: +56 2 5858743. Email: ricardo@maquis.cl. Website: www.maquis.cl

Established: 1997. Vineyard: 115ha (Carmenère, Syrah, Cabernet Sauvignon, Cabernet Franc, Malbec, Petit Verdot). Production: 700,000 litres.

Los Maquis is situated on what is effectively a triangular island of land to the north of Palmilla between two convergent watercourses. It is a late addition to the Colchagua fold and is still finding its way in wine-making terms; nonetheless, its initial efforts and overall game plan indicate there is good potential here.

The project was started in 1997 with the aim of producing bulk wine and one top-end though affordable red, Lien, the first of which was made in 2003. Around 120 hectares were planted in Palmilla between 1997 and 2004 in what winemaker and part-owner Ricardo Rivadeneira describes as different terrain to the surrounding area, slightly raised (the rivers lie around ten metres (thirty-three feet) below the level of the land) with relatively deep, fertile loam soil but well drained due to the alluvial sediments underlying. For now, this well-managed, all-red vineyard is the winery's main focus, though reds are also being planted in a 900-hectare estate in Marchihue.

The winemaking concept at Los Maquis is to make a red blend that is not stereotypically Colchagua in style, with more emphasis on fresh fruit, even florality in aromas, and concentration yet elegance on the palate. Tasting 2005 samples in the minimalist new winery, along with the 2003 and 2004 blends of Lien (mainly Syrah and Carmenère along with Petit Verdot and Malbec), freshness of fruit and invigorating acidity were indeed evident in all the individual components. What was lacking was a sense of easy harmony in the blend as well as overall complexity and all-round integration. The 2004 showed improvements over the 2003, perhaps due to the inclusion of Cabernet Franc, but in general the principal blending components of Syrah and Carmenère seemed to jar.

The sort of delicate balance between concentration and elegance that Lien is aiming for takes time and ongoing effort and experimentation to achieve, as well as an established vineyard and experience in the winemaking. For now, the wine is improving, and this is clearly a winery with a worthy aim as well as some good-quality fruit.

LOS VASCOS

Av Vitacura 2939, Of 1903, Las Condes, Santiago. Tel: +56 2 2326633. Email:
losvascos@losvascos.cl. Website: www.vinalosvascos.com

Established: 1988. Vineyard: 580ha (Cabernet Sauvignon, Chardonnay,
Carmenère, Syrah, Malbec). Production: 3.6 million litres.

While it seems that some wineries in Chile have been changing virtually by the day, Los Vascos has been managing its progress in a more
measured, even low-profile manner. It is a policy that has served the
wines well.

Los Vascos is majority owned by Domaines Barons de Rothschild
(owners of Lafite-Rothschild, among others), which bought into the
project in 1988 in a joint venture with the local Eyzaguirre-Echeñique
family, whose forty-three per cent share was later bought in 1996 by
the Claro group, owner of Santa Rita. It is based out of the 4,000-
hectare Cañeten estate in the western part of Colchagua, a north-facing
amphitheatre not far from Marchihue and around forty kilometres
(twenty-five miles) from the coast. The local climate tends to be warm
but rarely severely so, with moderating afternoon winds common.
Soils are of clay-loams of moderate fertility on the flat land, while on
the east-facing hillsides (the only ones to have currently been planted)
the soil is largely composed of granitic sands. Some 580 hectares have
been established here, predominantly with Cabernet Sauvignon but
also twenty-five hectares of Chardonnay, twenty-five of Carmenère,
eighteen of Syrah, and four of Malbec, along with other trials.

It's true to say that Cabernet Sauvignon has dominated proceedings
at Los Vascos, in keeping with its Bordelais direction. However, it is
interesting to see the subtle changes that have been taking place in
recent years, much of which is down to the winemaking stewardship
between 2001 and 2006 of Marco Puyo. For instance, where before the
winery made three different single-varietal Cabernets (varietal, Grande
Réserve, and le Dix), Puyo made a point of broadening the blend of the
Grande Réserve, adding four per cent Carmenère in the 2003, then sixteen per cent Carmenère and four per cent Syrah in the 2004, and then
with a further touch of Malbec in the 2005. Although I have yet to taste
the 2004 and 2005, I would applaud this move to flesh out at least one

Cabernet in the range with extra dimensions of flavour – the 2003 benefits from the touch of black fruit and peppery breadth that the Carmenère adds.

A further example of Puyo's influence can be seen in Le Dix, the winery's top wine, a single-vineyard Cabernet Sauvignon sourced from an eighteen-hectare plot of old vines. A vertical tasting in early 2006 of the wines from 1999 through to 2005 was a clear demonstration of how the wine has matured from a wannabe-claret into a refined, silky, complex Chilean Cabernet, with the major change in style being marked in 2001 (the most impressive wine in the line-up along with the 2003). Puyo describes his style as "New World perhaps, but always honest; Chilean but most importantly with the ultimate aim being elegance."

Although Puyo left in 2006 to join San Pedro, his belief in and improvement of Los Vascos' wines has rightly challenged the surprisingly sniffy attitude of the French owners towards the limit of their Chilean winery's ambitions. It is true that the basic line offers excellent value and character in the wines, from the peppery, blackberry-infused Cabernet to the enviably balanced Chardonnay, and the herbal, fresh Sauvignon Blanc. Beyond this, however, it is increasingly clear that Los Vascos does have both the ambition and ability to craft wines of complexity and class, and both the Grande Réserve and Le Dix are examples of this.

LUIS FELIPE EDWARDS

Vitacura 4130, Santiago. Tel: +56 2 4335700. Email: vinalfedwards@lfewines.com. Website: www.lfewines.com
Established: 1976. Vineyard: 426ha (Cabernet Sauvignon, Syrah, Merlot, Carmenère, Chardonnay). Production: 3.5 million litres.

LFE is a winery in the process of transforming itself from a conventional Colchagua producer into something more commercially focused and viticulturally diverse.

The aim, as outlined by managing director Luis Felipe Edwards Junior, is to double current production, to reach around seven million litres by 2008. Edwards, a former banker, notes that sales increased tenfold between 2000 and 2005 and states his priorities as consolidating distribution, minimizing costs, and ensuring quality in the wines. "Consolidation is a sensible option in Chile today," he comments. "It's necessary for the industry to improve as well as for mid-size producers to ensure their survival."

LFE has vineyards in westerly Colchagua (Pupilla) and has also recently bought a 162-hectare estate in San Antonio (Leyda), which, once planted and producing, should go some way to improving what has been a weak white wine portfolio. The winery is based in Puquillay, a self-contained estate south of Nancagua in warm central Colchagua. At the winery there are some old vines on the flat land, but in the late nineties plantings were begun on the lower foothills of the estate, an initiative that finally led in 2005 to ninety-six hectares being established between 800 and 980 metres (2,600–3,200 feet), some of the highest vineyards in the region. A proportion of these vineyards has been planted on terraces, mostly facing west and north (a warm exposure, though the winemakers point out that the elevation tends to lower temperatures and attract more wind). Installing irrigation has been a major cost but the idea is to produce fruit with greater concentration (no high-lying water table here) as well as a bit more diversity: Mourvèdre and Grenache have also been planted as trials.

The winery employs consultants from South Africa in the vineyard and Australia in the winery; its Chilean winemakers note that the winemaking style has evolved since 2000 toward shorter macerations, less extraction, and more approachable wines, especially at the lower end. In general, it does seem as if this is the case, making for satisfactory commercial wines, though in general LFE's portfolio could do with a boost in quality. This may well happen as the new vineyards come on line. For now, much of the interest is provided by wines like the Terraced Malbec – the name is misleading as Terraced in this case is a brand line; the fruit for this comes from old vines located on the flat land in Puquillay, giving attractive fresh red fruit and earthy, graphite character. Top-line Doña Bernarda also shows some quality and freshness on the palate in a traditional style.

MONTES

Av del Valle N 945, Of 2611, Cuidad Empresarial, Huechuraba, Santiago. Tel:
+56 2 2484805. Email: montes@monteswines.com. Website:
www.monteswines.com

Established: 1988. Vineyard: 550ha (Cabernet Sauvignon, Syrah, Carmenère,
Merlot, Petit Verdot). Production: 5 million litres.

Montes is a winery on the move. It has evolved at breakneck speed
since its foundation as Discover Wine in Curicó in 1988, switching its
name as well as its winemaking focus away from Curicó and onto
Colchagua – more specifically, Apalta and Marchihue – and producing
a raft of innovative, quality wines along the way. In 2003, it diversified
into Argentina with its Kaiken brand and has also been looking elsewhere – Australia, South Africa, and California – to study other possible projects.

Such prodigious investments, including a serene US$6.5 million
(£3.4 million) winery in Apalta designed on *feng shui* principles, have
so far been funded by operating profits and the owning partners,
though a listing on the stock exchange may at some stage prove a likely
option for the company. A principal partner in the winery is Aurelio
Montes, one of Chile's leading winemakers who began his career with
Undurraga, San Pedro, and Fundación Chile before co-founding what
would become his eponymous winery. He also carries out numerous
consultancies across the country.

It is Aurelio Montes' personal vision and energy that have been the
driving force behind the success of the wines. It was his experience
with Undurraga that led him first to Apalta; similarly, the potential of
Marchihue became clear while he was consulting for VEO in the area.
Currently, Montes has some 300 hectares of vineyard in Marchihue,
with a further 120 hectares being planted in 2006, as well as 129 in
Apalta. Both projects are impressive in their scope and ambition – in
Apalta, for example, vines have colonized the hillsides in the property
up to 370 metres (1,200 feet), some planted on slopes of up to forty-
nine per cent incline, with experiments including head-trained
Mourvèdre.

Neither do the two properties exist in isolation from each other. Two of Montes' most successful top-end wines of recent times to my mind, Purple Angel and Alpha Syrah, are entirely complementary blends of Apalta and Marchihue fruit. In both cases, the structure and power of Apalta are balanced and fleshed out by the fresher, juicy fruit of Marchihue. Purple Angel, for example, is predominantly Carmenère (forty-six per cent from lower Apalta slopes, forty-six per cent from Marchihue) with eight per cent Apalta Petit Verdot for acidity, tannin, and colour. Its first vintage, in 2003, is a very impressive marriage of roasted fruit and sweet pepper with a broad, structured yet lively and fresh palate. Aurelio Montes' winemaking style tends to be unapologetically ripe and full-on, so it is good to see an extra dimension in wines like these, the result of well-judged blends and promising new vineyards.

Elsewhere in the range, Montes' wines offer good value and much interest. The house Sauvignon Blanc style tends toward the crisp, herbaceous mould, though a new version in 2005 from Leyda (made from fruit at Garcés Silva, one of the winery's partners) shows more body and breadth – features it would be good to see the winery develop. Both the oak and malolactic influences have been toned down in the Alpha Chardonnay, to my mind a sound development, but one that still needs to go further for best results.

Pinot Noir and Malbec also offer some interest, but the winery's forte is with Cabernet, Carmenère, and Syrah. A good example of the latter is Folly, a wine made from hillside Apalta in weathered granite soils from vines planted as recently as 1998 but which, by its second vintage in 2003, was already showing intense, refined fruit, admirable structure, and potential for ageing. As for Carmenère, it is telling to see the how far this variety has developed in the hands of a winemaker who once described its main function as "a silent partner" in blends. It reminds me of a comment he once made to me, "You have to keep trying new things, moving on – nothing is set in stone just yet."

MONTGRAS

Av Eliodoro Yáñez 2962, Providencia, Santiago. Tel: +56 2 5204355. Email: info@montgras.cl. Website: www.montgras.cl

Established: 1992. Vineyard: 423ha (Cabernet Sauvignon, Syrah, Merlot, Carmenère, Malbec). Production: 3.9 million litres.

MontGras' aggressive commercial focus has seen it initiate an ambitious plan of expansion. Sales grew by forty per cent in 2004, from US$9 million to US$13.5 million (£4.7–7 million), and the aim is to reach a turnover of US$24 million (£12.7 million) by 2010. In order to meet these targets, new vineyards were purchased in 2004 and 2005 (an investment of US$15 million (£8 million)) which, if fully planted, would take MontGras' holding up to 1,560 hectares.

The new land is in Maipo (Linderos, 184 hectares), San Antonio (Leyda, 570 hectares), and other sites in Colchagua, including Pumanque with 400 hectares. The idea, according to Patricio Middleton, managing director and one of four owning partners, is to end up with one winery in each of the three regions and give each one a discrete identity and brand, but all under the MontGras umbrella. A similar strategy was developed by MontGras in the late nineties and early 2000s with the Ninquén brand, based on a hillside vineyard in Colchagua.

Winemaker Santiago Margozzini is all for the changes. "When MontGras started here in Colchagua in 1992, the approach to viticulture was completely different: winemakers believed we could make anything anywhere. But now we realize the importance of terroir; there's no doubt these investments will improve the wines." He cites the example of Linderos, which he describes as a better site for Cabernet Sauvignon than Colchagua, given its varied, well-drained alluvial soils and slightly fresher climate, which gives a longer growing season by around ten days. (Linderos already has an established vineyard, though more is being added.) Leyda, a site ten kilometres (six miles) from the ocean, is being planted mainly to Sauvignon Blanc, with some Chardonnay, Pinot Noir, and Syrah. Colchagua, Margozzini maintains, is best for Carmenère, Merlot, Syrah, and Viognier.

While it is difficult to comment on the commercial motivation behind this radical shake-up, it is hard not to be optimistic about the eventual development of MontGras' portfolio as a result. It has always been weak in terms of white wines, an aspect that the introduction of

Leyda fruit should address, and, having tasted the new, elegantly structured Linderos Cabernet up against its slightly awkward Colchagua
counterpart, it is clear that Maipo fruit will also serve the winery well.
It is crucial that, within all this, commercial targets do not hinder the
winemakers – for example, yields need to be kept within strict quality
parameters, as they have been on the high side in the past (especially
noticeable in the Reserva line which, while generally good quality, can
also be somewhat dilute). In addition, cellar hygiene needs to be kept
rigorous, as the wines (especially the Ninquéns) have occasionally
shown brettanomyces problems.

Changes are also taking place at the Ninquén project. Margozzini is
candid in admitting that the winery "went too far" in both the vineyard
and winery, over-stressing the vines and over-extracting the wines.
(The wines have been somewhat angular and clunky in the past.) The
plan for 2006 is to revert to a more easy-going viticulture and winemaking, also using an element of wild yeast fermentation, partly to
help reduce the alcohol – all methods that were apparently used for the
first, 2000 vintage. In addition, a two-hectare experiment is being
planted on south-facing slopes – a slightly cooler exposure than the
predominantly north- and east- facing hillsides where the current 100
hectares are located. A promising new brand, Antu Ninquén, was also
released in 2005 to make more use of the hillside fruit and sell at
around half the price of Ninquén.

NEYEN

Riesco 5711, Piso 9. Las Condes, Santiago. Tel: +56 2 2406300. Email:
jaime@neyen.cl.
Established: 2005. Vineyard: 125ha (Cabernet Sauvignon, Carmenère, Merlot,
Syrah). Production: 60,000 litres.

While its debut 2003 vintage, released in 2005, caused considerable
excitement, Neyen is not altogether a newcomer to the Colchagua
wine scene. Its vineyard, located at the far eastern end of Apalta, was
established in 1890 and traditionally the grapes have been sold to third
parties. The vineyard includes a thirty-hectare plot of old vines –
Carmenère (planted in 1980) and Cabernet Sauvignon, some of which

is thought to date back to the original planting. These dry-farmed, densely planted old vines are located on the flatter part of the 1,200-hectare property; newer plantings (twenty hectares in 1995, forty more in 1999 and 2000, and ten in 2004) have gone in around this vineyard and on the hillsides, taking the total to 125 hectares. A further twenty hectares are set to be added in 2007, mainly Carmenère and Syrah, with a final target vineyard of around 150 hectares.

The aim is to keep selling the majority of the grapes as a cash earner for the business, while retaining a percentage of fruit for the sole wine, Neyen. Between 2003 and 2005 the wine was sourced from two parcels of old vines, four hectares of Carmenère and two hectares of Cabernet. This was intended to keep volumes small initially to retain a niche appeal while driving interest. For 2006, however, the winery plans to use ten hectares for the wine, including new hillside fruit, and this total is set to rise to a thirty-hectare maximum by 2012.

It will be worth watching to see which fruit ends up being selected for future Neyen wines, especially when the hillside vines have had a chance to mature. It could well be that the fruit from the slopes ultimately trumps the old vines, and Syrah is already looking to be a firm favourite, giving good initial results from young vines (clone 174) planted in northeast-facing decomposed granite soils. It remains to be seen how elements such as this might work in a blend, though: 2006 will be the first when Merlot and Syrah could make the grade.

The 2003 vintage, the only wine I have tasted to date but on several occasions, is proving to be a very successful debut. Though the blend of seventy per cent Carmenère and thirty per cent Cabernet Sauvignon perhaps lacks a certain element of overall harmony, it already exhibits an excellent structure and a character that is a well-judged blend of ripe dark fruit, sturdy oak spice, and a certain appealing earthiness and pepper that emerges with time in the glass. Neyen's success will be determined by how the blend evolves; hopefully it will focus on harnessing the structure of the fruit with increasing complexity and integration. The debut wine has already set exacting standards – if it improves, it could set new standards for Chile.

An obvious comparison for the wine is with Clos Apalta, Casa

Lapostolle's icon wine, also made from the fruit of old Carmenère and Cabernet vines on the flatter Apalta land. Tasted side by side in 2006, the 2003 wines showed many similarities (steeped, heady fruit, spicy oak, broad and dense on the palate with refined tannin), though Clos Apalta showed more overt purity of dense fruit, majoring on warm alcohol and dense, ripe tannins on the palate; Neyen by contrast seemed more defined, less overtly fruit driven, and with a noticeably steelier structure.

Neyen's creative team include consultants Patrick Valette and Eduardo Silva. New winemaking facilities were completed on site in 2006.

SANTA HELENA

Av Vitacura 4380, Piso 5, Santiago. Tel: +56 2 4362400. Email: info@santahelena.cl. Website: www.santahelena.cl
Established: 1942. Vineyard: 90ha (Cabernet Sauvignon, Merlot, Carmenere, Malbec, Shiraz). Production: 12.1 million litres.

Santa Helena has been in existence since 1942 and owned by San Pedro since 1974 but the date that marks this winery's modern birthday is 2001. It was then that the San Pedro Wine Group restructured and Santa Helena was given the freedom to run itself effectively as an independent concern. It is an opportunity the winery has seized gamely, completing a range revamp, commercial makeover, and almost doubling in size and sales in just five years. (In 2004, the winery was the country's sixth-largest exporter by value.)

Santa Helena uses fruit from around the country to supply its sizeable annual production of twelve million litres, though its main focus is on Colchagua, from where it sources around two-thirds of its production. In 2004, the winery expanded its portfolio of single-varietal wines by introducing a new premium selection of wines under the Selección del Directorio, Vernus, Notas de Guarda, and DON brands.

Though it is fair to say that Santa Helena's wines have undergone a notable improvement over the last few years, it does seem as if its commercial ambitions are still some way ahead of its fundamental winemaking quality. The range, while generally sound, lacks real incisiveness and is often overly commercial in style – at the lower end especially the wines could do with more concentration and personality. Chardonnay, Viognier, and Cabernet work best in the cheaper wines, with the Selección del Directorio line offering a step up in quality (and price).

The top-end wines, by contrast, show more character and ambition but tend to lack elegance and integration. That said, fruit bought from Apalta gives good character in these lines, especially in the likes of Notas de Guarda Carmenère, and there is some sensitive blending of Maipo and Colchagua fruit in DON and Vernus. The potential is there; it would be good to see Santa Helena putting more of a focus on the vineyards to raise quality a notch or two across the range.

VINA SANTA CRUZ

Monseñor Escriva de Balaguer 6173, Vitacura, Santiago. Tel: +56 2 2199903. Email: info@vinasantacruz.cl. Website: www.vinasantacruz.cl
Established: 2004. Vineyard: 160ha (Carmenère, Cabernet Sauvignon, Syrah, Merlot, Malbec, Petit Verdot). Production: 300,000 litres.

Based in Lolol, Viña Santa Cruz is an eclectic mixture of tourist destination and winery, the brainchild of Chilean tycoon Carlos Cardoen.

Some background is necessary to understand Viña Santa Cruz. Cardoen is something of a controversial figure in recent Chilean history due to his involvement in the arms business. Later in life he began to invest in Colchagua (he was born in the town of Santa Cruz), building the Hotel Santa Cruz and its adjoining museum as well as co-founding the local wine train and, in 2005, the Colchagua Technological Institute for wine, food, and tourism education. A winery was a logical venture and so Cardoen bought a site on the southern side of Lolol complete with hillsides and an existing vineyard on the flat land. He knew the fruit well – it had supplied Misiones de Rengo, a winery that Cardoen had previously part-owned.

A grand plan for the site was rapidly implemented, beginning with a winery, gastronomic centre, and shop as well as a cable car leading to a hilltop overlooking the site. On this eyrie were installed re-creations of original homesteads belonging to Chile's various indigenous cultures – Rapa Nui, Aymara, and Mapuche – as well as an informal astronomical observatory. Further developments include a wine spa, restaurant, hotel and conference centre, and children's play area complete with Peruvian merry-go-round.

In 2005, a further eighty hectares were added to the existing ninety hectare vineyard (planted in 1997/8 and comprising Carmenère, Cabernet Sauvignon, Malbec, Syrah, and Pinot Noir). The Pinot was replaced by more Cabernet. Much of the new vineyard has gone in on hillside slopes, including some terraces, with Cabernet on the northern exposures and Syrah and Petit Verdot facing south. The location is windy and temperatures tend to vary between local sites, with the northern end of the farm (Guaico) generally warmer than the more exposed southern part (El Peral). A fifty-hectare white vineyard for Sauvignon Blanc, Chardonnay, and Viognier is also being developed farther west at Patacón, twenty kilometres (twelve miles) from the coast and near San Pedro de Alcantará.

Carmenère is the intended focus at Viña Santa Cruz and winemaker José Miguel Sotomayor believes the fruit will make for elegant, fresh styles of wine. The first vintage of Chamán (2004), a Carmenère/Cabernet blend, was decent if forgettable but barrel samples of the 2005 vintage, including a pre-bottling blend of Chamán, were fresher and more concentrated, indicating that good things may ultimately happen here. Gran Chamán, Tupú, and Santa Cruz are brands for future release.

VINEDOS EMILIANA

Av Nueva Tajamar 481, Of 701, Torre Sur, Santiago. Tel: +56 2 3539130. Email: info@emiliana.cl. Website: www.vinedosemiliana.cl
Established: 1986. Vineyard: 1,550ha (Cabernet Sauvignon, Merlot, Chardonnay, Carmenère, Syrah). Production: 7.8 million litres. *See also*: Emiliana Orgánico.

Formerly Santa Emiliana, the new-look Viñedos Emiliana has changed more than just its name. Its wines have taken a notable step up in quality over the last few years, the result of restructuring instigated in the late nineties by its parent company Concha y Toro.

Many of these changes have taken place in the vineyard. For example, in 1998, Emiliana adopted integrated pest management practices and also began the organic project that would lead to the formation of its important Emiliana Orgánico venture (*see above*). Although this organic subsidiary has appropriated many of its best vineyard sites, Emiliana has still managed to improve its wines – the Andes Peaks line, especially the reds, offers some excellent value. Where before the wines were often resolutely simple, now they have more character, yet still with the same soft, approachable house style.

This sizeable producer owns vineyards in Casablanca, Alto Maipo, Cachapoal, and Colchagua, and in addition sources some fruit from elsewhere, for example Sauvignon Blanc from the Guilisasti farm in Bío Bío.

VINEDOS ERRAZURIZ OVALLE (VEO, EOV)

Amunategui 178, Piso 4, Santiago. Tel: +56 2 5406057. Email: contact@eov.cl. Website: www.eov.cl

Established: 1992. Vineyard: 2,437ha (Cabernet Sauvignon, Merlot, Carmenère, Chardonnay, Syrah). Production: 18 million litres.

The first issue to clear up about VEO is the name, which can be confusing. VEO (Viñedos Errázuriz Ovalle), which is also known as EOV, is nothing to do with VOE (*see* Emiliana Orgánico) or Errázuriz (*see* Aconcagua). Instead, it is one of the largest family-owned wineries in Chile, controlled by Inversiones Errázuriz but in effect owned by Chilean businessman Francisco Javier Errázuriz and managed by his son, Matías.

In order to understand VEO, it helps to understand its owners. Inversiones Errázuriz owns several businesses in many sectors, including mining, supermarkets, forestry, and fisheries. Francisco Javier Errázuriz is a well-known, if controversial, figure in Chilean business and political circles, a man who ran for the right-wing ticket in the presidential elections of 1989 when Pinochet was stepping down, and who later became a senator.

It is certainly true that his winery has not done things by halves. Having decided to diversify into wine in the nineties, by 1996 VEO had some 2,000 hectares planted in Marchihue, an area where the family owns extensive property. This project was undertaken with the advice of Aurelio Montes, who later bought in the area himself. The winery also later planted 500 hectares in Lontué (Curicó) for whites, and new projects include vineyards on higher, windier elevations in Marchihue (mainly Cabernet Sauvignon and Shiraz in a site called Tierruca Alto, planted in 2005) as well as trial plantings some eight kilometres (five miles) from the coast near Pichilemu with Sauvignon Blanc, Chardonnay, and Riesling, and perhaps Pinot Noir eventually too.

VEO produced its first wines in the 2001 vintage, and as of 2006 was producing thirty thousand tonnes of grapes per year, some of which are sold to third parties. After something of a shaky start, the winery now seems to be settling into a more considered stride both in commercial and winemaking terms; the winemaking team is young and has been advised by consultant Hugh Ryman since 2004. Although I have not been able to try the wines as extensively as I would like, it seems that the reds tend toward a commercial, sweet-fruit style, while the whites need work. It will be interesting to see how the Marchihue vineyards mature, as well as the new Tierruca Alto and Pichilemu plantings.

VIU MANENT

Av Antonio Varas 2470, Santiago. Tel: +56 2 3790020. Email: export@viumanent.cl. Website: www.viumanent.cl
Established: 1935. Vineyard: 224ha (Cabernet Sauvignon, Malbec, Carmenère, Merlot, Syrah). Production: 1.6 million litres.

Viu Manent is a decidedly traditional Colchagua producer whose speciality is reliable reds made in a chunky style. There are signs, however, that things are changing – a necessary process for this winery if it is to improve and stake a claim to a place alongside Chile's better producers.

Although Viu was founded in 1935, it wasn't until 1966 that it settled into its present home on the flat valley floor in prime central Colchagua, near Cunaco. Vineyards were already in place, as evidenced by the old-vine Cabernet Sauvignon and Malbec, some of which is thought to date back up to a century. Since then, new vineyards have been added farther west, around Peralillo, with a variety of red grapes including recent plantings of Grenache, Tempranillo, Tannat, and Mourvèdre. In 2004, the winery purchased white grapes from Casablanca for the first time. The same year it launched a new line called Secreto, with vivid modern packaging, atypical varieties, shorter oak ageing, and the aim to broaden the winery's range and appeal.

These changes coincided with the arrival of Kiwi winemaker and restless live-wire Grant Phelps in 2003. Talking to Phelps in 2005, it was clear he was intent on innovation, reducing extraction times and length of oak ageing for the reds, and for the whites, picking earlier and working more reductively. "Chilean winemakers are so conservative," he told me, "they don't want to take risks. In New Zealand, it's the opposite, everyone wants to be an innovator. That's the reason I'm here: Chile still has huge potential for development." He added that the main reason Viu Manent had attracted him was its old-vine Malbec.

Malbec has traditionally been Viu's calling card, its densely planted old vines (like Cabernet) seemingly having adapted to the fertile loam-clay soils and high water table in the Cunaco estate. The wines, such as the Single Vineyard and Viu 1 (a blend of the oldest vines with ten per cent Cabernet Sauvignon) are powerful, chewy reds that need time to soften before revealing ginger, dark fruit, inky, tar, and nutmeg aromas – it is a style of wine that is not to everyone's taste, and often somewhat overdone.

Overdoing things is a criticism I would level at many of Viu's reds, though this may change under Phelps's hands-on winemaking influence and especially if more emphasis is placed on using fruit from western Colchagua, which seems to give more lift and freshness to the wines as well as a better balance on the palate. A good example of this is the Single Vineyard Cabernet Sauvignon, sourced from La Capilla near Peralillo: a spicy, juicy red whose profile complements the more austere, sturdy Cunaco fruit.

Elsewhere in the range, the whites still need work though the Secreto Viognier in particular shows signs of promise in its tropical, papaya character. The Secreto range is in general a very positive development for the winery and offers no shortage of vibrant character, though perhaps lacks elegance and integration, something that will hopefully be corrected in time. The Syrah is currently its most show-stopping wine, packed full of charred, meaty aromas and a big, spicy palate. This fruit comes from El Olivar, a young vineyard planted in the hills above Peralillo and which could prove to be a source of good-quality reds.

8

Curicó

BRIEF FACTS
Vineyard: 18,940ha (68% reds)
Main grape varieties (ha): Cabernet Sauvignon (6,754), Sauvignon Blanc (3,722), Merlot (2,937), Chardonnay (1,430), Carmenère (1,119)
Climate: temperate with annual rainfall of 700–850mm (28–34 inches)
Soils: mainly fertile clay-loams becoming coarser and sandier near the Andes and coast

INTRODUCTION

The Curicó winemaking region is bordered by Colchagua to the north and Maule to the south. It marks the start of Chile's cooler, rainier winemaking territory that extends to the south, though in summer this is by no means a cool-climate region. Warm summers, plentiful water, and often fertile soils have resulted in the region's two largest earners being forestry and agriculture.

Along with the Maule winemaking region, Curicó officially forms part of Chilean administrative Region VII, which is also known as Maule. Understandably, this tends to cause confusion. It has also not helped Curicó develop a clear-cut sense of individual identity as it tends to get lumped together with Maule in people's minds and not simply because of their proximity and comparable climates.

The two regions have also tended to share a reputation as Chile's engine room of wine production, good for driving volume but limited in their scope for fine wine. Between them, Curicó and Maule account for around forty-three per cent of the national vineyard – more in production terms due to high yields – though Curicó is significantly smaller than Maule in size, accounting for 18,940 hectares (versus 29,333 hectares). Both of these regions have continued to grow since 1997, however, proving their ongoing relevance to the modern Chilean wine industry and hopefully paving the way for improvements in the future. Such progress is urgently required in Curicó, which has lagged behind other Chilean winemaking regions.

Wine tourism has been one positive development for the region. This initiative was pioneered by the Miguel Torres winery, which early on introduced an open-door policy to visitors and has now developed a restaurant as well as other impressive visitor facilities. San Pedro as well as others have followed. *See* www.rvvc.cl for more details. Curicó also holds a popular annual harvest festival – in 2005, Chilean president Ricardo Lagos popped in to join in the festivities.

viii Curicó

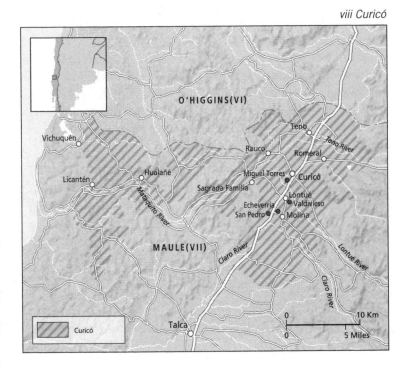

A PICTURE OF CURICO

In the cordillera southeast of Curicó is some of the loveliest scenery in Chile, where the Río Claro drops over a basalt escarpment into a series of pools known as the Siete Tazas or Seven Cups, the centrepiece of the 7,645 hectare reserve named after them. Daredevil kayakers run the Río Claro, including the Tazas, in spring, and others can view the Tazas, and the nearby Salta de la Leona, with short walks from the road. There are also superb longer hikes, to the Velo de la Novia (Bridal Veil falls), the Valle del Indio and elsewhere. The area is protected because of its ecological importance as a transition zone between the Mediterranean communities around Santiago and the moister Valdivian communities to the south; it marks the northern limit of Nothofagus (false beech), and 153 of the 322 vascular plant species are endemic.

Extract taken from Tim Burford, *Chile, The Bradt Travel Guide*, Bradt Travel Guides, 2005, Chalfont St Peter.

THE NATURE OF CURICO

In shape, the Curicó wine region resembles an egg-timer lying on its side, with two bulbous ends connected by a narrow mid-section. The eastern part of Curicó is where the vast majority of the region's wine activity takes place, in the flat lands situated in Chile's north–south central depression and into the foothills of the Andes. The western section is altogether more remote and less developed in wine terms, accounting for barely four per cent of the regional vineyard, and abutted in its westerly extremity by a broad coastal range of hills. In the middle lies hilly terrain intersected by a narrow corridor of cultivated land to the west of Sagrada Familia.

Curicó's eastern section is well watered. In the north runs the river Teno and its tributaries; in the centre section flows the river Lontué; and in the south the river Claro cuts through Curicó before turning abruptly south and becoming part of the Maule wine region. The confluence of the Teno and Lontué is located just north of Sagrada Familia, at which point the river takes the name Mataquito and runs along a meandering, broad path through hilly terrain before reaching its estuary just south of Iloca.

Officially, Curicó is subdivided into two zones, the Teno and Lontué valleys. The distinction is largely administrative and of little relevance to those seeking to make sense of the region's wines. A better way to consider Curicó is by looking at its localized areas such as Molina, Sagrada Familia, and Lontué. The two largest winemaking centres are Molina and Sagrada Familia, with around 5,000 hectares each.

Curicó is generally considered to be the start of Chile's cooler, rainier winemaking territory that gradually becomes more marked toward the south. While this is largely true, and in overall terms Curicó offers less in the way of climatic diversity than many other Chilean wine regions, conditions do vary between sites. For example, in some areas around Sagrada Familia, especially those in wind-protected sites in the lee of the hills to the west and south, conditions can be significantly warmer than in areas like Lontué, at night as well as during the day. Valdivieso winemaker Brett Jackson estimates that the temperature differential can reach up to 3–5°C (5–9°F), resulting in harvests up to four weeks apart for the same variety in Sagrada Familia and eastern Curicó.

Curicó's summers are well defined and warm, especially in the central areas around Curicó town and Sagrada Familia, where January daytime temperatures average 29–30°C/84–86°F (much the same as the warmer areas of Colchagua, for example). The region has a marked temperature fluctuation between day and night, especially in its easterly reaches, where the difference averages around 20°C (36°F). Closer to the Andes and the sea, temperatures decline and rainfall increases. Autumn conditions in Curicó from mid-April onward lead to temperatures dropping off relatively fast and rainfall increasing significantly (as is the case in Maule, for example, and regions farther south).

Frosts are a particular threat in Curicó. This is partly due to its topography, in that much of its vineyard lies in a flat area sandwiched between the Andes and the hills around Sagrada Familia. The maritime influence is minimal due to these hills and the coastal range farther west: moderating sea winds rarely reach the area. The main prevailing wind is southerly, which, when it turns bitterly cold and fuelled by a mass of freezing polar air (bringing one of Chile's rarer but most deadly types of frost), can lead to widespread damage. Other, more frequent frosts are those caused by cold night-time temperatures compounded by cloudless skies, a lack of wind, or low humidity. Flat, low-lying land is always the most vulnerable to frost – and much of Curicó's vineyard grows on this kind of terrain.

Soils in Curicó are relatively uniform because most of the vineyards are situated on similar kinds of terrain in the flat central depression. Alluvial clays and loams are the most common soil type. These can often be relatively deep and high in organic matter (especially in the so-called trumao soils nearer the Andes, which carry a high proportion of dark volcanic ash). On the other hand, as in many other parts of Chile's central depression, soils can be underlain by a hard pan of rock and clay that inhibits root growth – such as can be found around Lontué and Molina. Soils tend to become coarser in texture toward the Andes. The level of the water table varies between sites but can give high humidity in some soils on the flat land.

VITICULTURE AND WINES

Curicó is one of Chile's least dynamic winemaking regions. That is not to say that good wine is not being produced here or indeed that it lacks the potential to do great things. It simply means that the region desperately needs an injection of innovation and a sense of positive momentum driven by ambitious new projects, quality terroirs, and high-profile regional wines.

In a way, Curicó has had things a bit too easy. Warm summers, plentiful water for irrigation, and flat, often fertile land have proved all-too-attractive options for those who have developed the majority of the region's vineyards. High yields and relatively consistent, simple wines have been the most common result, which has led Curicó to gain a reputation – in similar fashion to Maule – as something of an unremarkable engine room for volume production.

Further issues inhibiting development have been plant stock purity and ill-conceived varietal site selection. For example, much of what is officially recorded as Sauvignon Blanc in the region is actually Sauvignonasse, a significantly inferior variety that lacks character and ages poorly. Carmenère is ill-suited to all but the region's warmest and least rain-affected pockets, giving green and lean wines as a result, yet it still accounts for nearly 1,000 hectares (and almost certainly more given that much is still registered as Merlot). There are many more examples of vine varieties ill-suited to their local conditions – for instance, Valdivieso is currently removing Pinot Noir from its warm Sagrada Familia site and installing Malbec.

It is exactly this kind of redevelopment and broadening of horizons that Curicó needs if it is to fulfil its potential beyond making acceptable if unremarkable wines. Until now, quality wines have been the exception and have largely stemmed from the rare occurrences of old vines in the region – Torres' Manso de Velasco, San Pedro's Cabo de Hornos, and Echeverría's Family Reserve are all cases in point. It is worth noting that all of these are single-varietal Cabernet Sauvignon wines made in a somewhat traditional style – this can either be considered an admirably faithful rendition of Curicó's terroir or a commentary on the region's diversity.

In all fairness, it seems that Curicó's best wines are reds made in a fresh though balanced style. The region's cool and rainy autumns can mean that some varieties, including Cabernet Sauvignon, struggle to ripen properly, especially in cooler sites and during wet vintages. However, it is the marginal sites that can end up giving the best results in viticulture so it is good to see producers persevering with this grape and making wines that major on balance and delicacy rather than ripeness and alcohol as can be the case in other Chilean regions. It is a difficult balance to strike well but maturing vines and increasing experience will help.

It would be good to see a broader range of varieties emerging from Curicó in the future. The likes of Cabernet Franc, Merlot, Malbec, and Syrah seem well-suited to the climate and soils here and are already giving good results, albeit on a limited scale. Of the whites, Viognier could surely prove worthwhile – especially given Cono Sur's success with the variety in similar territory just north of Curicó in Chimbarongo. Chardonnay and Sauvignon Blanc continue to give consistent results and some notable freshness, though the growing season can be too fast and short in the traditional viticultural areas for these varieties to gain real complexity.

One producer in particular working toward increasing plant and wine diversity in Curicó is Miguel Torres (*see* Case Study). In addition to developing Chilean plant material, Torres has imported varieties and now counts Gewurztraminer, Riesling, Viognier, Grenache, Garró, and Tempranillo among its planted varieties. The results can be seen in the wines: Don Miguel is a Gewurztraminer/Riesling blend, Conde de Superunda is a mixture of Tempranillo, Cabernet, Mourvèdre, and Carmenère. What is more, the winery also produces a successful fizz as well as sweet wine from its Curicó vineyards.

Diversifying Curicó's vineyards into more marginal territory is another challenge for the future. Incursions have begun into the Andean foothills, with mixed results so far, but the more coastal territory also offers significant potential. (Geological surveys show that around Licantén, for example, there are rare but prized metamorphic rocks including slate, which can offer good drainage and heat retention as well as complex soil profiles.) Valdivieso head winemaker Brett Jackson agrees that the area has much potential but warns that development won't be easy.

> *In areas like Casablanca and San Antonio there were at least roads and electricity; in coastal Curicó the limiting factor now is the logistical challenge due to a lack of infrastructure and the shortage of available water. But I feel certain it will happen given time; these are not insurmountable problems and this country is continually developing – just look at the progress it's made in the last decade.*

CASE STUDY: (SLOW) MARCH OF THE CLONES
Chile is a country that prizes its isolation. This is not a case of national aloofness; it is more to do with the fact that agriculture and its associated industries are vital to the country's economy – in 2003, total

exports were worth US$21 billion (£11 billion), out of which 7.9 per cent was fresh fruit, 11.8 per cent was forestry-related products, 5.3 per cent was salmon, and 3.2 per cent was wine. As a result, the country is aggressive in its attempts to keep potential viruses or pests from crossing its borders.

This policy has a direct impact on wine producers, who need plant material to establish new vineyards. Take Miguel Torres, a Spanish-owned winery based in Curicó that has been working on developing plant material since it was established in 1979. It has adopted two different approaches to dealing with this issue.

The first is what might be termed the old-fashioned approach. Realizing the difficulties of bringing in vines as well as the lack of proper work in this regard by the Chilean wine industry, Torres set to work on identifying the best vine selections it could find within Chile and isolating them for development and propagation. They chose six different varieties (Cabernet Sauvignon, Merlot, Sauvignon Blanc, Chardonnay, Riesling, and Gewurztraminer) and identified several supposedly different clones of each. Each plant selection was monitored and vinified separately over three years, and those that performed well were marked and noted. Those with three marks at the end were selected for propagation following in vitro multiplication. The winery now has a fifty-hectare vineyard of vines produced from this programme which it uses for further plantings.

"It's a long and expensive process," comments Torres winemaker Fernando Almeda.

> But if you don't do it yourself, you have to just have faith in the nursery you're buying from, and that's not always justified. Also, it was difficult initially because we didn't know if these were even separate clones we were dealing with. But recently we've been able to use genetic analysis to establish that these are in fact different clones of the same varieties.

The winery's second strategy is one of attrition. "We've been bringing in plants from abroad," explains Almeda.

> Varieties like Tempranillo, Garnacha, Sauvignon Blanc, Albariño. Every

year we send a batch and they go into mandatory quarantine, which lasts
two years. No vegetal material is allowed to have roots or green materi-
als when it arrives, so it's just wood cuttings that are sent. They are kept
in isolation and checked every month. If there's even a hint of something
untoward, the entire batch is burnt. Add to this the fact that the young
vines are struggling to acclimatize after changing hemisphere…we usu-
ally reckon on losing around half of the plants, so we then need to do fur-
ther propagation before planting. It all takes time. In truth, the whole
process is a real carry-on.

One of Chile's major failings is the haphazard quality of its plant material in the vineyard. The country needs to have a regular and certifiable supply of material available for planting in order to raise the overall quality of its vine stock as well as to introduce much-needed diversity. This means producers, nurseries, and institutions adopting both approaches illustrated above and working together for the long-term benefit of the Chilean wine industry. It is a process that is belatedly starting to happen in Chile and one that needs further encouragement. Almeda, for one, remains positive, noting with a wry smile, "Things should get easier in the future."

Noteworthy

Few external wineries have high profiles in Curicó. For those that do have a presence in the region, the fruit is frequently used in inexpensive whites or reds, either to lower costs or, in the case of the reds, to lend freshness and zip to a multi-regional blend.

Curicó used to be the base for Montes before it established itself wholeheartedly in Colchagua. The company retains a 6.5-million-litre winery here and also sources fruit from the area, mainly Sauvignon Blanc and Chardonnay. Errázuriz also maintains a presence in the region in the form of its 151-hectare El Descanso estate, mainly planted to Merlot, Chardonnay, and Sauvignon Blanc. This fruit is used for its basic Merlot as well as wines sold on the domestic market.

What used to be vineyards owned by Canepa – now property of TerraMater and its sister winery Millamán – are located in Sagrada

Familia. TerraMater also sources the Cabernet Sauvignon for its Altum line near Los Niches in eastern Curicó, the old vines in clay soils giving a fresh, tight-knit though linear style of wine. (It also makes some award-winning olive oil on its Peteroa farm.) Another winery sourcing a premium line from Curicó is Botalcura, whose La Porfia Carmenère is sourced in the region.

Chile's big players are also present here. Santa Rita owns 200 hectares of vineyards in Molina toward the mountains, of which 120 hectares are Sauvignon Blanc (used primarily in its 120 line). "It's too cold for reds," comments Carlos Gatica, Santa Rita's Curicó winemaker. Incidentally, Gatica notes that from 2000 the winery has been replacing its Sauvignon Vert with Sauvignon Blanc, meaning that the vineyard is now around eighty per cent Sauvignon Blanc. Concha y Toro has two vineyards in the region, one in Molina and the other near Rauco. Its best results according to winemaker Marcelo Papa are in whites and in particular Sauvignon Blanc, which is used for a small proportion of the Casillero blend. VEO has predominantly white vineyards near Lontué. Santa Helena, through its San Pedro connection, also sources fruit in the region.

Finally, one of Curicó's more eclectic and interesting projects is currently taking place high in its eastern reaches. English winemaker Julian Grubb is working with a local landowner and has planted several hectares of Merlot as a trial at 1,200 metres (3,900 feet) altitude in the middle of 4,000 hectares of pine forest. If the grapes ripen adequately, the plan is to plant Cabernet Franc and even Cabernet Sauvignon or Syrah. "It's a bit isolated so, for now, whites aren't the best option as the facilities are a bit rudimentary," comments Grubb.

Producer profiles

ECHEVERRIA

Av Apoquindo 3500, Of 204, Las Condes, Santiago. Tel: +56 2 2327889. Email: info@echewine.com. Website: www.echewine.com

Established: 1992. Vineyard: 80ha (Cabernet Sauvignon, Sauvignon Blanc, Chardonnay, Merlot, Carmenère, Cabernet Franc). Production: 1 million litres.

Echeverría is very much a traditional style of producer both in its wines and as a company. No fancy external consultants here: this is a winery that is family run from the winemaking through to the commercial side. The wines can be quite reserved in style and in some cases slightly austere, which does not lend them to mass appeal, but in general they work well in a fresh, food-friendly context.

The Echeverría family has owned vineyards on the outskirts of Molina since the early nineties, and started bottling wine in 1992. The eighty-hectare vineyard is mainly planted to Cabernet Sauvignon and the winery also buys fruit from a further sixty hectares in areas such as Maipo and Colchagua, which can provide a riper style of wine from that in the cooler Molina site. This synergy is put to good effect, for example, in the likes of the basic Carmenère, which is an appealing blend of freshness (grilled green pepper and sleek red fruit) from Molina together with the ripe fruit weight and round tannin of Colchagua. Syrah is also sourced from Colchagua and a new Limited Edition line is a blend of fruit from Maipo, Colchagua, and Curicó.

Cabernet Sauvignon is Echeverría's main focus and usually its most successful variety. The Reserva is a well-judged blend of fresh, earthy fruit and oak spice made in an elegant style; the Family Reserve, while it has more oak and concentration, is nonetheless a very similar style of structured, food-friendly, and ageworthy Cabernet. However, the fact that these wines are pure Cabernet Sauvignon sourced entirely from Molina means that they tend to be less successful in cooler vintages, lacking concentration and breadth. (The basic varietal Cabernet also suffers from the same problem.) The wines would surely benefit from an element of blending, however small, to broaden what can otherwise be a somewhat linear, if pleasant, style.

MIGUEL TORRES

Casilla 163, Curicó. Tel: +56 75 564100. Email: mailadmin@migueltorres.cl.
Website: www.migueltorres.cl
Established: 1979. Vineyard: 436ha (Cabernet Sauvignon, Sauvignon Blanc, Chardonnay, Merlot, Gewurztraminer). Production: 3 million litres.

Miguel Torres' Chilean operation is an exemplary winery in many ways, though it is by no means beyond criticism. There exists in its ethos a curious mixture of innovation and tradition that is at once appealing and frustrating; its wines can occasionally seem simultaneously impressive and unapproachable. Despite such apparent paradoxes, one thing is certain – this is a winery that continues to make wines that deserve time and attention. For that alone it is exemplary.

Miguel Torres arrived in Chile in the seventies with a brief to expand the family's wine interests beyond its traditional base in Catalonia. The USA and Argentina had also been considered but, having been introduced to Chile by his university friend Alejandro Parot, Torres took to the country and selected Curicó as the site for the new winery. The first wines were released in 1980. Torres was the first foreign winery to invest in Chile in the modern era and its impact on the local wine scene was considerable, not least for setting an important and much-followed example for temperature-controlled, reductive winemaking using modern presses, stainless-steel tanks, and hygienic cellar conditions.

If the eighties were a time of improvement in the wineries, then the nineties and subsequent years have been the time for improvement and diversification in the vineyard. Torres has been impressively active in this regard. It has been working on clonal selection programmes since the mid-eighties when such practices were virtually unheard of in Chile; it has also pursued a programme of vine material imports – never easy in Chile – that has seen it bring in the likes of Tempranillo, Grenache, Garró, Albariño, and Mencía (*see* Case Study). It has hunted out small parcels of old vines for wines like Cordillera and Manso de Velasco, as well as buying more vineyards in Curicó and Maule. Its most recent, and perhaps most exciting, acquisition was a 369-hectare parcel of land near Empedrado, in coastal Maule.

Empedrado is perhaps the first vineyard in Chile to be planted primarily on the basis of soil type – and probably the first vineyard in Chile to be planted on slate. It took three years of work with a geologist to find the site, which is thirty kilometres (nineteen miles) from the coast in virgin territory for wine-growing, on terraces with a range of exposures. (For a fuller explanation of the importance of slate and schist in winegrowing, *see* Maule, p. 276.) Torres was keen to find such soils because it had been developing vineyards in Priorat, Spain, where similar soils are the key to producing some outstanding wines. The idea in Empedrado, when initial trials are over, will be to end up with around 150 to 180 hectares of mainly reds, including Grenache, Tempranillo, Pinot Noir, and Merlot, which have all shown promising preliminary results. The fruit from here, as well as other vineyards that Torres has been developing in its favoured Curicó and Maule regions, looks set to maintain the winery's ongoing innovation in its wines.

Manso de Velasco is one of Miguel Torres' flagship wines. It is a single-vineyard, solo-varietal Cabernet Sauvignon made from very old vines growing near Lontué ("every one looks like a sculpture" comments Torres winemaker Fernando Almeda). It is a classic style of cooler-climate Chilean Cabernet, showing aromas of earthy cassis, bell pepper, leafy red fruit, and a touch of mint, with a taut, focused palate full of grainy but ripe tannin and a nervy, punchy acidity. It benefits from ageing – tasting in 2005, the 1995 vintage was showing better than the 1998 or 2000, having developed a pleasant tobacco and herby character along with a fused, elegant palate.

However, Manso is certainly not the most accessible of wine styles and in my opinion would benefit from a measure of judicious blending, perhaps with Merlot or Carmenère, to give the wine more breadth and complexity. It is a topic I broached with both Fernando Almeda and Miguel Torres himself. Almeda argues that the wine is unique as it stands and it would be a shame to tinker with it. "There are very few 100-year-old Cabernets in the world," he says. "It's unique and Chilean, so we try to extract all its quality because what we want above all is authenticity. Perhaps it can be rustic or with too much structure, even wild, but that's its style and we want wines with personality." Miguel Torres, meanwhile, clearly has a special affection for Manso and limits himself to saying, "We're in Chile to make Chilean wines."

Cordillera is another highly individual wine, made from dry-farmed, old-vine Carignan from Maule blended with Merlot and Syrah. Again, it is a wine that can be initially off-putting but rewards patience, with aromas of baked red and black fruit, earth, and clove and a warming palate that is grippy, juicy, and slightly leathery with firm tannin and well-integrated acidity. It is untamed but a different expression of Chilean identity from Manso.

The winery's range is generally impressive in its breadth and overall quality. The sparkling wine is fresh and balanced while a more recent innovation is the Late Harvest Riesling, an excellent, botrytis-affected wine with the much-needed fresh acidity to balance the lush apricot flavours. The Santa Digna range offers good-quality commercial wines – two classics of the range are the understated, workmanlike Sauvignon Blanc and a Cabernet rosé that works well but, to my mind, at nine grams per litre residual sugar is a little too sweet. Whites such as the Maquehua Chardonnay and Don Miguel Gewurztraminer/ Riesling could benefit from better integration. The new icon wine Conde de Superunda is a work in progress – its debut 2000 vintage, a blend of Tempranillo, Cabernet Sauvignon, Mourvèdre, and Carmenère, was a self-consciously New World style of wine that lacked structure and balance given its high price. (The blend is evolving; for example the 2001 vintage includes Grenache and Carignan.)

SAN PEDRO

Vitacura 4380, Piso 6, Vitacura, Santiago. Tel: +56 2 4775339. Email: info@sanpedro.cl. Website: www.sanpedro.cl

Established: 1865. Vineyard: 2,500ha (Cabernet Sauvignon, Merlot, Sauvignon Blanc, Chardonnay, Carmenère). Production: 80 million litres. *See also*: Altaïr, Santa Helena, Tabalí.

San Pedro is one of Chile's three largest wine producers, along with Santa Rita and Concha y Toro. Though its development faltered somewhat at the start of the twenty-first century, by 2006 it seemed as if the group was finally putting its house in order and developing a meaningful, positive strategy. In the midst of all these goings-on, the quality of the wines has remained largely unaffected and consistently sound, if somewhat underdeveloped. Credit for San Pedro's consistency should go to talented head winemaker Irene Paiva.

San Pedro was established in the mid-nineteenth century by the

Correa Albano brothers. In 1994, the winery went public and was acquired by Chilean brewing giant CCU, part of the corporate empire of the wealthy Luksic family. A concerted expansion programme saw San Pedro purchase Argentine winery Finca La Celia in 2000 and subsequently form two high-profile joint ventures, Altaïr (in 2001 with Château Dassault, *see* p. 197) and Tabalí (in 2003 with Guillermo Luksic, *see* p. 71). Around the same time, Santa Helena, which San Pedro had owned since 1974, was given a brief to develop independently. The San Pedro Wine Group was born.

Behind the scenes, however, all was not well. San Pedro's brand equity had been damaged by lowering prices to chase volume, despite which the winery was slipping in both export and domestic markets. To cap it all, a falling dollar meant profits were under pressure. Management changes ensued; finances were reviewed and regulated; further management changes took place. In 2005, retail guru Pablo Turner was installed as new general manager, a man with a reputation for a no-nonsense, frugal business approach and an expert eye for brand positioning. Shortly after his appointment, Turner stated his aims with San Pedro in the following terms: to make good wine, have a balanced brand portfolio, and raise prices. He also stressed the need to develop an aggressive approach to international marketing, focus on distribution, build brands in different value sectors, and consolidate to deliver economies of scale.

As a consequence, San Pedro appears to have been given a new lease of life, and it seems certain there are more changes ahead in what will be a critical time for the winery's long-term development. It will be interesting to see how the wine portfolio evolves, though for now the winery continues to offer some excellent value and consistency at the basic levels and sound quality at the middle and top end. It is in this more up-market segment that San Pedro now needs to focus its attention and ambition to make meaningful progress.

It would be good, for example, to see San Pedro looking to diversify and develop its own vineyards in more marginal, exciting winemaking areas in the way it has already done with its joint ventures. It currently owns some 2,500 hectares, half of which is around the winery in

Molina, a further 850 hectares are in Pencahue (Maule), and other major holdings are in Chépica (Colchagua) and Totihue (Cachapoal). While these vineyards deliver basic quality easily enough, real complexity and diversity are harder to find. The inevitable contrast is with the exciting ventures of Tabalí in Limarí's sun-drenched yet temperate climate or Altaïr's steep hillsides in fresh, challenging sub-Andean territory in Alto Cachapoal.

Cabo de Hornos is currently San Pedro's top wine, a single-varietal Cabernet Sauvignon sourced from dry-farmed old vines grown in a ten-hectare plot in Molina. It is a first-rate wine and a fresh, understated style of Cabernet that develops an attractive sweet spice and earthy-fruit character with age. Below this is the 1865 line comprising three varietal red wines, each sourced from a different region, which generally deliver plenty of character (a fresh yet ripe, spicy, ageworthy Carmenère is a highlight, along with an untamed Malbec from Curicó that is full of leathery, inky dark fruit and full-on flavours). At the lower levels (Castillo de Molina, 35 South, Gato) the wines offer consistently good value for money, often with commendable balance and weight, with Syrah standing out as the best-performing variety.

VALDIVIESO

Juan Mitjans 200, Macul, Santiago. Tel: +56 2 3819269. Email: csotomayor@valdiviesovineyard.com. Website: www.valdiviesovineyard.com
Established: 1993. Vineyard: 140ha (Pinot Noir, Chardonnay, Cabernet Sauvignon, Merlot, Syrah). Production: 5 million litres.

If wineries were athletes then Valdivieso would be a sprinter who, having competed in several frenetic 100-metre sprints, decided to retrain as a middle-distance runner. That reconditioning process is continuing – the wines, though generally sound and occasionally very good, are not yet quite fulfilling their intended potential at the top end, despite the company's laudable new aims. My inclination, however, is that, given time and the proper resources, Valdivieso could eventually become one of Chile's more interesting wine producers.

Valdivieso was launched in its modern incarnation in 1993 after the historic Chilean sparkling wine producer Champagne Alberto

Valdivieso (established in 1879 and owned since 1950 by the Mitjans spirits group) decided in the late eighties to start exporting its still wines. Chilean winemaker Luis Simian was hired along with US consultant Paul Hobbs and the winery was given a base near the company's vineyard in Curicó.

From the word go, Valdivieso's new export-focused still wine division was commercially aggressive and dedicated to rapid expansion, riding the wave of the Chilean export boom in the late nineties and almost critically over-reaching itself in the process. In 2003, a change of strategy was implemented, designed to slow volume growth and reposition the winery in a more up-market category. (It is worth noting that, by this time, the group had developed a new still wine operation targeting the volume sectors of the trade – Via – which effectively freed up Valdivieso to focus on a more niche market.)

One of Valdivieso's new releases since this transition is its Single Vineyard range, in which different varieties are sourced from individual sites, such as Cabernet Sauvignon from Maipo, Chardonnay from Casablanca, and Merlot from Curicó. It is a statement of intent from a winery that has traditionally sourced around ninety per cent of its fruit from contract growers and then blended much of it – a policy it has generally managed well over the years. (The other ten per cent comes from 140 hectares planted in Sagrada Familia, mainly Pinot Noir and Chardonnay, whose quality is at best mediocre in this warm area – this plantation was originally conceived for sparkling wine.)

Valdivieso is now looking to control more of its own vineyard as well as diversify its stock. Winemaker Brett Jackson says the company is "actively looking to expand its holdings", with one example being in Sagrada Familia where the vineyard is being enlarged and now includes Cabernets Sauvignon and Franc, Malbec, and Syrah planted on hillsides. Jackson notes that buying fruit from all around the country gives a good insight into which varieties work best where, "so we're now looking for specific sites to develop whites and reds".

Increased control over their own vineyards will inevitably mean improvements for Valdivieso's wines, especially in the mid to upper levels (Reserve, Single Vineyard, and above). For now, the entry-level wines remain sound if unexceptional. The Reserve range offers more concentration and interest, with the whites generally more impressive than the reds – the subtle, peachy Viognier looks promising. The Single Vineyard range needs time to develop as a project because, when I tasted these wines in 2005, they lacked that extra yard of complexity and individuality required of a terroir-specific line like this (although a complex, savoury Chardonnay from coastal Casablanca was a highlight). It is perhaps inevitable that such a project will take time to develop – a fact that Jackson cheerfully admits, describing these wines as "a wonderful learning experience".

At the top end, Caballo Loco is the winery's most renowned product, an eclectic red blend based loosely around Cabernets Sauvignon and Franc, Merlot, Malbec, and Carmenère that also includes other undisclosed ingredients and wine from previous vintages blended back in. A "solera Bordeaux" is how the winery describes it. The wine is a consistently alluring red that successfully blends maturity and freshness with its sweet spices and ripe fruit – it is a crowd pleaser and a somewhat traditional style of Chilean icon wine, but nonetheless one that showcases Valdivieso's knack for blending well. Eclat is a more recent release, a blend of old-vine Carignan from Maule (Linares) with Syrah, Merlot, and Malbec. Although an intriguing concept, the wine's initial release (2002) has tended to show quite funky and unfriendly characters, with the tannin a bit over-charged and the fruit somewhat leathery and soupy. Nevertheless, as with many other Valdivieso wines, it seems that there is good character and potential in there, though time is needed to hone the formula.

9

Maule

BRIEF FACTS

Vineyard: 29,333ha (82% reds)

Varieties (ha): Cabernet Sauvignon (9,139), País (8,427), Merlot (2,829), Sauvignon Blanc (1,494), Carmenère (1,441)

Climate: temperate with warm, dry summers and cool, rainy autumns and winters; annual rainfall 700–950mm (28–37 inches)

Soil: clays, loams, and silts in flat central areas with more varied soils in the west

INTRODUCTION

The political division that is Chilean Region VII – also, confusingly, known as Maule – comprises both the Curicó and Maule winemaking regions. This is the viticultural heartland of the country, containing 48,273 hectares, over forty per cent of the national wine vineyard. The majority of this is found in the Maule winemaking region, which occupies an extensive tract of land in the south of Region VII and is Chile's largest wine region with a total of 29,333 hectares. It continues to grow.

Maule is one of Chile's poorest regions, a determinedly rural area in which the primary source of income is agriculture, chiefly involving wine grapes but also fruit, vegetables, flowers, rice, sugar beet, and forestry. Electricity production is also a significant industry here – the Maule River feeds no less than five hydroelectric plants, including that at the mouth of the massive Colbún reservoir. Maule's main towns are Talca, San Javier, Linares, Cauquenes, and Parral, the latter renowned as the birthplace of poet Pablo Neruda.

Maule is often considered by more Santiago-centric Chileans as remote, parochial, and backward. Its wines are commonly stereotyped as basic and best used for bulk. While there is a certain element of truth in all of this, to view Maule in this way is too simplistic, not to mention increasingly dated. Given Maule's size and history it is inevitable that the quality of its wine is variable but in recent years the region has been undergoing something of a regenerative process, producing better, more consistent and ambitious wines, slowly shedding its traditional image and forging a new name for itself alongside Chile's more acclaimed regions. Maule deserves to be considered in this context and, if current trends continue, will surely be afforded an increasingly prominent role in winemakers' discourse, press coverage, and wine labels in a way that it has not until now.

Two important though quite different initiatives are also helping to raise Maule's profile. The first is the CTVV (Centro Tecnológico de la Vid y el Vino), a research and development unit attached to Talca University that has gradually assumed a role of some importance in Chilean wine, acting as a catalyst for technical advance in a country that has traditionally had little in the way of scientific rigour applied to its vinous development. Examples of CTVV's work are its research and evaluation of vine rootstocks, research into different varieties in different regions, as well as its clonal selection programme designed to identify and propagate useful clones for the industry. It also offers training programmes and acts as a focus for debate. The centre was established in 1996 under the auspices of agronomist Dr Yerko Moreno, who now also acts as a consultant for wineries across the country. The importance of establishments such as this cannot be overstated for Chilean wine: they are essential to its proper development, and the CTVV is doing an excellent job not just for Maule but for the whole country.

Wine tourism is the other progressive development in the region. Many individual wineries have been proactive in this field and the region has formed its own Wine Route, designed to co-ordinate visits to the area and promote the region's wineries (*see* www.valledelmaule for more details). There are now fifteen member wineries, with perhaps the most impressive from a tourism point of view being Gillmore, a veritable treasure trove of visitor delights, including wine-themed luxury guest houses, a wine spa with "vinotherapy", a range of outdoor activities, and an onsite menagerie of animals that range from skittish guanacos to pumas and parrots. Maule is a delightful area of Chile to visit and it is good to see wine as a prominent part of the region's attractions.

A PICTURE OF MAULE

We hear it first from the viticulturist: the Loncomilla Bridge has collapsed. So we take the alternative route, over the rickety one-lane puente mecano replacement bridge some distance upstream. Oblivious to our clanking progress, several families are swimming in the river, their clothes and bicycles strewn across the pebbly shore. The late-afternoon sunlight sparkles on the water.

Gillmore winery has changed in the five years since I last visited. Back then it was called Tabontinaja; I remember being taken to see bee-hives. Now it is clearly a grander operation and after being shown to my room I decide to take a quick dip in the pool. The poolside is made of wood; its latent heat stings the soles. Andrés the winemaker saunters over (beer in hand complementing his laid-back look of shorts, flip-flops, and baggy white vest): we talk about Argentine wine, the weather, beer.

Later, as I make my way over to dinner in the gathering dusk, exotic animal sounds ghost up the forested valley walls. Daniella, an effortlessly congenial hostess, warns me she will burn the chicken. We taste wine and home-brewed beer before another local producer joins us. The rosé is vibrant and moreish, and before we know it we are engaged in a passionate dispute about industry associations and the need for unity in Chilean wine. I admire their fierce independence but cannot bring myself to endorse their refusal to compromise for the greater good. Things get heated, at which point Daniella announces she has burned the chicken. She looks mortified; we all smile. The conversation turns to UFOs and bogeymen; outside, the stars pulse in a crowded night sky.

The next day, Andrés gives me a lift. He points out the local ice-cream factory and Concha y Toro's vineyard on the way to the Loncomilla Bridge, where we wait while the traffic is filtered slowly

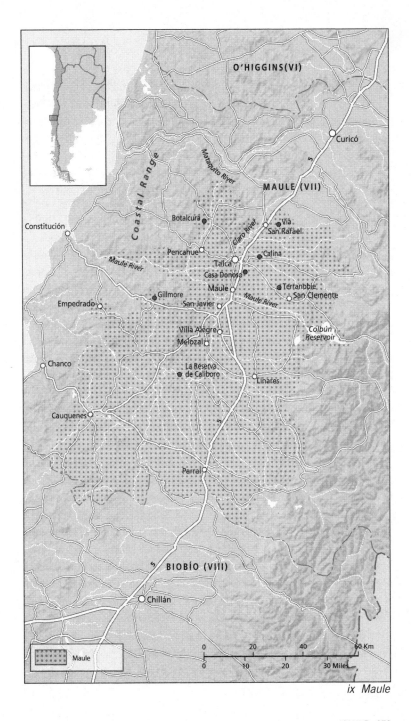

ix Maule

over the one carriageway left standing. Half the bridge is a road that plummets into the murky green water. Heavily laden forestry lorries thunder over the remaining lane, so Andrés winds his window down and intimates to the workman that this is why the bridge collapsed in the first place. Corruption and poor building techniques, he further explains, before turning to me abruptly and grinning in broad, carefree fashion. Eventually it is our turn to move across the bridge, and we do so cautiously, and with a slight longing for the rudimentary but reassuring simplicity of the puente mecano.

THE NATURE OF MAULE

At the heart of Maule is the broad flat expanse of the central depression, which opens out south of Curicó into a wide plain watered by an extensive network of rivers. The principal watercourse is the 240-kilometre (149-mile) Maule River, which flows almost directly east-west down from the Andes via the Colbún reservoir, passing south of San Clemente and north of San Javier before joining with the Claro River near Pencahue and flowing through the coastal range and into the Pacific at Constitución.

Maule is Chile's largest winemaking region and it is separated into three main sub-regions: Claro, Loncomilla, and Tutuvén. Broadly speaking, it is Claro and Loncomilla that are the most significant, the former occupying the northern part of the region and the latter the south, with both stretching between the coastal range and the Andes. Tutuvén occupies the region's southwestern extreme in the eastern lee of the coastal range.

The Claro sub-region extends south from Curicó's southern limit to the Maule River and takes its name from the Claro River, which flows southwest from Curicó. (There is also an area known as Río Claro in Curicó, which tends to confuse the issue.) Claro contains the major wine-growing centres of San Rafael, Talca, San Clemente, and Pencahue. Loncomilla's broad catchment area has its main focal points located in its northern central valley, around Villa Alegre and San Javier, while the south, toward the border with Itata, is less exploited. Tutuvén is centred on the town of Cauquenes and is an oddity in

Chilean viticulture given that its rivers flow west to east, running off the coastal range before turning north to join larger watercourses.

Generally speaking, Maule's climate is one of warm, dry summers that tail off quickly into mild, often rainy autumns come April. During the growing season the area experiences significant day–night temperature fluctuations, up to 20°C (36°F) in some central parts. Rainfall increases toward the west and south, with an overall average of around 700–950mm (twenty-eight to thrity-seven inches) per year, although this can vary significantly between years and sites – Gillmore winemaker Andrés Sánchez puts recent annual highs and lows in his coastal Loncomilla zone as 500 and 1,200mm (twenty to forty-seven inches).

Maule's warmest area is its central strip, in the prime mid-valley as well as in the eastern lee of the coastal range, including areas like Talca, Pencahue, San Javier, Villa Alegre, and Cauquenes. Here, January daytime temperatures average 29–30°C (84–86°F) with nights around 11–13°C (52–55°F). Farther to the east, toward the Andes foothills and around such zones as San Clemente and Linares, summer daytime highs tend to be less extreme (27–29°C/81–84°F) and nights also become cooler (10–12°C/50–54°F). In the west of the region, summer conditions become cooler and more maritime in the coastal ranges and over toward the Pacific, with higher humidity and less day–night differential. This is so far the least developed area of Maule, especially in its most westerly reaches, though the area around Empedrado being developed by Torres is in a zone where January daytime temperatures are 21–24°C (70–75°F), rainfall is 1,000–1,200mm (thirty-nine to forty seven inches), and latent humidity registers around fifty per cent during the growing season.

The typical soil profile in Maule is one of deep, rich alluvium, the result of deposits by the many rivers that cross the central depression. The material is often volcanic in origin – a common component is rhyolite, a rock associated with violent volcanic explosions. (Further reminders of this element of Maule's make-up come in the form of the black sand beaches on the coast and ubiquitous volcanoes on the horizon.) The finest and therefore heaviest clays tend to occur in the central parts of the mid-valley, often with hard pans underlying. It is the west of the region, in the coastal range toward the ocean, where the soils become the most varied and interesting. As well as further volcanic material (basalts and rhyolites) there are granites, which are commonly found in the coastal range, and raised sedimentary marine terraces. In addition to this there is also something very rare in Chilean wine-growing territory, and certainly unheard of in the Central Valley: slate and schist.

Slate and schist are both foliated metamorphic rocks, the latter showing visible mineral content, and prized by viticulturists because they offer many beneficial qualities for the vine, including allowing roots to penetrate easily, fast drainage, and good heat retention. Slate and schist are found in vineyard areas like Priorat in Spain, the Douro in Portugal, and Alsace in France. This particular vein of Carboniferous slate and schist runs up the western side of Chile's coastal range from Chiloé to around Pichilemu in coastal Colchagua, occasionally breaking surface level. This area has yet to be seriously explored for the vine, the one notable exception being Miguel Torres' project near Empedrado. Torres, which has extensive vineyards in Priorat, employed a geologist and viticultural team which spent three years looking for just such a soil in Chile – the first vines were planted in 2003.

VITICULTURE AND WINES
Maule has a large vineyard and a long history, neither of which are talismanic portents of good-quality wine in Chile. However, this is a region that is in the process of reinventing itself in impressive fashion, starting to produce some excellent wines in a range of styles, and it is reasonable to expect better things to come.

In recent years, three distinct winemaking strata have emerged in Maule's vinous landscape. The first, and least regarded, is made up of the region's many smallholders and producers of low-grade grapes, often from the likes of País, a legacy of colonial times that persists with surprising fortitude. The second is that sphere occupied by the better-quality but volume-driven wines sourced from extensive holdings usually by large wineries based outside the region and sold under the

Central Valley appellation. The third is Maule's most recent and encouraging development – a number of producers dedicated to quality and promoting Maule in its own right. Most of these are based in the region but increasingly, producers from outside Maule are also coming here to source top-end wines with a hallmark of origin.

Maule is Chile's largest winemaking region; its 29,333 hectares represent well over a quarter of the national total. Much of this area was added during Chile's planting boom in the late nineties (in 1997, Maule's planted area was 17,534 hectares) primarily to fuel growth of volume wines in a region where land and labour are still cheap, and a flat, expansive central depression enjoys the last reliably warm summer climate before the cool, rainy autumns set in farther south. Many of Chile's major export brands are sourced largely from here.

Red varieties occupy eighty-two per cent of the region's vineyard, with Cabernet Sauvignon the most planted, followed by País, then Merlot, then Carmenère. There is a gradual shift of focus occurring in the vineyard, with earlier-cropping varieties such as Cabernet Franc becoming increasingly popular, especially in the cooler sites, as autumn rains can complicate the maturation of Cabernet Sauvignon and Carmenère. Some producers, such as Calina and Via, are increasingly looking to warmer regions to source the longer-cycle varieties. Blending is then an option that can work well. Maule fruit is also advantageous to growers from outside the region and is often used in pan-regional blends to give a freshness and lift to the wines.

As a general rule, Maule's reds tend to be lighter in body and higher in acidity than the Chilean norm, majoring on fresh red fruits rather than ripe black fruits. Of course, when harvested too early and poorly made the result can be thin, mean wines, but with the necessary experience and hard work, it can also make for complex, ageworthy wines. This has taken time in Maule. Felipe García was until recently winemaker at Calina, a winery that sources fruit from all over the country and as a result gives a good perspective on the relative values of each region. "I'm fanatical about Maule," he says.

We can get excellent pH and also tannin which can make special,

*ageworthy wines. I'm a big fan of freshness and acidity in my wines;
I don't like heavy, tiring ones. My concept of an ideal wine is more
about elegance, and it's for this kind of wine that the rest of Chile is
starting to look to the south.*

While Calina tends to blend its wines from across sites for complexity, a more specialized, individual-terroir focus is in place at Gillmore, a fifty-five-hectare estate in coastal Loncomilla with dry-farmed vines. Winemaker Andrés Sánchez, a former Calina employee himself, shares García's view that Maule's best attributes are its freshness and balance.

*Chilean winemakers often forget acidity in reds; they say that for the
structural backbone, acidity is more important in whites and tannin
in reds. But wine has to have balance in all things and, for me, acidity is crucial to the backbone of good reds. The problem is that it's difficult to get fruit where the acidity is naturally balanced with the
ripeness, but we do here. It sometimes means the wines are more difficult when they're young, but they age well.*

With Maule's evolution just beginning in terms of establishing the best varieties for the individual areas, it is good to see experimentation afoot. In 2004, Carta Vieja planted or grafted Malbec, Riesling, Viognier, Gewurztraminer, Petit Verdot, and Nebbiolo into its various vineyards. Torres has been trying out Syrah, Tempranillo, Grenache, and Carignan in its new vineyard near Empedrado (from initial results it seems Grenache and Merlot work best). La Reserva de Caliboro is currently majoring on Cabernet Sauvignon, Merlot, and Cabernet Franc but is also conducting trials with Petit Verdot, Mourvèdre, Barbera, Montepulciano, Tempranillo, Syrah, and Teroldego. Its owner Francesco Marone Cinzano is optimistic about the potential for development and diversity: "In Maule there's a lot to be discovered; it's a great opportunity for Chilean wine."

Such discoveries include a broadening of Maule's traditional territory, mainly toward the west into cooler, more humid mesoclimates that are challenging winemaking terrain but could give interesting results when well managed and dry farmed. Torres' new vineyard near

Empedrado is the clearest case in point and it seems reasonable to expect others to follow in time. For the moment, however, Torres winemaker Fernando Almeda comments, "Other wineries are watching us to see how we're getting on, making discreet enquiries, but no one's made a move in the area yet. It's all very Chilean!"

In addition to its newer attractions, Maule has a valuable resource in its old vines. The likes of Carignan and Malbec are starting to show startling quality from old vines, many of which have been discovered in small plots growing in intermixed vineyards, which would originally have been harvested and vinified together. Now a reversal of fortunes is taking place and they are rightly becoming the main focus. Maipo-based De Martino sources its impressive Single Vineyard Malbec from eighty-year-old, free-standing, dry-farmed vines in granitic soils in the warm north of the region. Yields are less than one kilo (2.2 pounds) per plant and no acid adjustment is necessary. Odfjell, also a Maipo winery, was so impressed with the quality of the old-vine Carignan it was buying in Maule that it bought the farm. "Carignan from young vines can be green and sharp," explains winemaker Arnaud Hereu. "But with old vineyards in dry, warm conditions with good exposure, low yields, and proper ripening, it can be amazing."

White wine production in Maule has hitherto been significantly less successful than red, largely due to a lack of experience and investment as well as inadequate sites and poor-quality plant material (Sauvignonasse instead of Sauvignon Blanc, for example). For now, the best examples are crisp and simple. There is no reason why this could not change given the right planning and development (apt sites, sound plant material, sensitive winemaking) though much remains to be done on this front.

With the shift in wine tastes generally moving away from overripe, heavy wines, Maule could be well placed to capitalize with its more restrained styles of red.

CASE STUDY: TO WATER OR NOT TO WATER
Symptomatic of the progress that has and is being made in Maule is the increasing sensitivity toward the issue of irrigation. Traditionally in

Maule there have been two major approaches to irrigation: doing it big or not doing it at all (let's call them liberal and conservative, respectively). Both systems are now being refined to suit individual sites.

Cheerful celebrants of water's bounty in Maule, the liberals are content to irrigate often via their traditional flooding or ditch systems. One producer refining this method is Terranoble, a winery located in the east of the region near San Clemente. Soils here are mainly alluvial clays of varying depth and with low organic content. Winemaker Ignacio Conca realized he had an issue to address when his Merlot, harvested in mid-March at an acceptable fouteen per cent alcohol, regularly showed hard tannins and an angular, rustic character with baked fruit and herbaceous aromas. "The problem was simple," says Conca:

The roots were too shallow. The frequent flood irrigation encouraged them to stay high, and as the uppermost soil dries out quickly, the result is the vine does not have enough water to tap while ripening and the berries lose water but gain sugar, meaning alcoholic ripeness is swift but phenological ripeness just doesn't happen.

So we changed. Now we irrigate less often but in bigger doses to encourage the water to penetrate deeper into the soil. We fill narrow channels for eight to ten hours, creating humidity down to 1.2–1.5 metres [four to five feet], and follow this up by ploughing and using cover crops. Just doing this has enabled us to harvest our Merlot one month later (mid April) but with one degree less alcohol and we have a wine with better acidity and mature fruit. Other winemakers say you have to irrigate less for better quality but we are doing double what we did five years ago and the quality is better. Before, we weren't getting the right balance in the wines; now we're focused on getting that balance through the right irrigation practices.

Such a focus, though with a very different method, is also evident in the conservative west of the region. Many vineyards here are in what's known as Chile's *secano costero*, a broad strip of land that hugs Chile's westerly coastal range and in which vines are dry farmed. Although most of these vineyards have traditionally been used for low-grade production, quality producers are now starting to take a risk and abandon the safe, reliable comforts of irrigation in what is undoubtedly a highly positive move for Chilean viticulture.

One modern exponent of this method is the new La Reserva de Caliboro estate, which was planted from 1998 onward in coastal range territory some forty-five kilometres (twenty-eight miles) southwest of San Javier. "We do things differently from the rest of Chile; we are the purists here," affirms joint owner Francesco Marone Cinzano, an Italian count whose winemaking background is in Tuscany.

> Dry farming is a major difference – it means vine growth is more natural, not being prolonged artificially by irrigation, so the vines are very healthy and need fewer treatments to resist pests and diseases. To acclimatize the young vines to dry farming we used micro-aspersion [fine spray] systems to mimic rain, but now the vines are coping well on their own. Yields are necessarily low and we get good natural acidity and balance in the wines.

Speaking with Marone Cinzano, I was reminded of a conversation I'd had with Burgundian producer Louis-Michel Liger-Belair, who had recently toured Chile's wine lands. "Chile irrigates too much," he told me:

> It means they make average or good wine every year, when they could be making better wines with some middling and some great vintages. Vines need to suffer a bit to get the best quality – to make great wines, you have to take a risk.

Noteworthy

At a recent seminar, Maule was described by a senior Chilean winemaker as "Chile's largest wine region but one which has played a minor role in Chilean wine development". This is a questionable statement given that Maule has for some time been supplying significant quantities of fruit for the large-volume players. Perhaps what was meant was that Maule just hasn't been publicly credited as such, and this would indeed be true. However, just as the large producers are now increasingly willing to talk about Maule fruit in their wines, so too Maule is beginning to be championed by producers aiming for more high-quality niche wines.

Among the larger players, San Pedro owns some 850 hectares of vines in the dry-farmed Pencahue area. "It's a very warm spot and can be up to 5–6°C (9–11°F) warmer than our base in Molina," says San Pedro winemaker Irene Paiva. The winery uses the land predominantly for reds such as Syrah, Carmenère, and Cabernet Sauvignon, and not just for lower lines like Gato Negro but also for more prestigious lines such as Castillo de Molina (Cabernet Sauvignon) and 1865 (Carmenère).

Santa Rita and Santa Carolina also source fruit from Maule, as does Concha y Toro, which owns over 1,700 hectares, mainly in Pencahue as well as Villa Alegre and San Clemente. It also sources a considerable amount of fruit from other growers. In fact, Concha y Toro winemakers Marcelo Papa and Max Weinlaub both used to work at Calina so know the area well. The fruit is mainly used for the entry-level Sunrise and Frontera ranges, though Casillero del Diablo uses Cabernet Sauvignon from San Clemente and Syrah from Villa Alegre. Tasting Concha's 2005 vintage samples from around the country in late 2005, it was clear that the Merlot and Cabernet Franc sourced from western Loncomilla showed excellent quality. "We get crisp, fresh, varietal character in the wines as well as a sense of the area," commented Weinlaub.

Those producers sourcing fruit with more of a niche focus in mind are the likes of Odfjell, De Martino, and Valdivieso. In 2004, Odfjell purchased sixty hectares near Cauquenes to ensure its supply of old bush-vine Carignan from a four-hectare plot as well as to plant Syrah, Malbec, Cabernet Sauvignon, and more Carignan. Arnaud Hereu recalls that the first time he vinified Maule Carignan, it raised a few eyebrows. "Our consultant Paul Hobbs questioned the decision but when he tasted the grapes during cold soak he said it was the most beautiful juice he'd tried." A similar opinion emerges from Valdivieso, which sources old bush-vine Carignan from near Linares that is primarily used for its Eclat red blend. "You have to fight your way through the vineyards but the aromatics you get from the fruit at these low yields are incredible," comments winemaker Brett Jackson. De Martino sources old-vine Malbec for its prestigious Single Vineyard line from the north of the region.

Surely the most ambitious development of late in Maule by an external producer, however, has to be that undertaken by Torres in its Empedrado vineyard. Pushing back the boundaries of Maule's western frontier, this is a virgin site hewn out of a pine forest on steep-sloping hillsides and with a relatively cool, humid climate. It is the slate-based soils, however, that are generating the real excitement in Torres' ranks – these are the first vineyards in Chile to have been planted on this type of soil and so may prove a significant evolution in its vinous diversity. Torres and his Chilean winemaker Fernando Almeda hope that the soils' fast drainage, low fertility, good heat retention, and ease of root penetration will give the wines a unique character.

After the 369-hectare plot was purchased in 2002, terraces were installed and initial plantings in 2003 included Syrah, Cabernet Sauvignon, Carmenère, Riesling, Garró, and even some fifteen-year-old Carignan vines that had been uprooted and transplanted from Melozal. According to Almeda, initial results point to Merlot, Tempranillo, Grenache, and Pinot Noir working best here, giving a style of wine that he terms as "like Priorato, but fresher". Further developments are expected as more land is planted on different exposures and the vines gradually adapt to the local conditions.

Producer profiles

BOTALCURA
Fundo el Delirio S/N, Lote 1 – A, Pencahue, Talca. Tel: +56 2 5604978. Email: info@botalcura.cl. Website: www.botalcura.cl
Established: 2001. Vineyard: 0ha. Production: 400,000 litres.
Private investment plus the winemaking talent of Philippe Debrus are what lies at the heart of Botalcura, a small winery located a short distance northwest of Talca, in the warm, dry-farmed lands around Pencahue. The winery's financing came from two shipping magnates,

Jochen Dohle and Juan Fernando Waidele, though Dohle has now left the project. The first vintage was 2002.

Spring-heeled Debrus, a Frenchman but resident in Chile since 1996 and also a partner in Botalcura, previously made wine at Valdivieso, where he gained extensive experience in the concept of sourcing fruit from growers around the country. It is precisely this practice he has instigated at Botalcura, purchasing all fruit used for the wines. However, this arrangement is not always as conventional as it may seem – for example, officially the winery buys grapes from Waidele, but his forty-two-hectare vineyard is adjacent to the winery and to all intents and purposes managed as if it were self-owned. The winery may look to buy land eventually.

El Delirio is the winery's basic range (though pointedly marketed as a "reserve"), La Porfia is a step up ("grand reserve"), and two new lines are expected in the near future, a "super premium" (for 2006) and "icon" (for 2007), in the winery's terminology.

The El Delirio and La Porfia wines tend to be characterful and fairly priced, though they can vary from year to year as fruit origin is switched or fine tuning occurs between vintages. For example, the El Delirio Sauvignon Blanc 2004 is from coastal Casablanca where the 2003 was from Maule, and it is a definite step up in quality with more zip and character all round. A well-judged Chardonnay/Viognier blend is the other highlight of this winery's whites, managing to match broad, exotic flavours with fresh acidity and an appealing balance – Debrus says the secret is to use the Chardonnay for palate freshness (no malo-lactic allowed) with the Viognier barrel fermented for aromatic complexity.

Though they are sold as varietal wines, the winery's reds almost always include small amounts of other varieties blended in for complexity, an excellent strategy in Chile. That said, the El Delirio line can be somewhat commercial in style, lacking freshness and length even though the interesting Syrah/Malbec blend shows promise and the Cabernet Sauvignon benefits from a touch of Cabernet Franc and Carignan. The La Porfia reds, on the other hand, show more concentration and complexity, with highlights including the spicy, juicy

Cabernet Franc grown in Sagrada Familia (Curicó) from eighty- to ninety-year-old dry-farmed vines, and the Maipo-sourced Malbec, a vibrant and perfumed red with plenty of power and fifteen per cent Syrah. The disjointed Curicó Carmenère is the only question mark in the line-up, while the Colchagua Cabernet Sauvignon is made in a pleasant, traditional style of ripe fruit and sweet spice.

CALINA
Fundo el Maitén, Camino Las Rastras km 7, Casilla 482, Talca. Tel: +56 71 263126. Email: info@calina.cl. Website: www.calina.cl
Established: 1993. Vineyard: 60ha (Merlot, Carmenère, Cabernet Sauvignon, Petit Verdot). Production: 450,000 litres.

One of Maule's best producers, Calina was established in 1993 when family-owned US winery Kendall-Jackson decided to diversify into Chile. The project was initially undertaken with purchased fruit vinified in rented winemaking facilities, though in 1999 the winery finally found a home at the ninety-hectare El Maitén estate a short distance east of Talca near the Lircay River. At the same time it bought three other properties, two near Cauquenes and one in Itata. Although El Maitén came with its own established Carmenère and Merlot vineyard and the other properties are now also being developed, Calina has continued its policy of buying fruit from across the country at the same time as developing its own vines. The balance of own and bought fruit is now fifty/fifty.

Calina is a quietly influential winery on the Chilean wine scene. It has been patiently raising the profile of Maule since its inception as well as pioneering other areas such as Limarí, where it started sourcing fine wine as early as 1995, a contract it continues with its Chardonnay from Camarico. In addition, Calina has been a formative influence for several dynamic young Chilean winemakers, including Marcelo Papa (Concha y Toro) and Andrés Sánchez (Gillmore), as well as Felipe García, who left in 2006. Winemaking at Calina has been by overseen Kendall-Jackson's American oenologist Randy Ullom since the start. Three quarters of the winery's US$2.2 million (£1.2 million) annual sales are to the USA.

Fruit is sourced from Limarí, Casablanca, Colchagua, Itata, and Maule, though the latter is assuming increasing prominence in the wines. This is partly because the El Maitén vineyard has developed. Cabernet Sauvignon, Merlot, and Petit Verdot have been added, all carefully chosen clones planted on rootstocks (to minimize vigour in these deep, rich soils), drip irrigation has been installed, and growing experience with the Carmenère (much of which is trained in a Geneva Double Curtain to reduce vigour and improve light exposure) has meant more consistent ripening. García has also been a vocal fan of Maule's more westerly reaches for its "elegance and freshness" – Cauquenes and western Loncomilla are two favourite spots for Merlot and Cabernet Sauvignon. In addition, new plantings of Chardonnay and Pinot Noir are being undertaken in coastal Itata, not far south of Cauquenes in an area called Quirihue.

Calina's wines are generally considered and well integrated; it is clear that the emphasis on retaining freshness of fruit and sensitive blending is helping create wines of increasing intricacy. Bravura is the top wine, a red blend of Cabernet Sauvignon and Merlot that has evolved since being sourced entirely from Itata in 2000 to being a blend of Cauquenes and Loncomilla fruit in 2001 and, in 2003, Colchagua and Loncomilla with a dash of Maule Carmenère to boot. (This change was partly enforced, as Calina used to source fruit from Fundación Chile vineyards in Itata that were later grubbed up when the Celco wood pulp factory was built; see p. 298.) The 2001 is an excellent blend of sleek, firm, fresh fruit and spice. Below this is the Alcance line, a consistently high-quality range that has in the past been a blend of Colchagua and Maule fruit, but the latter now takes precedence as fruit from Calina's own vineyard comes on stream. The Merlot is a particular highlight. The Calina Reserve range is the winery's most commercial offering though still gives good quality from the four varieties (Chardonnay, Merlot, Carmenère, and Cabernet Sauvignon).

CASA DONOSO

Fundo La Oriental S/N, Casilla 864, Talca. Tel: +56 71 341400. Email: info@casadonoso.com. Website: www.casadonoso.com

Established: 1989. Vineyard: 149ha (Cabernet Sauvignon, Carmenère, Merlot, Syrah, Malbec). Production: 1 million litres.

Casa Donoso is not one of Maule's most celebrated names, perhaps a legacy of changes that have been afoot (it used to be called Domaine Oriental), but it is showing signs of ambition and quality in the top-end wines.

The ninety-hectare property and vineyard used to belong to the Donoso family until they were bought in 1989 by a group of Polynesian wine-lovers including luxury hotelier Louis Wane, economy minister Michel Paoletti, and Robert Wan, the largest producer of black pearls in the world. Both the estate house and vineyard have a somewhat timeless feel, indeed some vines in this property are over a century old, so it is then odd to see the modern Scott Henry training system employed in the same vineyards. (This Oregon-developed system is used to decrease vine vigour by using four fruiting canes per plant to create two canopies, one trained up and one down; the result is better ripening and higher yields. It is rarely used in Chile.) The winery also owns an estate called Las Casas in the westerly part of the Loncomilla Valley.

Casa Donoso is trying to pull off a tricky double act by both increasing its volumes significantly at the lower end and at the same time maintaining the quality image of its top-end wines. There is no reason why this won't work, although such a transformation requires a watertight business plan and an obsessive focus on basic wine quality at all levels. While I have yet to try the more commercial wines, the higher-end wines maintain an attractive, amicable style that majors on ripe fruit and plenty of sweet oak spice (which can become somewhat dominant in wines like the Reserva Carmenère). Both the 1810 line and top wine Donoso D, a blend of old-vine Cabernet Sauvignon and Carmenère, are enjoyable examples of this style.

The winery has been proactive on the promotion side, opening up its estate house and pretty gardens to visits, with accommodation now available, as well as a shop and wine spa, which offers bathing in a mixture of water, red wine, milk, and rose petals, and a wine massage that uses grape extracts for exfoliation.

GILLMORE

Casilla 75, San Javier. Tel: +56 73 1975539. Email: daniela@tabonko.cl.
Websites: www.gillmore.cl, www.tabonko.cl
Established: 1990. Vineyard: 54.5ha (Cabernet Franc, Cabernet Sauvignon,
Merlot, Carmenère, Carignan). Production: 100,000 litres.

Gillmore is a rising star in the Chilean wine firmament and deserves to
be better known than it is. The winery's hallmark is ageworthy, serious
red wine made with increasing deftness from a single vineyard set in
the hills of the *secano* (dry-farmed) area of western Loncomilla under
the Hacedor de Mundos and Cobre labels. The wines show an almost
Italianate perfume matched by ripe fruit and crisp underlying acidity.

Owner Francisco Gillmore bought the farm in 1990 and grafted old
País vines to noble stock including Cabernets Sauvignon and Franc.
The first production was in 1993 but for around a decade, though
promising in their natural freshness, the wines lacked the kind of
breadth and depth needed for real balance. A change in circumstances
in 2002 paved the way for progress: Francisco's daughter Daniella took
over the winery in conjunction with her husband, the former Calina
winemaker Andrés Sánchez.

This move seems to have injected the kind of focus and dynamism
needed to make complex wines in what is a challenging area. Much of
this is down to the talents of Sánchez, an up-and-coming oenologist
who has made wine in Italy and Argentina, and also consults for the
likes of Calina, La Reserva de Caliboro, and Santa Carolina. His most
pressing task when assuming control was to coax more complexity into
the wines without losing their characteristic freshness, a feat that he
has clearly managed with the 2003 vintage – a year that marks a water-
shed in Gillmore's evolution as a result. I tried these new-era wines
before release at the winery in early 2005 against earlier versions and
the difference was clear: better fruit definition, more concentration
and character. The red Cobre blend (Cabernets Sauvignon and Franc
with a touch of Carmenère) stood out, showing excellent integration
and plenty of potential for further development.

Around sixty per cent of the fruit from Gillmore's Tabontinaja vineyard is sold to third parties. The majority of the vines are grafts onto old País roots, dry-farmed and wide spaced. Being a relatively cool part of Maule, this area tends to give low pH in the fruit come harvest time – Sánchez puts the figure at 3.3, versus 3.9–4 as a norm in Colchagua. Rainfall is usually around 800mm (thirty-two inches) though according to Sánchez this can vary from 500 to 1,200mm (20–48 inches) in any given year. Sánchez defines his winemaking style as "simple, non-interventionist".

Gillmore has also been proactive in broadening its appeal via its laudable development of wine tourism (*see* Introduction).

LA RESERVA DE CALIBORO (ERASMO)

CP 177, San Javier, Maule. Tel: +56 73 1970400. Email: info@caliboro.com. Website: www.caliboro.com

Established: 1998. Vineyard: 50ha (Cabernet Sauvignon, Merlot, Cabernet Franc). Production: 45,000 litres.

Caliboro is just what Maule needs: a small-scale, foreign-owned wine producer dedicated to terroir-driven wine and prepared to champion the region as a result.

The man behind Caliboro is Francesco Marone Cinzano, an Italian count and vermouth heir whose family has a long winemaking history and owns the renowned Tuscan estate of Col d'Orcia. In the early nineties he was looking to diversify the business outside Italy and visited several countries with his winemaking consultant Maurizio Castelli; on arrival in Chile they rejected better-known regions in favour of western Maule's rolling raised plain. According to Marone, what motivated this choice were factors including the area's high luminosity and dry winds, with just enough rainfall to allow dry farming. ("A typical Mediterranean climate," he notes.) Trying the local wines lent further strength to Castelli's convictions.

Marone took on a majority-holding joint venture with the Manzanos, a local landowning family, who set aside 230 hectares for the wine project.

Planting began in 1998 with French vine clones – sixteen hectares of Cabernet Sauvignon (clones 337, 191, 341), Cabernet Franc (312), and Merlot (181, 347, 343). A further thirty-four hectares were added in 2001, including other varieties such as Mourvèdre, Petit Verdot, Barbera, Montepulciano, Teroldego, Tempranillo, and Syrah. All vines were planted without rootstocks, though in 2002 Marone initiated a comparative trial with the same clones of Merlot and Cabernet Franc planted on rootstocks, the results of which will be apparent from 2007 onward. The policy in the vineyard is of high-density planting (5,000 plants per hectare) and low yields (under one bottle of wine per vine), allowing the plants to find a natural balance. Soils are alluvial terraces with a mixture of clay, loam, and silt.

The first release was a single wine, the 2001 Erasmo, a blend of sixty per cent Cabernet Sauvignon, thirty per cent Merlot, and ten per cent Cabernet Franc. For a debut vintage it shows astounding class, depth, and intensity, with a ripe, steeped fruit and roasted herb character matched by a tight-knit, stylish palate. It somehow manages to reflect the warmth and rusticity of the Maule terroir while retaining a structure and style more readily associated with Europe.

It will be interesting to see how Caliboro progresses with time. Marone certainly believes there is more to come as the vines age and more is learned of the site, and it is a sentiment he also associates with the broader Chilean wine scene. In a conversation in 2005 he told me:

In my view, Chilean wines have not yet shown their full potential in terms of quality. Search for terroirs, use of a greater number of varieties, selection of genetic material, and development in the management of the vineyards are areas with room for improvement.

The eventual aim at Caliboro is to reach a production of 250,000 bottles or over; in 2005 an old winery on site was renovated to cater for this. Apart from its inherent quality, the wine's early success owes much to what Marone terms as "piggy-backing" on established distribution routes for his Italian wines. Neither is he totally alone in his family connections in this part of the world as his sister Noemi owns the Noemía winery in Río Negro (Argentine Patagonia).

TERRANOBLE

Av Andres Bello 2777, Of 901, Santiago. Tel: +56 2 2033628. Email:
terranoble@terranoble.cl. Website: www.terranoble.cl

Established: 1993. Vineyard: 140ha (Cabernet Sauvignon, Merlot, Carmenère,
Sauvignon Blanc, Chardonnay, Syrah, Petit Verdot, Malbec). Production: 1.6
million litres.

In the past, Terranoble has hardly been the most exciting of Maule's
wineries, regularly producing wines of acceptable standard from its
base near San Clemente in Maule's cooler easterly reaches toward the
Andes, but little better. However, it seems to have turned something of
a corner recently and is now setting its standards higher.

Much of this progress is down to a re-evaluation of the vineyard.
When it was planted in 1993, the Maule vineyard included Carmenère
(not pure Merlot as intended), Cabernet Sauvignon, and Sauvignon
Blanc. But being a cooler area of Maule, prone to late-season rains and
cool autumns, it gradually became apparent that this was not the most
propitious site for either Carmenère or Cabernet Sauvignon.
(Winemaker Ignacio Conca notes that Carmenère, for example, ripens
properly one year in two on their estate.)

In 1998, pure Merlot began to replace the Carmenère, though this
merely led to a different set of challenges (*see* Case Study) with a lack
of root development in the vines and underripeness in the wines.
However, this is being addressed with improved irrigation, cover
crops, ploughing, and lower yields (fifty to sixty hectolitres per
hectare), to the extent that Conca is now bullish about initial results.
"It's a bet but I think Merlot will prove our best variety here," he says.
"I'm not looking for an overripe, big wine; I want to make a ripe, juicy,
smooth Merlot with good acidity that tastes of the variety and doesn't
overwhelm the palate."

The search for riper late-season reds took Terranoble to Colchagua,
where in 2002 and 2004 it bought land in two different sites in the
eastern end of the valley near San Fernando. To complement bought-in
fruit, the main focus here has been on Cabernet Sauvignon,
Carmenère, and Syrah. At the same time, the winery began to buy

Carmenère and Syrah from coastal Maipo (Puangue) in what is a warm area but with a long growing season for good retention of acidity. In addition, Chardonnay is now sourced from Casablanca and the winery is looking to buy in this coastal area to plant more Chardonnay and possibly Syrah. Conca is looking to blend the fruit across valleys in some lines, noting that reds from Maule give good freshness, Colchagua fills the mid-palate, and Maipo provides the back palate.

The focus in the Maule estate will now be on Merlot and Sauvignon Blanc. The latter shows good freshness and herbaceous tones but is simple on the palate – Conca is working on harvesting later to develop palate breadth again by working in the vineyard. The Merlot, on the other hand, is looking increasingly interesting – comparing the 2003 against the 2004 was like night and day, the latter showing far more vibrant fruit and appealing balance. This may well prove to be the winery's forte, though I have yet to try the results of the Colchagua and Maipo ventures.

VIA

Av Kennedy 5618, Santiago. Tel: +56 2 2121125. Email: info@viawines.com. Website: www.viawines.com

Established: 1998. Vineyard: 1,500ha (Cabernet Sauvignon, Syrah, Chardonnay, Cabernet Franc, Carmenère). Production: 23 million litres. *See also*: Valdivieso.

Very much a commercially minded, market-orientated producer, Via is a sizeable operation based out of northern Maule (San Rafael) that is a relatively recent arrival on the scene but already creating quite an impact. "We want to be the one-stop shop provider for the world's major clients" is how commercial manager Alex Huber puts it, and the winery has been aggressive in securing major commercial deals as well as expanding its winemaking operations within Chile.

Via was established in 1998 when Valdivieso supremo Jorge Coderch decided to head up another wine project and secured the backing of investors including his brother Juan, US businessman Richard Huber, and television star Mario Kreutzberger, among others. Since then Via has grown and continues to do so at a startling rate, in 2006 crushing thirty-two million kilograms of grapes (around twenty-three million litres), sourcing fruit from 4,000 hectares, and establishing a selection of contracted grape growers (for around sixty per cent of supply). Partner vineyards and owned vineyards now stretch from Limarí to Bío Bío, plus there is also a joint winemaking venture in Brazil.

Via's operations are based out of the scenic 2,500-hectare Chilcas estate in San Rafael, which as well as playing host to the majority of its owned vineyards also harbours substantial quantities of olive trees, corn, and cattle. Via chose Maule as an operations base mainly due to economic reasons – cheaper land and labour – though Huber also professes a desire to "put Maule on the map". The estate was planted in 1998 though changes are now taking place, with for example the emphasis being moved away from Cabernet Sauvignon and onto the likes of Syrah, Cabernet Franc, and Viognier, which have adapted better to the cool autumns and late-season rain in the area. Via also has wineries in Curicó, Colchagua, and Casablanca, where it has major vineyard bases. Former Errázuriz winemaker Ed Flaherty took the reins in 2004 and is now assisted by the likes of viticulturist Yerko Moreno.

The wines tend to be commercial in style and are usually very acceptable as such. The range is broad, including many own-label wines for different countries, though the winery's own brands have been given increasing prominence as the commercial operation has been able to support the investment they need. The well-presented Oveja Negra offers some pleasant drinking, as do the Chilensis Reservas. Organic wines are also now an increasing part of the line-up as part of an initiative whose instigation Huber describes as "to do with our philosophy of being a full-service provider". A significant proportion of production is sold as bulk.

It is refreshing to see a can-do attitude and hearty dose of commercial realism being introduced to Maule. However, Via should be wary of becoming too subservient to the margin-squeezing tendencies of global buyers, a path that can only lead to lower-quality wine being produced at the price. Such a move could potentially damage not only Via but also the entire Chilean category. It would be good to see it building brands at all levels and investing in quality as well as volume.

10

The South

Chile's Southern Region is a transitional zone in many senses. In one respect, it marks the transition between the warm, dry Mediterranean climates of areas to its north and the cooler, rainy conditions of the south. In another, it is a wine region undergoing a period of change, experimentation and vinous renaissance.

ITATA, BIO BIO, AND MALLECO

The three wine regions of Itata, Bío Bío, and Malleco comprise what is officially known in Chilean wine law as the Southern Region (Región del Sur). Though this area is generally cooler and rainier than the regions to the north, its well-defined summers and mild autumns allow grapes to ripen before the autumn rains and winter chills set in. The more marginal nature of these regions does nevertheless mean that vintage variation can be a more significant factor than farther north.

The commercial heartbeat of this area is the coastal city of Concepción and its surrounding ports. This is a massive centre of industry, including fishing, manufacturing, oil refining, and other large-scale business. Elsewhere in the region, forestry is the most noticeable commerce, with thousands of hectares of pine and eucalyptus stands spread over the countryside awaiting processing into wood pulp or timber. (Some of Chile's indigenous forests can also be found here.) Agriculture and livestock are traditional occupations.

It is impossible to speak of these regions in Chile's southern heartlands and not mention its indigenous people, collectively known as the Mapuche. The Mapuche were driven south when the Spanish arrived in the mid-sixteenth century and there ensued a bitter power struggle in which the dogged and resourceful Mapuche more than held their own, the result being that for three centuries the area south of the Bío Bío River remained under Mapuche control. They were finally forced to recognize the Chilean state, in the face of overwhelming firepower, in an 1881 treaty that consigned them to some 500,000 hectares of land – the government, meanwhile, appropriated millions.

Since then the Mapuche's fate has largely been a sorry one, reduced to poverty and protests over land rights in this southern region, to which the Chilean government has made scant concession. It is a social issue that needs to be addressed urgently by Chile's political leaders. The Mapuche culture is an important part of Chile's identity that should be nurtured, not marginalized: its most striking legacy is in the wonderfully evocative names that bring Chile's geography to life, such as Bío Bío, Puyuhuapi, Cachapoal, Lolol. The wine industry may well have a role to play in this process, having already started to embrace Mapuche culture and identity in its wine labels and promotional activity. Perhaps the wine industry can offer the Mapuche an outlet for their frustrated sense of identity and land ownership in southern Chile.

For now, the wine reality of the south remains a curious mix of old-fashioned, congenitally mediocre winemaking (continuing the legacy of the original Spanish settlers) and a handful of dynamic, forward-looking producers. The impetus toward progress has, it is worth noting, largely come from outside the region – Aquitania, the Concha y Toro group, Córpora, and before them Fundación Chile are all examples of wine producers that have put this area firmly on Chile's fine wine map. Some of these laudable initiatives, like similar exciting wine developments across Chile, originally started out life as somewhat happy coincidences, such as planting family farms – the Quitralman and SoldeSol properties are two cases in point – but now a more reasoned, concerted programme of expansion and consolidation is called for.

The administrative region of Biobío, which includes the wine regions of Itata and Bío Bío, contains 13,908 hectares in an almost exactly even split between reds and whites. (This total is around twelve per cent of the national vineyard.) The most planted varieties are País and Moscatel de Alejandría; among the main noble varieties are Cabernet Sauvignon and Chardonnay. Nearly eighty-five per cent of the vineyard is head trained; over ninety per cent is dry farmed; the average vineyard property size is just over two hectares. Malleco has just thirteen hectares of vines.

THE FAR SOUTH

Chile's process of vinous self-discovery is seeing its wine frontiers being extended in all directions of the compass, and south is no exception. Aquitania's SoldeSol has pioneered wines from Malleco, in the Araucanía Region (IX) of Chile, and now it seems there are more developments even farther south. Though the wisdom of moving into Chile's far south is consistently questioned by the majority of its winemakers – who reason that the cold and rain will prevent the grapes reaching proper ripeness – it may well be that there is more to come from the south in specific sites that are warmer and dryer than the rest, making for more restrained and elegant styles of wine. The search goes on, and rightly so.

Meanwhile, evidence of this movement comes in the shape of Viña Momberg, which in 2005 launched its first wines, made from a vineyard in utterly uncharted territory for wine near San Pablo, just north of Osorno. This is the lakes region (X), some 900 kilometres (560 miles) south of Santiago – in other words around 300 kilometres (190 miles) farther south than Traiguén in Malleco and roughly the same latitude as the northern tip of New Zealand's South Island. Though the wine is not yet commercially available, it is a declaration of intent. Currently plantings include Sauvignon Blanc, Sauvignon Gris, Viognier, Chardonnay, Pinot Noir, Merlot, and Zinfandel.

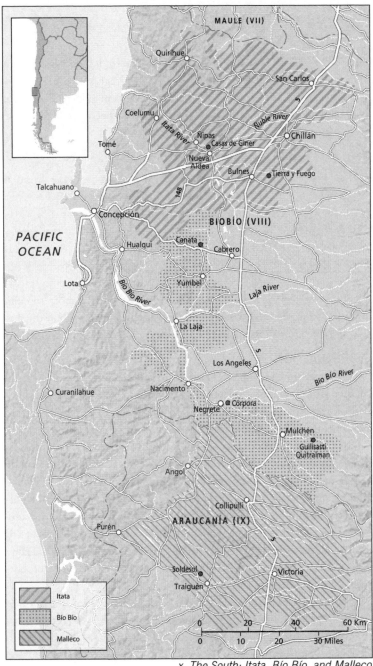

x The South: Itata, Bío Bío, and Malleco

10a

Itata

BRIEF FACTS

Vineyard: 12,036ha (54% whites)

Varieties (ha): Moscatel de Alejandría (5,540), País (4,552), Cabernet Sauvignon (410), Chasselas (374), Chardonnay (199)

Climate: mild temperate with annual rainfall of 1,000–1,200mm (39–47 inches)

Soil: fine-grained alluvial loams, sands, silts, and clay on the flat land with granitic sands on hillsides

INTRODUCTION

That this section on Itata is shorter than Bío Bío and Malleco – far smaller wine regions – reflects the somewhat ramshackle reality of a wine region that desperately needs to break with the past if it is to avoid being left behind by Chile's modern wine juggernaut.

Itata has had its fair share of ups and downs. Nowhere is this captured better than in the story of Fundación Chile in the region. Fundación Chile, a non-profit development agency with public Chilean and private American backing, came to Itata in the mid-eighties with the aim of establishing an ethos of professional modern winegrowing in a region whose wine industry was in a dilapidated state. It did so successfully, even setting up its own well-managed 100-hectare vineyard near Nueva Aldea in the early nineties with a range of varieties. Itata's stock began to rise.

But then a bewildering development took place: Fundación Chile decided to withdraw from the initiative. What was most galling, however, was that the land was not sold to another winery but instead to Celco, a wood-pulp manufacturing firm whose US$1 billion (£500 million) development project on the Itata River has been bitterly opposed from many quarters, not least the local population, with wine-growers prominent among them. They argued that Celco would have a profoundly damaging impact on the local environment and economy, buying up water rights to the detriment of local enterprise and posing a major pollution threat. (Celco's Río Cruces plant near Valdivia was temporarily shut down in 2005 after the black-necked swans in a nearby nature reserve began to die, allegedly as a result of toxic run-off.)

Casas de Giner is the nearest winery to the plant, with vineyards just 500 metres (a third of a mile) away; owner Fernando Giner was furious when I asked him about the sale in late 2005:

> I believe that once the plant starts work, the gases and dioxins emit-
> ted by it will present a clear danger to the quality of our wines. They
> will probably contaminate the plant leaves and may even spoil the
> wines by erasing varietal character with other undesirable aromas.

This event was a body blow for the valuable momentum that had been gathered in building the foundations for Itata's wine future. "It's terrible," another local wine-grower groaned.

> This is a monstrous development. Despite assurances to the contrary, it
> is certain to have some sort of social and environmental impact in what
> is a traditional area of small-scale, artisan production. Fundación
> Chile did a great job in showing the region's wine growers that quality
> viticulture could work here, and now it's all gone. It's a sad paradox.

Forestry and its related industry are big business in this region: the Biobío administrative region (VIII), which includes Itata, contains nearly half of Chile's forestry plantations, of which over eighty per cent are the fast-growing, non-indigenous radiata pine (*Pinus radiata*). The wood is destined for a variety of purposes including pulp, used to manufacture paper, or timber. It is these extensive forestry plantations that are the most common focus of the frequent protests by the indigenous population claiming ancestral land rights.

Fishing, manufacturing (petrochemicals, iron, steel, ships), oil refining, and other industries are concentrated around the coastal city of Concepción and its four major ports. This is Chile's hidden hive of industry. Concepción is the country's third-largest city and it was the first to be founded in southern Chile, in 1550, when it gained its full name of Concepción de María Purísima del Nuevo Extremo (locals refer to themselves as *penquistas* for short, since the original settlement of Concepción was near a place called Penco, although it was later moved in the late eighteenth century due to frequent earthquakes). Tourism is also a significant business in the region, with the skiing resort at Termas de Chillán a major draw. Wine-growers would be well advised to take advantage of this constant flux of people to the region by promoting wine tourism.

A PICTURE OF ITATA

The drive has been long, with dust blowing through the juddering open windows and the holes in the bodywork of the rusty old truck. Though we have talked the whole way, in reality it has been more of a monologue, the product of a careering, prodigious train of thought. My host is larger than life.

As we arrive at the winery, he reveals that there was a wedding there last night. He stayed up carousing with the bride and groom until the early hours yet, though it is still not mid-morning, he bears no visible traces of the previous night. He strides into the winery and I follow.

We are to taste from the barrels, so we need a pipette. Vigorous rummaging ensues. Various staff members are summoned to give their account; none know the whereabouts of the *pipeta*, *señor*. Frustration begins to creep in. It must be here somewhere. But it isn't. A length of garden hose is identified underneath the substantial remnants of the wedding cake, still in its many tiers, in the kitchen sink. This will do. It is extracted and rinsed. I follow him into the barrel room. One end of the hose is inserted into the barrel, the other is raised to the lips. Vigorous sucking ensues.

A short while later we emerge. We both stand, stained, in the warming mid-morning sunlight, as aromas of damp cloth and red wine gently steal off into the clean air and out over the vineyards.

THE NATURE OF ITATA

At the heart of Itata are two major rivers: the Nuble and Itata, both of which flow over long and diffuse courses from the Andes across a wide central depression. They converge near the village of Nueva Aldea, at which point a sparse and low-slung coastal range begins to rise out of the flat land to the west.

Itata shares many climatic characteristics with Bío Bío and Malleco, such as cold winters, warm days, and cool nights during a well-defined summer, rainy late autumns, and substantial precipitation. However, being the most northerly wine-growing area in the Southern Region, Itata generally has slightly more of the summer heat and marginally less of the rain than its counterparts to the south.

The central and northern part of the region is the warmest, with average summer temperatures in January around 27–29°C (81–84°F), with conditions gradually cooling and becoming more humid toward the ocean in the west. The area between Nueva Aldea and Coelemu in the coastal range, for example, has average January temperatures of 24–27°C (75–81°F), and farther west the mean reaches 21–24°C (70–75°F). (This maritime climate in the west of the region is a point of difference with Bío Bío and Malleco, which do not experience a direct coastal influence to the same extent.) Chilly nights (8–12°C/46–54°F) are the norm in all areas during the summer, and this day–night temperature fluctuation becomes increasingly marked away from the ocean, in the central and eastern parts of Itata.

Rainfall is concentrated in the winter months, with summer remaining relatively dry, though precipitation is common in spring and autumn. Annual rainfall comes in at around 1,000–1,200mm (thirty-nine to forty-seven inches) though this can vary between vintages.

Soils are generally fine-grained, water-retentive loams and clays on the flat land, with rockier content near the river courses and finer textured sands, often of granitic origin, on the hillsides. The region seems to be fairly homogeneous in terms of its underlying geology, in a way that many Chilean regions are not, with little diversity beyond an extensive alluvial central depression and a broad, granitic-based coastal range.

VITICULTURE AND WINES

Production in Itata is still dominated by dry-farmed, untrained, high-yielding, non-noble varieties cultivated in a host of small holdings (*see* Case Study). Nevertheless, those few wine-growers who are working well are producing results that are starting to give an idea of the region's strengths and weaknesses.

The best thing to happen to Itata in wine terms was Fundación Chile. Its project was established from scratch and came complete with drip irrigation, a range of modern training techniques such as Lyre for greater sun exposure and ventilation, plant material from France, and several nurseries. The focus in the plantings was on Cabernet Sauvignon and Chardonnay, with small amounts of Merlot, Sauvignon Blanc, Cabernet Franc, Syrah, and Mourvèdre. A decent sweet wine was also made from old-vine Moscatel. The initiative proved that a range of good wine could be made in the right places with the right varieties, sound viticulture, and modern winemaking techniques.

When the majority of these vineyards were then sold to and largely grubbed up by Celco (*see* Introduction), it was a massive setback for the region. However, both local and national winemakers view Fundación Chile's enlightened legacy with positive eyes. Aurelio Montes, for example, praises how "by the time Fundación Chile left, it had made its point that Itata did have the potential to make fine wine". Former Fundación Chile winemaker Carlos Andrade is of a similar opinion: "I believe that the Fundación Chile initiative fundamentally advanced the technological development not just in this area but also those farther south, where today there are wines with established reputations for quality."

It is a legacy with a slow burn. While Itata's wines are still yet to convince on a widespread basis, progress is happening behind the scenes. For example, in 2004 a group of five of the region's more forward-looking wineries (Casas de Giner, Viñedos del Larqui, Valle de Itata, Tierras de Arrau, and Tierra y Fuego) undertook a project in conjunction with the Precision Agriculture Programme (PROGAP) to study the region's vineyards and consequently draw up detailed conclusions regarding Itata's future. Data from aerial vigour mapping as well as subsequent physical and chemical analysis of soils are being used to improve the producers' understanding of and approach to key issues such as microclimates, irrigation, canopy management, yields, harvest times, and both site and varietal selection.

With regard to varieties, Cabernet Sauvignon, Cabernet Franc, and Syrah seem to have good potential in the warmer areas, making mid-weight wines with good balance between fresh acidity and ripe fruit. In this regard, it is interesting to note the comments of Carlos Andrade when he says:

> When we first came to the region, our official climatic information from the state told us this would be a cool-climate area. However, once we had set up there we realized that the summer climate was warmer and dryer than expected so it was better for the reds. It rapidly became clear that Cabernet Sauvignon was working very well and, later, Syrah.

Maule-based Calina has been buying fruit from all over Chile since the mid nineties and has consistently used Itata as a source for its top-line Cabernet Sauvignon. Former winemaker Felipe García explains:

> Cabernet from Itata has better tannins and natural acidity, and therefore balance, than other areas of Chile. They're not big, power-ful wines; instead, they're elegant, with good acidity and firm, chalky tannin, which enables the wines to age well. For example, at harvest in Itata the pH is around 3.5–3.6 – in Colchagua, it's more like 3.8–3.9, and acidification of one gram per litre and over is almost automatic if the wines are to have any kind of shelf life. In Itata, it's a more natural, more European style.

Chardonnay is a work in progress. Its largest plantings are currently centred on Chillán, but its most propitious natural habitat is probably nearer the coast. In this regard, Calina is developing a vineyard in

Quirihue, some twenty kilometres (twelve miles) from the Pacific, for Chardonnay and Pinot Noir. Other reds such as Merlot could be a sound bet here (Casas de Giner has been doing some good work in this regard) as well as Malbec, with good results also notable in the rare instances of old-vine Carignan.

CASE STUDY: THE BURDEN OF HISTORY

History is both Itata's pride and its downfall. Its winemakers will tell you that their region has one of the longest wine-growing traditions in Chile; that this was the original Chilean wine country, favoured by the Spanish long before the advent of the French and the fashion for regions nearer the country's commercial hub around Santiago.

There is truth in all of this. But, when you stop to think about it, the sobering thought is the following. Itata's vineyards have been culti-vated for nearly half a millennium, since the Spanish arrival in the mid-sixteenth century. That's around a century longer than the Médoc. So, by rights, Itata should be producing some of the best wine Chile has to offer, given its long history and ample time to discover the finest terroirs and extract every nuance of subtlety and flavour from them. Sadly, this is not the case.

Five centuries after it was originally planted with indifferent grape varieties in enthusiastic though ill-considered fashion, with the emphasis firmly on quantity over quality, much of Itata has changed very little. The briefest glance at the facts confirms this: the Southern Region, which is dominated by Itata, has a mere fifteen per cent of its vineyard trained to modern systems (the remainder is almost all free standing) and under ten per cent is equipped with irrigation. In addi-tion, what are considered non-noble varieties in Chile (País, Moscatel de Alejandría, Torontel, Chasselas, and others) account for ninety per cent of plantings, and their surface area has in fact remained stable over the last decade. Finally, the average size of vineyard property is just over two hectares, making for a fragmented, torpid producer base.

How has this situation arisen? The reasons are manifold, but among the principal ones are a fundamental lack of investment compounded by the distance from the money centres of Santiago, challenging natural conditions, and a parochial attitude devoid of ambition that seems to be endemic among the majority of the region's producers as well as its wine drinkers.

How can this situation best be resolved? To start with, the basic remedy lies in those fundamental features and values of all good wine enterprises: investment, time, patience, humility, self-criticism, awareness, communication, hard graft, and ambition. A radical overhaul of the region's vineyard is required, with detailed studies establishing the fundamentals for a thorough plan to phase out ill-suited varieties and replace them either with pine trees or noble vine varieties that benefit from proper training, irrigation, plant material, and viticultural management. (This is already starting to happen – *see* Viticulture and Wines.)

In addition, bottled wine must replace the over-reliance on bulk wine. Every successful wine region needs its flag-wavers: Itata desperately needs producers prepared to shout its qualities from the rooftops – and, more importantly, to back this up with the wines to match. The momentum for this may well have to come from non-native producers.

Malleco, Bío Bío, and Maule are all showing how it's done and there is no reason why Itata cannot follow suit. Its producers have a bright future to work toward; they simply need to shrug off their burden of history.

Noteworthy

One long-term backer of Itata is Calina, the Maule-based winery owned by US winemaking firm Kendall-Jackson. Since its inception in 1994, Calina has sourced fruit from Itata, mainly Cabernet Sauvignon and Chardonnay. Now the winery is planting its own Itata vineyard in a 300-hectare property in rolling hills near Quirihue, where former winemaker Felipe García explains that the sandy soils and cool coastal climate are similar to the westerly end of Casablanca. Chardonnay and Pinot Noir are the focus here. "The wines I like to make are fresh, balanced, and more elegant than powerful," explains García, adding,

"These are the kind of wines this area can give, which is why other wineries are now looking to the south of Chile, too."

On a different note, local producer Casanueva has a unique sales pitch: its wines are matured in the Pacific Ocean. The bottles are kept underwater with specially developed seals for at least six months, a process that the winery claims imparts a special flavour to the wines. Customers can then come and dive for their wines.

Producer profiles

CASAS DE GINER

Fundo Cucha-Cucha, km 35 Camino a Confluencia, Portezuelo. Tel: +56 42 351025. Email: informa@casasdeginer.cl. Website: www.casasdeginer.cl
Established: 1983. Vineyard: 250ha (Cabernet Sauvignon, Carmenère, Merlot, Chardonnay, Sauvignon Blanc). Production: 1.8 million litres.

Located not far from the confluence of the Ñuble and Itata rivers in the delightfully named Cucha-Cucha estate, Casas de Giner is a traditional winery attempting the transition to fine winemaking. For example, 130-year-old free-standing País vines are being grafted to noble stock and training is being introduced; old *rauli* beech vats are now used only for the most basic wines, or are being made into furniture. Currently, all the production is sold on the domestic market and only ten per cent is bottled wine.

Merlot and Chardonnay make the best wines. However, more sensitivity is needed in the winemaking if Casas de Giner is to make its transition successfully. Essentially, this means tailoring the processes to get the best out of the fruit from this area, in other words majoring not on power but instead aromatic breadth and a delicate palate presence. It is to be hoped that the new Celco developments do not impede development (*see* Introduction).

TIERRA Y FUEGO

Km 7 Camino a Tres Esquinas, Casilla 70, Bulnes. Tel: +56 42 1971573. Email: tierrayfuego@terra.cl. Website: www.tierrayfuego.cl

Established: 1999. Vineyard: 40ha (Tintoreras, Carmenère, Syrah, Merlot, Cabernet Sauvignon). Production: 120,000 litres.

Tierra y Fuego is owned by four Swiss investors, Karin Lenz, Rudolf Ruesch, Roland Lenz, and Michele Ruefenacht, with the latter running the operation, which is located thirty kilometres (nineteen miles) south of Chillán, just east of Bulnes in Itata's warm central heartland.

A certain cheery mania and fixation with novelty characterizes this winery. Production is sourced from no fewer than fifteen varieties and includes a white Carmenère, port-style sweet wines, grappa, and a medium-sweet Zinfandel/Torontel red–white blend known as La Vida Loca. "Our customers appreciate novelty, as well as a story behind the wines," explains Ruefenacht.

Well-meaning but ultimately uninspiring oddities aside, there are signs that Tierra y Fuego could produce wines of decent quality. Malbec in particular looks to be a potential forte – the company buys from a four-hectare parcel of vines thought to be over a century old, and the style is invitingly fresh and fragrant, though more palate presence is required. A barrel tasting at the winery in 2005 showed the potential of Malbec, Pinot Noir, and Cabernet Sauvignon, though Syrah and Carmenère were disappointing. The best wine is Quarteto, an equal blend of Merlot, Malbec, Cabernet Sauvignon, and Syrah.

10b

Bío Bío

BRIEF FACTS

Vineyard: 1,872ha (81% reds)

Varieties (ha): País (1,144), Pinot Noir (158), Moscatel de Alejandría (143), Cabernet Sauvignon (131), Chardonnay (107)

Climate: mild temperate with annual rainfall of 1,000–1,500mm (39–59 inches).

Soil: clays, silts, and loams in flat areas with gravels and sands near river courses

INTRODUCTION

Bío Bío is a region that does things in twos. Firstly, there is its name, an evocative Mapudungun phrase that either means "big river" or was coined from the term fiu-fiu, an onomatopoeic name for a local bird. Then there are its two major rivers: Laja and Bío Bío. Furthermore, there are its two broad areas of wine-related interest: the first in the south of the region that includes Negrete and Mulchén, the second in the north around Yumbel. Finally, it has two contrasting sides to its vinous character: one, the historic, rustic school of winemaking that caters for the undiscriminating local market, the other an ambitious attempt to establish Bío Bío as a bona fide fine wine region.

Of all Chile's southern winemaking regions, it has been Bío Bío that has caught the attention and imagination of wine watchers. While this may in some small measure be helped by a catchy name, it is in reality more to do with the excellent work of producers such as the Córpora and Concha y Toro groups. As Bío Bío is an extensive region but with only three significant producers, it is worth homing in on their operations in order to set the focus for this chapter.

Córpora – the producer of the Gracia, Porta, Agustinos, and Veranda labels – is located in Negrete, by the banks of the Bío Bío River. Farther upstream toward the Andes is Mulchén, site of the Quitralman property owned by the powerful Guilisasti family, who control Chile's largest producer Concha y Toro and, by extension, its independent subsidiaries of Cono Sur, Emiliana, and others. The only winery based in this region is Canata, which is to be found in the north (both Mulchén and Negrete are in the south) in the beginnings of the coastal range, near a town called Paso Hondo in the Yumbel area.

Plantings in Bío Bío are still dominated by País and Moscatel de Alejandría, mainly the former, which accounts for nearly two-thirds of the vineyard. This is a throw-back to colonial days, when huge swathes of Chile were planted with these two varieties, mostly in the north and south of the country. País is also known as Mission in California, and indeed its original and ostensible role was to make sacramental wine – though its rapid spread was encouraged by the Spanish not simply for pious purposes but also as a means of promoting settled, established communities in order to solidify their conquest. These days, País and Moscatel serve little purpose other than making the most basic of wine, such as *pipeño* and *chicha*, sold in plastic receptacles to locals.

Forestry is a key trade in the region and the majority of its raw material is the fast-growing, non-indigenous radiata pine. Agriculture and livestock (mainly dairy and beef) are also important to the local economy. Hydroelectric power serves sixty per cent of Chile's energy needs and a significant proportion of this is supplied by a series of five plants along the Laja and Bío Bío rivers. However, this issue has been divisive as there was stiff opposition to the construction of these dams, especially Ralco on the upper Bío Bío, by the local indigenous population as well as environmentalists and the tourist industry.

A potential point of confusion to clear up concerns the name Bío Bío and its dual use for political and wine purposes in this part of Chile. Chilean Region VIII, one of the country's thirteen administrative areas, is known as Biobío; within this administrative region are located the smaller wine regions of Bío Bío and Itata.

A PICTURE OF BIO BIO

From the air, Bío Bío seems a considered landscape. Its curves and undulations are gentle; its volcanoes distant, obligingly snow-capped and conical. Even the clouds seem summery and unthreatening as they drift past the windows of the plane. Where farther north the scrub is parched like hyena skin, here all around there is green. The pyrazinic green of the pastureland; the lichen-like grey-green of the eucalyptus stands; the deep green of the pine forest that runs hard to the ocean edge and then pulls up, abruptly, as if in amazement that it has been outdone: the shallow water shines vivid emerald green in the piercing sunlight.

Bío Bío's palette is far from monotone. Grey abounds; the stern lines of industry litter the landscape, grinding wood pulp, milling timber, processing fish, honing metalwork, refining chemicals. Five massive ports huddle around Concepción, and all the time the broad Bío Bío River slips down from the simmering Andes: all along its course there are banks, islands, and beaches of chattering grey pebbles. Its water is a thoughtful navy-grey, oblivious to the gaudy oranges, blues, and yellows of the rowing boats that occasionally crease its surface. Overhead, the southern sky is blue.

Autumn comes, and clouds gather their greyness. The leaves of the Carmenère vines turn first yellow, then amber, then russet, and finally scarlet. Their flames echo the forest fires of the summer that have scoured hills and mountainside. The wheat fields lie golden and shorn. Lactic mists congregate and dissipate. A chestnut mare trudges along the roadside, cart and driver in tow, her destination unknown, leaving a peaceful, colourful world in her wake.

THE NATURE OF BIO BIO

Bío Bío takes its name from the diffuse and languorous river that is Chile's second longest at 380 kilometres (236 miles) and a major topographical presence in the region. It affects both climate and soils in its vicinity, although it should be added that this is a large region and considerable parts of it lie away from the river.

Like Itata and Malleco, Bío Bío has a transitional climate between the dry Mediterranean conditions of central Chile and the rainy, cooler climate of the south. This means that the summers are generally warm and dry, though short in duration and with cool nights, with rains common in both autumn and spring. Frosts are also a risk during spring. Winds are relatively frequent in the growing season and the area benefits from long daylight hours owing to its southerly latitude.

The coastal influence is minimal in any of Bío Bío's wine areas due to their location in the central depression and the presence of the Nahuelbuta coastal range, which restricts the ocean's cold and humid intrusion. As a result the climate is predominantly continental in character, with warm days and cold nights in summer; this thermal fluctuation increases toward the Andes in the east. Mean January temperatures vary between 24 and 29°C (75–84°F) in the daytime and 8 to 11°C (46–52°F) at night. The warmest areas tend to be those in the middle and northern tract of the central depression; the temperatures drop somewhat in the far south and the west. Rainfall also increases toward the south.

As regards soils, close to the Bío Bío and other rivers on floodplains or terraces there are significant areas of alluvium, characterized by gravel and sandy soils with some loam. Away from the rivers, the soils tend to be heavy red clay, with loam in places and weathered granite in the coastal range.

VITICULTURE AND WINES

Winemaking in Bío Bío is not for the faint-hearted. The region makes many demands of its serious vinous practitioners, in a way that Chilean winemakers have not traditionally been tested. Nevertheless, it looks probable that, in time, it will also bestow commensurate rewards on those who have taken it seriously.

In a climate that can be relatively cool and rainy, especially in the autumn, it is imperative to practise scrupulous viticulture. This means selecting the right varieties and training systems for each site, maintaining fastidiously low yields, de-leafing, sulphur spraying, adequate pruning, and reacting quickly and decisively to challenges such as frosts and rains. Nematode infestations can be a problem in the sandy riverside soils. Judging harvest times well to get the best out of the grapes is critical. It is an investment of time, energy, patience, and money. As Canata's Salvador Domenech comments wistfully, "This is a region that makes us work hard."

"Our biggest challenge", Domenech adds, "is achieving full ripeness before the rains come at the end of April." Bío Bío's winemakers do not have particularly fond memories of 2004, for example, a vintage in which it rained in March and then steadily throughout April. This can be particularly problematic for the producers that then have to truck the fruit some distance by road before it can be vinified, compounding the risk of rot spoilage. Córpora vineyard manager Carlos Carrasco is keen to play down the effect of this, though:

> It's not too bad here when it rains because our soils, especially near the river, are free-draining sands and gravels. Plus, we usually have winds and it's not too warm in the autumn, both factors that reduce the risk of fungal spread. In 2004 we just had to harvest between the rains.

Winemaker T J Evans adds, "Rains are a real problem if you're not prepared for them; in the south, we expect them."

By contrast, 2005 in both Bío Bío and Malleco saw an almost total absence of rains at harvest and was consequently touted as one of the best vintages of recent times in southern Chile. (In Negrete, only 600mm (twenty-four inches) of rain were recorded during the year measured from harvest to harvest, when the average is 900–1,100mm (thrity-five to forty-three inches).) It has been said in the past of Chile that it has very little vintage variation; however, as the country's wine-makers move increasingly into more promising marginal terroirs such as Bío Bío, vintage differences will become increasingly apparent.

Bío Bío's best white wines tend to major less on aromatic power and more on a soft yet beguilingly structured and generous palate. Córpora's best Santa Ana Chardonnay is a good example (both Gracia and Porta have it as their top labels), a gentle, enveloping, and food-friendly style. Cono Sur's Riesling and Gewurztraminer are two further instances of characterful but ultimately restrained aromatics and dense, thrilling palates.

Winemakers constantly refer to the "minerality" of these whites; take Gracia winemaker T J Evans, who describes his Reserva Lo Mejor Chardonnay as "like picking up one of the stones from the vineyard and sucking on it". Major attributes of the better wines I have tasted from the area are firm structure, palate density, and subtle flavours. One option to improve the aromatics in some wines is to blend more aromatic fruit from elsewhere to complement Bío Bío's palate structure. This is what Cono Sur does with its Gewurztraminer; Evans is also contemplating blending a small amount of Viognier or Chardonnay from Totihue to lift the aromatics of his Bío Bío Chardonnay.

The worthwhile reds, on the other hand, show a notable freshness and vibrancy of fruit character; Merlot, for example, is showing some good, bright-fruit potential. One version is made by Córpora, and T J Evans notes:

> We're on the limit for ripening Merlot here. We usually look to harvest it in late April or early May, so if it rains in April then it won't be great. It depends on the season and the block. But when it doesn't rain, it's very good.

Part of Merlot's problem in Chile has been its tendency to dehydrate; Carlos Carrasco suggests that the lower temperatures and higher humidity in Bío Bío, with greater availability of moisture in the sub-soil during the growing season, might counteract this.

Malbec also looks to have a future in the perfumed, fresh-fruit style. Syrah, though yet to be planted in any serious quantities, is playing on winemakers' minds. "I'd really like to plant a few hectares of Syrah," ventures Evans. "It would be a gamble, but it might work with a north-facing site on well-drained soil. Site selection is critical in Bío Bío." Pinot Noir needs more work and, while there is some promising delicacy already evident in the wines, they need more complexity, breadth, and balance all round. This can be improved by work in the vineyard, especially that involving proper site selection and diversity of clonal material. Exactly this kind of work is being conducted at Córpora, and is already producing wines of better weight and balance.

CASE STUDY: OUT WITH THE OLD

A detailed consideration of Bío Bío's vineyard statistics can be a useful exercise in getting to know this region. The first, fairly clear feature of note is the still-dominant though steadily declining presence of País and Moscatel de Alejandría, which point to Bío Bío's past. (Sauvignon Vert would also come into this category; it still outhectares Sauvignon Blanc, although it too is being reduced or replanted.)

Then we come onto the more contemporary horizon, and this is where it gets interesting. Pinot Noir is ahead of the pack in vineyard area, concentrated almost exclusively in Negrete and Mulchén. While these relatively cool, continental-climate areas might seem to offer a promising niche for Pinot, many of the original plantings have been with rather uninspiring Chilean clones, some of which originated in sparkling wine production. This is now changing as Córpora and Concha are introducing superior clonal material, and allocating considerable time and effort to coaxing better quality out of this fickle variety.

Furthermore, there is the curious prominence of both Cabernet Sauvignon and Carmenère, late-ripening varieties that seem out of place in this region of cool and rainy autumns. On closer inspection, it becomes clear that almost all of these plantings occur around Yumbel and in fact belong to the Canata winery, which when I visited in 2005 was busy re-grafting its Cabernet to Pinot Noir and Merlot. The team at Canata were admirably frank in conceding that when they had originally planted, they were being guided by the market rather than local conditions. "We've got to know the land a bit better now," they dutifully informed me, "and so we're undergoing a period of re-adjustment."

It is also instructive to look at which varieties do not yet feature but which could well prosper given the climate and soils. Cabernet Franc, Syrah, and Pinot Gris have yet to appear on the scene but would seem to be sound options. Riesling has performed well and surely deserves more of a run – it is intensely disappointing to hear, as I have, producers bemoaning Riesling's poor reputation worldwide as a reason not to plant, when it clearly has such excellent potential here.

Understanding terroir, especially that of Chile's southern wine lands, is a learning process that can be successful only if producers are prepared to take the failures along with the successes and to learn from both. It is a process that takes time, patience, and investment. Bío Bío is only just embarking on that journey, but it already has many positives to work with and should take heart that the reward at the end is a vinous identity, and a consequent place in the market, that no one or nowhere can replicate. As Córpora winemaker T J Evans says, "Chile's winemaking history is in the hot Central Valley; its future is in the more marginal, cooler sites such as Bío Bío."

Noteworthy

CORPORA

Vines: 240ha (mainly Chardonnay, Pinot Noir, Sauvignon Blanc, with Merlot, Malbec, Gewurztraminer). Farm manager: Carlos Carrasco. *See*: Córpora (Cachapoal).

Córpora is multifaceted in wine terms, producing wine under four labels (Gracia, Porta, Agustinos, and Veranda) from vineyards across Chile (Aconcagua, Casablanca, Maipo, Cachapoal, and Bío Bío). However, it seems that Bío Bío has become a favourite focus for the group and its dynamic young winemaking team. Considerable investment is being committed to the company's vineyard holdings near the town of Negrete and the company aims to arrive at its final total of 370 hectares of vineyards producing around four million kilograms (four thousand tonnes) of fruit by 2008, with the focus on Chardonnay, Sauvignon Blanc, and Pinot Noir.

The first vines were planted in 1993, in the predominantly sandy loams and gravelly sub-soil of the Santa Ana estate on the banks of the Bío Bío River. Varieties included Chardonnay, Pinot Noir, Sauvignon Blanc, Gewurztraminer, Merlot, and Malbec, though this combination is now being fine tuned. For example, Pinot Noir planted in low-lying, frost-, and nematode-affected sandy soils has been grubbed up or grafted to Sauvignon Blanc. In addition, planting has begun at the brand new Miraflores estate, little more than rolling, golden wheat fields when I visited in 2005, but now being transformed with plans for

240 hectares of predominantly Chardonnay, Sauvignon Blanc, and Pinot Noir, with some Merlot and Malbec. Soils here are mainly clay-based, though small areas on the hilltops have a high rock content and good drainage: there are high hopes for these sites.

Much time and effort have been invested in detailed studies of the land and vines. Soil structure and water retention capacity have been precisely mapped. Infra-red aerial surveys have been carried out to measure vine vigour; rootstock trials are underway; choice of new clones has been detailed and varied. There is also an extensive plant nursery with nearly one million vines, which supplies all of Córpora's planting needs across the country.

The project is undoubtedly ambitious and deserves praise for it. As regards the wines, there are signs that the hard work is paying off but it is clear there is still more to be done and the focus on quality needs to be maintained. An on-site winery would benefit this drive greatly, and plans are afoot in this regard, with a possible start date of 2007 – currently the grapes have to be trucked some seven hours north to Totihue for vinification.

The Pinot Noir needs more complexity and staying power if its deliberately delicate style is to be a success, though a tasting of some newly established clones in 2005 was impressive, and vine age will also help in this regard. Sauvignon Blanc also needs more character; again, growing clonal diversity and a range of sites for blending will help here. Chardonnay is looking promising (the best styles from Santa Ana are engagingly subtle, elegantly structured, and long), as indeed are Merlot and Malbec which, when properly ripened and blended, show a scented, sleek fruit style packed with fresh berries and dark chocolate.

Providing they stick with it, Córpora's four young winemakers and vineyard manager Carlos Carrasco should grow in experience and benefit the wines accordingly. One final suggestion would be to cut the eucalyptus trees down, as they do tend to influence the character of the reds, sometimes overpoweringly so.

QUITRALMAN (GUILISASTI)

Vines: 150ha (Sauvignon Blanc, Pinot Noir, Riesling, Chardonnay, Gewurztraminer). Farm manager: Marcelo Yañez. *See*: Concha y Toro, Cono Sur.

The Guilisasti family are the controlling shareholders and management of Chile's largest winery Concha y Toro, as well as its independent subsidiaries Cono Sur, Viñedos Emiliana, and others. This farm belongs to the family and, though traditionally an apple farm, it was planted with grapes in the eighties, many of which were high-yielding Riesling vines destined for sparkling wine.

The property is located near the town of Mulchén and sits with a view over the Bío Bío River and distant volcanoes. The vineyard is arranged on two levels: the higher one with red clay soils and planted mainly to Riesling and Sauvignon Blanc, the lower part with sandy soils near the river hosting mainly Chardonnay, Gewurztraminer, and Pinot Noir.

Much of the credit for discovering this property's potential for fine wine should go to Adolfo Hurtado, Cono Sur's ambitious winemaker, who has found considerable success with Riesling and Gewurztraminer. The first fine table wine made from the property was Cono Sur's varietal Gewurztraminer, as early on as 1996; it was followed by the Visión Riesling 2002, made from the 1986 vines with yields lowered from the previous eleven to twelve tonnes per hectare to six. Both Hurtado and Concha y Toro winemaker Marcelo Papa are firm believers in the potential of Riesling here.

Though Cono Sur at present takes the lion's share of the Mulchén grapes, other wineries are starting to make wines from this property's fruit, including Concha y Toro, Emiliana, and Baron Philippe de Rothschild Maipo Chile. For now it is Riesling and Gewurztraminer that have performed the best, though it will be interesting to monitor progress with other grapes such as Pinot Noir, Chardonnay, and clonal selections of Sauvignon Blanc (planted from 2002 to start replacing Sauvignon Vert).

Producer profile

CANATA

Hernando de Santillán 153, Lomas de San Andrés, Concepción. Tel: +56 41
912170. Email: canata@canata.cl. Website: www.vinoscanata.cl
Established: 1996. Vineyard: 270ha (Cabernet Sauvignon, Carmenère, Sauvignon
Blanc, Merlot, Chardonnay). Production: 1.7 million litres.

Canata is a winery finding its feet. It was set up in 1996 by Esteban
Canata, a Concepción-based businessman who had made his money in
the fishing and construction industries. The land was bought between
1993 and 1996 and the majority of the planting took place between
1997 and 1999 in three estates (Santa Carla, Huinganal, Quinel), with
the operation based around the town of Paso Hondo in the northern
area of Bío Bío.

However, much of the winery's early plans have been subject to re-
assessment under the guidance of viticultural consultant Yerko
Moreno, and until recently former winemaker Eugenia Díaz. The
extensive plantings of Cabernet and Carmenère are slowly being converted to more suitable varieties like Merlot and Pinot Noir. The winery is sticking with its Sauvignonasse but also planting selected clones
of Sauvignon Blanc, some of which are being grafted onto Cinsault
vines originally intended for rosé production.

Moreno has soundly advised experimentation as a means of discovering which varieties will work best here, in a region where fine wine
production is still something of a novelty. As a result, Canata now has
a wide range of varieties planted. Díaz, who left in 2006, stated that her
aim with Canata was "to develop a style of wine unique to Bío Bío".
Her enthusiasm even extended to Carmenère although, like Cabernet,
it can struggle to reach full ripeness.

Canata needs time before it can become a serious player in Bío Bío.
For now, Chardonnay, Merlot, and Malbec are performing moderately
well in its Paso Hondo and Hacienda del Rey brands. Half of the wine
is sold as bulk on the national market.

10c

Malleco

BRIEF FACTS
Vineyard: 13ha (60% reds)
Varieties (ha): Chardonnay (5), Pinot Noir (8)
Climate: mild temperate with annual rainfall of 1,100–2,000mm (43–79 inches)
Soils: red clay and decomposed granite

INTRODUCTION

Malleco is a province within a larger Chilean region whose very name is enlightening. This is Araucanía (IX), a land closely associated with the araucanos, the Spanish name for the indigenous Mapuche people, as well as the giant, ancient araucarias, or monkey puzzle trees (*Araucaria araucana*).

Araucanía has long been a landscape of dense and diverse vegetal life, with ample rain and rich soils creating a perfect environment for all kinds of flora to thrive, including temperate forest. The majestic araucarias are just one species to prosper; they are also called pehuén and their edible pine nuts are a traditional staple for the local Penhuenche tribe. Coigüe, raulí, and tepa trees also flourish. Non-indigenous imports include the pine and eucalyptus trees, designed to serve the increasingly important forestry industry.

Despite this vegetal diversity, the vine is a stranger to these lands. Like the pine trees, horses, and Spanish conquistadors, it is a non-native interloper – and with all these things there has been indigenous resistance to their spread. The responsibility for this lies primarily with the belligerent Mapuche, who in successfully resisting incursions into their land for three centuries also barred the way to vineyard development. (Vineyards were considered prime targets for destruction by the Mapuche, along with other foreign agriculture, as it encouraged permanent settlement on their land.)

By the time the Mapuche were finally brought into the Chilean national fold in the 1880s and their land summarily redistributed, vineyard expansion was not so much on people's minds as more immediately profitable industry such as mining and non-wine-related agriculture like barley and wheat (Malleco later became known as "Chile's granary" at a time when Chile was exporting wheat to the USA and Australia). For a long time this was still considered an underdeveloped hinterland with an unwelcoming population and far from the commercial hubs of Santiago and Valparaíso (it still is, to a certain extent). Though the forestry and fishing industries have developed significantly, it was not until the twenty-first century that wine would make its presence felt in Araucanía, when the first vintages of a new vineyard began to make headlines.

"We had no experience of wine-growing in the region. No one had, because no vines had ever been grown there before. This was virgin land." These are the words of Paul Pontallier, head winemaker at Château Margaux in Bordeaux and partner in Aquitania, the Maipo-based winery that makes SoldeSol Chardonnay, Araucanía's first wine. The first commercial vintage was 2000, the vines having been planted in 1995.

To date, SoldeSol constitutes Malleco's only fine wine project, so any discussion of the region in wine terms must focus exclusively on this vineyard and producer. The vineyard is located in Traiguén, a designated wine area within Malleco that was incorporated into Chilean wine legislation in 1998 specifically to include this one property. As French winemaker and Aquitania partner Bruno Prats comments, with an implicit reference to the notorious strictness of the Gallic wine laws, "It shows the flexibility of the Chilean wine system – they created an appellation just for us!"

A PICTURE OF MALLECO

Under the volcanoes, beside the snow-capped mountains, among the huge lakes, the fragrant, the silent, the tangled Chilean forest...My feet sink down into the dead leaves, a fragile twig crackles, the giant rauli trees rise in all their bristling height, a bird from the cold jungle passes over, flaps its wings, and stops in the sunless branches. And then, from its hideaway, it sings like an oboe...The wild scent of the laurel, the dark scent of the boldo herb, enter my nostrils and flood my whole being...The cypress of the Guaitecas blocks my way...This is a vertical world: a nation of birds, a plenitude of leaves...

Anyone who hasn't been in the Chilean forest doesn't know this planet.

I have come out of that landscape, that mud, that silence, to roam, to go singing through the world.

Pablo Neruda, *Memoirs*, trans. Hardie St Martin, Souvenir Press, London, 2004

THE NATURE OF MALLECO

It is a commonly held belief that Malleco is little more than cold and rainy, but this is a misleading and simplistic conviction. Malleco's climate, like Bío Bío's, is in fact a transitional one between Chile's warm, dry Mediterranean centre and its cool, rainy south. This makes for a complex climatic make-up that can vary markedly from year to year and from area to area.

The land around the town of Traiguén, the region's only wine centre, is gently undulating, set in the beginnings of the Nahuelbuta coastal range and at the western edge of the broad, flat central depression that is curtailed in the east by the Andes, which at this latitude are relatively low but contain many active volcanoes.

It is true that Malleco receives more annual precipitation than most other wine-growing regions of Chile: contrast Limarí's 100mm (four inches) with Traiguén's 1,500mm (fifty-nine inches). However, much of this falls during the winter months, and even this far south there is a clearly defined dry summer period of around two to three months (December to February). Figures from Aquitania show that precipitation during the all-important growing season is around 350mm (fourteen inches), of which around half comes during the autumn months of March and April. In fact, Felipe de Solminihac makes the point that one challenge he faces during the summer is a shortage of irrigation water.

As regards temperature, while Malleco can certainly be cold, especially during the winter, it is relatively warm in summer, and Traiguén is among the warmest spots in the region. The picture that emerges from the figures and winemakers' comments is of a fluctuating, continental-style temperature chart, with summer averages notably moderate or even balmy in the daytime (24–27°C/75–81°F) but matched by cool nights (9–10°C/48–50°F). Some sources record summer nighttime absolute lows as cold as 2°C (36°F), and summer daytime highs as over 40°C (104°F) (a record for the area, registered in 2005). In the autumn, during March and April, when the fruit is at its most critical maturation period, temperatures rarely exceed 18–20°C (64–68°F) in the day and 8°C (46°F) at night, according to de Solminihac.

De Solminihac compares the growing-season climate of Traiguén in broad terms to that of Marlborough, Geisenheim, or Beaune. (It was a trip to New Zealand that convinced him to plant at this southerly latitude in the first place.) Statistics compiled by Aquitania in this regard indicate that Traiguén is warmer than all of these areas (marginally so in the case of Beaune; more significantly in the case of Marlborough and, especially, Geisenheim) and with less rainfall. Aquitania partner and Château Margaux winemaker Paul Pontallier explicitly compares Traiguén's climate with that of Burgundy, contrasting it with the more maritime-affected nature of Casablanca.

Further climatic aspects of note are the frequent winds in the area, often southerly, which help to moderate high summer daytime temperatures as well as dry the vines after rains. Winds from the north, meanwhile, herald rain. The Nahuelbuta range tends to restrain the cool coastal influence.

With regard to soils, a combination of tectonic, volcanic, glacial, and river activity has left an undulating landscape in the central depression characterized by red clay soils underlain by coarse granitic rock that varies between 1 and 1.5 metres (three to five feet) in depth and can extrude on the surface in weathered form. The soil is fertile and rich in organic material, with a pH of around 5.8 and high humidity retention.

VITICULTURE AND WINES

Considering that both de Solminihac and Pontallier liken Traiguén's climate to Burgundy, it comes as no surprise to learn that the two varieties currently planted in the SoldeSol vineyard are Chardonnay and Pinot Noir. However, de Solminihac has also expressed an interest in growing varieties like Gewurztraminer, Riesling, and Sauvignon Blanc here. It seems that the region's identity is not yet firmly defined, which can only be logical given its vinous infancy.

Nevertheless, for now it is Chardonnay that has the hegemony on the region's wines. The feature of this wine that de Solminihac constantly returns to is its acidity. "We get fantastic natural acidity here," he says, specifying that at harvest, the Chardonnay fruit has around 9 g/l of tartaric acid. He compares this with 6.9 g/l in Casablanca, where he maintains that warmer summers and autumns burn off the malic acid. The pH in the final wine is usually around 3.2 – strikingly low for a Chilean wine.

At the end of March I have a good concentration of sugar, enough to harvest, but I wait an extra month to lower the acid and harvest at the end of April. The acidity is still strong, but it declines during the primary fermentation and then I do a certain amount of malolactic fermentation to soften the edges and make it more approachable. How much malolactic? It depends on what I like, to be honest.

(It is interesting to note that in 2000, two-thirds of the wine underwent malolactic whereas by 2004 that total was down to thirty per cent, reflecting a desire to retain much of that striking natural acidity and reduce the lactic tones.)

While acidification is often the norm in Chile and when well handled can be fine, de Solminihac emphasizes that these wines' natural acidity means they are better equipped to age than acidified wines. Pontallier adds, "We can get the freshness in the wines without the harshness of tartaric acid additions that you often find in Chardonnay from warmer parts."

But is this spotlight on natural acidity simply another way of saying that the grapes aren't properly ripe at harvest time? De Solminihac disagrees, pointing to his delayed harvest time and long growing season as more than enough to ensure proper maturation while retaining high natural acidity. He also affirms that high luminosity in the area aids ripening, a product of a clean atmosphere and depleted ozone layer as well as long daylight hours at this latitude, which means that photosynthesis can carry on until as late as 10pm in the summer. In addition, he argues that increasing vine age – the first Chardonnay vines were planted in 1995 – means that his plants are slowly adapting to the vagaries of the climate.

While summers can be warm in Traiguén, de Solminihac points out that veraison takes place only after the hottest period of January-February, and as a result fragile aromas that might risk being burned off in warmer regions are retained during the cooler maturation period of March and April. This fact also enables liberal de-leafing, as sunburn due to excess heat is less of a worry. De-leafing is necessary, along with a regime of low yields (no more than six tons per hectare, usually around five), and sulphur spraying to counteract any potentially negative effects of autumn rains. Southerly winds help dry out the fruit, and this ventilation is also encouraged by the low planting density (2,666 plants per hectare – not a deliberate ploy as the "pilot" vines were originally tended by farm machinery used for wheat). Nonetheless, botrytis is still a constant threat – de Solminihac notes some of this character in the rain-affected 2000 vintage, and is wary of planting Sauvignon Blanc as a result.

Vigour is also moderated by controlled irrigation during the growing season. As described above, irrigation is necessary in this otherwise rainy area because the majority of the rain falls in winter and summers, though brief, are usually warm and dry. The vineyard has a small rain-fed reservoir, though if winters are dry and evaporation high, this supply can run scarce. As a result, de Solminihac is planning to install a new water system from the nearby Traiguén River to supply his needs, which would also then allow him to expand the vineyard. (It has been a lack of irrigation water that has limited expansion until now.)

Although the soils are generally high in organic material, additions of nitrogen and phosphorus are still necessary. The acid, water-retentive soils can also prevent uptake of iron by the plants, leading to chlorosis, though this is usually only a problem in spring. Water saturation can also be a problem, though again usually only in winter and spring, and in the summer the soils dry out naturally. Spring frosts are a threat until early November and, even though de Solminihac claims only one serious frost in ten years, he is introducing a micro-aspersion system into the new vineyards for protection.

De Solminihac describes the wines of Araucanía as being distinctive, with more mineral than tropical character and a good ageing potential. Though it is still early days, the increasing quality of the SoldeSol Chardonnay does bode well. Its high natural acidity gives it the backbone to support oak flavours as well as an enviable intensity and length. The oak influence has been reduced since the first vintages (from fifty per cent new oak in 2000 to twenty-five per cent in 2004), as well as the percentage of malolactic fermentation, making for an increasingly fresh, zingy style full of mouth-jangling acidity though the nutty, creamy complexity is retained.

As for its ageing ability, time is needed to form a firm opinion. Although the 2000 has developed gracefully, this was the first wine made at the property and I would recommend waiting for a more rounded vintage, like the 2003 or 2004, to spend time in the bottle before making a judgment. Both vintages seem to have all the requisite balance and concentration to mature well.

CASE STUDY: THE BENEFIT OF THE MARGINAL

"A difficult region in which to grow grapes" is how Felipe de Solminihac characterizes Araucanía, the region in which Malleco is located. Given that de Solminihac is a thoughtful and deliberate man, the implications of this statement are far-reaching.

His reasons are various, but they can be summarized. Firstly, rain. Water-retentive heavy clay soils. Spring frosts. Icy winters. Potential water shortage for irrigation during the growing season. A low annual heat summation. Then there is the considerable distance from Santiago to contend with (the fruit has to be trucked over 650 kilometres (400 miles) to the capital before it can be vinified at Aquitania). Also, a total absence of wine-growing history in the region, along with a consequent lack of local wine culture and experienced workers. All this, and then he has his in-laws to deal with (they own the farm).

Against such overwhelming odds, you might think that de Solminihac's vinous efforts were destined for little more than in-house, medicinal consumption. Far from it: SoldeSol Chardonnay has gone down a storm both in Chile and abroad, vaunted for its excellent structure, freshness, and invigorating breadth of flavour. A new style of white wine from Chile, they say. There are plans for expansion. How can this be?

It is a truism that the best wines are made in marginal climates. The concept of pushing the vine to the limit to achieve the best results does seem to have its benefits, provided the viticulturists and winemakers are skilled in their management, and the plants well adapted to the conditions. Chile has only recently started to leave the comfort zone of the warm, flat central depression and push east, west, north, and south into more marginal areas in an attempt to move away from acceptable if unambitious styles toward more complex, challenging wines. SoldeSol is just such a project and it represents a trend that should be encouraged.

"Other wineries are doing research down here," comments de Solminihac. And indeed they are: no longer is SoldeSol the most southerly winery in Chile, because Viña Momberg released its first wines in 2005 from an area near Osorno, some 300 kilometres (186 miles) farther south. These are positive developments, and I for one would like to see more vineyards going into Malleco as well as farther south. Only when this spirit pervades the whole country will we as wine drinkers discover what diversity and quality Chile really has to offer.

Noteworthy

SOLDESOL

Vines: 10ha (Chardonnay, Pinot Noir). Winemaker: Felipe de Solminihac.
Production: 18,000 litres. *See*: Aquitania.

SoldeSol is not a winery; it is a brand made by Maipo-based producer Aquitania. The arrangement works as follows: Chilean winemaker Felipe de Solminihac is one of four partners in Aquitania; his in-laws own a farm near Traiguén and Felipe planted five hectares of Chardonnay there in 1995 as an experiment; now Aquitania buys the grapes from Felipe's in-laws and he then makes the wine in Santiago.

At first, Aquitania's partners were not convinced about the project's credentials. "We weren't optimistic at the start," admits Bruno Prats, "so we sold off the fruit." However, after the first Chardonnay was made in 2000, Prats and the other partners were enthused by what he terms "the combination of high natural acidity and richness of structure", and the wine was well received in the market. A further five hectares of Pinot Noir were planted in 2002 and there is a potential for growth up to and over 110 hectares once a new irrigation system is installed. Other varieties being considered include Sauvignon Blanc, Gewurztraminer, and Riesling.

It is fair to say that, though Aquitania's three founding partners were joined by a fourth, Ghislain de Montgolfier, in 2001, de Solminihac remains the mainstay of the company, especially in the south. He is a prodigiously experienced winemaker and, having consulted all over Chile, has a privileged insight into its many varied terroirs; he deserves credit for his brave initiative with SoldeSol. It has added a useful string to Aquitania's bow.

11

OTHER WINERIES

The following is a compilation of further Chilean wine producers.

ALTA CIMA (CURICO)

Casilla 70, Lontué, Septima region. Tel: +56 75 471034. Email:
info@altacima.cl. Website: www.altacima.cl

Established: 2002. Vineyard: 59ha (Cabernet Sauvignon, Gewurztraminer, Merlot,
Chardonnay, Syrah, Petit Verdot). Production: 780,000 litres.

Winemaker Klaus Schröder does much consulting in Curicó; his winery mainly sells in bulk to Germany.

APALTAGUA (COLCHAGUA)

Casilla 114, Santa Cruz. Tel: +56 72 824595. Email: apaltagua@apaltagua.cl.

Established: 1974. Vineyard: 59ha (Carmenère, Cabernet Sauvignon).

Production: 400,000 litres. Brands: Grial, Envero.

Some good-quality reds at the top end from this Apalta-based winery but it has lacked direction.

ARESTI (CURICO)

Alcántara 107, Las Condes, Santiago. Tel: +56 2 4614330. Email:
infowine@arestichile.cl. Website: www.arestichilewine.cl

Established: 1951. Vineyard: 346ha (Cabernet Sauvignon, Sauvignon Blanc,
Merlot, Chardonnay, Gewurztraminer).

Curicó's most southerly winery is undergoing changes in its winemaking and vineyard strategy; a fresh style of Cabernet has so far been its strongest suit.

BALDUZZI (MAULE)

Av Balmaceda 1189, San Javier. Tel: +56 73 322138. Email:
info@balduzziwines.com. Website: www.balduzziwines.com
Established: 1988. Vineyard: 600ha (Cabernet Sauvignon, Carmenère, Merlot,
Syrah, Sauvignon Blanc). Production: 4 million litres.

BISQUERTT (COLCHAGUA)

Padre Mariano 401, Providencia, Santiago. Tel: +56 2 9461540. Email:
jruiz@bisquertt.cl. Website: www.bisquertt.cl
Established: 1960. Vineyard: 800ha (Cabernet Sauvignon, Merlot, Syrah,
Carmenère, Malbec). Production: 6 million litres.

Commercially orientated, large-scale producer; wines are formulaic
though some decent reds are made in a traditional, sweet-fruit style.
Also makes the Chilcaya brand for US giant Gallo.

BUTRON BUDINICH (CACHAPOAL)

Av La Campañía S/N, Rancagua. Tel: +56 72 222947. Email: avalencia@bbw.cl.
Website: www.bbw.cl
Established: 2000. Vineyard: 98ha (Cabernet Sauvignon, Sauvignon Blanc,
Merlot, Malbec, Carmenère, Chardonnay). Production: 800,000 litres.

Bulk producer turning to bottled wine; quality is generally very sound,
with some good Carmenère and old-vine Malbec.

CAMINO REAL (CACHAPOAL)

Camino La Punta S/N Viña 3, San Francisco de Mostazal. Tel: +56 2 9551518.
Email: caminoreal@caminoreal.cl. Website: www.caminoreal.cl
Established: 1879. Vineyard: 100ha (Cabernet Sauvignon, Carmenère, Merlot,
Chardonnay, Sauvignon Blanc). Production: 650,000 litres.

CANDELARIA (COLCHAGUA)

Providencia 1930, Of 33, Santiago. Tel: +56 2 3353325. Email:
egidi@candelariawines.com. Website: www.candelariawines.com
Established: 2001. Vineyard: 30ha (Cabernet Sauvignon, Merlot). Production:
270,000 litres.

CARTA VIEJA (MAULE)

Av Francisco Antonio Encina 231, Villa Alegre de Loncomilla. Tel: +56 73 560500. Email: info@cartavieja.cl. Website: www.cartavieja.com

Established: 1825. Vineyard: 600ha (Cabernet Sauvignon, Carmenère, Merlot, Syrah, Cabernet Franc...). Production: 1 million litres.

Historic Maule producer owned by the del Pedregal family and starting to show signs of a renaissance under the winemaking guidance of consultant Pascal Marty.

CASAL DE GORCHS (MAIPO)

Av Vicuña Mackenna 2289, Santiago. Tel: +56 2 7504000. Email: info@casaldegorchs.com. Website: www.casaldegorchs.com

Formerly Viña Manquehue, Casal de Gorchs was established in 2003 by the Rabat family after they withdrew from the joint venture in Casa Lapostolle; still and sparkling wines are produced.

CASANUEVA (ITATA)

Av Vitacura 3568, Of 801, Vitacura, Santiago. Tel: +56 2 9535060. Email: info@vinacasanueva.com. Website: www.vinacasanueva.com

Established: 1998. 125ha (Cabernet Sauvignon, Merlot, Chardonnay, Sauvignon Blanc). Production: 600,000 litres.

A producer with a novel angle: wines are matured in the Pacific Ocean.

CASAS DEL MAULE (MAULE)

PO Box 540, Talca. Tel: +56 71 631023. Email: info@casasdelmaule.com. Website: www.casasdelmaule.com

Established: 1948. 56ha. Production: 400,000 litres.

CASAS DEL TOQUI (CACHAPOAL)

Fundo Santa Anita de Totihue, Requínoa. Tel: +56 72 321870. Email: oficina@casasdeltoqui.cl. Website: www.casasdeltoqui.cl

Established: 1994. Vineyard: 100ha (Cabernet Sauvignon, Chardonnay, Merlot, Semillon, Syrah). Production: 1 million litres.

Joint venture between the Chilean Granella family and Bordeaux's Château Larose-Trintaudon; seems to have lacked direction of late and wines have disappointed, though the top Cabernets from old vines still offer good quality.

CAVAS DEL MAIPO (MAIPO)

Camino al Volcán 0121, Puente Alto, Santiago. Tel: +56 2 8711508. Email: cavasdelmaipo@ntelchile.net. Website: www.cavasdelmaipo.cl

Established: 1985. Vineyard: 30ha (Chardonnay, Cabernet Sauvignon, Sauvignon Blanc, Semillon). Production: 250,000 litres.

CHATEAU LOS BOLDOS (CACHAPOAL)

Camino Los Boldos S/N, Casilla 73, Requínoa. Tel: +56 72 551230. Email: boldos@clb.cl. Website: www.chateaulosboldos.com

Established: 1990. Vineyard: 390ha (Cabernet Sauvignon, Carmenère, Merlot, Syrah, Sauvignon Blanc, Chardonnay). Production: 3 million litres.

Owned by the French Massenez family famed for their fruit liqueurs, this normally sound winery has been producing some worryingly lacklustre wines recently; improvements are called for.

CHILEAN WINES (MAULE)

2 Sur 665, Of 1301, Talca. Tel: +56 71 232730. Email: export@chileanwinescompany.com. Website: www.chileanwinescompany.com

Established: 1979. Vineyard: 600ha (Cabernet Sauvignon, Merlot, Syrah, Pinot Noir, Carmenère...). Production: 5 million litres.

CREMASCHI FURLOTTI (MAULE)

Estado 359, Piso 4, Santiago. Tel: +56 2 586 2510. Email: informaciones@cf.cl. Website: www.cf.cl

Established: 1975. Vineyard: 400ha. Production: 4 million litres.

Some increasingly good wines from this producer, including top Venere blend of Carmenère, Syrah, and Cabernet Sauvignon.

DONA JAVIERA (MAIPO)

Luis Thayer Ojeda 073, Of 1001, Providencia, Santiago. Tel: +56 2 8181470. Email: vinadonajaviera@vdj.tie.cl. Website: www.donajaviera.cl

Established: 1993. Vineyard: 50ha (Cabernet Sauvignon, Merlot, Carmenère, Chardonnay, Sauvignon Blanc). Production: 500,000 litres.

Traditional winery near El Monte in central Maipo making moves toward more modern styles of wine.

EL HUIQUE (COLCHAGUA)

Alcántara 200, Of 306, Las Condes, Santiago. Tel: +56 2 2078410. Email: info@elhuique.com. Website: www.elhuique.com

Established: 1970. Vineyard: 100ha (Cabernet Sauvignon, Carmenère, Chardonnay, Syrah, Merlot...). Production: 800,000 litres.

ESTAMPA (COLCHAGUA)

Av Presidente Kennedy 5735, Of 606, Santiago. Tel: +56 2 2027000. Email: info@estampa.com. Website: www.estampa.com

Established: 2001. Vineyard: 270ha (Cabernet Sauvignon, Carmenère, Syrah, Merlot, Viognier...). Production: 940,000 litres.

New Colchagua winery that specializes in blended wines and looks to be improving its hitherto pleasantly commercial style; new fruit from Marchihue is being used from the 2006 vintage.

INDOMITA (CASABLANCA)

Lote B Parcela 12 B 2, Mundo Nuevo, Casablanca. Tel: +56 32 754400. Email: contacto@indomita.cl. Website: www.indomita.cl

Established: 2000. 400ha (Sauvignon Blanc, Chardonnay, Pinot Noir, Merlot, Cabernet Sauvignon, Carmenère). Production: 3.5 million litres.

Formerly owned by fruit producer David del Curto; recent management and ownership changes may lead to better wines.

J BOUCHON (MAULE)

Evaristo Lillo 178, Of 23, Las Condes, Santiago. Tel: +56 2 2469778. Email: jbouchon@jbouchon.cl. Website: www.jbouchon.cl

Established: 1892. Vineyard: 370ha (Cabernet Sauvignon, Sauvignon Blanc, Merlot, Carmenère, Chardonnay...). Production: 3 million litres.

Another historic Maule winery revamping itself, this time with the help of top consultants Patrick Valette and Eduardo Silva.

KORTA (CURICO)

Casilla 450, Curicó. Tel: +56 75 520505. Email: info@korta.cl. Website: www.korta.cl

Established: 1998. Vineyard: 97ha (Cabernet Sauvignon, Cabernet Franc, Carmenère, Merlot, Syrah...). Production: 700,000 litres.

Promising new producer based in Sagrada Familia whose owners are also in the fruit and tannery business.

LA FORTUNA (CURICO)
Av Kennedy 5454, Of 903, Vitacura, Santiago. Tel: +56 2 9538271. Email: jefortuna@manquehue.net. Website: www.lafortuna.cl
Established: 1942. Vineyard: 250ha (Cabernet Sauvignon, Sauvignon Blanc, Malbec, Merlot, Semillon...). Production: 1.5 million litres.
Organically managed vineyards; wines need improvement.

LAURA HARTWIG (SANTA LAURA) (COLCHAGUA)
Casilla 150, Santa Cruz. Tel: +56 72 823179. Email: alejandr@laurahartwig.cl. Website: www.laurahartwig.cl
Established: 1994. Vineyard: 75ha (Cabernet Sauvignon, Merlot, Carmenère, Chardonnay). Production: 220,000 litres.

LOMA LARGA (CASABLANCA)
Gertrudis Echeñique 348, Las Condes, Santiago. Tel: +56 2 2065253. Email: info@lomalarga.com. Website: www.lomalarga.com
Established: 1999. Vineyard: 110ha (Sauvignon Blanc, Chardonnay, Pinot Noir, Syrah, Cabernet Sauvignon).
New coastal Casablanca enterprise selling fruit and making small quantities of premium reds and whites, the 2005 vintage of which shows excellent quality and considerable promise.

LOMAS DE CAUQUENES (COVICA) (MAULE)
Av Ruperto Pinochet 690, Cauquenes. Tel: +56 73 560000. Email: export@covica.cl. Website: www.covica.cl
Established: 1939. Vineyard: 2,527ha.
Large cooperative focused on Cauquenes producing organic and fair-trade wines within a broad and sometimes eclectic range; Cabernet and Carignan show promise.

LOS ACANTOS (MAULE)
Chorrillos Sur S/N, San Javier. Tel: +56 73 324113. Email: info@losacantos.cl. Website: www.losacantos.cl
Established: 2000. Vineyard: 40ha (Cabernet Sauvignon, Merlot, Carmenère, Syrah, Pinot Noir). Production: 500,000 litres.

LOS ROBLES (CURICO)

Balmaceda 565, Casilla 8 – D, Curicó. Tel: +56 75 310047. Email: vinoslosrobles@losrobles.cl. Website: www.losrobles.cl

Established: 1942. Vineyard: 1,000ha (Cabernet Sauvignon, Sauvignon Blanc, Merlot, Carmenère, Semillon...). Production: 8.7 million litres.

Historic cooperative based in downtown Curicó that is in the process of reinventing itself with the aid of high-profile consultants; has accredited fair-trade status.

MILLAMAN (HACIENDA EL CONDOR) (CURICO)

Luis Thayer Ojeda 236, Piso 6, Providencia, Santiago. Tel: +56 2 4380031. Email: info@millaman.cl. Website: www.millaman.cl

Established: 1946. Vineyard: 200ha (Cabernet Sauvignon, Sauvignon Blanc, Merlot, Malbec, Syrah...). Production: 1 million litres.

Sister winery to TerraMater; wines can be formulaic and dilute so need work, but the Malbec and Zinfandel inject some appeal into the line-up.

OCHO TIERRAS (LIMARI)

Independencia 664, Ovalle. Tel: +56 53 633202. Email: info@ochotierras.cl. Website: www.ochotierras.cl

Established: 2002. 157ha (Cabernet Sauvignon, Chardonnay). Production: 70,000 litres.

PERALILLO (COLCHAGUA)

Fundo Santa María S/N, El Olivar, Rancagua. Tel: +56 72 391344. Email: info@peralillowines.cl. Website: www.peralillowines.cl

Established: 2002. Vineyard: 170ha (Cabernet Sauvignon, Carmenère, Cabernet Franc, Chardonnay).

Principally sells its fruit to other producers but also makes wine for its partners, including Spanish winery Guelbenzu.

POLKURA (COLCHAGUA)

Av Kennedy 5454, Of 804, Santiago. Tel: +56 2 9538171. Email: info@polkura.cl. Website: www.polkura.cl

Established: 2002. Vineyard: 12ha (Syrah, Malbec, Cabernet Sauvignon, Tempranillo, Grenache). Production: 28,000 litres.

Promising micro-project co-owned by winemaker Sven Bruchfeld and based in Marchihue with just one Syrah so far made in a ripe, toasty style.

PORTAL DEL ALTO (MAIPO)

Casilla 182, Buin. Tel: +56 2 8213363. Email: ventas@portaldelalto.cl. Website: www.portaldelalto.cl

Established: 1971. Vineyard: 160ha (Cabernet Sauvignon, Carmenère, Merlot, Sauvignon Blanc, Chardonnay...). Production: 800,000 litres.

The wines made at this property owned by Chilean winemaking authority Alejandro Hernández are simple at best.

RAVANAL (COLCHAGUA)

Av Los Conquistadores 2595, Santiago. Tel: +56 2 4744074. Email: info@ravanal.cl. Website: www.ravanal.cl

Established: 1936. Vineyard: 120ha (Cabernet Sauvignon, Carmenère, Merlot, Chardonnay, Sauvignon Blanc...). Production: 1 million litres.

REQUINGUA (CURICO)

Estado 337, Piso 9, Santiago. Tel: +56 2 6327984. Email: mlong@requingua.cl. Website: www.requingua.cl

Established: 1961. Vineyard: 380ha (Cabernet Sauvignon, Carmenère, Merlot, Sauvignon Blanc, Chardonnay...). Production: 10 million litres.

Bulk producer turning to bottled wine; its self-contained estate near Sagrada Familia is producing some decent wines, the best being Cabernet Sauvignon.

SAN JOSE DE APALTA (CACHAPOAL)

Av Miguel Ramírez 199, Rancagua. Tel: +56 72 213338. Email: contacto@sanjosedeapalta.cl. Website: www.sanjosedeapalta.cl

Established: 1970. Vineyard: 200ha (Cabernet Sauvignon, Carmenère, Merlot, Syrah, Chardonnay, Sauvignon Blanc). Production: 1.6 million litres.

SANTA ALICIA (MAIPO)

Camino Las Rosas, Pirque, Santiago. Tel: +56 2 8546021. Email: diego@santa-alicia.com. Website: www.santa-alicia.com

Established: 1954. Vineyard: 140ha (Cabernet Sauvignon, Merlot, Chardonnay, Sauvignon Blanc...). Production: 2.5 million litres.

SIEGEL (COLCHAGUA)

Casilla 132, Correo de Santa Cruz. Tel: +56 72 933112. Email:
info@siegelvinos.com. Website: www.siegelvinos.com

Established: 1980. Vineyard: 225ha (Cabernet Sauvignon, Merlot, Carmenère,
Sauvignon Blanc, Chardonnay). Production: 7 million litres.

Wine and grape broker Alberto Siegel went into the bottling business
in the late nineties; the wines are fairly commercial in character though
with some quality in the Crucero and Gran Crucero lines.

SUTIL/LA PLAYA (COLCHAGUA)

Av 11 de Septiembre 1860, Of 131, Providencia, Santiago. Tel: +56 2
3730606. Email: njarpa@topwinechile.tie.cl. Website: www.topwinechile.com

Established: 1990. Vineyard: 473ha (Cabernet Sauvignon, Chardonnay,
Carmenère, Merlot, Cabernet Franc...).

Former grower; wines need more character, balance, and fresh fruit.

TERRA ANDINA (SUR ANDINO) (CURICO)

Apoquindo 3669, Piso 16, Las Condes, Santiago. Tel: +56 2 3622122. Email:
info@terraandina.cl. Website: www.terraandina.com

Established: 1996. Vineyard: 0ha. Production: 2.2 million litres.

Commercial but generally reliable winery developed by Pernod Ricard
and bought by the Claro group (Santa Rita) in 2001; fruit is sourced
from around the country and blended into easy-going wines with some
good character in the Alto range.

VALLE DEL ITATA (ITATA)

Casilla 271, Chillán. Tel: +56 42 432222. Email: vitata@valledeitata.cl

Established: 1995. Vineyard: 120ha (Cabernet Sauvignon, Carmenère,
Chardonnay, Merlot, Sauvignon Blanc). Production: 600,000 litres.

VALLE FRIO (MAULE)

Fundo los Pocillos, Camino San Clemente km 12, Casilla 874, Talca. Tel: +56 2
5820540. Email: sebastianmoreno@vallefrio.cl. Website: www.vallefrio.cl

Established: 1998. Vineyard: 200ha (Cabernet Sauvignon, Merlot, Sauvignon
Blanc, Chardonnay, Carmenère, Pinot Noir). Production: 1.4 million litres.

VINA MAIPO (MAIPO)

Av Nueva Tajamar 481, Torre Sur, Piso N° 9, Las Condes, Santiago. Tel: +56 2 4765104. Established: 1948.

Subsidiary of Concha y Toro, based nearby in Pirque.

VINA MAR (CASABLANCA)

Los Conquistadores 1700, Piso 16, Providencia, Santiago. Tel: +56 2 7076288. Email: info@southernsunwine.com. Website: www.southernsunwine.com Established: 2002. Vineyard: 70ha (Chardonnay, Sauvignon Blanc, Pinot Noir, Merlot, Cabernet Sauvignon...). Production: 900,000 litres.

Commercially minded off-shoot of the Southern Sun Wine Group; wines are commercial in style, too, but some of the Casablanca reds show promise.

VINEDOS DE EL TAMBO (CACHAPOAL)

Manuel Montt 1452, Providencia, Santiago. Tel: +56 2 3433607. Email: cesarfredes@mi.cl.
Established: 1996. Vineyard: 9.5ha (Cabernet Sauvignon, Carmenère).
Production: 25,000 litres.

WILLIAM FEVRE (MAIPO)

Huelen 56-B, Providencia, Santiago. Tel: +56 2 2351919. Email: info@wfchile.cl. Website: www.wfchile.cl
Established: 1991. Vineyard: 70ha (Cabernet Sauvignon, Merlot, Chardonnay, Pinot Noir, Carmenère, Sauvignon Blanc). Production: 500,000 litres.

Joint venture between the Chilean Pino family and French investors including Chablis producer William Fèvre; wines are restrained in style.

Glossary

This glossary does not aim to be the most authoritative of its kind. There are excellent books that fulfil this purpose to a far more comprehensive degree, such as the fine *Oxford Companion to Wine*, which I have used as a principal source for this glossary. This is more of a simple guide to help clarify words I have used in the text, especially in those cases in which I have given a particular slant to terms, and also provides specific relevance to Chile.

Acidification: a common procedure in warm-climate viticultural zones including Chile, especially for red wines, wherein acid, usually tartaric, is added to a must or wine to adjust pH

Alluvial: deposited by flowing water, such as rivers

Alto: high or tall, literally, though when used in conjunction with a Chilean wine region, such as Alto Maipo, it refers to the vineyard zone near the Andes

Amarone: powerful wine made from dried grapes in the Italian region of Valpolicella

Anaerobic: in the absence of oxygen

Anticyclone: high-pressure body of moving air that brings clear skies and fine weather

Appellation: a delimited area of controlled viticultural production; in Chile, the controls are not as strict or wide-ranging as Europe, mainly focusing on permitted grape varieties and defined areas

Aquifer: underground water reserve

Arcilla: clay

Arena: sand

Astringency: negative tasting term referring to a hard or drying sensation in the mouth

Bacterial spoilage: wine fault caused by inadequate hygiene in the winemaking process

Bajo: low or small, literally, though when used in conjunction with a Chilean wine region (such as Bajo Maipo) it refers to an area near the coast

Batholith: a large body of intrusive or plutonic igneous rock, such as granite, formed from magma that cooled deep in the earth's crust

Biodynamic: an extension of organic viticulture focused on promoting the natural health of the soil and vines by treating the farm as a symbiotic entity, using homeopathic remedies and specific composts, and observing the cycles of the cosmos

Biodynamic preparations: natural composts and homeopathic remedies used in Biodynamic viticulture

Blanco: white (as in *vino blanco*)

Blind tasting: this is simply a wine tasting in which the tasters do not know the identity of the wines

Botrytis: a fungus that attacks grapes; in most cases it is undesirable (grey rot) but in a few specific cases, when it is known as "noble rot", it can cause a concentration of flavours in the grapes and give sweet wines – though this is rare in Chile

Brettanomyces: aka "brett", a yeast that can cause animal or farmyard aromas in wines

Bud-break: the first emergence of green shoots from buds on the vine in spring; usually takes place in September in Chile

Calicata: a hole dug in the ground to study the soil

Camanchaca: the coastal mist and low cloud that regularly form in Chile's maritime areas, especially in the mornings

Canopy: the vine's above-ground structure, including leaves, stems, and fruit

Canopy management: tending and arranging the vine's canopy to achieve desired ripeness in the fruit and taste in the wine, as well as to avoid diseases and pests

Catar: to taste (wine)

Cepa: vine or grape variety

Chicha: crude fermented drink historically made by indigenous Andean cultures from a range of produce including maize, though in Chile it is most commonly made from grapes or apples and drunk during the national independence day celebrations on September 18

Chips: not the eating sort, these are small chips of wood or oak that are suspended in bags within wine tanks to impart flavour

Chlorosis: disease of the vine in which leaves turn yellow due to lack of chlorophyll, often caused by iron deficiency

Clay: fine-grained particle soil or sediment

Clonal selection: the process of propagating clones from a single parent vine

Clone: a vine derived by propagation from a single parent vine and identifiable as such, as opposed to mass/massal or field selections that may include a number of mutations; examples of clonal vine material in Chile include Pinot Noir clone 777 and Sauvignon Blanc clone 242

Cold soak: the technique of macerating (soaking) the solid matter of grapes with the juice prior to fermentation in cool conditions; it often gives a softer extraction than post-fermentive soaks

Colluvial: the product of erosion from cliffs and slopes

Consultant: external adviser on wine matters, normally either on viticultural or winemaking issues

Continental: a term used somewhat loosely in this book, indicating a type of climate in which extremes of temperature are notable, both between night and day as well as summer and winter

Cooper: barrel-maker

Co-operative: winemaking operations owned and managed by shareholding farmers

Co-pigmentation: a technique still under scrutiny that aims to give better depth and stability of colour to red wines by fermenting red wine with the skins of white grapes

Cosecha: harvest

Costa: coast – often used to denote a coastal area of a Chilean wine region (such as Maipo Costa)

Cover crop: plants grown between vine rows to provide soil nutrition and attract beneficial insects

CTVV (Centro Tecnológico de la Vid y el Vino): a research and development unit attached to Talca University that focuses specifically on viticulture and wine and is of increasing importance to the Chilean wine industry as a whole

Denominación: denomination or appellation; a defined and controlled winemaking region

Dry-farmed: farmed without the use of irrigation, see Secano

Dulce: sweet

El Niño: oceano-atmospheric phenomenon in which uncommonly warm coastal waters in the eastern Pacific lead, among other things, to unusually rainy weather in western Latin America

Embalse: reservoir

Empresa: firm or company

Espaldera: the support structure of the vines, or trellis system, which usually refers to a simple wire-trained system with plants in a vertical shoot position (VSP)

Extraction: the transfer of compounds in grape skins, seeds, and stems to the must by maceration; it can also refer to oak

Filtering: the process of straining the wine by passing it through filters, which can be very fine if required

Free standing: a method of vine training in which the vines have no trellis system and stand alone as plants; this is a traditional method of vine-growing in Chile

Fruit set: the stage when grape berries form on the fertilized flowers and which occurs around December in Chile

Geneva Double Curtain: a form of vine training in which the canopy is divided into two blocks or curtains that hang down from high canes; often used to counter vigour

Grafting: the process of connecting two pieces of living plant tissue so that they unite and grow as one plant; this can be done when planting a scion on a rootstock to grow a vine from new, or by the common practice in Chile of inserting a new vine stock on older plant roots (e.g. Syrah over País)

Granite: coarse-grained intrusive igneous rock common in Chile, especially in the coastal range, where it is often found in weathered form at ground level and known as *maicillo*

Grub up: pull out (vines)

Habitat breaks: areas of varied vegetation cultivated in the vineyard to diminish the extent of vine monoculture and promote plant and insect diversity

Hang time: the length of time the grapes are left to hang on the vine before being harvested; a long hang time can result in high alcohol and very ripe flavours

Hard pan: hard layer of rock or compacted soil that prevents root growth

Head trained: a method of vine training in which the fruiting canes grow from a vine head stump rather than cordons (the vines are usually free standing, *see above*)

Hectolitre: one hundred litres

Hot: negative tasting term indicating an imbalance of alcohol in the wine, giving the sensation of heat on the back of the palate

Hydric stress: strain exerted on a vine's mechanism specifically due to a lack of water

Icon: top-level or prestige wine, normally highly priced and made in small quantities

Integrated pest management: an eco-friendly method of viticulture that aims to control pests, diseases, and weeds via natural methods, but which stops short of organic due to the permitted use of some agro-chemical treatments

Irrigation, ditch: water supplied to vines via a system of channels or ditches

Irrigation, drip: water supplied to vines via a system of pipes suspended above ground level out of which the water drips through small holes

Irrigation, flood: water supplied to vines by flooding the entire vineyard area

La Niña: oceano-atmospheric phenomenon in which uncommonly cool coastal waters in the eastern Pacific lead, among other things, to unusually dry weather in western Latin America

Lago: lake

Leafroll virus: non-lethal vine disease widespread in wine-growing countries that can have a negative impact on wine quality

Leaf-to-fruit ratio: a measurement of the amount of leaves to each bunch of fruit on a vine; good growers learn with experience what the ideal balance is in any given year – problems with ripening will occur if the ratio is either too high or too low

Lees: dregs or sediment that form during fermentation or maturation, primarily composed of dead yeast cells as well as grape seeds, pulp, and skin; when kept in contact with wine it can give a buttery, creamy, yeasty character, such as in lees-stirred Chardonnay

Limo: silt

Linear: negative tasting term indicating a wine that is somewhat lacking in breadth or dimensions

Loam: soil mixture containing sand, clay, and organic matter

Lyre: a vine-training method in which the canopy is divided into two blocks with shoots positioned vertically and the vine trunk forming a T-shape in the middle; improves sun exposure and acts as a counter to vigour

Maceration: the process by which solid matter from grapes is soaked with the grape juice or wine in order to extract constituent parts such as colour, tannins, or flavour; this can happen before (pre-) or after (post-) alcoholic fermentation, but because some compounds are more soluble in alcohol than water, extraction levels tend to be higher during and after fermentation

Maicillo: a term used broadly in Chile but more often than not refers to a coarse-grained, sand-like soil derived from weathered or decomposed granite

Malolactic fermentation: the transformation of the zesty malic acid into the softer lactic acid by bacteria, a process that usually occurs after the alcoholic fermentation but can either be encouraged or blocked by winemakers depending on the required results in the wine (in Chile, it is increasingly being blocked in Chardonnay to retain crispness)

Margarodes vitis: insect pest that infests vine roots in a similar way to phylloxera

Maturation: term that refers both to the ripening of grapes and ageing of wines in the cellar

Mealybug: small white insects that feed on vine sap

Medio: medium or middle, literally, though often used to denote the central part of the country, between the Andes and coast, when used in conjunction with a Chilean wine region (e.g. Medio Maipo)

Mesoclimate: term between macroclimate (regional) and microclimate (highly localized) in scale, referring to the climate in a medium-sized area; the *Oxford Companion* suggests a scale of tens or hundreds of metres, *e.g.* a vineyard or site

Micro-aspersion: fine spray

Microclimate: the smallest climatic designation, can be as specific as the conditions within a particular vine's canopy, but more often refers to specific points in a vineyard

Micro-oxygenation: the process by which small amounts of oxygen are passed through wine in tank for various reasons, including building yeast populations, stabilizing colour, reducing "green" or unripe aromas, and mimicking the effects of barrel ageing

Must: crushed grape juice that is being transformed into wine

National selection: broad term used in Chilean viticulture to refer to certain roughly defined strains of vine varieties that are of uncertain origin but have been grown in Chile for some time – such as "national selection Pinot Noir"

Nematodes: microscopic roundworms that can feed on vine roots and are a particular risk in sandy soils, *e.g.* Casablanca

Noble (vine) stock: those vine varieties considered to be apt for quality wine production, as opposed to basic wine – thus Pinot Noir is noble, Thompson Seedless is not

Oak: the tough though pliable and watertight wood of the *Quercus* tree, used as barrels, staves, or chips to influence the taste and nature of a wine

Oenologist: fancy name for a winemaker

Oidio: Spanish for oidium

Oidium: synonym for the vine fungal disease powdery mildew

Old vines: imprecise and relative term that refers to established vines; as a vine's yield tends to decrease and its root system expand with age, it can produce concentrated and better-quality fruit, hence wine-growers' enthusiasm to identify their vines as old

Organic: system of grape growing that does not use synthetic or chemically manufactured products such as herbicides, pesticides, fungicides, or chemical fertilizers

Oxidative: either the liability to oxidation or the allowance of controlled oxidation in the winemaking process

Parra: vine

Parrón or *Parronal*: Spanish term referring to the pergola vine-training method, in which the vines' canopy and fruit are trained in a ceiling-type structure

Passito: wine made partially or wholly from dried grapes

Pergola: vine-training method in which the vines' canopy and fruit are trained in a ceiling-type structure

pH: an indication of acidity or alkalinity measured on a scale of 0–12, with higher being more alkaline, lower more acid, and 7 as neutral

Phenolics: *see* Polyphenols

Phenological ripeness: a somewhat elliptical term to refer to the maturity of grapes as measured by the nature of the polyphenols as opposed to simply the concentration of sugar and alcohol

Phylloxera: small aphid that feeds on vine roots and can prove lethal to the plants; its infestation proved devastating to European viticulture in the nineteenth century until American rootstocks were found to be a solution

Pinta: Spanish word for veraison (*see below*)

Pisco: grape brandy, a speciality of Peru and Chile

Planting boom: the swift and substantial growth in the Chilean wine vineyard between 1995 and 2000, which saw plantings increase from 54,393 to 103,876 hectares

Polyphenols: a large group of reactive chemical compounds found in grape skins that includes tannins and anthocyanins and which can have a substantial impact on wine aroma, flavour, and colour, especially in red wines

Powdery mildew: fungal disease of the vine

Pyrazines: used in this book in the sense of methoxypyrazines, compounds that give so-called "green" or vegetal aromas and flavours to wines, such as Sauvignon Blanc

Racking: moving wine from one container to another in the cellar, usually to remove the sediment or lees in a container but can also be used for aeration

Raulí: type of southern beech tree (*Nothofagus*), a commonly found hardwood in Chile, used in the past to make fermentation and maturation vessels for wine

Reduction: the opposite of, or complement to, oxidation; in winemaking this term is often used in a broader, less scientific sense to refer to states or reactions, often undesirable, that are the result of a relative absence of oxygen

Reserva: ill-defined term often used to denote wine that has been aged in oak, although it can also simply be used as an arbitrary term intended to signify "better-quality" wine

Río: river

Rootstock: the root system of a grape vine, onto which a scion is grafted to grow as a fully functioning vine; the grafting system became widespread after phylloxera hit Europe and only American or hybrid vine roots proved resistant, thus noble vine stock was grafted onto these rootstocks. Uniquely, they are the exception rather than the norm in Chile, which has never suffered from phylloxera, though they are increasingly being used to promote homogeneity in the vineyard.

Rosado: rosé

Sand: large-grained particle soil

Scion: piece of a fruiting vine that is grafted onto a rootstock

Secano: areas of agricultural land in Chile in which irrigation is not used; most commonly it refers to the *secano costero*, a broad swathe of land in the eastern parts of central Chile's coastal range

Seco: dry

Silt: medium-grained particle soil

Split canopy: vine-training methods in which the canopy is trained in separated form, for example Geneva Double Curtain or Lyre

Stainless steel: metal commonly used as a fermentation tank or storage vessel in modern wine production; in Chile it is also being used in barrel form to carry out lees contact without the oxidative character of oak, for example with Sauvignon Blanc

Staves: planks of wood that are suspended in wine tanks to impart flavour

Stress (vine): the strain on a vine's working mechanism caused, for example, by lack of water or excess heat; this situation can be manipulated by wine-growers to force the plant to yield less in order to promote quality

Structure: tasting term denoting the overall make-up of the wine as an impression on the palate; the combination of acidity, flavour, tannin (if applicable), and other major components

Stuck fermentation: a fermentation that stops or slows down prematurely

Sulphur/sulphur dioxide: a naturally-occurring preservative used in the vineyard to counter powdery mildew and in winemaking as a preservative and disinfectant

Synthetic closure: any method of sealing a bottle of wine that does not use natural cork, hence screwcap, plastic cork, etc.

Temperate: a climate in between that of polar and tropical in nature; moderate in temperature

Temperature-controlled fermentation: winemaking technique in which fermentation temperatures are controlled by cooling mechanisms such as plate or pipe systems inserted into tanks, or by jackets on stainless steel tanks; fermentations are cooled in order to preserve wine aromas

Terroir: the vine's world – in other words, the combination of the climate, soil, exposure, topography, and human intervention, all of which influence the nature and quality of the grapes

Tinto: red (as in *vino tinto*)

Toast: the extent to which oak used in the winemaking process has been heated and thus charred or caramelized, which affects the flavour it imparts to the wine; toast can be light, medium, or high

Topography: the shape and nature of the land surface in any given area

Training: the process by which the vine is adapted to the growing system in a given vineyard

Trellis: structure consisting of wood and wires that supports the vine; there are many different kinds of trellis systems (*see Espaldera, Parrón*)

Uva: grape

Vendimia: harvest

Veraison: also known as *pinta* in Spanish, the stage when a grape berry acquires its colour, which occurs around January in Chile

Vertical Shoot Position (VSP): also known as vertical trellis, a common vine-training system in Chile in which shoots are trained upward in a single canopy on a simple wire system

Vertical tasting: a tasting of exactly the same wine from a number of different vintages

Vigour: the vine's propensity for growing vegetative material; medium vigour is optimum for wine quality, whereas overly high or low vigour can reflect imbalances in the vine or its environment and have a negative effect

Viña: winery. (In peninsular Spanish the equivalent would be bodega; to specify vineyard in Chile, one should use *viñedo*.)

Viñedo: vineyard

Vinification: the process of making wine

Vino: wine

Vinotherapy: broad term encompassing a range of health and beauty treatments that use wine grape ingredients

Vinous: relating to wine

Vintage: a specific year or harvest

Viticulture: the science and practice of grape growing

Viticulturist: a practitioner of viticulture; vine tender

Water rights: legal requirement in Chile needed to draw on water reserves, such as rivers or aquifers, in order to irrigate land

Water table: subterranean layer of humidity

Wild ferment: fermentations carried out without the use of commercial or cultured yeast – instead, ambient or "wild" yeast is allowed to carry out the fermentation; it is thought to imbue wine with greater complexity, though it is still under scrutiny

Wine route: collection of tourist attractions including wineries and vineyards that organize tours and visits

Wire trained (vine): almost all vine trellis systems use wire to arrange the vine's canopy; simple wire-trained trellises are those such as VSP (*see above*)

Wooded: a wine that has been in contact with oak during its vinification

Yeast: single-celled organism that plays a key role in alcoholic fermentation, transforming sugar to alcohol; in modern winemaking it is common to use commercial or cultured yeasts to carry out fermentation, as these give more predictable and reliable results than ambient yeasts

Yield: the quantity of fruit produced by a vine or vineyard; often measured in Chile as tonnes or kilograms per hectare (and in Europe as hectolitres per hectare)

APPENDIX 1

CHILE'S BIG COMMERCIAL CHALLENGE

The context of Chilean wine production and sales has changed significantly in recent years. Production has boomed, as have exports. The structure of the industry has modified, with far more small and medium-sized producers than before. The global wine context has also been changing. The issue for Chile now is how and where to sell best.

At the beginning of the nineties, Chile was producing around 300 million litres of wine annually, of which some twenty per cent was exported. By 2005, production had more than doubled, reaching 788 million litres, with exports fluctuating between fifty to seventy-five per cent of production by volume. Production is expected to increase as a result of a steadily growing national vineyard, which by 2004 covered 112,056 hectares. A study in 2005 by government body Odepa projected total Chilean wine production by 2014 to be 1–1.2 billion litres.

To put these figures into context, in 2004 the world vineyard covered around 7.9 million hectares, with global wine production of some 29.5 billion litres. Chile sits around tenth or eleventh position in terms of wine-producing countries though, due to its high relative export rate, it is the wine world's fifth-largest exporter. Chile's two main markets by far are the USA and UK, with other European countries, Canada, Brazil, and Japan also prominent buyers of Chilean wine. The Chilean domestic market has been declining or static since the mid-twentieth century, when annual consumption was over fifty litres per capita – by 2003 it was around sixteen litres per capita.

The commercial challenges facing the Chilean wine industry in the early twenty-first century are varied. Chile is looking to further establish and consolidate its position in an increasingly competitive and over-supplied global wine market. Margins for bulk and entry-level wines have come under pressure as a result of an ongoing global wine over-supply. Currency fluctuations remain a potential Achilles heel for a wine industry heavily beholden to export markets, when a weak dollar and strong peso can have a debilitating impact on profits. A lack of unity in the wine industry has also impeded development, with big and small producers often at loggerheads.

The growth of the modern Chilean wine industry has been fast and furious; there has been a concomitant need to develop the commercial aspects of the business. There are several key areas that the Chilean wine industry is looking to target.

Chile needs to retain its image for producing good-value wines while increasingly targeting the more premium sectors of the market, thus moving away from the commodity business of big-volume, low-margin wines, where the odds are stacked in favour of larger-scale pro-ducers and countries. Inherent in this strategy is the production of wines that offer increasing quality, diversity, and added value. Ongoing improvement and measured growth are required in the vineyards and wineries, fostered by a variety of research and development initiatives.

Greater unity and strategic awareness would be of significant bene-fit to Chilean wine producers. While there is undoubted progress being made in this regard, there remains much to be done. In a competitive market, Chile needs to accentuate its differences, develop key strategic aims, and effectively communicate its identity. This should relate as much to the domestic as the export market. Growing national con-sumption in Chile would not only make for a more balanced sales strategy but may also lead to other positive effects such as developing Chilean gastronomy both at home and abroad, a powerful tool for con-veying national identity and image. Wine tourism can also prove a valuable asset and Chile has made good progress in this regard.

Chile has many commercial challenges ahead of it as well as signifi-cant commercial advantages. As of 2006 it was one of the most open economies in the world, having signed up to no less than forty-three free trade agreements, significant among them those with the USA, China, and the EU. After a period of sustained growth, the wine indus-try is working on developing its commercial reach. There is a need for ongoing innovation, cooperation, and development.

APPENDIX 2

A SHORT GUIDE TO CHILEAN PRONUNCIATION

Chilean Spanish can appear a daunting language to the uninitiated, hard enough to read on the page, let alone pronounce. I remember when my parents came to visit me in Chile and we were planning our trip, looking at the map and discussing places to go. My mother's finger paused over a large lake named Llanquihue, her lips moved silently in preparation and then she gave it a good go. "Why don't we go to lu-lanky-hoo?" she asked.

And why not indeed. If there is one piece of advice that I would give to anyone approaching a foreign language, it would be the following: don't be afraid to give it a go. If you get things wrong, that's fine, and you'll end up learning far faster than if you don't. (For the record, my mother, who has a very good ear anyway, swiftly learned that our destination would be "yang-kee-way".) People, and especially Chileans, always appreciate you making the effort, however rudimentary the attempt.

By way of background, Chilean Spanish is essentially a fusion of Latin American Spanish with the native tongues that were spoken before the arrival of the Europeans. In Chile, there were several indigenous languages but the main one is known as Mapudungun, the language spoken by the Mapuche. These indigenous words are almost entirely restricted to place names, but they invest the Chilean language with a rare sense of poetry and linguistic richness, for example in wonderfully evocative, lilting words such as Lolol, Cachapoal, Chimbarongo.

It is worth noting that Mapudungun and its fellow languages were entirely oral and in their pure state were never written down; this is the reason that many places in Chile have variant spellings, as they are simply approximations of Spanish orthography to a spoken word. A useful tip is that the Mapudungun suffix "-*hue*" means "place", and hence often crops up in place names, such as Llanquihue, which thus rather delightfully means "submerged place". (A similar point could be made about the suffix "-*che*", which means people, hence *mapuche*, meaning "people of the land".)

The good thing about Chilean Spanish is that, if you follow a few basic rules and learn a few initial pronunciation guides, things become a good deal easier. Hence this short guide. It is by no means a definitive treatment of the subject – the pronunciation guide here is a system entirely of my own devising and does not measure up to the high standards of the proper International Phonetic Association (which can be found in any good dictionary). It is instead a collection of general rules as well as a more specific guide to pronouncing the trickier elements of the wine-related Chilean lexicon. They are brief tips to help dispel the nerves and engender a basic confidence with what is ultimately a beautiful, evocative, and rewarding language.

Stress

• Try not to worry too much about pronouncing Spanish well. As a language, in general it doesn't hold too many horrors for the uninitiated. It translates fairly easily from the page to speech and is pronounced exactly how it is written more often than not. Energy, enthusiasm, eye contact, confidence – and often some gesticulation – are often more important to communication in Spanish than impeccable pronunciation.

• In this guide, a syllable in bold type denotes the stress in the word: hence *amigo* ('a-**mee**-go') is stressed on the middle syllable.

• In the majority of cases in Spanish, the stress falls on the penultimate syllable of the word (this comes quite naturally to English speakers). The more specific rule is that if the Spanish word ends in a vowel, or in "n" or "s", the penultimate syllable is stressed.

- If the word ends in a consonant other than "n" or "s", the last syllable is stressed.
- If the word is to be stressed in some other way than the two rules above, an accent is written over the vowel to be stressed, such as *paralítico*.

A few peculiarities of the Spanish language

- The curvaceous little devil that is the letter ñ (pronounced "**en-ye**") crops up quite often in Spanish. Essentially it indicates a "y" sound that follows immediately after the "n" (as in the English "onion"). Thus, the word *niño* is pronounced "**nee**-nyo" and *niña* is "**nee**-nya".
- Another potential spanner in the works is written as "ll" in Spanish. This is a tricky one for English speakers to get their tongues around, as we don't have an equivalent sound in our language. The best and easiest approximation is to simply substitute the "ll" for a "y" sound as in "you".
- The letter "j" can be a tough one for us Anglophones. Its proper pronunciation involves a sound rather like that you make when you clear your throat (a bit like the "ch" sound in the Scottish "loch"). The simplest equivalent is simply to substitute it with a heavy "h" as in "hail". (The letter "g", when it comes before "i" and "e", is pronounced the same as "j": hence *general* is "heh-neh-**ral**".)
- In Latin American Spanish, when the letter "c" comes before the letters "i" or "e" it is pronounced like the letter "s" in "see". (This contrasts with Castilian Spanish, where it is pronounced with a lisping sound, like "th" in "theatre".) Thus, Concepción is pronounced "kon-sep-**syon**".
- Similarly, the letter "z" in Latin American Spanish is always a sibilant "s" and not lisped, so *zapato* is "sah-**pah**-toh".
- The letter "h" in Spanish is silent.
- The letter "u" is, by contrast, more forceful than its English counterpart. It is pronounced like the English "w" in "well" – hence Marchihue is "mar-**chee**-way".
- The double "rr" is a rolled "r", a sound entirely foreign to English

speakers, though not perhaps Scots. Some of us can do it; others can't. Just give it a go and see what comes out.

Aconcagua – a-cong-**ka**-gwah
Alhué – al-**way**
Cachapoal – catch-a-po-**al**
Choapa – cho-**a**-pah
Colchagua – kol-**cha**-gwah
Cousiño – coo-**see**-nyo
Curicó – koo-ree-**ko**
Errázuriz – eh-**rra**-soo-reece
Guanta – **wan**-tah
Huasco – **wass**-ko
Huaso – **wa**-so
Huelquén – well-**ken**
Huique – **wee**-kay
Limarí – lee-mar-**ee**
Llaillay – yai-**yai**
Lontué – lon-**tway**
Maipo – **my**-poh
Malleco – ma-**yeh**-koh
Mapudungun – ma-poo-**doon**-goon
Marchihue (also spelt Marchigüe) – mar-**chee**-way
Maule – **mao**-lay
Melipilla – meh-lee-**pee**-yah
Mulchén – mool-**chen**
Nahuelbuta – na-well-**boo**-tah
Ninquén – ning-**ken**
Paine – **pie**-nay
País – pie-**eace**
Panquehue – pang-**keh**-way
Peñalolén – pe-nya-loe-**len**
Peumo – pay-**oo**-mo
Tapihue – ta-**pee**-way

Totihue – toh-**tee**-way
Traiguén – try-**gen**
Valparaíso – val-pa-ra-**eace**-o
Viña – **vee**-nya
Viñedo – vee-**nyeh**-doh

Bibliography

Allende, Isabel, *My Invented Country, A Memoir* (Mi País Inventado), Harper
Perennial, London, 2004

Alvarado, Rodrigo, *Chilean Wine, The Heritage,* Origo Ediciones, Santiago,
2004

Alvarado, Rodrigo, *Los Caminos del Vino,* Editorial Universitaria, Santiago,
1999

Ariste G, Jacqueline and Castillo P, Jorge, *Flora y Fauna del Alto Cachapoal,*
Chile, 2005

Burford, Tim, *Chile, The Bradt Travel Guide,* Bradt Travel Guides, Chalfont St
Peter, 2005

CTVV (Centro Tecnológico de la Vid y el Vino), *Informe Final Diagnóstico de
Recursos Genéticos, Variedades, Clones y Portainjertos, para el Valle de
Cachapoal,* Talca, 2006

del Río, María Paz (Ed), *Apec Chile 2004, A Country in the Making,* Santiago,
2004

Duijker, Hubrecht, *The Wines of Chile,* Spectrum/Seagrave Foulkes, Utrecht,
1999

Fielden, Christopher, *The Wines of Argentina, Chile and Latin America,* Faber
and Faber, London, 2001

Green, Toby and Jani, Janak, *Footprint Chile,* Footprint Handbooks, Bath,
2004

Hickman, John, *News from the End of the Earth, A Portrait of Chile,* C Hurst &
Co London, 1998

Lagos, Ricardo *The 21st Century, A View from the South,* First, London, 2005

Le Blanc, Magdalena, *El Vino Chileno, Una Geografía Optima,* Ocho Libros,
Santiago, 2000

Moncada, X et al, *Análisis Genético Aplicado en la Identificación de Cultivares y
Clones de Vid,* INIA La Platina/INRA Colmar/Viña Miguel Torres, Chile,
2005

Neruda, Pablo, *Memoirs (Confieso que he Vivido),* trans. Hardie St Martin,

Souvenir Press, London, 2004

Neruda, Pablo, *Residence on Earth* (*Residencia en la Tierra*), trans. Pablo Neruda and Donald D Walsh, Souvenir Press, London, 2003

Odepa, *Agricultura Chilena 2014*, Ministerio de Agricultura/Oficina de Estudios y Políticas Agrarias, Santiago, 2005

Origo, *Chilean Wine Regions 2006, 2005*, Origo Ediciones, Santiago, 2006, 2005

Read, Jan, *Chilean Wines,* Sotheby's Publications, London, 1988

Robinson, Jancis (Ed), *The Oxford Companion to Wine*, OUP, Second Edition, Oxford 1999

Rubio S, Andrés and Heijbroek, Arend *The Chilean Wine Industry*, Rabobank International, 2003

Sánchez, Alfredo and Morales, Roberto, *Las Regiones de Chile,* Editorial Universitaria, fourth edition, Santiago, 2004

Sernageomin, *Mapa Geológico de Chile*, Chile, 2000

Silva, José Manuel (Ed), *Sector Vitivinícola Chileno*, LarraínVial SA, Santiago 2003

Tagle A, Blanca and del Rio P, Carmen, *La Vid en Tierra de Promaucaes*, Chile, 2004

Tapia, Patricio, *Descorchados, Guía de Vinos Chilenos 2005* and *2006*, Origo/Planetavino, Santiago, 2005, 2006

Tapia, Patricio, *San Antonio Valley*, Comunik/Wine Travel Chile, Chile 2004

Tapia, Patricio, *The Wines of Colchagua Valley*, PMC Pinnacle Worldwide/Ediciones Planetavino, Santiago 2001,

Various, *Compendio Vitivinícola de Chile 2004*, Nuevos Mundos, Santiago

Various, *Guía de Vinos de Chile 2005*, Turismo y Comunicaciones, Santiago, 2004

Various, *Maipo Alto, Un Terroir Privilegiado*, Viñas del Maipo Alto, Santiago, 2005

Various, *Turistel, La Guía Turística de Chile 2005*, Turismo y Comunicaciones, Santiago, 2004

Waldin, Monty, *Wines of South America*, Mitchell Beazley, London, 2003

Index

Profiled producers are shown in **bold**.